The upheavals of the international political economy during the last decade have fundamentally altered the relationships among states and multinational enterprises. Growing interdependence now means that the rivalry between states and the rivalry between firms for a secure place in the world has become fiercer. As a result, governments have come to recognise their increased dependence on the scarce resources controlled by firms.

In this original theoretical work, two distinguished authors explore this mutual interdependence of states and firms throughout the world. They show how global structural changes – in finance, technology, knowledge and politics – often impel governments to seek the help and co-operation of managers of multinational enterprises. Yet, as Professors Stopford and Strange demonstrate, this is constrained by each country's economic resources, its social structures and its political history. Based on grass-roots research into the experience of over 50 multinationals and more than 100 investment projects in three developing countries – Brazil, Malaysia and Kenya – the authors develop a matrix of agendas. They present the impact on projects of the multiple factors affecting the bargaining relationships between the government and the foreign firm at different times and in a variety of economic sectors. In a conclusion they offer some guidelines for actions to both governments and firms and some points to future interdisciplinary research.

In this study of negotiation and bargaining, Professors Stopford and Strange synthesise the insights derived from international relations and international business. *Rival states, rival firms* will, therefore, be essential reading for students and specialists of international political economy, international relations and international business. This work will also be an invaluable resource for managers of international business and will help to explain to government policy makers how and why foreign firms decide to expand or contract their operations in foreign countries.

D0561851

CAMBRIDGE STUDIES IN INTERNATIONAL RELATIONS: 18

RIVAL STATES, RIVAL FIRMS

Cambridge Studies in International Relations is a joint initiative of Cambridge University Press and the British International Studies Association (BISA). The series will include a wide range of material, from undergraduate textbooks and surveys to research-based monographs and collaborative volumes. The aim of the series is to publish the best new scholarship in International Studies from Europe, North America and the rest of the world.

CAMBRIDGE STUDIES IN INTERNATIONAL RELATIONS

RIVAL STATES, RIVAL FIRMS

Competition for world market shares

JOHN M. STOPFORD
London Business School

SUSAN STRANGE
European University Institute, Florence

with **JOHN S. HENLEY**
University of Edinburgh

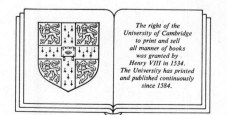

The right of the
University of Cambridge
to print and sell
all manner of books
was granted by
Henry VIII in 1534.
The University has printed
and published continuously
since 1584.

CAMBRIDGE UNIVERSITY PRESS

**Cambridge   New York   Port Chester
Melbourne   Sydney**

Published by the Press Syndicate of the University of Cambridge
The Pitt Building, Trumpington Street, Cambridge CB2 1RP
40 West 20th Street, New York, NY 10011–4211, USA
10 Stamford Road, Oakleigh, Melbourne 3166, Australia

First published 1991

Printed in Great Britain at the University Press, Cambridge

A catalogue record for this book is available from the British Library

Library of Congress cataloguing in publication data

Stopford, John M.
  Rival states, rival firms: competition for world shares market /
John M. Stopford, Susan Strange with John S. Henley.
     p.   cm. – (Cambridge studies in international relations: 18)
  Includes bibliographical references.
  ISBN 0 521 41022 3. – ISBN 0 521 42386 4 (pbk.)
  1. International business enterprise – Developing countries.
2. Developing countries – international economic relations.
3. Investments, Foreign – Government policy – Developing countries.
4. Competition, International. I. Strange, Susan. 1923–
II. Henley, Johns. III. Title. IV. Series.
HD2932.S76   1992
338.8′881724–dc20   91–11012   CIP

ISBN 0 521 41022 3 hardback
ISBN 0 521 42386 4 paperback

CE

CONTENTS

FIGURES

TABLES

ACKNOWLEDGEMENTS

This book grew out of a rare collaboration between two teachers, one at the London Business School and the other formerly at the London School of Economics and Political Science. We found that students of international business knew too little about world politics, and students of international relations had little grasp of the problems faced by international firms. So we began our collaboration by appearing in each other's classroom to try to interpret our experience of business to students of international relations, and vice versa. We hope our attempt to unite two academic disciplines will be followed by others.

To make possible field research in three developing countries, both the Leverhulme Trust in London and the Nakamae Research Institute in Tokyo generously contributed funding. We acknowledge both that debt and their moral support with gratitude.

John Henley of Edinburgh University wrote the chapter on social issues, and collected the Kenyan data. His contribution went further to ensure that due attention was paid to the human resource issues throughout the book.

Hans Mathieu provided much of the data from Brazil. In Malaysia, John Stopford was asked to oversee a United Nations study, conducted by Anuwar Ali and Wong Poh Kam. That study has been presented as a confidential report to the Malaysian Government and does not provide a resource base for this book. None the less, on frequent visits to Malaysia, John Stopford talked to many investors and government officials, thus gaining additional insight into government/business relations there.

We also acknowledge our debt to countless managers and officials, both in the three countries and at headquarters level, who gave their time so generously. Their judgments and the facts they provided helped form our own opinion by challenging preconceived notions. So, too, many scholars generously shared their own earlier work and sharpened our thoughts by debate and challenge. In particular, we acknowledge the contributions of Ted Moran and John Cline at Georgetown University, Mike Hodges at the London School of Economics, Patrizio Bianchi at Nomisma, Bologna, and Lou Wells at Harvard. Mike Sadler and Mark Curtis helped us compile the data in the appendix. Throughout the work, we were dependent on Jenny Lewis for help in making our own typing intelligible and for ensuring that communications happened roughly as planned. She played a major part in shaping the final form of the manuscript and collating the bibliography.

Even with so much help, we remain responsible for the opinions expressed in this book. Specialists in international relations, in international business and in development economics will find much that is already familiar to them. We hope, however, that our attempt to synthesise known literatures and to add fresh data and alternative models will provoke further debate and will advance a broader understanding of the complex forces that shape our lives.

1   THE NEW DIPLOMACY

The upheavals of the international political economy during the last decade have altered, irreversibly we believe, the relationships among states and multinational enterprises. Growing interdependence – that much abused word – now means that the rivalry between states and the rivalry between firms for a secure place in the world economy has become much fiercer, far more intense. As a result, firms have become more involved with governments and governments have come to recognise their increased dependence on the scarce resources controlled by firms. This mutual interdependence of states and firms throughout the world is the subject of this book; even though the detailed material is drawn from just three countries – Brazil, Kenya, Malaysia – we believe it raises new and universal questions just as relevant in Eastern Europe, the Soviet Union or China as in the third world.

We start our questioning with six general propositions. The first is that states are now competing more for the means to create wealth within their territory than for power over more territory. Where they used to compete for power as a means to wealth, they now compete more for wealth as a means to power – but more for the power to maintain internal order and social cohesion than for the power to conduct foreign conquest or to defend themselves against attack.[1] The implication is that national choices of industrial policy and efficiency in economic management are beginning to override choices of foreign or defence policy as the primary influences on how resources are allocated.

The second is that the emergence of new forms of global competition among firms also affects how states compete for wealth. As firms harness the power of new technology to create systems of activity linked directly across borders, so they increasingly concentrate on those territories offering the greatest potential for recovering their investments. Moreover, in a growing number of key sectors, the basis of competition is shifting to emphasise product quality, not just

1

costs. Attractive sites for new investment are increasingly those supplying skilled workers and efficient infrastructures. These new demands from firms affect how governments allocate resources to attract wealth-generating investment.

The third is that small, poor countries face increased barriers to entry in industries most subject to global forces of competition. They must look to their investments in skills as a primary means of hooking into the growing international systems and avoiding constant relegation to the periphery of investors' concerns.

The fourth is that these changes have added two new dimensions to diplomacy. No longer do states merely negotiate among themselves; they now must also negotiate – if not as supplicants then certainly as suitors seeking a marriage settlement – with foreign firms. Furthermore, multinational firms themselves are increasingly having to become more statesmanlike as they seek corporate alliances, permanent, partial or temporary, to enhance their combined capacities to compete with others for world market shares. The interaction of all three dimensions, in 'triangular diplomacy', calls for new skills in management and government that challenge the old order.

The fifth is that these new dimensions have multiplied the number of possible policy options for governments and for firms, and thus have greatly complicated the problems for both of managing multiple agendas. The administrative capacity of both has now become an important determinant of who can gain most from the changes in the world economy.

The sixth is that all of these shifts have acted to increase the volatility of change and the divergence of outcomes of the new diplomacy. Many developing countries are poorly placed to respond effectively, *not* for reasons of lack of factor-cost advantages, but because of deep-seated internal obstacles. These are born of traditional attitudes, political structures and often a lack of political will to confront and resolve inherent dilemmas of choice: policies aimed at enhancing internal welfare seldom sit comfortably with those designed to enhance the efficiency needed to compete in world markets. Development thus becomes a function of nations' abilities to link and control their economic affairs co-operatively with others: policies of autarky are increasingly ineffective.

These propositions all suggest reasons why policy must become more outward-looking if states are to find a place in the sun. But *how* states both resolve increasingly intractable dilemmas and implement policy becomes a critical determinant of success. For many, the prevailing attitude expressed in more liberal attitudes towards the multinationals seems to be, perhaps grudgingly, that of saying, 'if you cannot beat them, then join them'. Yet, at the same time, many are also saying that the struggle for self-reliance must go on. There are, thus, countervailing forces at work. The creation of fruitful partnerships in production will be, we believe, a fitful process and suffer many setbacks in the years ahead. But the direction of progress seems clearly charted, even if the details are blurred.

Outline for the book

In this introductory chapter, we summarise the general line of argument to amplify these initial propositions. In chapter 2, we elaborate our contention that global structural changes – in finance, technology, knowledge and politics – have exerted a dominant influence on the behaviour of governments and firms and pushed multinational enterprises more centre-stage in the evolving international political economy. In chapter 3, we examine how structures of global competition among firms have been affected by these shifts and why they have been evolving at different rates and in different forms. We argue that governments need to understand more fully that differences in firms' abilities to master change are more important than are differences among industries. Only by looking at the relative strength of firms in an industry can the basis of lasting bargains be discerned.

The next two chapters focus on the nitty-gritty detail of action and response at local levels. In chapter 4, we examine how our three governments have formulated national and sectoral policy and attempted to resolve the dilemmas inherent in their dealings with foreign firms and with international institutions such as the World Bank, the IMF and the web of treaty organisations such as the GATT. The need for control – to ensure that firms do not cheat, as well as to ensure order in managing economic and social transformation – can conflict with the promotion of entrepreneurship. The divergence of policies and outcomes in these countries seems to us especially striking and not susceptible to interpretation by any single model of bargaining power. Chapter 5 examines the impact of the global strategies of firms on their policies in developing countries. In the specific relationships between firms and governments, how the policies of each affect the responses of the other, whether positively or negatively, is illustrated. From this it will be clear that firms seek governments that provide a stable, temperate environment, while governments look for firms that will be good citizens, productive, expanding and loyal. Chapter 6, written by John Henley, examines the

3

social dimensions of the government–corporate relationship. Working with the grain of what is socially and politically acceptable in each country is essential if policies are to be stable and to have a chance of surviving external shocks.

In the concluding chapter we return to our six propositions and amplify them in the light of the evidence presented. Here, we expand on the notions of the new dimensions to diplomacy and examine the implications of the additive and growing matrix of agendas that determine the interaction between firms and governments. We aim to persuade our readers that a few simple models can cut through much of the complexity by linking together agendas previously kept separate. The new questions thus provoked can help to identify and explain future sources of opportunity and risk for both parties.

THE CHANGING GAME

Our propositions suggest that structural change in the international political economy has altered the nature of the game by affecting the actions and responses among firms and states. What we mean by structural change will be explained in some detail in the next chapter. But for the moment we would point to some of the more visible outcomes of greater volatility in a world of more mobile financial resources and faster technical change.

A brief catalogue of some of the major sources of dynamism in world markets illustrates the difficulties of forecasting when determining appropriate policy for developing countries with differing resources. For example, modern designs and technology allow firms to save on materials. By 1984, Japanese firms had reduced by 40 per cent the raw materials needed for each unit of industrial production in 1973 (Drucker, 1986). Such a massive reduction directly affects the commodity-exporting countries: much of the persistent weakness in the prices for many commodities seems to have as much to do with this effect as with the production cycle. Simultaneously, the costs of labour as a proportion of total costs have been falling in all developed countries. In many fabricating industries, they have fallen from 25 per cent to under 10 per cent within the last decade (Ohmae, 1985); in TV, they fell to 5 per cent in Japan by 1980 and have fallen further since. Similar falls are endemic in the information-technology industry.[2] Developing countries that have based their export strategies on low labour costs now find those advantages to be eroding. Indeed, there have been some instances where investors have pulled back

4

their labour-intensive operations from developing to developed countries (UNCTAD, 1989).

The real costs of transport and communication have also been falling. That firms have taken advantage of the reduced costs of running a far-flung corporate empire and altered the balance between trade and investment in their strategies is shown, for example, by the fact that the value of air freight across the Pacific overtook passenger revenues in 1986. Moreover, reduced communication costs allow new *systems* of global information management to become feasible. If the 1980s were the decade of the personal computer – 110 million sold worldwide – the 1990s look set to be the decade of telecoms and other forms of electronic communication. Advantage will shift to those who can take advantage of collapsing time scales and harness the value of the signals received by innovative action.

In some sectors, these shifts have stimulated trade in intermediate goods; in others, more trade in finished goods and less in the intermediates previously produced in developing countries. Added to these changes are the increasing costs of R & D, the shortening life for many products, the new possibilities for producing variety at lower cost, and the increase in the risks for many new product ventures. These and other factors have combined to create novel, and often unpredicted, divisions of labour within and among developed and developing countries.[3] They have also changed the structure of entire industries. In the pursuit of ever lower costs and greater shares of an increasingly open world market, many firms have been propelled into taking on the challenges of what has become known as global competition.

Shifting opinion

As these changes have unfolded, the tone and substance of the debates about the role of multinational companies in developing countries have been revised. It is hard to remember that only a decade ago politicians in third world countries were almost unanimous in their castigation and condemnation of foreign companies, and that the heads of many of these companies, especially the American and European ones, held inflexible views on how they would operate in a developing country. In place of the old bitterness, bigotry and mutual incomprehension,[4] we find a new pragmatism in their mutual attitude.

For the firms, competition for a secure place in the world market has become much more acute. Managers' attitudes are adjusting as they

5

seek new sources of competitiveness, either by internal development or in partnership. Their operations reflect, as in a mirror, the growing interdependence of national economies perceived by their opposite numbers in national governments. Few can afford to ignore the developing world, either as a market, or a source of supply, or indeed as a source of new competition. As buyers, developing countries as a whole account for a quarter of world imports, the majority of which comes from developed countries. For many multinationals, such as Komatsu in earth-moving machinery and GEC in electrical machinery, trade with developing countries can spell the difference between profit and loss. As suppliers, they provide nearly 30 per cent of world exports, 60 per cent of which is in manufactures, the more capital-intensive parts of which go to developed countries.[5] And as third world multinationals gain in stature, they add further pressure to change the rules of the competitive game. Most multinational firms recognise the importance of these issues, even those who remain unwilling to invest in developing countries.

Similarly, most developing countries feel the pressure to re-examine how foreign firms with their command of finance and technology and their access to rich markets can help offset the dire consequences of the failure of sovereign borrowing to provide a reliable and secure engine of growth. As we show in chapter 4, many have relaxed their previously stringent criteria for screening potential investors and added more generous incentives. By their actions, they are showing how far opinion has moved from the early 1980s, when one study could report that three-quarters of diplomats thought that all multi-nationals employed corrupt practices and policies detrimental to development.[6] They are also rejecting the conclusions of many quite recent academic studies, one of which asserted that 'the multi-nationals have undermined local economic and social autonomy' (Dixon et al., 1986: p. 16). It is not the firms per se that have constrained autonomy; it is the world system in which the firms are but one set of players and are increasingly recognised as such.

There is a new hope that firms can provide poor countries with both the stimulus and some of the resources they need for economic development without unduly undermining national self-esteem. The dynamism of global structural change offers states new options and makes the future seem altogether brighter. Yesterday's straitjacket of fixed opinion can be shrugged off. Yet there are risks and uncertainties. As the next chapter shows, structural change both helps and hinders aspirations for development. Moreover, beneath the veneer of growing pragmatism and collaboration, there often lurk fears that the old possibilities for exploitation by foreign interests remain as strong as ever. Many government officials to whom we talked expressed the hope that their countries would eventually be able to break away from the current reliance on foreigners to promote their exports. The necessity they feel to dash for export-led growth can call for bedfellows that prove only temporary.

Optimism about a new rapprochement can thus be overstated: a latent hostility may remain. Besides, it is perhaps ironic that while the official climate for inward investment has improved, the investment flows into most developing countries have declined. In part, this seems to reflect the fact that most of the policy changes address the problems of the 1970s and ignore the opportunities of the 1980s. In the service sectors, where much of the new dynamism lies, old attitudes and restrictions seem as firmly implanted as ever. This is an issue that we address at the end of the book when we have shown the evidence for both optimism and pessimism about the possibilities.

Where does government policy fit in?

Liberalisation of policy combined with falling costs of cross-border transactions has rekindled old fears in many quarters that the multinationals are becoming more mobile and more stateless world citizens, divorced from the competition-distorting effects of national policy. This depiction of the multinational has been promoted by such observers as Ohmae (1990), who point to some of the outcomes described in chapter 3. In our opinion, however, Ohmae's view is perhaps no more than a portent of the long-run future: closer inspection of the evidence shows that only a few firms can hope to operate in a 'borderless' world. Governments, both host and home, continue to play a crucial, and perhaps paradoxically, an increasing role.

Porter (1990), in particular, has advanced strong arguments to show that firms draw their vitality from the conditioning forces in their home markets. He asks why some nations are more prosperous than others and why some national sectors flourish while others stagnate. He focuses attention on four factors. One is the basic structure of national factor costs, including the supply of skilled workers and an efficient infrastructure. For this he draws on earlier work in trade economics to question many of the basic assumptions of comparative advantage (Ohlin, 1933). Another is the structure of demand conditions, affected by national macro-economic policy and in turn affecting the composition of trade in ways shown earlier by such scholars as Linder (1961). Equally important are the effects of com-

7

petition (echoing Schumpeter, 1942) and the impact of related and supporting industries (familiar to students of Marshall in terms of 'externalities'). His central thesis is that competitiveness is born of fierce local rivalry, an active anti-trust policy and avoidance of protectionism. 'Competing domestic rivals will keep each other honest in obtaining government support. Companies are less likely to get hooked on the narcotic of government contracts or creeping industry protectionism'. Despite the title of Porter's work, *The Competitive Advantage of Nations*, the main lines of argument apply at the level of the firm. No country can be good at everything, for only some firms and some sectors thrive within the framework established by economic management and the workings of a national culture.

Porter's analysis provides only a point of departure for many of the lines of argument advanced here. Though the basic analysis is contained in the older ESP paradigm (Koopmans and Montias, 1971), his analysis takes life from the detailed analyses of contemporary conditions. None the less, he omits detailed consideration of entrepreneurship and investment. More seriously for our purposes, he almost wholly ignores the changes in the world system outside the countries and fails to recognise the composition of government as groups of parties with different interests. He also fails to examine the interaction between the international competitiveness of local firms and government policy; a crucial issue in many developing countries (Aggarwal and Agmon, 1990). Yet his analysis can be adapted to host, developing countries. For this one needs to add more explicit treatment of government policies that balance economic with social conditions. Small, poor countries cannot afford the luxury of letting market forces determine outcomes. Besides, even in the USA, it is recognised that government action can alter the balance of factor cost advantage through intervention (Zysman and Tyson, 1983). Adding explicitly the role of government policy and the shifts of global competition to Porter's four factors produces the diagram of related influences shown in figure 1.1 below.

Rather like Toynbee's concept of challenge and response, the diagram suggests the possibility of an explanatory framework: it is not the basis of a deterministic theory. Its meaning emerges from the interactions among the variables, more in terms of what is contradicted than definitively established. By suggesting new questions, it can help articulate, but not resolve, the long-standing debate about the lines of causality between policies to create growth and those aimed at structural reform.

Causality can be seen to run in both directions. Governments may

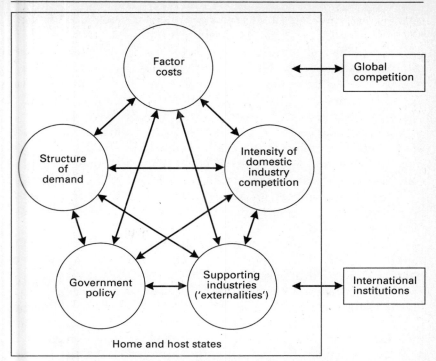

Figure 1.1 Primary factors influencing a nation's competitiveness.
Adapted from Porter (1990).

either take the initiative to influence the composition of output or trade, or feel forced to respond to external changes they regard as undesirable.[7] There is therefore great uncertainty about the appropriateness of conventional prescriptions for development policy. Besides, the ability of forecasters and policy makers to pick 'winners' is low. Who would have forecasted in the 1950s that South Korea would maintain a real growth rate of 5.7 per cent for thirty years? More likely, economists would have looked at the low savings rate and considered South Korea a likely loser (Crook, 1989). Malaysia would probably have been written off on the same basis, especially given its security problems at that time.

By focusing on the role of the firm, figure 1.1 can also be used to challenge the theory of comparative advantage that has formed the basis of so much official thinking. Many economists have begun to develop new models that accord more closely with actual trade behaviour.[8] As Krugman (1987: p. 131) has said, 'these new models call into doubt the extent to which actual trade can be explained by comparative advantage: they also open the possibility that government intervention in trade ... may under certain circumstances be in the national interest after all'. For example, in capital-intensive industries such as chemicals, the decision to build a new export-oriented refinery can disturb existing trade patterns. The location of such lumpy investments is chosen as much by the investor's calculation of advantage relative to all its existing refineries as by the national factor costs and demand function in the host country. Though we do not set out to build an omnibus theory that can embrace such calculation, we recognise that trade and national advantage must be seen in the context of the bargain struck between the investor and the host nation. Countries now compete for scarce managerial resources more by providing a favourable investment 'climate' than simply relying on factor cost advantages.

A further issue in any analysis of policy choice is the *power* of the state to implement its choices and overcome social, religious and political obstacles to change. How Brazil and South Korea responded to the problem of spiralling debt and reduced inflows of foreign capital illustrates the impact of domestic circumstance on policy and thus on the investment climate. In 1982, the Brazilian government, afraid of the social effects of the decline in capital inflows, cut investment even more severely than they cut consumption. By contrast, the Korean government, more confident of its ability to contain and suppress social unrest, acted to increase domestic saving and stepped up domestic investment to take the place of foreign loans, even though this meant a cut in real wages and consumption. Growth rates in Korea stayed high: they declined in Brazil. Brazil's choices in the 1980s reflected in part the relative weakness of its government in the aftermath of the transition to civilian rule. Weak states usually resort to approaches that can be regarded as 'making policy by default'.

Related to these choices of internal policy are those affecting attitudes towards 'outward-looking' policies. Despite the claim of bodies such as the IMF, some countries hold the view that an 'outward-looking' policy framework does not always promote growth and that inward-looking approaches can be superior. Lall (1987: p. 28) asked, 'can Tanzania become Korea only by adopting an outward-looking trade policy?'. Clearly not, when the necessary technical abilities and entrepreneurial drive is absent. The spread of growth rates under each policy regime shown in figure 1.2 below supports such agnosticism and illustrates the difficulty of drawing general conclusions. As the 1989 United Nations Conference on Trade and Development (UNCTAD) trade and development report stated,

1963-73

Outward-oriented		Inward-oriented	
STRONGLY	MODERATELY	MODERATELY	STRONGLY

Scale: 10, 8, 6, 4, 2, +, 0, −, 2, 4

Strongly outward-oriented: Singapore; S. Korea; Hongkong

Moderately outward-oriented: Brazil; Israel; Thailand; Indonesia; Costa Rica; Malaysia; Ivory Coast; Colombia; Guatemala; Cameroun

Moderately inward-oriented: Yugoslavia; Mexico; Nigeria; Tunisia; Kenya; Philippines; Bolivia; Honduras; El Salvador; Madagascar/; Nicaragua; Senegal

Strongly inward-oriented: Turkey; Dominican Republic; Burundi; Argentina/Pakistan; Sri Lanka; Tanzania; Ethiopia; Chile; Peru/; Uruguay; Zambia; India; Ghana; Bangladesh; Sudan

1973-85

Outward-oriented		Inward-oriented	
STRONGLY	MODERATELY	MODERATELY	STRONGLY

Scale: 10, 8, 6, 4, 2, +, 0, −, 2, 4

Strongly outward-oriented: Singapore; Hongkong; S. Korea

Moderately outward-oriented: Malaysia; Thailand; Tunisia; Brazil; Turkey; Israel/; Uruguay; Chile

Moderately inward-oriented: Cameroun; Indonesia; Sri Lanka; Pakistan; Yugoslavia; Colombia; Mexico; Philippines; Kenya; Honduras; Senegal; Costa Rica/; Guatemala; Ivory Coast; El Salvador; Nicaragua

Strongly inward-oriented: Bangladesh/; India; Burundi; Dominican Republic; Ethiopia/; Sudan; Peru; Tanzania; Argentina; Zambia; Nigeria; Bolivia; Ghana; Madagascar

Strongly outward-oriented
Trade controls are either non-existent or very low in the sense that any disincentives to export resulting from import barriers are more or less counterbalanced by export incentives. There is little or no use of direct controls and licensing arrangements, and the effective exchange rates for imports and exports are roughly equal.

Moderately outward-oriented
Incentives favour production for domestic rather than export markets. But the average rate of effective protection for the home markets is relatively low and the range of effective protection rates relatively narrow. The use of direct controls and licensing arrangements is limited. The effective exchange rate is higher for imports, but only slightly.

Moderately inward-oriented
Incentives clearly favour production for the domestic market. The average rate of effective protection for home markets is fairly high and the range of effective protection rates relatively wide. Direct import controls are extensive. The exchange rate is somewhat overvalued.

Strongly inward-oriented
Incentives strongly favour production for the domestic market. The average rate of effective protection for home markets is high and the range of effective protection rates wide. Direct controls and licensing disincentives to the traditional export sector are pervasive, positive incentives to nontraditional exports are few or nonexisting, and the exchange rate is substantially overvalued.

Figure 1.2 Trade regimes and growth. Adapted from *The Economist*, 23 September 1989, based on data from the World Bank.

'export reforms are no guarantee of economic growth'. Besides, some of the external choices clash uncomfortably with domestic priorities. Developing effective external policy to gain internationally calculated *efficiency* to support an export drive can conflict with domestic priorities for *equity* or racial justice.

Resolving such clashes cannot be solved by rational economics alone; they must be regarded as political choices. An interview with India's prime minister in 1990 provided an illuminating vignette of the dilemma. Mr Singh had publicly acknowledged his awareness that the events in Eastern Europe and the USSR were shaking India too, and that India risked being left further behind if it did not accept the new international challenge. When asked why he had not liberalised and deregulated faster, he replied, 'We are politicians. We know our place. The people have to be persuaded first: they will understand what is confronting them when it is explained . . . but it will take time.'[9]

India's long-run performance has been much poorer than South Korea's. In 1950, both were miles behind the industrialised countries and it seemed then almost impossible for either to attain high standards of living. Today India has a per capita income of about $250 (in 1980 $) and South Korea's is roughly $2,900. Similar differences show up in Korea's far greater levels of social gains, such as greater life expectancy, education and change in the structure of the domestic economy. What caused the difference?

Though it might be tempting to attribute South Korea's greater success to its outward orientation and India's problems to its inward-looking priorities, the many differences in social and economic conditions make it impossible to provide a single answer. Besides, aggregate statistics run the risk of provoking sweeping generalisations; they obscure sectors of relative growth or relative decline. None the less, there are some important similarities and contrasts that seem to bear on the issue. For instance, both governments followed policies of strong intervention in their markets – an outward-looking policy does not necessarily mean *laissez faire*. The crucial difference is that India constrained competition, whereas South Korea actively promoted both domestic rivalry and the international development of local firms.

There is a balance to be struck. As Lawrence (1987: p. 102) said, 'an industry needs to experience rigorous competition if it is to be economically strong. Either too little or too much competitive pressure can lead an industry to a predictably weak economic performance characterized by its becoming inefficient and/or non-innovative.' This sense of required balance is a repetitive theme in the chapters that

12

follow, for countries need to steer carefully between the scylla of many-headed foreign competitors (as in Brazil) and the charybdis of government protection (as in Kenya).

We believe that sustained investments in building an educated society whose *mores* are those of competition (as in Japan) provide the best means of steering a middle course and of achieving a quality of growth that is sustainable even in the face of external shocks. Sustainability depends largely on underlying skills, on social equity, and on the avoidance of the careless exploitation of natural resources and environmental damage that will harm later generations. The Ivory Coast illustrates how temporary success can be. For a time, it was the darling of the development agencies as its outward-looking policies generated growth. So strong was the economy in 1979 that, for example, one large multinational made 10 per cent of its world-wide profits there, largely because of its ability to supply neighbouring Nigeria with a wide variety of standard products that could not satisfactorily be produced under the then chaotic Nigerian conditions. Those exports have now dried up as Nigeria has put its own house more in order. Moreover, the Ivory Coast placed much reliance on the same commodities as its neighbours, thus entering a zero-sum game that worsened its plight when prices fell. And its exchange rate, pegged to the French franc, turned from an advantage to a constraint in the ensuing phase of enforced adjustment. From looking outwards, the Ivory Coast has now turned inwards. Robustness of policy combined with an ability to adapt systematically to changing external circumstance are qualities just as important for states as they are for firms.[10]

THE GROWING REACH OF THE MULTINATIONALS

International business is an ancient feature of the world economy. The Phoenicians opened up new trade routes and stimulated new sources of production. Indeed, the travelling merchant has been one of history's unsung heroes in providing the initial contacts among entire cultures. It is only in the last century that the multinational corporation has emerged in forms we would recognise today. Led by pioneers such as the American firm, Colt, which established a revolver factory in Britain in 1852, these firms began to change the old order of trade and finance as the primary weapons of international business. They added international production of goods and services and began to manage their overseas assets as part of an integrated unit rather than as passive investments in a portfolio.

More recently, there has been an explosion of FDI (foreign direct investment). While world trade volumes grew at a compound annual rate of 5 per cent between 1983 and 1988, FDI grew at 20 per cent annually in real terms. Why this occurred has much to do with the structural changes described in chapter 2. The consequence has been to tie more closely together the determinants of trade and investment flows. A milestone was reached in the mid-1980s, when the volume of international production for the first time exceeded the volume of international trade. The increased FDI flows have, as Julius (1990: p. 36) claimed, 'reached the threshold where they create a qualitatively different set of linkages among advanced countries ... [A]s a means of international economic integration, FDI is in its take-off phase, perhaps in a position comparable to world trade at the end of the 1940s.'

The change is significant as it diminishes the power of states to control economic events. States retain considerable *negative* power to disrupt, manage or distort trade by controlling entry to the territory in which the *national* market functions. They cannot so easily control production which is aimed at a *world* market and which does not necessarily take place within their frontiers. And even when most of the supply is under control, the market may not be, as OPEC discovered to its cost in the 1980s. In other words, states' *positive* power to harness internal resources is decidedly constrained when they try to influence where and how international production takes place. They find they cannot direct; they can only bargain. And the costs to themselves can be very much higher than those of trade protection. For example, when the Brazilian government introduced its Informatics Laws to prevent the international computer enterprises from producing in Brazil, it imposed a very high cost on those local enterprises needing to use the latest and best computers in order to keep up with *their* competitors. The outcome of bargaining may be to the state's advantage, or to the multinationals'. It is still a bargain.

How powerful the multinationals have become is a notoriously difficult question to answer. It is not solely a question of the statistics on FDI, the asset base of the multinationals.[11] These understate the growing reach of the multinationals by ignoring other ways these firms affect performance. Yet much official attention concentrates on these figures. In the hey-day of sovereign lending to developing countries, when FDI accounted for less than 10 percent of the resource transfers in some years during the 1970s, many thought that the multinationals were of little consequence for development. Figure 1.3 shows the trends as measured by the IMF. An even smaller role might

14

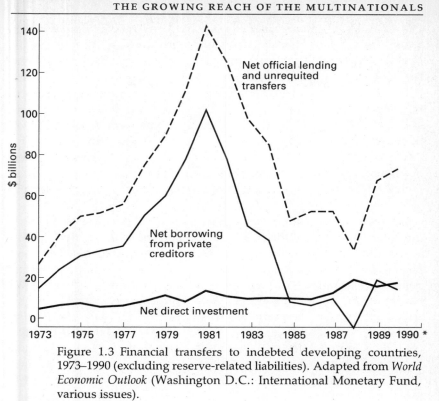

Figure 1.3 Financial transfers to indebted developing countries, 1973–1990 (excluding reserve-related liabilities). Adapted from *World Economic Outlook* (Washington D.C.: International Monetary Fund, various issues).
* Forecast

be accorded to the multinationals as a source of finance if one deducts the remission of profits from the FDI flows. In most years during the 1980s, the IMF data show that the 'real' transfer has seldom exceeded $3 billion.[12] Perhaps this was why the authors of the Brandt Reports (1980, 1983, 1985) ignored almost totally the phenomenon we address in this book.

There are three basic reasons why such statistics misrepresent the role of the multinationals in development. The first is that the multinationals' share of and influence over world production and trade is far greater than their share of the capital transfers. Directly or indirectly, they have been estimated to control over one quarter of the world's economic activity *outside* their home countries;[13] over half the world trade in manufactured goods and even more of the growing trade in services; 80 per cent of the world's land cultivated for export crops, and the lion's share of the world's technological innovations. The accumulated stock of FDI was estimated to have exceeded $1 trillion by the end of 1988. Table 1.1 gives some detail on the growth of

15

FDI, where it originates and where it is invested. The picture is one where the concentration of activity is increasingly within the developed world, leaving all but a few developing countries outside the reach of the new dynamism. The early post-war dominance of the USA as the source of FDI has been reduced as Europeans and the Japanese have invested in the USA. Indeed, if one excludes US-sourced FDI, the USA alone has attracted 60 per cent of all FDI flows during the 1980s. The declining US share of FDI is leading to a more diffused structure of economic power and a more fiercely contested international market. Though these estimates should not be taken too literally, they indicate the orders of magnitude of the multinationals' activities.

Impressive as $1 trillion sounds, the real asset base is even higher if one takes into account the effects of debt and the indirect effects of the non-equity and contractual forms of association, the so-called New Forms of Investment (NFI) that have been growing rapidly in recent years. For example, Reuber (1973) found in the years before the bank-lending boom that 54 per cent of the capital raised for the sixty-eight projects he examined was in the form of debt and that 40 per cent of the equity was raised in the developing countries. Thus, the total resources affected by the multinationals far exceeded the total suggested by their equity base. Though some observers hold the view that NFI opens the door to more equitable arrangements (Oman, 1984, 1989), recent analysis suggests that, for many classes of activity, these arrangements are inherently inefficient (Hennart, 1989). NFI may be no more than a second-best solution to distortions in international markets, capable of alleviating some problems but worsening others. Much depends on the individual firm, whether it is defending or attacking an established market position. The issues are discussed in chapter 5, for they have a large bearing on attitudes that form the basis for policy choice.

An alternative measure of the multinationals' significance is in terms of their employment. They are estimated to account for only 10 per cent of employment in developed countries. In developing countries, they employ perhaps twenty-one million men and women directly. When indirect employment provided through sub-contractors and suppliers is included, the International Labour Office (ILO, 1984) estimates this still only doubles the employment base, to perhaps 2 per cent.[14] These estimates overlook the influence exerted on host economies through multiplier and similarly indirect mechanisms.

The second reason for underestimating the multinationals' reach is

Table 1.1. *Stock of Foreign Direct Investment, 1960–1988 ($ Billions)*

	1960	1971	1980	1987	1988
A. *By source country*					
United States	33	83	215	314	334
United Kingdom	10	24	74	179	184
Netherlands	7	14	40	79	70
W. Germany	0.8	7	38	100	97
Japan	0.5	4	37	77	111
Other developed countries	15	36	93	179	199
Developing countries	0.7	4	14	40	45
Total (estimated)	67	172	512	968	1,040
B. *By host country*					
United States	8	14	68	272	328
Canada	13	28	46	100	N/A
United Kingdom	5	13	45	95	110
Other developed countries	11	60	165	N/A	N/A
Developing countries	18	51	117	N/A	N/A
Total	55	166	441	N/A	N/A

Note: The data for source and host countries differ due to different national reporting procedures; annual estimates vary according to currency translations into US $.

Source: These data are drawn from many sources. The principal ones are national official sources, plus Stopford and Dunning (1983) (for 1960–1980 data); JETRO, White Paper on Overseas Investment (annual series); UNCTC (1988a); and authors' estimates.

their growing role as agents of integration with the world system. A large and growing share of merchandise and financial trade is managed within the firms' networks, either as part of their operations or ancillary to the rapidly expanding service activities both within the manufacturers and among service specialists. Data from many nations show that over 40 per cent of their external trade in manufactures is managed as transactions among firms' affiliates and that the figure could be increased by adding in the trade among multinationals.[15] For example, over 80 per cent of the technology payments received by the United States are royalties paid by affiliates to their US parent companies.

Table 1.2. *Concentration of flows of FDI to developing countries (% share of worldwide inflows)*

	1981–3	1984–7
All developing countries	27.5	21.2
Latin America and Caribbean (of which, Argentina, Bermuda, Brazil, Colombia & Mexico)	13 (82)	8 (93)
South and East Asia (of which, China, Hong Kong, Malaysia, Singapore)	11 (78)	9 (72)
Africa (of which, 8 oil-exporting countries)	1 (70)	1 (83)

Source: UNCTC, (1989), 'FDI Flows in the Mid-1980's', UNCTC Reporter, No. 27, Spring.

These 'hidden' consequences of the spread of FDI are part of the general trends that limit the ability of governments to control events.

The third reason for not taking the FDI figures too literally is that, like all aggregates, they hide more than they reveal. As table 1.2 shows, a few countries attract the bulk of the investment in developing countries. Of the total flow during the 1980s, nearly 90 per cent went to just twenty countries, compared to 70 per cent in the early 1970s (UNCTC, 1988a; IMF, 1985). That concentration is increasing as multinationals seek the best prospects for growth and focus their interest on those countries with abundant natural resources, large internal markets, plentiful skilled but relatively cheap labour, and favourable regulatory regimes. This trend reflects the fact that the multinationals tend to be influenced by and in turn influence the ability of countries to grow.

The multinationals' impact on those countries receiving the greatest investment attention has been considerable relative to GDP, as figure 1.4 indicates for a few countries. Yet these aggregates hide major sectoral differences. These are due as much to regulatory variations as to availability. In Brazil, for example, 62 per cent has been in manufacturing, whereas in Chile, services together with mining and oil have taken the lion's share. Moreover, the accumulating stock of investments have produced quite different impacts on the proportion of sectors controlled from abroad. Thus, while over 60 per cent of

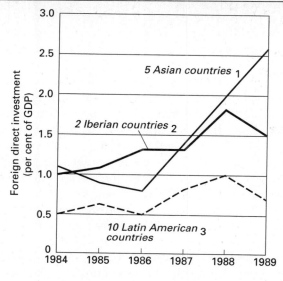

1 Indonesia, Malaysia, Phillipines,Singapore, and Thailand.

2 Portugal and Spain

3 Argentina, Brazil, Chile, Columbia, Costa Rica, Equador, Mexico, Peru, Uruguay, and Venezuela

Figure 1.4 South-East Asia lures investors. Adapted from 'Fostering Foreign Direct Investment in Latin America', mimeo, Institute of International Finance, Washington D.C..

Singapore's manufacturing is foreign-controlled, in India the equivalent figure is well below 10 per cent.[16] In short, generalisations obscure the dynamics of adjustment. Why this should have been so and how these firms might affect the course of development in the future is the focus of all that follows.

TRIANGULAR DIPLOMACY

Cross-border competition is intensifying for both firms and states. For firms, decisions in one country are now more frequently influenced by choices made elsewhere. For example, Firestone, the US tyre producer, renegotiated its position in Kenya in part because of the competitive battles it was fighting in the industrialised markets. As we show below, the effect of global competition on Firestone's cash flows acted powerfully to change managers' opinions about previous policies of ownership and control. States are also competing among

19

themselves to woo new investors. Malaysia, for example, has stated publicly that its recently enhanced incentive packages are calculated with a clear knowledge of what other governments in the region are offering.

The ideas that interdependence necessarily involves closer inter-action among governments and firms is not new; it was suggested nearly twenty years ago by a German scholar, Karl Kaiser, when the debate first opened on the meaning and significance of 'inter-dependence' (Kaiser, 1971). Implicitly criticising much of the then-current discussion, Kaiser pointed to the asymmetry of government power in transnational politics. He drew on the work of Aron who had introduced the concept of 'transnational society' to international relations to indicate that states' options are affected by developments in the flow of ideas and beliefs across borders and by non-national organisations (Aron, 1966; p. 105).[17] To this he added Perroux's ideas on dominant economies (1950) and drew a diagram (shown in slightly modified form in figure 1.5 below) to illustrate how all these ideas could apply to the power and influence of foreign companies in less developed countries. His arrows indicate attempts by one group to influence others. Some point downward, implying direction, coer-cion, regulation, rather than dialogue. But they also point upward, implying some reverse influence of business on government within countries.

Kaiser's diagram shows only a two-way relationship to indicate that some states have more influence than others over the conduct of international organisations and firms. What he omits is the nature of the interactions within his 'transnational society' and how these affect the options and power of states. More recent developments have shown that these interactions have developed strongly both to add a third dimension to the phenomenon and to suggest further limits to the power of the state.

These interactions are indicated by the difficulty states increasingly have in controlling population movements: witness the illegal immi-grants in the USA and southern Europe. Still less can they control the flow of ideas. Much of the recent change in the Eastern Europe and the USSR has been sparked by individuals' heightened awareness of their relative material backwardness, let alone political constriction. Rising consumer expectations in developing countries add pressure on governments barely able to cope with basic needs. Labour unions have also exported their ideas. Though their attempts to organise labour internationally, as in the International Metalworkers Federation, have not amounted to much, their ideas are pervasive.

20

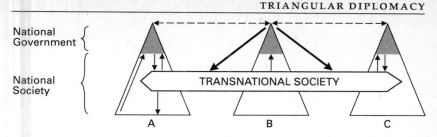

National Government {

National Society {

TRANSNATIONAL SOCIETY

A   B   C

A, B, C stand for nation states: see text for definition of 'transnational society' and the arrows.

Figure 1.5 .Transnational politics. Adapted from Kaiser (1971).

Of particular note has been the emergence of a privileged transnational business civilisation, or what Sunkel (1973) labelled the 'transnational kernel'. Its US core is in New York – not Washington – and in Chicago and Los Angeles, where the social and political elites most wholeheartedly accept the values, the *mores*, the customs and taboos of the business civilisation. So do their counterparts in London, Tokyo, Sao Paulo, Sydney and Taipei. Their values are both economic (efficiency, speed and responsiveness to changes in demand) and social (openness to competition, opportunity for social advancement regardless of race and parentage, and soon, perhaps, of sex). Particularly on the latter issue, practice, as always, falls short of ideology. Women are not yet given equal opportunity; nor are blacks, as a headcount of business class passengers on any airline will show. But the significance of each of these values is that the core is in the lead in bringing about social and economic change. American women have more opportunities than Japanese women; American blacks more opportunity than Japanese of Korean origin. There seems little doubt that where the core has led, the business civilisation will follow. Far from acting to preserve dependency in small 'peripheral' states, even radical analysts now seem to be accepting that this privileged class can play a crucial and positive role in economic transformation (Weiss, 1988: p. 159).

These three sets of forces are transforming the old game of Diplomacy. No longer can national boundaries define the rules, for the game is now one where negotiation and action is carried out on a triangular basis. The traditional players in the embassies and foreign ministries are still in business, but they have been joined by members of other government ministries and by the executives of firms, both local and multinational All are now involved in both bilateral and multilateral negotiation. Figure 1.6 shows the three dimensions of the game in a simple form. Later on, in chapter 4, we complicate the

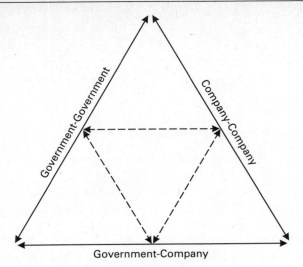

Figure 1.6 Triads of relationships.

diagram to distinguish the nature of the relationships affecting local and foreign firms.

Changes in the international political economy create new sources of asymmetry in the relative importance of the three sides of the triangle. The growth of global competition can be seen as moving the world towards a position where events are conditioned more by an emerging managerial technocracy than by traditional notions of state power. In this new technocracy, firms feature prominently but are only one component of a wider network that links them to the educational and skills infrastructure and the financial system. Competition is increasingly among different production and institutional systems and contrasting social organisations. Further challenges to the role of the nation state are provided by the Europe of 1992 and North American debates about a free-trade area to run from Canada to Mexico. Supra-national bodies could emerge to offset the growing power of the world market. We are not attempting to forecast from among these and other possible 'meta' structures; we merely indicate that new triangular relationships will continue to evolve.

In the explicit bargaining between host governments and foreign enterprises, sometimes one and sometimes the other has the whip hand. Frequently, as in inter-state diplomacy, elements of both conflict and cooperation exist simultaneously in the bargaining process.[18] The asymmetry of the process makes the choice of partner critical. For states, a sickly corporate partner may be just as damaging as an alliance with a weak or vacillating state. The other side of the coin is the firm's choice of national site. Before the 1980s, corporations looking for compatible hosts shopped for tax breaks and docile, low-paid labour. More recent experience has demonstrated that neither could compensate for administrative incompetence or for official intervention, either by internal price control or tariffs or other barriers to efficient operations.

Recent scholarly interest in economic organisation has spawned a controversial view of the modern corporation as a 'nexus of contracts' (Aoki et al., 1990). We have gone further, regarding state–firm bargaining as the nexus of international treaties affecting the balance of power; the lasting effectiveness of the deal is determined by the success or failure of bargaining on all three sides of the triangle. When we examined the record of many investors in our three countries, we found that we could not understand much of what had been decided and done without explicitly taking into account shifts elsewhere. If one looks at only one side of the triangle, one misses important factors.

Three examples make the point. Some years ago, Britain infuriated the Indonesian government by reducing its (already small) import quota for T-shirts as part of one of the endless rounds of renegotiating the Multi-Fibre Arrangement. Indonesia sought ways of retaliation and found that one British firm, Davy International, was constructing a large chemical plant in their country. They embargoed the project as a way of voicing their displeasure and put at risk a contract worth many times the value of the trade in T-shirts. Davy might have foreseen the risk had they been monitoring the state–state negotiations, but who in that industry then would have considered the cost of such monitoring worthwhile? Malaysia also illustrates how unexpected risk can be created on another side of the diplomatic 'triangle'. Malaysian anger over British 'colonial' attitudes and especially over the decision to raise the fees for foreign students in Britain led to Dr Mahatir's 'buy-British-last' policy. British exporters were affected much more than the investors, but both were hurt by the consequences of a state–state dispute that had little, at least initially, to do with economic relations. A third example concerns Kenya. When the British Foreign Secretary announced that British aid would be reduced to countries abusing human rights, the British High Commission in Nairobi had to lobby strenuously to get the UK government to back off, so as to protect British investors' interests.

A MATRIX OF AGENDAS

To begin to capture the sense of this complexity, we tried to model our initial propositions, but found that we could not cope systematically and simultaneously with all three sides of the triangular relationships. We therefore concentrated on the direct relations between states and firms, leaving considerations of state–state and firm–firm bargaining as modifying factors in specific circumstances. The result was a simple matrix that provides a snapshot of the range and scope of the interests of both sets of players at a given time. Figure 1.7 shows nine possible combinations of circumstance. The concentration is on trade policy as a proxy variable for other critical issues affecting negotiations. Though this is a simplification of reality, we chose to focus on trade, as export creation is now one of the most urgent needs of developing countries. The matrix is not, however, designed to define all possible roles for multinationals in development, but to identify some of the major arenas in which bargaining takes place. We complicate the model in later chapters, most particularly in terms of the dynamics of change on either axis and in terms of issues that reflect the interactions with the other two sides of the triangular diplomacy, but for now the simple version can serve to introduce the ideas.

Governments are placed on the horizontal axis in figure 1.9 in terms of their trade policy 'Intent'. They are considered to have three primary options. One is to regard inward foreign investment as a means of replacing imports and to provide encouragement for that by offering tariff protection or other barriers to competition. This was the traditional view, dominant in the 1950s and 1960s. Developing countries typically used import-replacement as an initial step to create the industrial infrastructure needed for later exporting (Chenery et al., 1986; Page, 1986; Stewart, 1982). Yet, some economists have argued that to equate industrialisation with import-substitution has been mistaken, because of the high costs of the transformation needed later on (Krueger, 1983; Pazos, 1985). This is an issue to which we return in chapters 4 and 5, for both states and firms find that eliminating the bad habits engendered by operating behind protective barriers is far from easy, and sometimes impossible. In many cases, national firms cannot change for lack of resources and multinationals are resistant to change for fear of upsetting arrangements elsewhere. None the less, many states would consider they had no other initial option.

More recently, many developing countries have actively sought to add export-creating investments without going through the stage of

24

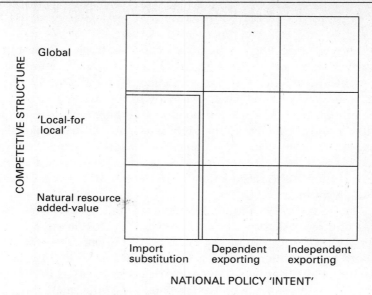

Figure 1.7 Nine possible bargaining sites.

import-substitution. They have done so in a great variety of ways, but all have been spurred by the need to earn hard currency to finance domestic investments and service payments on prior loans. We draw a critical distinction between policies designed to replace imports and those for export-creation, for they have much to do with the questions of efficiency, appropriate technology, managerial competence and the likely effectiveness of alternative forms of incentive.

We also draw a distinction between two basic approaches to creating exports. A country can recognise its reliance on foreigners, either by ownership or by contract. Multinationals possess power by virtue of prior investments in distribution systems to serve the world market. Equally, states can benefit from the power of distribution groups in industrialised countries who offer long-term or seasonal contracts for supply of goods at pre-determined specifications. Sears Roebuck in the USA, for example, has for long supported local entrepreneurs in South-East Asia by providing engineering drawings and even assistance in factory layout for a wide variety of products. Some contract farming of cash crops has similar features. In addition, manufacturing companies like Amstrad in consumer electronics and Courtaulds in textiles now have wholly locally-owned factories producing exclusively for them. Such exports are labelled as *dependent*, for they will only continue to exist for so long as the foreign entity considers them economically viable.

25

By contrast, some countries like South Korea have actively sought to promote exports from indigenous producers. They have valued *independent* exporting for the freedom it gives them to determine their own position in world markets. Malaysia sought some of these benefits by buying the parent companies of politically important subsidiaries, such as Sime Darby, which now promotes itself as 'South-East Asia's largest multinational'. Whereas *dependent* exporting allows countries to avoid the high entry costs to international selling and distribution, policies designed for *independent* exporting explicitly recognise these costs and the associated risks that local firms must bear if they are to reach and sustain the required levels of efficiency and performance.

On the vertical axis in figure 1.7, firms are considered to operate in one of three basic structures of competition. Most manufacturing and service industries can be regarded as having either of two configurations of international activity. One, labelled as 'local-for-local', refers to those industries where the primary locus of activity is close to each market, with relatively little interaction with other markets. Accounting services and toiletries are examples, even though the transfer of skills and the firm's international reputation or brand are important. 'Local-for-local' production was the predominant structure during the early expansion of FDI up to the 1960s. Many industries have subsequently shifted into a 'global' configuration, where the interaction among markets is much greater. These interactions involve trade in components as well as finished goods together with the use of cash-flows and managerial systems as competitive weapons for competing across borders. Electronics, automobiles and specialised machinery are examples. There is a third category of competition, the local added-value processing of natural resources. We exclude the production of basic commodities and concentrate on later stages of the processing, for which there are choices as to the location of the plants. The power of the local country to affect decisions about such added-value processing is considerable and generally greater than for other types of manufacturing or services.[19]

The bargaining agenda in each of the nine 'cells' of the matrix is subject to different balances of consideration. Table 1.3 provides a crude identification of some of the important variables affecting which side holds power in the negotiation. The reality is, to be sure, more complex. One problem is that relative power changes *over time*. Governments may hold power to control and regulate the outcomes when a firm first enters the country, especially if there are many competitors who can be played off one against the other, but may lose

Table 1.3. *Factors influencing relative bargaining advantage*

	Advantage held by	Likely regulation
Factor		
Dependence on local resources	Government	High
Dependence on local markets	Government	High
Political 'salience'	Government	High
Industry structure		
Many competitors	Government (at entry)	Variable by product
Global 'linkage'	Firm	Low
Business dependent on:		
Proprietary knowledge	Firm	Low
Highly complex process	Firm	Low
Labour-intensity	Government	Low–high
Capital-intensity	Firm	High
Marketing skills	Firm	Low
Mobility of facilities	Firm	Low
Costs/efficiency	Firm	Indeterminate
International information	Firm	Variable by product

influence later on as operations become established. Conversely, in risky projects such as exploring for oil or other minerals, the firm may hold the initial advantage but lose it once the project has been successfully completed. This, latter, case is what Vernon (1977) has labelled the 'obsolescing bargain'. As we explore in later chapters, such obsolescence does not occur so markedly in other sectors.

A second major problem has to do with determining the long-term purpose of the project. A project may start its life to replace imports in a 'local-for-local' industry, but later be under pressure to start exporting, either because the government's objectives have changed or the industry has become more globally integrated. Initial negotiations typically emphasise how access to the market is to be regulated and the degree of protection offered. Firms may be willing to cede some or all of the ownership of the venture in exchange for market access and some sense of stability in the operating regime. Quite opposite conditions apply for the establishment of 'dependent' exporting in a global industry. Failure to anticipate the possibilities of such a shift in the original deal not only incurs high costs of transition, but may also create conflicting expectations that cannot readily be resolved by subsequent re-negotiation.

The changing nature of the bargaining requirements challenges governments' use of the 'blunt instrument' of general policy, for inflexibility in its application can be counterproductive. Kenya, for example, operates a system of queuing for foreign exchange approvals that slows down decisions and creates uncertainties that impede exports. Malaysia and many other countries have policies of supporting prices for agricultural products, designed among other things to maintain their least efficient farmers. Processing industries using such inputs suffer cost penalties that also impede exports. Further difficulties are created when a shift in international competition upsets the status quo: a firm that operated profitably but inefficiently in a protected local market may find that its very survival is threatened. Even if conflict can be avoided, the government then faces the dilemma of whether it should increase the level of protection, or permit the cheaper, perhaps more technologically advanced, imports to land, or provide adjustment assistance to allow the firm to gain new capabilities.

One of the striking features of the 1980s has been the speed with which many industries have been shifting towards some form of global structure. Equally striking has been the willingness of governments, despite all the obstacles, to change their policy orientation and to move from left to right in figure 1.7. Simultaneous change on both axes can create confusion: the policies adopted are *additive* and force hard choices for governments. None the less, many are adopting much more pragmatic approaches and are becoming more adept in managing selective policies towards those industries and firms that can bring the greatest benefits. For them, as in Brazil, the calculation is not just in terms of today's output but also in terms of gaining greater access to more of the skills needed for tomorrow's competitiveness in an increasingly information- and skill-intensive world.

Managing change of this type requires governments to confront a further issue: taking care to make sure that policy aimed at one of the nine 'cells' in the matrix does not inadvertently wash over to affect behaviour in another. The need to 'ring-fence' agendas can be illustrated by the experience of Malaysia. Ownership restrictions have for long been in place for projects serving the local market, but exporters (mainly in the Export Processing Zones) have been exempt from these provisions, subject to stringent performance targets. When the government introduced its Industrial Coordination Act in the mid-1970s, the exporters feared that the new regulations would apply equally to them. They quickly made it clear that they would reduce future investments and induced the government to revise some of the provisions in the Act and to reaffirm the exemptions.[20]

More generally, the difficulty of keeping agendas separate in this climate of change can be shown by the increasing use of the so-called trade-related investment measures (TRIMS) that link together government incentives and policies for a broad range of trade, investment and financial issues. The emergence of debt-to-equity swaps made contingent on export performance and the debates about how to manage the trade effects of financial institutions are other manifestations of the growing interdependence of previously separate policies. International institutions like the World Bank, IMF, and OECD all have to adjust their policies and reconsider the effectiveness of their loan conditions and structural adjustment programmes.

In a world of increasing divergence among the fortunes of nation states, the role of the international institutions becomes ever more important. Weak institutions will inhibit the development of the kinds of partnership we seek and indeed hope for. How they, too, will adjust to the new challenges will also affect the existing balance in the triangular diplomacy.

LOOKING AHEAD

Change in the international political economy points one way: states are losing power to pursue independent policies and now must master the new game of triangular bargaining. At the same time, the outcomes of the bargaining have been markedly divergent. Indeed, divergence is a *leitmotif* of this book – divergence between continents, between countries in the same continent or region, even within countries over time and among sectors and, finally, divergence between firms – not necessarily in accordance with their national origin. Hardly surprising that, with so many intervening variables, there has been so much variety in the opportunities for change and in the speed with which moves could be made.

The main arguments that follow, therefore, concern the effect of the structural changes on states and firms as interdependencies have multiplied. We aim to show how interdependence affects the options open to both, and why the criteria they use for choice and action can only usefully be considered in the framework first of the triangular nature of the bargaining and second of the matrix of multiple, but related agendas affecting their relationships.

It follows from the above that the skills of managing multiple agendas simultaneously are at a growing premium – for governments, and also for firms. Governments need to manage a series of difficult trade-offs among competing internal and external objectives. They run considerable risk if they fail either to keep some of these agendas separate or to manage the separation in such a way as to appear inconsistent and thus to lose the confidence of prospective investors. Judging where and how to 'ring-fence' the individual agendas stretches the administrative capacity of government. They also run considerable risks if they limit their sights to sectoral preference and fail to perceive that they must also identify strong firms as partners in development.

The more complex the economy, the greater the difficulty in establishing and maintaining explicit policies. Complexity leads to greater reliance on implicit policy, or even in extreme cases to policy setting by default; one can tell only with hindsight what the policy was in the first place. One observer concluded recently that 'the state's most crucial task by far is to provide the rule of law' (Crook, 1989). But the rule of law has to be one that appears reasonably stable and not plagued by frequent, arbitrary alteration.

We also find that many governments adopting more outward-looking, export-promoting policies lack the political will or necessary national consensus to implement them. Central among the many obstacles is that of changing established administrative practice. There can be too many vested interests in the status quo. When change will create too many local 'losers', it will be resisted no matter how strong are the rational arguments. How to address this knotty problem is an issue we pick up at the end of the book, for we believe that all too few observers pay adequate attention to the behavioural aspects of government. The risk that policy pronouncements will not be enacted often lies in the realm of the civil service.

Firms face exactly the same problems of growing complexity. They may seem better equipped for the necessary juggling act because of the greater focus on a limited number of objectives and greater abilities to implement policy in a command structure. Yet even firms are finding that their ability to command from the centre is being challenged by their managers at local levels. Multinationals are far from the monolithic actors they are often deemed to be.

Implicit in these arguments is a general concern about the adequacy of existing theory to explain what has been happening. By working at the micro-level of individual firms and investment projects, we found many instances where we could not have anticipated the outcomes had we predicted them using received wisdom. Our concern is not that the theories are wrong, but incomplete and insufficient to reflect

30

the changes we observe. Because the way the question is asked has much to do with the answer produced, we start the next chapter with a review of theory and a statement of what we see as the critical issues on which progress is needed. Those readers already familiar with the theory may wish to skip over this section; alternatively they may wish to test our ideas against their own.

2 STRUCTURAL CHANGES

The new diplomacy we sketched in chapter 1 has three critical and intertwined ingredients: the bargaining among states for power and influence, the competition among firms contesting the world market and the specific bargaining between states and firms for the use or creation of wealth-producing resources. All three are critically influenced by and in turn influence the world structures of security, finance and knowledge (Cox, 1987; Strange, 1988). The changes in these structures during the last few decades have altered the ground rules for everyone. Structural change has not, however, had a uniform effect on either firms or countries. Though the experience of structural change is common to all, the consequences have been sharply different for both countries and firms.

To make the point, consider the striking contrast during the period 1973–85 'between the serious economic setbacks suffered by the newly oil-rich Mexico and the notable strides made by the oil-poor and oil-hungry Brazil' (Hirschman, 1986). While Mexico's political weakness was excused and its economy helped out by the US, Brazil's relationship with Washington steadily deteriorated and its policies came under American attack. Hirschman's explanation, influenced by the radical Brazilian economist, Antonio Barros de Castro, lay in the fortunate coincidence for Brazil of the 1983 devaluation with the moment when prior investments in heavy industry and infrastructure planned by the military government in the 1970s came to fruition (Lowenthal, 1987). Growth resumed strongly after the hiccup of the debt shock, and expanded industrial exports combined with harsh decisions to reduce imports financed enough of the debt service to maintain trade credit. By contrast, Mexico allowed imports to flood the domestic market and to crowd out capital investment so that growth was slow to get started again on a scale sufficient to keep pace with population growth and urbanisation. Though there were other factors involved, as we discuss in chapter 4, one may conclude that Mexico 'was one of the most active

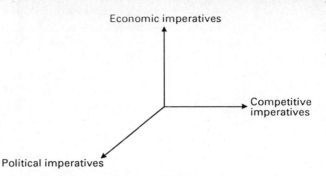

Figure 2.1 A three-way tug-of-war.

borrowers and one of the most careless in its use of funds' (Congdon, 1988: p. 121).

The central argument in this chapter is that change in world structures has created both new possibilities for creating wealth, and new dilemmas for governments as to how to balance the conflicting demands of their domestic and international agendas. Though all three sides of the new diplomatic 'triangle' are interconnected, all too often, states find less connectivity and more a sense of contradictory pulls among the imperatives of choices that cannot be avoided, as figure 2.1 illustrates.

Economic imperatives drive change in the structure of product and financial markets and affect the international division of labour. Competitive imperatives drive firms' choices of strategy and may, as we illustrate later on, have little to do with short-run considerations of national economic factors. The political imperatives are those choices faced by states, either solely or in alliance with others. Whereas many developed countries are learning to resolve the contradictions and find new sources of advantage, we found that in our three countries the choices forced on them were not readily perceived as necessarily beneficial.

To explore why developing countries have such difficulty in resolving these contradictory pulls, we first review some of the most pressing economic and competitive shifts. The combination of greater mobility of critical factors of production, notably technology and finance, creates tensions and uncertainties for firms as they develop their global strategies. These tensions also inform the nature of the political imperatives, both international and national. For example, greater capital mobility has permitted many governments, for good or ill, to initiate development projects that previously had been starved by capital shortage and has helped raise the levels of ambition for future competitiveness and importance on the world stage. Most critically, the clash between mobile resources and the largely immobile labour base of an economy has changed the ground rules for determining the attractiveness of a country to potential investors. It is here that the nature of the structural changes raises troubling questions about what defines the 'state' and creates great uncertainty about the validity of many previous ideas and policy prescriptions. The emphasis throughout the chapter is on developments at the world level to provide the backdrop for the more detailed discussions about individual firms and individual states in subsequent chapters.

ECONOMIC AND COMPETITIVE IMPERATIVES

The economic and competitive imperatives that shape the world system are born of two fundamental shifts that have in turn spawned a raft of consequential changes that affect deep-seated attitudes and behaviour. We single out technology and the structure of international finance as the primary driving forces for change. It is impossible to be certain, however, whether it is always technology that has caused change or whether technical innovation has been spurred by changes elsewhere. Causality irrespective, we argue that many of the competitive innovations made possible by new technology could not be realised in corporate strategy without the simultaneous changes in finance. Both, in tandem, have transformed who does what and where they do it to create the wealth governments now seek.

Technology shapes the division of labour

'The international division of labour' is only a fancy way of describing what people do when they go to work. It is no more than the sum of forces – institutions and markets – which determine who is going to produce what goods and services, on what terms and by what combination of the four major factors of production: land, labour, capital and technology. Of these, technology has had by far the greatest impact, by permitting structural changes in internationally linked production systems. These could be described as a New Form of Production. Accelerating change in technology has enhanced the capacity of producers to supply the market with new products and services, and to produce old ones by new processes. For example, recall that when anyone aged thirty today was born, computers were rare; the standard equipment in all offices was a manual typewriter; jumbo jets were only at the development stage; transatlantic phone calls went by cable, not satellite; and television was virtually unseen outside the developed world.

Rapid change in the new supply possibilities unleashed by technical innovation has increased the risks for corporations of equally rapid elimination from the competitive game. Choosing the wrong technology, or failing to take the necessary adaptive measures in management, production or marketing can quickly lead to falling profits, dwindling market shares and finally to takeover or closure. Like the Cheshire cat, many great industrial enterprises, such as Firestone and Dunlop in tyres, have already vanished, leaving behind only their brand names as images to be exploited by their new owners. Many have failed by being slow to realise that commanding a high market share in a single country is seldom enough. As product lives shorten, there is less time to recoup investments in new processes or new products. Besides, investments in innovation are becoming costlier. The combination has impelled manufacturing and service enterprises in almost all sectors to search for larger markets abroad, and to establish themselves there in an 'insider position' (Best, 1990: p. 260; Milner and Yoffie, 1989). It is that, or go under.

Everyone, it would now seem, is in the race to build positions abroad. Though it used to be thought that internationalism was the preserve of the large, private corporation, today they have been joined by small firms and many state enterprises. Declining barriers to trade and investment have made this possible. Not all are American, Japanese or European; some have bases in Taiwan or Korea, or India or Hungary even. The net result is that enterprises with some form of linkage to the global market now account for the largest part of the global production structure – in raw materials, manufactures and services. As vertical integration between producer and seller grows, so the ability of governments and systems such as the GATT to regulate trade declines.[1]

Global production has not become integrated overnight. Though the antecedents are ancient, it was not until the 1960s that one could begin to see the beginnings of what we now call global competition in other than oil and similar natural resource-processing industries. There had, to be sure, been many cross-border investments, but in the main these were to replace imports and were based on exploiting competitive advantage only within a particular country.[2] In the 1960s some firms started investing abroad in forms that linked together production, trade and finance. These linkages provided a source of

Table 2.1. *The changing nature of global competition*

Decade	Factor	Threatened national industries
Pre-1960	Natural resources	Oil, aluminium
1960s	Labour-intensity	Textiles, shoes, simple assembly
1970s	Capital-intensity	Automobiles, machinery, chemicals
1980s	Technology	Consumer electronics, telecoms
1900s	Information	Financial services, media, 'systems' businesses

new competitive advantage for the entire corporate *system* and threatened the foundations of powerful national firms. The beginnings were slow and limited to a few sectors where differences in labour costs were important. From the 1970s onwards, however, the moves began to accelerate and involved quite different factors. Table 2.1 suggests, in simplified form, the changing factors that have shifted particular industries at different times towards global competition.

The first wave of export-creating investments were predominantly in developing countries. Led by, but not restricted to, the Japanese, these were what Michalet (1976) labelled 'workshop' affiliates, to distinguish them from the earlier 'relay' affiliates that 'cloned' the business in the foreign country. These workshops were responsible for only that part of the production process or those components of the final product most sensitive to labour cost differentials, and have been located principally in South-East Asia and parts of Latin America (Grunwald and Flamm, 1985). The gains in the host countries have sometimes proved short-lived, with the initial advantages being eroded by competition from other countries, as we elaborate in chapter 4. Some countries like Malaysia have, however, managed to hang on to the advantages of being early recipients of such investments by virtue of their installed base of experienced workers who could help attract later entrants.

It is the developments from the 1970s onwards that have provided the greatest impetus to transform industries by linking activities ever more tightly across borders. There has been continuous and continuing innovation in competitive strategy to change the 'rules of the game', as we show in the next chapter. Three critical developments were needed to make these innovations possible. One was the impact of information and transport technologies on lowering the real costs – and risks – of managing at a distance. A second has been the creation of new technologies that have altered the scale needed for efficient operation. The third has been the provision of an ever-increasing variety of financial instruments needed to support the growing complexity of cross-border transactions.

Not surprisingly, these developments have been most widely exploited among the developed countries where the barriers to integration have been least. Some of them, particularly in the information-intensive industries, had to wait until deregulation took hold. For example, the deregulation of brokers' commissions on Wall Street in 1975 started a revolution in other financial capitals – the 'big bang' in London – and made possible the rise in international competition in sectors previously reserved for nationals. Japanese security houses such as Nomura now challenge such US financial giants as Merrill Lynch in their own back yard, while the US giants together with the Japanese challenge the European leaders each in their own *chasse gardée*. Similarly, the global development of the telecommunications industry was blunted until the land-mark US anti-trust decision in 1984 to dismember its monopoly supplier, AT&T. With matching moves in Britain and Japan designed to galvanise their moribund monopolists, all the leading players have been propelled into a global contest. The European moves towards 1992 have had similar consequences on a regional scale in those sectors, like defence, pharmaceuticals and informatics, where the barriers of regulation and restrictive public purchasing has been greatest. In other sectors, the regulatory barriers were lower, allowing an earlier flowering of innovative, integrating strategy.

The consequence has been an explosion of FDI flows among the developed countries, as we noted in chapter 1. Only Japan remains relatively isolated in terms of its low receipts of inward investment. The attraction of the USA as a site for 60 per cent of the 1980s investment flows is not only the size of its market but also its favourable and stable political environment for business.[3] Just the opposite, in fact, of corporate perceptions of many developing countries. Indeed, so strong have the differential views on advantageous locations become that one recent assessment of the total stock of foreign capital in developing countries suggests that it is less today than it was in 1900, measured in relation to GNP (Maddison, 1990).[4]

It is noticeable, however, that whereas the G-5 countries now account for 75 per cent of the world's FDI flow, their position as the five major exporters is a much less concentrated 45 per cent. The implications of the imbalance for the future growth of FDI in developing countries and for an expanded trading role are considerable and discussed later on.

Where information technology permits operational integration across borders, other forms of technology are transforming what happens within each operation. They have created new capabilities for the production of widening ranges of goods and services without paying the cost penalties or producing variety in yesterday's inflexible plants. Moreover, system technology is capable of reducing the time needed to respond to changes in demand or to serve orders. These systems apply both within the factories and in the linking of the factories to the markets. Where technology may have reduced the minimum efficient scale within factories, the creation of corporate-wide systems of communication and control have served in many instances to increase the minimum efficient scale of the enterprise as a whole. As chapter 3 shows, however, such developments have been possible in only some industries and to varying degrees.

These New Forms of Production (NFP) have caused significant adjustments within leading multinationals that spell both good and bad news for developing countries. The bad news has at least three components. The first is that, where they exist, they have created a new barrier to entry, making it more difficult for third world firms to compete. Second is that, as the costs of developing the NFP has risen, many firms have had to face up to hard choices of priority about where to concentrate their efforts. Few can afford to compete everywhere, and many have chosen to concentrate on those businesses and markets they know best. Some have withdrawn from smaller territories. Burned by their experience of the volatility of the capital markets, many leading banks such as Bank of America and Lloyds are pulling back from the periphery of their systems to defend their home bases.

The third negative applies in the high-technology sectors. Even if – which in some cases is a big 'if' – the patent system does not give away the vital clue to an innovative product of process, innovating enterprises now increasingly prefer to keep their knowledge to themselves in order to preserve their options on when, where and how to market it. For developing countries, this internalisation of innovation makes it more desirable to strike a bargain with the innovator, because the alternative of paying patent fees simply does not exist. Offsetting this cost is the possibility for some to make their own developments off the back of previous transfers of knowledge. As Lall (1985) and others have noted, some developing countries have been able to create 'localised technical advances' that emphasise their relatively greater knowledge of low-wage countries and so establish advantage in neighbouring markets. But these offsets are seldom adequate to compensate for the inability to afford the technological investments needed to compete globally.

The good news for developing countries is that change has opened up unforeseen opportunities. One comes from change in the methods of manufacturing. In the 1960s, for example, it was often argued that the prospects of developing a car industry in Latin America were poor because the small size of the local market meant that small local plants could never compete on cost with imported cars. What this argument did not anticipate was that new, flexible methods of manufacturing made possible by electronics sharply reduced the minimum economies of plant scale. These opened up new opportunities of producing components either for export to the big car companies in America or Europe, or for sale to the local affiliates of those same companies. In Brazil, for example, the change has meant a vast increase in the added-value part of the supply chain in local hands. Their exports of auto components have risen sharply as VW, Ford and other majors have altered their supply policies.[5] These exports are still, to be sure, 'dependent', in the terms of the matrix in chapter 1, but they are none the less valuable and help to explain the asymmetry of the multinationals' share of investment and their share of trade.

A second source of opportunity has been created as innovative third world firms such as Comcraft from Kenya have found that the systems of their much larger, multinational rivals have become overly complicated and expensive and can be simplified. The consequently enlarged margins, especially when tied to the acquisition of operations shed by their rivals in peripheral territories, open up new avenues of growth unsuspected by 'rational' calculations of advantage. A third source of opportunity has opened up by the increased willingness of many firms to contemplate non-traditional forms of investment (NFI), also in their marginal territories. Similar attitudes may be adopted by newer, weaker rivals as they seek novel forms of alliance to overcome the disadvantages they face in tackling the world leaders head-on. These opportunities have risks and costs as well as gains. A fuller discussion of the balance of effect is, therefore, deferred until chapter 5 when a greater range of consideration can be entertained.

Managing all these new systems and new options places great demands on executive ability. To develop adequate and growing capability requires investment in human skills and provides a new kind of barrier to the entry of more newcomers into the international system. As later chapters show, these barriers are beginning to differentiate the corporate winners from the losers. There are, however, limits to the capability of any one firm to cope with all the new challenges. Many of the largest firms, such as Fujitsu and General Electric, are finding that they have had to enter into alliances with competitors to create an adequate spectrum of global advantages. Alliances bring new problems: as the Japanese say 'same bed: different dreams'. Learning how to reconcile the conflicting interests of the partners is a new challenge that is as yet imperfectly understood. Like ministers new to government, managers are learning how to become statesmen and to reject the certainties that 'winning' strategies can endure without new alliances.

No matter how skilled the executives, these shifts in the production structure would not have been possible without complementary adjustments in the way firms can organise their financial affairs. As competition shifts towards a more frenetic pace of activity, so the need to clear the cash balances speedily increases. Inefficiency in the financial function can erode the benefits offered by the new technologies. The communications and information revolution has permitted progressively greater central control over their financial affairs. Moreover, the leading multinationals have been able to gain critical efficiencies in financing the whole system. They now go to international markets, especially the Euro-currency markets, not just their national ones. With more recent developments such as currency swaps and loans based on a basket of currencies, they have been able to lower their cost of capital and reduce the risks of their asset exposure in multiple currencies. Thus, it is to the financial structure that we now turn.

INTERNATIONAL FINANCIAL STRUCTURE

By the international financial structure we mean the system by which in a market-based economy, credit is created, bought and sold and by which, therefore, the use of capital is determined. This is not to be confused with the international monetary system which is usually understood to mean the system that governs exchange rate parities. The two may interact with one another – for instance when countries try to control capital outflows in order to maintain a given exchange rate. But, conceptually they are quite different. Both are important in affecting state-enterprise bargaining, but they need to be assessed separately.

It is in the international financial structure that change in the past two decades has proceeded fastest, away from nationally-centred credit systems toward a single system of integrated financial markets. Instead of a series of national financial systems linked by a few operators buying and selling credit across the exchanges, we now have a global system, in which national markets, physically separate, function as if they were all in the same place. The balance has shifted from a financial structure which was predominantly state-based with some transnational links, to a predominantly global system in which some residual local differences in markets, institutions and regulations persist as vestiges of a bygone age. The pressures for greater convergence of national policy, at least among the developed countries, are irresistible.

Peter Drucker may have overstated his case when he observed that 'capital movements rather than trade ... have become the driving force of the world economy' (Drucker, 1986: p. 768), but he has pointed the finger at a central issue in the global environment. The world economy controls events, not the macro-economics of the nation state. Consequently, developments in the international financial structure have had a decisive influence on how wealth-creating activities are divided among nations.

Twenty years ago, many of the smaller economies were more or less cut off from the world market economy. Today, there are virtually none, apart from extreme cases such as Albania and Myanmar.[6] Yet, though most developing countries have created ties to the international system for sovereign borrowing and for accommodating the demands of the World Bank and others for the adoption of more 'outward-looking' policies, many retain features of the old system of financial isolationism and inefficiency (Dooley and Mathieson, 1987). Elaborate systems of exchange control, combined with politically-influenced procedures of domestic credit rationing can serve to keep critical parts of the domestic economy sheltered from the demands of the international economy. Where these domestic effects are strong, the country has prevented any far-reaching adjustments of the domestic economy at the micro-economic level. In particular, national desires to shift from import-replacing investments to export-creating ones may be confounded by administrative impossibility. In short, failure to adjust fully to the demands of the newly-integrated global financial system can be a specific handicap to future development.

The consequences of structural change in international finance can be summed up in two words: Innovation and Mobility. Together they were the necessary and sufficient conditions for the surge in bank loans to the developing countries in the 1970s, and together they provide much of the explanation for the reverse flow of funds, from South to North, that followed in the 1980s (see figure 1.3).

Innovation

To gauge the full significance of recent innovations in the international financial system, recall that in all market economies, it has always been possible to 'buy' money, like any other commodity. Money for use today can be bought in exchange for money to be repaid some time in the future. (By contrast, in a socialist or command economy, credit, like any other commodity, is allocated by the agencies of the state; the market does not come into it.) In market economies, the key is that the very process of trading credit actually creates money. The money-traders (bankers) take deposits from savers and then issue promises-to-pay to borrowers. Ever since the Middle Ages, bankers' promises-to-pay, issued first as instruments of credit, have turned into money by being used as a means of exchange in their own right. The same thing happened later with governments' promises-to-pay. These too started as promises to exchange paper for gold, but soon became currency, a normal medium for exchange of goods and services. After a while, and usually in wartime, governments were able to suspend the promise, so that the paper became simply paper money.

Over the last thirty years or so, a similar evolution by which credit instruments become money has rapidly taken place for the world market economy as a whole. It began with the Eurodollar market. By creating new credit instruments – at first Eurodollar loans, then Certificates of Deposit and more recently all sorts of commercial paper (i.e. more promises-to-pay issued direct by enterprises), banks began creating money in a new, unregulated international banking system, thus adding to the world's money supply. For, as before, the credit instruments soon became used as means of exchange. The availability of credit sustained investment and lubricated the channels of trade.

The results were all good for so long as the growth in output kept pace with the expansion of the new 'money'. While much economic theory ascribes the sustained economic growth of post-war decades to the liberalisation of trade and the lowering of tariff barriers through GATT negotiations, it seems far more likely that the real engine of growth has been credit-creation, begun by governments through the Marshall Plan and other state-initiated measures but continued through the combined efforts at financial innovation of transnational corporations and banks in issuing tradeable commercial paper.

Trouble came after 1973 when much of the credits landed up in the hands of oil-producing sheiks who did not know how to spend all this new-found wealth. The world economy was given a deflationary jolt.

42

The unwillingness of oil-consuming societies to check their spending resulted in the phenomenon of stagflation: slow growth combined with inflation. The stagnation would have been much worse had the banks, with whom the sheiks deposited their unspent dollars, not quickly recycled them to governments and enterprises in developing countries where rates of return on invested capital were high and the potential growth seemed relatively high, at least initially.

Such rapid recycling simply could not have happened either in socialist systems (dependent on credit-by-*fiat*), or by Western governments attempting to get the taxpayers' democratically elected representatives in government to vote the funds for expanded government-to-government loans, i.e. foreign aid. Nor could it have happened on such a scale had the banks' powers of credit-creation been constrained by the prudential rules governing national financial structures. This is not to deny that – as the rude awakening for the debtor countries of 1982 showed only too clearly – there were risks in unregulated credit creation. The risks, as always, are of two kinds: that too much credit is created and inflation results; or that too little credit is created and deflation results.

The expanded scale of the banks' operations depended on two significant types of innovation: technical and structural (Enkyo, 1989). Technical innovations have included the idea of arranging money transfers by issuing chequebooks, the use of plastic credit and cheque cards or the automatic, electronic transfer of funds and cheque-clearing systems between banks. Structural innovation means the introduction of new credit instruments or the development of new kinds of business by banks, such as the invention by Citibank of Certificates of Deposit in 1965 or the introduction of Money Market Funds and NOW accounts by Merrill Lynch in the mid-1970s.

Structural innovation began with the creation of offshore, relatively unregulated Eurocurrency markets in the 1960s, as US banks searched for ways to get round irksome (and costly) domestic restrictions. The second stage brought in much more fundamental and hard-to-reverse changes. The banks developed a new role as providers of financial services, such as arranging leveraged buyouts, marketing commercial paper for corporate clients or advising LDCs on their rescheduling strategy. They ceased to act solely as intermediators between savers and investors. They became suppliers of financial services and more or less autonomous, internationally spread, gatekeepers to the Aladdin's Cave of the financial markets.

Further innovation began in the 1970s as banks came to regard their foreign branches as profit centres in their own right, not just as

43

overseas service counters for domestic clients with overseas interests. The enhanced mobility of dollar funds and other short- and medium-term credit enlarged opportunities for commercial enterprises. But at the same time, it increased risks for national governments, both as helmsmen for the national economy and as the ultimate authority responsible for maintaining or improving the creditworthiness of the state as a debtor seeking finance from the system.

This was the scenario of the 1980s against which the mini-dramas of our company-government bargaining was played out. The bargaining was affected both by the new opportunities opened up in the 1970s and by the growing risks attendant on the 1980s. In both periods, the decision making of governments and enterprises was greatly complicated by the changes in the financial structure.

Mobility

The altered financial structure greatly enhanced the mobility of capital. Instead of most loans being made and credit instruments issued and traded within national systems under national authorities and in accordance with recognised, fairly stable rules, the new system is a worldwide network of banks and financial operators linked together by cheap, reliable and instant means of communication – but operating under far less well-defined and exigent rules.

The opportunities opened up by the technical innovations are so large and exciting that it is hard to grasp the full extent of the change. Instead of a world of national economies linked mainly by trade, we have a world linked more closely by flows of funds across national frontiers. In any week or month, these international financial flows are fifty times greater in value than the flow of goods (Spero, 1988). By comparison with the mobility of labour or of goods, the accelerated mobility of capital in the world market economy is of an altogether different order.

Greater mobility has bred greater volatility. Whereas conventional economic theory predicted that a change to flexible exchange rates would eliminate financial crises and allow markets to ease and soften adjustment to change, the opposite happened. Volatility increased, and the extent as well as the direction of change became less predictable. Expert advice proliferated, but in contradictory ways. Where, and how far up or down, exchange rates or interest rates would go became matters of great importance to government and business. For developing countries, volatility increased the direct impact on their domestic policies and plans. Openness, urged on them by the hegemonic power, the United States, and the international organisations it dominated, and implicitly accepted by their own decisions to borrow heavily from foreign banks, multiplied their vulnerability. Corporations, having greater advantages of physical and financial mobility were also exposed, but to a lesser extent. The sense of impotence and frustration experienced by the policy makers in developing – as, indeed, in developed – countries, has often encouraged nationalist reactions. As with so many other aspects of the new international political economy, weak international institutions will continue to allow the divergence and unpredictability of the impact of global change on individual nations.

The debt crisis

Structural change combined with greater mobility increased the role of financial markets (and market operators) at the expense of states. By facilitating the recycling of resources from surplus to deficit economies, the system's stability was placed in jeopardy unless the flows could be maintained. The consequences of this dependence were seen when the flow was cut off so abruptly after 1982. The banking system – and with it the whole world market economy – was subjected to new risks of insolvency if debtors defaulted or delayed repayment.

The uneven impact of the debt crisis on developing countries can be seen in each of four groups. The first group includes those countries, like India, that had not borrowed heavily in relation to their size. Though they missed the opportunity for a rapid spurt in growth in the 1970s, they were spared the social and political strains of vulnerability to the subsequent cut-off in bank credit. India's foreign debt per head in the early 1980s was about $30; Brazil's was $480 (Nunnenkamp, 1986: p. 25). In the second group, there were those countries, like Kenya, who had never been able to borrow much from the banks. Their needs for funding, however, grew as interest charges rose, commodity prices fell and competition for export market shares from the indebted countries intensified. The international organisations and aid donors did what they could to fill the gap by giving them special status and new credit facilities, but it was only just enough to keep them financially afloat. This closer relationship incidentally increased the role of the state in most of these economies, but subjected it to the risks inherent in the political strings which the lending institutions attached to their 'aid'.

The other two groups were the 'heavily indebted' borrowers. They can be divided into the safe and the unsafe. Some were 'safe', because, like Malaysia, they had not borrowed beyond their capacity to repay. Others were also 'safe' by virtue of being able to count on diplomatic help during the post-1982 adjustment. The United States, moved by geo-political motives, came up with massive government aid for Mexico.[7] South Korea also got special help from Japan under the formal guise of reparations. The fact that the postwar treaty had been a dead letter for many years did not worry either party. The Japanese government was aware that putting up $3 billion to help Korea service its large foreign debt was going to be in the long-term interests of the many Japanese companies with investments and joint ventures in Korea. The result was that in subsequent phases of the debt 'crisis', the Korean government never had to negotiate with foreign bankers or with the IMF.

The 'unsafe', heavily indebted countries were those who had over-borrowed but got no special international diplomatic help. For these countries, the impacts of what has been dubbed the 'forced adjustment phase' (Mentre, 1984) were reflected internally, with the main burden of adjustment often falling on wage-earners. In the first two years of the debt crisis, Brazilian per-capita GDP fell by 8 per cent, unemployment rose by 13 per cent, and consumer prices doubled. The large role of foreign banks in Brazilian development in the 1970s earned them a central role in the later adjustment period. Their behaviour in Brazil was, however, complicated by the monetary authorities and policies of their home government – primarily, that of the United States since it was US banks who had taken the lead and were therefore the most exposed (Frieden, 1987; Nunnenkamp, 1986).

It was thus the internal policies of the United States that determined to a great extent who among the indebted nations won and who lost out in the long debt crisis of the 1980s (Wellons, 1987). A recent study of US banking supervision policies in the 1980s shows how domestic policies, adopted to safeguard the solvency of the domestic banking system, could exacerbate the pains of adjustment for the debtors (Pauly, 1990). In theory, the US prudential rules prevented banks from lending more than 15 (later 10) per cent of their capital to any one borrower. But in practice these rules were not properly enforced, allowing banks to 'pretend' that loans to state-owned enterprises were not loans to a 'country'. Though an Interagency Country Risk Exposure Review Committee was set up in 1978 to assemble the facts, no one insisted that the banks took notice of them or acted accordingly. Instead of reducing their exposure to Brazil, for example, after the second oil shock in 1979, some US banks who had already lent 100 per cent or more of their capital to Mexico and Brazil, actually increased their exposure.

They did so under pressure of increased competition. Greedy for profits and market share, they shaved profit margins and incurred unwarranted risks. Fearful of the growing possibilities of default, the US monetary authorities then pulled sharply on the reins by insisting on tougher capital/asset ratios. This forced the US banks to set aside more of their profits as reserves. With lesser ability to lend, they exacerbated the plight of their indebted customers. As Pauly (1990: p. 41) concluded, 'regulatory reforms designed to enhance market efficiency and institutional competitiveness ... effectively provided distinct incentives for most banks to get out of the business of development finance'.

This would not have mattered if the US government, instead of giving special bilateral help only to Mexico had taken earlier, bigger steps to ease the pain of adjustment for all the major debtors. The Baker Plan of 1986 was a move in the right direction but came only *after* what the IMF called the painful adjustment phase of 1983–4 was over. Besides, the Plan was not big enough to convince the banks that the risks of co-financing were acceptable. The 1989 Brady Plan proposed financial support from the Fund and Bank, supplemented by Japan, to relieve the debtors, provided they initiated economic reforms. It, too, sounded good but eighteen months later had been applied to only four favoured countries – Mexico, Venezuela, Costa Rica and the Philippines.

The prime concern for the adjustments was the preservation of the banks and the international financial system. The impact of the credit famine on indebted countries was secondary. This indifference was naturally felt most acutely by the countries like Kenya in the second group of borrowers and by countries like Brazil in the fourth. The knock-on consequences were even more severe. The various plans failed to restore the confidence of either foreign banks or foreign investors. They became less willing to transfer capital to the most troubled borrowers by the conventional means of foreign direct investment. For example, many of the foreign firms we talked to in Brazil had adopted policies of limiting their capital budgets to locally generated profits, less dividends remitted home. Such risk-avoiding moves did not, however, stop them from continuing to deepen their involvement in the economy by other means.

Alternatives to financial transfers

As the UNCTC notes, 'the sharp decline in FDI flows to developing countries does not mean that TNCs have been ignoring those areas. In fact, ... they have expanded their contacts with developing countries through the use of a variety of business arrangements other than direct investment. [These non-equity arrangements] include licensing agreements, franchising, sub-contracting, management contracts and joint ventures.' Quite how much these New Forms of Investment (NFI) have expanded is open to debate, for there are no reliable estimates. None the less, they are an important new feature of the global financial structure. They are 'invisible investments', just as earnings of foreign exchange by the sale of banking, insurance and other services to foreigners are described as 'invisible exports'. Essentially, what the firm is doing is to reap an additional return on the capital already invested at home in developing the product by transferring its know-how across frontiers. However disembodied, it is still capital.

From the host country's point of view, although no capital has been transferred, the licence payments are the exact equivalent of dividends paid on debenture shares or to payments of interest on a loan. But there are no hard and fast definitions of NFI; the distinction between a sale by the investor which represents some sort of invisible investment and one which does not is not always easy to see, especially with turn-key contracts. Oman (1984, 1989) suggests that the crucial test is whether the arrangement involves some element of risk to the seller – and some prospect of a share in future income. But, unlike equity investments of the traditional kind, there need not be in NFI arrangements a direct correspondence between the degree of risk assumed by each party and the degree of control exercised by them. This would be something to be bargained over.

Where the NFI is very important to the multinational, it may be in a position to exert total control. An example is how NFI-type arrangements have made possible the development of Brazil's automobile component industry. General Motors has increased its sourcing of components from local subcontractors. To make sure that these components met the quality standards needed by the main plant, the company despatched, at its own expense, what they described to us with only mild exaggeration as 'a regiment of engineers' from Detroit, some of whom stayed down in Brazil for months advising the subcontractors on how to meet the company's standards. In corporate accounting, this would go down under salaries or labour costs; while for Brazil it represented an investment of time and resources as well as a transfer of technology. GM has reduced its financial exposure in Brazil, but it has not reduced its long-term commitment: the continuing success of its assembly plants there depend crucially on the quality and reliability of its local suppliers, all of whom need continuing sources of assistance to upgrade their capabilities as technologies and competitive standards shift.

In other cases, as we more fully discuss in chapter 5, the use of NFI alternatives to capital transfers incur distinctly second-best solutions to the problem. None the less, the fact that such alternatives are being employed means that one must look beyond both debt and FDI flows to capture a fuller sense of how multinationals are extending their reach into even the most troubled countries. The decline of LDC's share of the investment flows reflects the uncertainties consequent on the debt problem and is the counterpart to the strikingly increased concentration in intra-OECD FDI noted earlier. But that would not necessarily be inconsistent, in some sectors at least, with an expansion of multinationals' activities in developing countries where growth rates were better or markets protected and where they could do so without transferring fresh capital. Whether by some form of contract or by increasing local capital, firms can continue expanding their economic involvement. They are also changing the nature of the risks they choose to manage. Yet, however disembodied, these are still transactions involving foreign capital.

POLITICAL IMPERATIVES

We turn now to the third of the imperatives that shape the bargaining climate: the political context. For developing countries especially, the contradictory tugs from the imperatives of economics and competition pose dilemmas of choice. In many instances, the choices are not of their own making, but the product of the world system, and are often perceived as contrary to the national interest. To explore why this should be so, we first have to be a bit more precise. What do we mean by 'the political context'?

Clearly, there are two parts to it: the international, and the national. Political economists would say that both are aspects of a security structure. Just as the production structure consists of arrangements governing what is produced where and by whom, so the security structure consists of the arrangements governing the provision of security, for persons and property, for states and for enterprises. On the international level, such security as there is derives from some sort

49

of balance of power between states. When it breaks down, war may result. At the national level, the degree of security provided for firms and individuals usually derives from the government's maintenance of law, order and increasingly regulatory behaviour. Yet at the same time, governments may threaten to take away or violate the security of firms or individuals, in their person or in their property. Thus, in political economy terms, change in the global security structure – the context of bargaining – may take place both at the international level (as relations among states change) and at the national level as a result of the changing relations between the state and what sociologists call civil society (Cox and Jacobson, 1973).

For example, if the firm's home state and the host state go to war, bargaining with the latter is bound to be gravely affected, as British firms experienced recently in Argentina. The company's property may even be forfeit, as happened to German corporate property in America or Britain in 1946. Equally, bargaining may be affected by internal political change. If the host government appears to lose authority, or the legitimacy of its authority, over its civil society, the firm's security will be at risk. An example was the effect of the Soweto riots in 1976 in South Africa. Foreign companies immediately became less ready to invest in the country. A less extreme example was the waning legitimacy and sense of control of the Sarney government in Brazil in the late 1980s, which undoubtedly stimulated some of the capital flight. This in turn reinforced the vicious circle of foreign debt, exchange controls, administrative impediments to corporate planning and the reluctance of foreigners to increase investment in the country.

International politics

The main changes in the international political system are well known and understood. The first is often described as the change from a bipolar to a multipolar world, though it is debatable whether there really are multiple, more or less equal power centres as the phrase implies. What is actually meant is that the world is no longer so clearly divided as it was in the 1950s and 1960s into two armed camps of allies, with China, after 1960, causing something of a schism in the Russian camp. Each superpower's dominance over its associated allies rested on its ability to provide a nuclear umbrella. That dominance began significantly to diminish once the superpowers started to negotiate arms controls.

If the superpowers are still perceived as dominant, it is for other reasons. For instance, US domination over South Korea is now less exclusively based on the military protection it offers against invasion from the North: it is increasingly based on the threat of closure of the US domestic market to Korean exports. More subtly, the United States has created an alternative form of economic hegemony through the market position of its multinationals. As the US share of world exports has declined, the US multinationals' share of world trade of manufactured goods actually increased between 1966 and 1984 (Lipsey and Kravis, 1987). Nye (1984) made the same point when he observed that the agenda for examining the power of US firms in the 1980s was little different from that of the early 1970s, despite the relative loss of US power. He argued that the success of US multinationals had become much less dependent upon US hegemony and challenged Gilpin's earlier claims (1971: p. 54) that 'a diminution of the Pax Americana and the rise of powers hostile to the global activities of multinational corporations would bring their reign over international economic relations to an end'.

The workings of these changes have had quite different effects on our three countries. Kenya has been the least affected, because it had never occupied a strategically important corner of a continent that had largely been ignored in the bipolar world of the superpowers.[8] They have had most effect on Malaysia. The political context for investors there has shifted from that of a favoured frontline position on the Western side of the Bamboo Curtain in the 1950s to that of an emergent player in a dynamic, economically important region in the 1980s. In the 1950s, the civil war with the Communists had made the newly independent government nervous about its future defence and security. Britain was a member of SEATO, the US alliance organisation in the region, and shared the US interest in containing the Asian spread of communism. It also had a more direct interest in keeping Malaysia in the sterling area. The result, in 1957, was 'a bargain unique in the history of the unscrambling of the British empire' under which Malaya (as it then still was) agreed to bank her foreign exchange surpluses from exporting rubber and tin in sterling in London, while Britain undertook responsibility for Malaysian security. Thus, colonial dependence was prolonged beyond independence, with marked effects on British investment in Malaysia. Only after the dissolution of the Malaysian Federation, did the Malaysian government take over control of monetary policy and reserve management from the old colonial currency board (Strange, 1971). The lingering effects of Malaysia's earlier position in the security structure go far to explain some of the subsequent changes both in the investment strategies of corporations and in the policies of the government.

51

For Brazil, which had been the US's chief Latin American ally among surrounding neutrals in World War II, the decline of the bipolar alliance system has been part of a long, slow process of growing mutual disenchantment. The signing of the Rio Treaty in 1947 guaranteed US defence of the Western Hemisphere in peace as in war. In the subsequent decade, a boom in US FDI in Brazil placed US corporations far ahead of others. Subsequently, the American share of both influence and investment has shrunk. Though there were other important factors at work some part of this decline can reasonably be attributed to Brazil's diminished sense of dependence on US military aid and protection (Lowenthal, 1987).

The impact of the international politics of the cold war upon most developing countries was rather distant. The exceptions were those few developing countries where America feared most the possibilities of Soviet or Chinese expansion. In particular, South Korea and Taiwan both got a kick-start to economic growth from lavish American aid and easy access to the US market. Both made the most of their chance. Others, like Iran or Pakistan, were unable or unwilling to do so. In the development game, only a few countries benefited substantially from the conflict between the superpowers.

Of much more direct relevance to all developing countries has been the burial of third world hopes for an effective political alliance of the poor against the rich. Born in the 1960s, the UN's decade of development, these hopes had been reinforced by the success of OPEC in the 1970s, only to be buried in the course of the 1980s. By the time the debt crisis hit in 1982, it was already clear that solidarity among the delegations of developing countries at the United Nations and in other international forums was not enough. The Group of 77, as the developing countries called themselves, had already discovered the capacity of the opposing phalanx of rich, aid-giving industrialised countries either to stonewall their demands for more aid or for preferential trading arrangements, or to fob them off with empty, symbolic gestures.

Recall that in 1964 the developing countries used their voting power in the UN to call the first United Nations Conference of Trade and Development (UNCTAD), because they had been frustrated by the rules operating in the GATT. These rules stipulated that negotiations on trade matters could only be initiated by principal suppliers. When developing countries wanted better terms of access for their exports of manufactures, they found that the principal supplier was invariably an industrialised country. Moreover, even when negotiations were opened, the principle of reciprocal bargaining introduced by the

United States as a result of its own domestic legislation from the 1930s, meant that the LDC's had little to bargain with. Their markets were small and concessions were rated by combining the size of the proposed tariff cut with the size of the market. The equality of treatment boasted by GATT worked only among equals and to the detriment of the small.

Superficially, the rich countries appeared to make two concessions to the UNCTAD complaint of inequality in international trade. One was to acknowledge that GATT's rules should take account of levels of economic development, and that developing countries henceforward would not invariably be expected to make reciprocal concessions to the rich, developed countries. When it came to practice, however, the concession meant little. In the 1960s Kennedy Round of multilateral trade negotiations, the much-acclaimed reductions in barriers to manufactures' trade did little for those LDC's that were poorly placed to produce, let alone export them. A trend had already been set in textiles, where the comparative advantage of cheap labour was becoming important. The Long Term Cotton Textile Agreement of 1962 (LTA) permitted the developed countries to check imports from developing countries. By the 1970s, when the more comprehensive MultiFibre Arrangement (MFA) of 1974 took the place of the LTA, these quotas put a virtual stop to further export growth of the most successful textile producers.

The second concession was to exempt from most GATT rules those developing countries who could benefit from preferential trade arrangements offered by some rich countries, such as the European Community's Lomé Conventions, or by regional agreements like the Latin American Free Trade Area (LAFTA) or the Central American Common Market (CACM), both established in 1960. But because most of the LDC's exports were primary products sold in open, competitive markets, and because when it came to their nascent manufacturing industries they were in hot competition with each other, these concessions brought little benefit.

High as their hopes had been after the OPEC price rise of 1973, the Group of 77 failed to get substantial support for its proposed Integrated Programme for Commodities. Under pressure from France and other Europeans, the US reluctantly agreed to a North–South dialogue to consider this and other matters. At the ensuing Conference on International Economic Cooperation (CIEC) in Paris in 1976, the only small concession made to the demand for a New International Economic Order (NIEO) was a grudging and procrastinating acceptance of the idea of a Common Fund to support price stabilisation

53

arrangements for eighteen of the most important commodities exported from developing countries. Setting up such a Common Fund proved even more difficult and it was not until 1986 that the required number of states ratified the agreement. Even then, major subscribers like the US and the USSR had not come up with the necessary money. By that time, the writing on the wall for the G–77 was clear for all to see. Little was to be expected from combining forces and votes in international organisations. It was each for himself in a hard, competitive world.

One significant casualty of the collective defeat of the G-77 was the attempt to use international organisations, specifically the United Nations, to put shackles on the multinational enterprise by means of an agreed Code of Conduct. But by the mid-1980s, after more than a decade of discussion the G-77 had been unable to get the industrialised countries to agree to substitute the mandatory 'shall' for the advisory 'should' in the draft Code (Zacher and Finlayson, 1988: ch. 2). The liberal, non-mandatory OECD Code of 1976, together with the ILO's Tripartite Declaration dealing with social issues were left as the only general guideline for foreign investors in developing countries.[9] Neither have much influence over those countries most concerned with getting what they can from the colder world of *sauve qui peut*.

Domestic politics

In this new world of each for himself, the influence of domestic politics on state–firm bargaining has correspondingly grown. The gap between stable, competent states (whether large or small) and unstable, incompetent and often corrupt states incapable of inspiring confidence whether as political or economic partners has widened. Far from lessening the role of domestic politics, the growing interdependence of the world economy has put new pressure on the national political authority. The essence of the change is that the intermediating function between social and economic forces is no longer one that a government can renounce or let go by default.

One might consider the primary choices for domestic policy to be those affecting autonomy, security, efficiency and the distribution of wealth. In the early postwar decades it seemed that governments had some clear options. States could choose to join the Soviet Union or the People's Republic of China in the non-market part of the world economy. They could also choose to maintain barriers to trade, to investment and to other financial transactions with the outside world.

They could also match political neutrality with economic autarky as a means to maintaining the autonomy of the state and its immunity to external pressures.

Most of these options have been closed out in the last two decades. Economic growth in the open world market economy has been so great that few governments are now in strong enough control over their civil societies to be able to deny them the chance to participate in this wealth-creating system. Khrushchev's boast in the 1960s that socialism would bury capitalism sounds laughable now, as Poland and Hungary scramble ahead of the Soviet Union in economic reforms. Even Gorbachev proclaimed the Soviet Unions' interest in participating in the management of the world market economy. The radical change in Soviet policy was epitomised when Western investors were warmly invited to buy into state-owned enterprises (SOEs) or to set up new ventures, all with the ability freely to repatriate their profits. Here, we see the state as an ardent suitor, suddenly aware of the rich dowry the multinational can bring to the national economy.

Opinions may differ on the relative contributions of different factors to the changes, but of the pressures pushing governments further and faster into the arms of the multinationals there can be little doubt. These pressures complicate the choices for domestic policy and add new dilemmas. Should political authority be managed for national independence or for collaboration? Should considerations of efficiency dominate those of welfare? Should regulation, based on international principles, supersede political intervention in the name of the national interest? Whose interests within the state are of paramount importance? These and other similarly familiar issues are examined in chapter 4 in the light of changing international circumstance.

It seems clear that the USSR, like many developing countries, has been revising its opinion about the nature of what bargaining with firms entails. Instead of thinking of it as a zero-sum game in which one side gains what the other loses, they are beginning to regard it as a positive-sum game from which both sides may gain, provided both play with skill and finesse.[10] They have no illusions about the difficult choices that lie ahead, especially in terms of the distribution of the gains throughout the civil society. The rewards, however, are seen to be worth the effort to master the new game.

What now defines the state?

The reader might conclude from this that we are arguing that Hayek (1979) and Friedman (1962) have won the ideological battle for a diminished role for the state. Their view that the less the state interferes with the market, the better for everyone is a totally different argument, especially as it applies to the developing countries. In any particular society, real life suggests to us that the answers are neither black nor white but rather shades of grey. How much welfare, and in what form, are questions that different societies with different resources and different ambitions will always answer differently. The importance of the shift for the purposes of this book is that the growing competition among states-as-suitors means that government has shed some powers, but taken on others. Their role in fostering education and R & D assumes far greater proportion than hitherto in conditioning their success in attracting those foreign firms who might assist in achieving national aims. This is the basis of our earlier argument that states are being drawn, willy-nilly, into a new game with more complex rules and far greater demands on the skills of public servants.

The new game of competing for world market shares alters the order of importance of the functions of the state. In the long run, the defensive function wanes as the welfare function waxes in importance. Armed forces increasingly take on the role of internal policemen – as they often have in several countries. Where states need armed forces to maintain internal order, as in China or South Africa or Northern Ireland, the military will continue to play a political role. Neighbouring states, observing these forces as a potential threat to themselves as well as to the internal dissidents, will hesitate before dismantling their own forces. But the trends in the global security structure must be toward a demotion of the military functions of the state.

Conversely, in most states the economic functions of the state become more important and more powerful. The capacity to produce internal wealth and to create exports to finance purchases of needed goods and services eases the pressures for social and political change. The dilemma in many countries, though, is that the civil society is itself becoming more fragmented. Whose interests are best being served? Can one think of the state as a giant labour union with an uncommitted workforce? Social divisions, described in chapter 6, complicate the job of those who discharge the functions of the state. They are more interested in tending the cow rather than milking it – the cow being the national economy. Finance ministers and central bankers will be more concerned than generals and defence ministers to keep the cow healthy, well fed and growing than to extract more milk in the form of taxation from the wretched animal.[11]

The problem for analysts here is to define precisely what is the 'cow'. If the aim of states hence forward is to maximise the share of world demand being satisfied from their national territory, industrial policy grows in importance. The European propensity to discriminate in favour of 'national champions' has been strong, as it has been in Japan and to a lesser extent in North America. The power and effectiveness of such discrimination, however, is eroding as the 'national champions' increasingly go offshore either to produce or to procure technologies.[12] The result, both in some sectors where there are producers who are purely home-based and others who are foreign-based, and in whole states, is a political tug-of-war to define the 'cow' according to either the stay-at-home or to the go-abroad interests. The more there are of the latter, the less powerful the pleas of the former for protection against imports or foreign ownership. The more there are of the stay-at-homes, the less warm the welcome for foreign rivals on the home ground.

We see already this battle joined within and between the United States and the European Community. The weapons are competition policy and regulation of trade and services. In both, there are contending forces in each direction and the final outcome for economies as a whole and for particular sectors is still in doubt. In both, too, there are problems of defining the state. In the EEC, there are the member states and increasingly regions, such as the Mezzogiorno or Scotland, whose interests diverge. Within the USA, the states are increasingly flexing their muscles in the form of rushing through anti-takeover laws when a favoured local firm is threatened.[13] The 'state' thus becomes literally a bone of contention between opposed interests, both of whom want control over it in order to decide what precisely its role shall be and in whose interest the market shall be managed. Precisely the same sorts of divisions of opinion plague policy making in less developed countries, though in many the lines of demarcation may lie along racial lines or involve the role of the traditional elites.

In short, a sufficient explanation of the differences in bargaining relations between states and enterprises must include consideration of changes in the security structure as well as to changes in the financial and production structures. It is not enough to say, as successive reports from the IMF or the World Bank have tended to do, that it all depends on governments and that it is up to them how the economy prospers. That is to beg the question of why any particular government was able to act or was constrained from acting in an economically optimal way. The political economist has to look behind policy choices to the structural context of international relations and to the context of the security structure influencing the definition of the role of the state in relation to markets, domestic and global. Managers would be well advised to do the same, for otherwise they will be blind to many of the causal forces at work.

THE REALM OF IDEAS

'A bonfire of the certainties' – the phrase was coined by a British politician in 1989.[14] It aptly describes the structural change that took place in the realm of ideas in the course of the 1980s, and which, no less than the more tangible structural changes in production, finance and politics, made up the context within which foreign firms and host governments bargained over the terms of their association. In the 1970s, most Keynesians, monetarists and marxists still believed firmly in the validity of their diagnoses and the efficacy of their remedies. But by the end of the 1980s none of them – not even the marxists and dependistas – were quite so sure. The evidence before them – literally, thanks to television, before their eyes – was equivocal and contradictory. A comparable uncertainty about the conventional wisdom of past decades can be found among political scientists concerning the forces shaping the state and influencing its responses both to the market and to civil society. There were no more clear guidelines, no simple models, no surefire prescriptions for success. The same is equally true for managers as they wrestle with the new demands of innovations in global competition that we describe in the next chapter.

A brief reminder to the reader of the nature of these uncertainties, without going into a lengthy digression on them, may serve to emphasise the point that this structural change, as much as the other kinds, added to the dilemmas of decision makers both in business and in government. For while the other structural changes altered the range of options open to states and to firms, this one cast a shadow of doubt over which of the available options to choose within the range. The uncertainties concerned not only the ends to be sought but also the means chosen to achieve them.

We see three really major issues on which ideas have undergone change, but without, as yet, reaching a firm verdict either way.

* whether democracy is a help or a hindrance in the pursuit of economic growth. Does a free, politically liberal regime provide a more stable environment for foreign firms than an authoritarian one?

58

* whether in its style of economic management a weak state or a strong one is best for the economy. Do governments throw sand in the works, so that the less they interfere the better? Or, does the economy do better if they act as gardeners, nourishing the soil, pulling out the weeds, selecting the plants?
* whether free trade is superior to protectionism. Given that a totally closed economy is no longer a feasible option, questions remain about the optimal timing, the sectoral priorities and the best forms of liberalisation.

On all three issues, the accumulation of conflicting evidence is the main reason for the discomfiture of the dogmatists, the discrediting of easy, universal theories about economic growth or political progress. On the first issue of political liberalism vs bureaucratic-authoritarianism, the popular dogma of the 1960s and 1970s – in Latin America especially – held that in poor countries, the ruling elites were mainly concerned to hang on to power and also to increase their own wealth, if necessary at the expense of the peasants and the urban proletariat. The elite – bureaucrats as well as politicians – needed, it was asserted, alliances with local business and foreign multinationals. The alliance would sustain the authoritarian political regime. Economically, there would be growth, but also continuing poverty.

But by the 1980s, it was clear that there were contradictory permutations to this simple model of third world backwardness. There had been some authoritarian regimes that were also populist and had been sustained by votes not repressive force. And some of the authoritarian oligarchies had been good for economic growth – as in Brazil in the 1970s, or Singapore under Lee Kuan Yew – while others, like the Greek colonels, had not. Some dictators had been keen to forge triple alliances including foreign firms; other had kept them at arms' length. The diversity of political systems and of economic records in developing countries suggested that international capitalism was not the sole deciding factor. General theories were suspect.

In an influential book, *Bringing the State Back In*, one of the editors, Theda Skocpol (Evans, Rueschmeyer and Skocpol, 1987: p. 28) concluded, 'we do not need a new or refurbished grand theory of The State. Rather, we need solidly grounded and analytically sharp understanding of the causal regularities that underlie the histories of states, societies and structures and transnational relations in the modern world'. This book reflected a growing disenchantment with sociologists' abstract generalities of earlier years. The editors' work had emphasised the divergent consequences on political development of historical experience, of culture and social structures and of external threat. Policy choices reflected what governments perceived as the major threats to the cohesion and survival of the state. This might be foreign invasion, as in Israel or South Korea, or internal strife and divisive conflict as in Sri Lanka. Evans concluded that in some developing countries, the foreign multinationals might be a help and not a hindrance to the state. Their transnational linkages created new problems but also a new role and function for government (1987: p. 193). These linkages moreover could even strengthen the hand of the state against humiliating interference by the US-dominated international financial organisations like the IMF or the World Bank.

The second disputed issue – really Keynesian interventionism vs Hayek-Friedman minimalism – was perhaps the dominant ideological issue of the 1980s. Until well into the 1970s, the almost universal conventional wisdom – except perhaps in the United States – was that the government should stand ready to act as a *deus ex machina*, stepping in to save the capitalist system from its inherent defects of inequality in the distribution of the wealth it created, of unbalanced investment that created private affluence and public squalor, and or vulnerability to cyclical downturn, slump and unemployment (for example, Shonfield, 1965; Galbraith, 1956). By the 1980s, in the wake of the stagflation and slow growth in even the rich economies of the Western Europe, came an equally almost universal loss of faith in the capacity of any individual state to intervene decisively and effectively.

More than that, state intervention, and especially public ownership of the means of production, had sadly disappointed socialist hopes. Instead of balancing and sustaining the economy, it was stunting growth and obstructing innovative flexibility and creativeness to respond to market signals. The most dramatic demonstration of the disillusion came from Eastern Europe at the close of the 1980s. Though some reformers wanted to keep the social democratic welfare-oriented interventions of the state, all were united in wanting to free the production and distribution system from administrative meddling, incompetence and inefficiency. There was wide disagreement about where and how to start dismantling the command economy, but none about the direction for progress.

Such disillusion is not confined to what UN statisticians call the centrally planned economies (CPEs). From Latin America came a devastating critique of the consequences of excessive state intervention through the administration of licences and permits. Hernando de Soto's (1989) study of Peru concluded that government had created a large and costly informal economy by insisting on licenses for everything from building a house or driving a taxi, to starting a shop or business. Rather than pay the bribes and suffer the losses resulting from delays, people took the risk of fines for disobeying the law. In Peru, there were half a million laws, some conflicting, but all administrative. Nearly two-thirds the work force opted to work outside the law, producing a hidden uncounted 29 per cent of the country's GNP.

The evidence we have from foreign firms' experiences in Kenya bear out de Soto's thesis: state intervention can be costly and corrupting. Moreover, the excessive resort to public ownership is a drag on economic development. One World Bank study estimated that in sub-Saharan Africa the public sector accounted for an average 30 per cent of GDP – but appropriated 60 per cent of capital available for investment.

Yet not all the evidence supports the minimalist, Friedmanite conclusion. In Japan and South Korea, and in some sectors in Taiwan, government played an important part in accelerating industrialisation and developing exports. In Taiwan, steel and shipbuilding had both been state-owned. In Korea, industrial policy had clear priorities and had used political power to make sure that firms complied with what the planners wanted. In Japan, the industrial policy of the ruling Liberal Democratic Party worked through industry-wide business associations, and disputes were arbitrated by a strong, meritocratic central bureaucracy.

> The central bureaucracy performed this arbitrating function mainly by developing long-term, multi-issued inter-relationship between each industry and the ministry of jurisdiction with minimal dependence on parliamentary legislation . . . The system appeared elitist but it was mass-inclusionary because bureaucratic rationality was, through the LDP, subject to constituency demands at the constituency level. (Murakami, 1987: pp. 68–9)

These varying forms of state intervention, rather clumsily described as 'bureaucracy-led, mass-inclusionary pluralism' worked well from the 1950s into the 1980s. How they might continue to function is, however, a different matter. Some analysts like Murakami are unsure of the effects as the new, wealthier mass middle class begins to use its political power. And in Korea, the repression of opposition parties and of student and workers' protest suggested that policies suitable to early phases of industrialisation might not continue to be so acceptable.

All in all, state ownership and state intervention with prices has come out with a generally, but not totally, bad record. Some state enterprises have been efficient state enterprises, and some price controls (usually highly selective) effective. For the rest, the Keynesian/monetarist debate is unfinished and inconclusive so far as any particular policy by any individual state is concerned.

Much the same can be said of the third issue, of free trade vs protectionism. It was certainly not so simple an issue as supposed by the old ideologues on either side – the neo-mercantilists in favour of protection and the neo-classical liberals in favour of open, free trade. By comparison with some of their Asian neighbours, the four 'Little Tigers' seemed comparatively liberal in trade matters. Moreover, the record was mixed. South Korea maintained barriers to imports of consumer goods well into the 1980s. Taiwan kept some tariffs high, and until coerced by the United States had used the still more effective trade weapon of an undervalued currency. Even Japan had such a low ratio of imports to GNP that it was repeatedly accused by Washington of covert protectionism, worked through its opaque distribution system. Protectionism it seemed, was not necessarily a hindrance and could even be a help in the transformation of an economy.

That conclusion leaves open the question of what sort of trans-formation is best for the society. By the mid-1980s, some development economists were beginning to question what was meant by successful economic growth. There could be a rise in GNP per head without the poor being any better off than before (Streeten, 1981). Sen, for instance, considered national economic development to be only a means to the end of better living standards. He pointed out that some countries – mainland China, Sri Lanka, Mexico, India, for instance – had failed to achieve as dramatic increases in terms of GNP per head as, say, Korea, but had nevertheless progressed in terms of individual entitlements to food, housing, literacy, health and life expectancy (Sen, 1984, p. 485). Their exports were not always spectacular but their industries produced enough for a growing domestic market. In the case of India, in fact, a highly protected market had been highly competitive in some key sectors of the economy. Local private firms had built up a skilled work force that eventually drew in foreign multinationals on terms acceptable to the government. Hirschman, too, stressed that Latin American countries who by and large had disregarded the wisdom of the liberals had nevertheless managed to improve material standards for most if not all their people (Hirsch-man, 1986).

Perhaps the question is not that of choosing the right theory, but of getting the timing right. Some development economists, hitting at the liberal dogmatism of the Bank and the Fund, were arguing in the late

1980s that the choice was not a simple either-or choice between Import Substitution or Export Promotion. Rather, protecting some selected local markets was a necessary stage in the progress to successful exporting. The difficult decisions for policy makers were when to make the switch of emphasis; and what policy measure to choose to make it effective.

The problem of specifying the timing and the form of effective state action is essentially political, not economic. A government's ability to act coherently and consistently with a predetermined economic strategy, is circumscribed by its dual political role: as both judge and advocate. It is the arbiter of market forces, gatekeeper to the domestic market, and umpire, in the last resort, between conflicting vested interests. And at the same time, it owes its very existence to an alliance of social forces that sees government as the instrument of social domination – whether by a ruling class, a small party or tribal elite or a coalition of either with the bureaucracy of the state. Consequently, choices judged politically feasible are not always economically optimal. One can see the effects of such political calculation in the choices made by each of our three countries, whether it is Malaysian domination of the Chinese, Brazilian bureaucratic domination of unorganised workers, or Kenyan domination of those outside the inner ring of presidential favourites.

As always, the range of politically practicable options open to policy makers at any time is circumscribed by local circumstances, the power base on which they depend and by external forces beyond their control. To that extent, it could be argued that the current disarray of the theorists is a minor factor. Yet because the function of theory in social science is not just to explain, clarify and add to understanding, but also to legitimate some courses of action over others, the contemporary 'bonfire of the certainties' adds one more difficulty to the normal dilemmas of policy making in developing countries. Theory needs to deal more adequately with how general structural change has been a vital ingredient in the transformation of the role multinationals play in their dealings with states.

Global competition is much more than rivalry among firms, for it involves the 'structural competitiveness' of states within the world system. The continuous confrontation is, as Fajnzylber (1988: p. 2) put it

> between different production systems, institutions, schemes and
> social organisations in which business enterprises figure promi-
> nently but are nonetheless only one component of a network that
> links them with the educational system, the technological infra-

structure, management/labour relations, the relations between the public and private sectors, and the financial system.

The structural shifts we have described are pushing business enterprises to the centre of the stage in the evolution of the international political economy. So it is to the consequences of structural change for the economics of global competition and the adjustments of firms' strategies that we now turn.

3   GLOBAL COMPETITION

The accelerating pace of structural change thrusting multinationals more squarely centre-stage in world affairs means that the economics of competition in many industries have been altered fundamentally, and probably irreversibly. What is loosely termed 'global competition' is the outcome of how individual firms have reacted over time to the changing balance of opportunity and threat. The opportunities have been pervasive, given the declining regulatory and technical obstacles to the internationalisation of firms' activities. But so too have been the threats, for not all were able to respond adequately to the new standards set by the leaders. The actions taken by both leaders and followers have, at each turn of the wheel of fortune, helped to create the next round of change. Though most enterprises in developing countries have been by-standers in many rounds, more are now coming forward to play their part for the future. That a Taiwanese enterprise, the Evergreen Marine Corporation, has emerged as the world's largest container shipper reflects the new opportunities, even for latecomers in established industries.

This chapter explores why external change in the international political economy has had the uneven impact on industries we showed in the previous chapter. Some reasons are not hard to find. For example, electronics has transformed many industries, but left others like agriculture relatively unmarked. If during the last twenty years, the costs of automobiles had declined as fast as those for memory capacity in computers, today a Rolls-Royce would cost 50 cents (van Tulder and Junne, 1988). Equally, regulatory change transformed financial services, but had lesser impact on chemicals. Such changes radically alter firms' options for choosing how to serve their foreign markets and create alternative structures of increasingly global competition.

Other reasons are less obvious, for firms have not merely reacted to change in their external environments; many have actively sought to create new, internal sources of advantage. As they jockey for position, firms often adopt quite different strategies within the same industry. Their investments in *competitive innovation* have proved decisive in determining who gains leadership on the world stage and who loses. For example, the US firm, RCA, one of the pioneers of TV technology and the first to produce a commercial monochrome TV set in 1946, could not keep up with later developments, was bought by GE during the 1980s and is now owned by the French firm, Thomson. The dynamics of competition are such that firms' capacities to invest in next-generation skills and capabilities can be regarded as more important than industry-level economics in determining the international division of labour for specific projects.

The new competition created by all these external and internal forces has increased the barriers to entry and thus the degree of global concentration in many industries. In many cases, as illustrated by examples from a few industries, the issue of the advantages of scale has shifted from the level of the factory to the firm as a whole. The New Forms of Production (NFP) can be seen to be of increasing power in certain circumstances. Where they have been most developed, they act to divorce the firm from the factor costs of a national location, and thus provide a further challenge to older notions of comparative advantage determining the outcomes for countries.

This plurality of possibility and change among industries, and most particularly for firms *within* an industry, creates added complexity that government officials need to understand. Anticipating *future* sources of competitiveness is at the heart of successful negotiations between firms and states.

ALTERNATIVE STRUCTURES OF COMPETITION

Competitive structures are shaped by the sum of the actions taken by the firms contesting the market. They reflect managers' choices about how best to serve markets. Essentially, they have three options: exporting, local supply or licensing. Exporting is common when the costs of transport are low and the benefits of creating scale in a single location are high, as, for example, for Boeing and Airbus. Alternatively, the firm can choose to set up a local operation and simply 'clone' the domestic business in the foreign country. This investment option is favoured when the costs of transport and tariffs are very high in relation to the product, as in detergents and many simple household products, or when the need for local service is high, as in accountancy services and retail banking. The third option is to offer a licence or franchise to independent local firms, as is common in fast food services, hotels and parts of branded businesses like Coca Cola.

For the same business, firms vary their choices across countries, depending upon local regulations, the size of the local market and the existence of both local competitors and suppliers. Thus, for example, McDonalds has some franchises, owns some of its foreign outlets and, for its new outlet in Moscow, has been obliged to set up its own supply chain for beef and other items not readily available locally in the needed quantities and qualities. In Malaysia, ICI's industrial chemicals business combines all three: it imports scale-dependent products such as chlorine; manufactures simple pesticides; and has licensed locals to manufacture other products. Brazil's informatics policy has obliged industry leaders like IBM and DEC to adopt policies in Brazil that they tend to avoid elsewhere.

Decisions about suppliers also affect the overall structure of competition. Boeing's US exports are based in part on the supply of components from Canada, Britain, Japan and elsewhere. Some of these are the result of political negotiation on offset agreements – as in the cases of their sale of AWACS planes to the UK – and some reflect the economics of scale and specialisation among independent suppliers. Where firms use 'workshop' affiliates in developing countries, they may lower their total costs below those of stay-at-home rivals. In other words, a complete picture of the structure of competition must be built up from consideration of the location and form of the whole chain of activities that go together to make up a business. Merely looking at the final stage of supply can obscure the full range of options open to a particular firm in its choice of serving foreign markets.

Taken together all these effects have produced a widely varying balance of choice between exports and local production across industries, as figure 3.1 illustrates. Only the general tendency for an industry is shown; there are always exceptions, as for example the development (though usually only temporarily) of some international chains of hairdressing salons in an otherwise 'domestic' industry. Omitted are a whole host of major industries where the dominant pattern is less readily discernible. Automobiles, machinery, electronics, chemicals and many others are somewhere in the middle: the choices made by individual firms are scattered all across the map.

'Global' is included in two guises in figure 3.1, for there are many possible variants of the phenomenon. They all share the characteristic that decisions taken in one country directly affect decisions elsewhere. When, for example, Matsushita decided to build an export-oriented

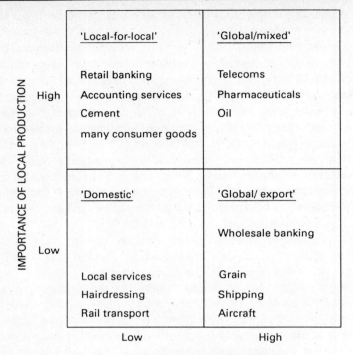

IMPORTANCE OF EXPORTS

Figure 3.1 Balancing exports and local production.

air-conditioner plant in Malaysia, it also had to adjust its plans for investment in Mexico and its export policies from Japan. Matsushita's competitors were also affected for they had to make compensating decisions to protect their own market positions. The American competitor, Carrier, had to adjust its investments in South Korea and Singapore as well as its trading policies in the USA.

Great care is needed in interpreting such diagrams, for what one sees depends critically on how the 'industry' is defined. Automobiles are made of thousands of components, many of which are produced by small firms and sold to the assemblers like Toyota. Should one talk about the auto assembly business or the carburettor business? The former is global and one where Brazil's industry is exclusive to the multinationals: the latter is much more local and dominated in Brazil by indigenous entrepreneurs. Another problem lies in the definition of 'product segments' within an industry. What it takes to succeed in the PC market differs sharply from that for mainframe computers. Moreover, the 'boundaries' that separate industries are shifting continuously. For example, the computer industry and telecommunications are now converging as technology advances. NEC in Japan has adopted the corporate slogan 'C & C' – computers *and* communications – to indicate the basis on which it is setting out to compete across the world with IBM and many others.

Global structures of competition are not god-given. They are created as firms seek new advantages by linking together markets and activities that previously were kept separate. In newspapers, for example, *The Financial Times* is now printed simultaneously in London, Frankfurt, the USA, and recently Tokyo, thus greatly extending the scope of the market it can serve. Its development of a form of NFP harnesses the twin developments of declining scale in printing and growing scale advantages in a global network of information. Often the changes come from managers' innovations in thinking. Commenting on the fact that the industrial gas separation business had conventionally been regarded as 'local-for-local', because of the economic supply radius of 200 miles for the distribution of gas, the Chairman of BOC said,

> we learned that the conventional wisdom was wrong. Overlaid on local costs are substantial costs for the maintenance of technology. We recognised that we could export technology and managerial skills internationally . . . These one-time costs once met could be leveraged over much more business activity around the globe than we then enjoyed. (Giordano, 1990).

Figure 3.1 provides a simple snap-shot of only two dimensions that distinguish one industry from another. In reality, the picture is more akin to a movie full of life and detail. Leaders emerge from a bruising contest. Like others, BOC was seeking to create advantages from an international presence and make it possible to do things a purely local operator could not afford.

Why do firms expand abroad?

The basic driving forces propelling firms abroad come from managers' desires for growth, for cost reduction and for control. These are the same as in domestic competition, but assume greater complexity and risk once the firm strays from its known market. Why then do managers take on these extra burdens? They must set up costly systems of command and control that can work effectively over large distances and deal with the hazards of markets that differ from their own. Managers must feel that the gains will outweigh the costs.

The balance of effect depends largely on what the firm is trying to

69

do. The firm may be *market-seeking*, in the sense that it wishes to gain access to more customers and consumers. Alternatively, it may be *resource-seeking*, in the sense that it wishes to gain access to raw materials that are not readily available without investment. For firms that have already invested abroad, there is a third motivation: *efficiency-seeking* from investments that transform the workings of their international network. This last motivation is explored later on in the section on 'scope' advantages. For now, attention is focused on the first two reasons why firms invest, rather than rely purely on third-party trade.

In the hunt for both markets and resources, managers invest to create three basic kinds of new advantage that make it more difficult for others to compete. First, they may create an 'internal' market that allows them to *control* all the activities involved in cross-border transactions. They do this when they believe they can operate more profitably and with greater stability than could be achieved by reliance on the workings of imperfect international markets (Buckley and Casson, 1985). Second, they may wish to exploit advantages of scale. A third reason is the desire to spread risks by diversifying sources of supply or markets.

Exploiting a technical lead or a brand name are common spurs to creating an internal market. Typically, technology innovators emphasise exports as the initial route for expansion and set up local sales subsidiaries to ensure proper control. Few use licenses, for fear of creating future competitors by giving them a 'free ride' on ideas that cannot adequately be recovered by the fee (Magee, 1977). Similar reasons apply to brands. The perceived need to create an internal market and eschew licensing is also strong when there are concerns about ensuring the reliability and quality of the product. Over time, however, the balance of effect may change as the technology matures, competitors develop rival products or regulations shift. Trade can be replaced by import-substituting investments.

Exploiting the advantages of large scale, where they exist, is a second major force propelling firms abroad. For example, in capital-intensive industries like oil refining and industrial chemicals, the largest plants can provide substantial unit-cost saving over smaller plants. These plants can exceed the size of some national markets, leading producers to concentrate their production on a few sites and export to small markets: some chemical plants in Brazil or Mexico serve other parts of the Latin American market.[1] Alternatively, when the costs of transport are high and local production can be justified only by the creation of a single plant, competitors may choose to collaborate, as in the case of consortium oil refineries. Scale advantages are also created by the rising costs of development of the product or the process. Both types of scale can provide advantages to only the largest players and lead to a concentration in the industry. They are, however, offset in many cases where customers and consumers around the world want variety.[2] As we show later, the question of scale is complex and subject to rapid alteration in contemporary markets.

The third motivation – lowering risks – has several components. Market-seeking investors often wish to smooth out the risks of fluctuating demand by serving multiple markets: decline in one market can be offset by growth in another. The same considerations apply to the diversification of sources of supply for resource-seeking investors (see, for example, Rugman, 1979; Vernon, 1983).

Many investors also try to reduce risk by vertical integration. Where scale has created high fixed costs, producers of standardised products have a strong incentive to stabilise demand: small variations in volume have a large impact on profits. Owners of facilities such as a mine or oil well can reduce uncertainty by acquiring customers, or integrating 'forwards'. Although this does not eliminate the uncertainty, it reduces customers' abilities to switch among suppliers. To protect their captive customers, they may also offer advantageous terms not available to others in the market. These benefits can, however, be limited by producer countries' actions, as OPEC's countervailing power showed for the oil industry. Attempts to create producer cartels for copper, aluminium and other commodities have, however, been less successful for lack of diplomatic solidarity. The benefits are further reduced when competitors respond by integrating 'backwards'. As the oil majors integrated forwards into petrochemicals, some chemical companies such as Du Pont bought oil companies to give them access to captive sources of petrochemical feedstock. Such action and reaction creates turbulence in many markets.

Technology drives change

Technological change is one of the most potent forces for upsetting existing industry structures. It is driven by competition, for necessity has always been the mother of invention. Though much attention has been focused on critical 'breakthroughs' in such areas as micro-electronics, biotechnology and new materials where the potential for creating dramatic changes is obvious, change can also be created in small steps as firms find new ways of upgrading efficiencies. Over time, less glamorous 'tortoises' can change the rules of

71

competition and the structures of industry just as much as the 'hares' of rapid change.

For the purposes of this book, it is important to define what we mean by technology and why time scale and the extent of change in any one step is important. Our concern is not with the creation of technology, but with its diffusion to developing countries. We share the view of Ernst and O'Connor (1989: p. 20) that

> technology cannot be reduced to machines. It has to do with certain kinds of knowledge, which allows the adaptation of means to ends. Part of this knowledge is embodied in machines, but most of it is not. It is embodied elsewhere – in the brains of people, in organisational structures and in behavioural patterns, which in turn are conditioned by the strategies of different social factors and their patterns in conflict and co-operation. Understood in this broader sense, techno-logical change cannot be separated from market structures, patterns of competition and social regulation, and from the quality of the educational system and of the labour force.

Technology is a double-edged sword. It can create new advantages for innovators; it can also erode the position of incumbents by altering the 'rules' of supply and encouraging new entrants. Sometimes, new entrants can come from 'latecomer' countries that previously had been excluded from the industry.[3] Whether developing countries can become competitive latecomers is a pressing issue that we discuss in later chapters when we look more deeply into the issues of social structures and human skills. Our concern here is to sketch the broad trends.

With some notable exceptions, the costs of innovation have been rising to reinforce the barriers to entry and further concentrate already strongly oligopolistic industries. Hi-tech leaders like IBM and Fujitsu spend close to 10 percent of turnover on R & D, and in the pharma-ceutical industry spending is closer to 20 per cent. Some large firms have found it impossible to match competitors' spending: Jaguar found it could not afford the costs of developing the next generation of engines and models and was forced to sell out to Ford in 1989 for £1.6 billion. Sometimes the development costs exceed the resources of even the largest firms. For example, a new large passenger aircraft can cost over $3 billion, requiring government assistance, either directly or indirectly. Goldstar's new wafer fabrication facility being developed in South Korea will probably cost more than $2 billion before it is opened in 1996 and is dependent on generous government support (Hayashi, 1989).

Offsetting this barrier is the possibility that the costs of imitating the leaders' original innovations can be much cheaper. For example, EMI spent millions of pounds developing its Nobel Prize-winning medical scanner in the early 1970s, only to find that competitors found ways around the complex wall of protecting patents for several hundred thousand pounds. Similarly, the entry cost for new mini-computers used to be $25 million and five years' work, but has now fallen to below $5 million and one year. Latecomers can take advantage of the effects of the broad diffusion of the ideas behind the original concept. The same has been happening in the steel industry with the advent of the mini-mills. Whereas Nigeria followed the classic pattern of building large plants with the latest equipment, and then suffering from overcapacity, Togo has been operating a mini-mill profitably for some years and has begun to export to neighbouring countries, even those with large, underused plants of their own. Similarly, small plants were built in the late 1980s in the Ivory Coast and Benin. These African developments owe much to an American entrepreneur who has personally provided the necessary technology transfer and opened up new possibilities for breaking old structures of trade that were dominated by the large producers in developed countries.[4]

The application of technology to managerial systems provides the basis for creating the many possible NFP structures. Even though the advent of computer-controlled equipment has lowered the minimum efficient scale in many factories, it has usually increased the need for greater scale elsewhere in the system. Shortening lead times and the possibilities of widening the product range made on a single set of machines adds considerable complexity to the operation. Some models of hand calculators, for example, are on the market today for six months or less, whereas a life of several years or more was common during the 1970s. Further complexity is added because the factories have to be linked more closely to the markets, otherwise the advantages of better factory management would be eroded by inefficiencies in the supply system. Managing such complexity usually requires efficiency-seeking investments that permeate the whole enterprise. In both manufacturing and service industries alike, firms are becoming more critically dependent on advances in communications and office automation to make these systems work effectively. For example, international insurers compete in part by deploying the abilities to manage large-scale systems they have built up by investment in equipment and human skills over many years. Such investments, though less obvious than product development costs, provide equally stiff barriers to entry.

With smaller scale in the producing unit, the entry costs to many component businesses have declined and allowed a proliferation of new entrants scattered across the globe. Moreover, greater efficiencies in communication can make it relatively easier to control subcontractors and to separate parts of the vertical chain of supply into more bite-sized pieces. Whether these entry positions can, in turn, be levered into positions of more than a new dependency on the technological leaders is an open question and one that cannot be answered in the general case. Much depends on the specific conditions of both the technology and the state of competition. Yet some new options have been created for developing countries.

Economic explanations

During the last three decades, many economists have built models that link together many of the factors affecting both trade and investment flows. Their models have been evolving as circumstances have changed and explain much of what has been happening at the level of the industry, but say little about the behaviour of individual firms. Economists are more concerned to find similarities among firms than to explain the differences. As we argue many times in this book, it is the differences that concern government officials in negotiating lasting deals. None the less, the concepts are powerful and provide a way into understanding the more detailed *managerial* explanations that follow later.

Economists consider the advantages described above to be created by inherent market imperfections; in a perfect market, all firm-specific advantages would be traded away by competition and the world would have remained in the state of Adam Smith's atomistic market. Consequently, multinationals are concentrated in oligopolistic industries and have been larger than firms that stay at home (Bergsten et al., 1978). Without the development of oligopoly at home first, multinationals would not exist. There are, to be sure, a growing list of exceptions, but seldom are oligopoly considerations far removed from the picture. After all, multinationals are essentially 'monopolists' in their use of their specific advantages, otherwise they would need neither internal markets nor contractual arrangements.

One school of thought concentrates on defining the conditions for creating power by building the internal market and thus overcoming the 'market failure' in many cross-border transactions. Economists such as Buckley and Casson (1985), Caves (1982), Casson (1987), Rugman (1986), and Teece (1985) have explored how international production is affected by the relative costs of transactions inside and outside the firm. They place much stress on the distinction between 'intangible' advantages and those from large scale in production. Intangible advantages are created by investments in technology, marketing and skills of organisation. These provide firms with product and service differentiation that allow them to compete on other bases than merely those of costs and prices. These 'intangibles' are growing in importance in NFP structures to provide alternative forms of scale benefit to leading firms and erect further barriers to entry. The converse of barriers to entry are barriers to exit: it may cost firms more to quit than to stay in the market. As we show in chapter 5, exit barriers make multinationals less mobile in practice than they are theoretically capable of being.

A related school of thought asks questions about how the competitive advantages of firms interact with those of countries to help explain the level and pattern of cross-border activities of firms. Dunning's (1988a) 'eclectic paradigm' contrasts a country's resource endowment and geographical position (providing 'locational' advantages) with firms' resources ('ownership' advantages). In his model, countries can be shown to face one of the four outcomes shown in figure 3.2.

In the top, right hand box of figure 3.2, local firms possess competitive strengths, but the home domicile has higher factor and transport costs than foreign locations. The firms, therefore, invest abroad to capture the rents from their advantages. But if the country has locational advantages, strong local firms are more likely to emphasise exporting. The possibilities when the nation has only weak firms, as in most developing countries, leads to the opposite outcomes. These conditions are similar to those suggested by Porter's (1990) 'diamond' of national competitiveness, discussed in chapter 1.

Dunning and Porter help one to understand *average* national competitiveness, but fail to explain why competitors in the same country often adopt quite different strategies. Moreover, national conditions have quite different effects on firms, depending on whether they are seeking markets, resources or efficiency. Further, as we show below, the general theory needs modification to allow for the ability of some firms to escape from the average of national industry economics by internationalising their systems of management. More generally, this effect means that multinationals are cushioned to a degree from the effects of exchange rate shifts and other determinants of national competitiveness (Lipsey and Kravis, 1987).

A major problem with such economists' models is that they are essentially static. One exception is Vernon's (1966) international product life-cycle model.[5] Based on US data, this model treated

75

LOCATION ADVANTAGES

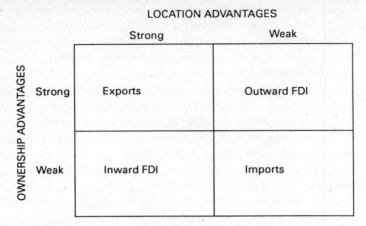

Figure 3.2 Trade and FDI patterns for industries and countries.

investment motivations as primarily *defensive*; to protect export markets threatened by either tariff barriers or competitive moves. For income-elastic products and services, demand first arises in high-income countries. Firms in those countries become the world leaders and begin to export as rising incomes spur demand elsewhere. At some stage, demand in a particular country grows to the point where it can more profitably be exploited by trade-replacing investments. Later on, products mature and become more price-elastic, allowing production advantage to shift to lower-income countries that may later begin exporting on their own account. The timing of the shifts depends on the growth of the local market, the extent of tariffs imposed and the fear on the part of one player that if he does not invest, others will and thereby capture the market. This leads to a 'bandwagon' or 'follow-the-leader' effect in which many firms invest in the same markets at roughly the same time (Knickerbocker, 1973; Graham, 1990).

These lines of reasoning emphasise the innovative capacity of firms and challenges static neo-classical economic explanations of national competitiveness. This is the force that Schumpeter (1942: p. 84) describes as

> competition from the new commodity, the new technology, the new source of supply, the new type of organization . . . competition which commands a decisive cost or quality advantage and which strikes not at the margins of the profits and the outputs of the existing firms (and possibly even entire national economies) but at their foundations and their very lives.

Johnson (1975b) picked up this theme: 'Innovative capacity should be viewed as a basic source of difference in comparative advantage, and technological change as a chronic disturber of existing patterns of comparative advantage'.

Even Vernon's model has fallen foul of the continuing disturbance to existing patterns, as he himself acknowledged (1979). Though it captured much of the dynamic of British and American FDI in the pre-oil shock world, it failed to anticipate subsequent developments in corporate strategy or indeed what had motivated investors from other countries. A critical reason has been the exploitation of new advantages of 'scope', permitted by the declining costs of information.

New 'scope' advantages

Technology has permitted firms to link together more closely the three basic means of serving foreign markets – exporting, local production and licensing – within more complex 'internal' markets. A global perspective allows firms both to spot opportunities faster than others and to build networks of supply that combine the strengths of various locations and so further reduce total supply costs. This combination is sometimes called the economy of 'scope' and should not be confused with scale. Because some firms are better equipped than others to create new advantages of this kind, the differences in corporate strategy have widened. So too has the gap separating winners and losers.

Early analysis concentrated on the multinationals' invested position abroad. For example, Vernon (1971) defined a multinational to be a firm with wholly or partly owned production facilities in a minimum of six foreign countries. More recently, attention has shifted to considering the combination of FDI and world market share. The idea is that, just as brands provide suppliers with enduring benefits, so command of significant shares of world markets can confer lasting advantage even if the supply choices change over time.

The success of many Japanese and German firms in gaining global market leadership has helped shape this re-appraisal. Initially, they emphasised export strategies as an alternative to the leaders' investment-based approach. They were helped by their post-war cost advantages – rapid reconstruction at home meant they had newer facilities than many of their competitors – but they were also pre-disposed towards exporting by the Allies' confiscation of their pre-war overseas assets. When the Japanese returned to investing in the 1960s, they first concentrated on Asian markets that had largely been ignored

Table 3.1. *World market share of Japanese companies, 1985 (selected products)*

Product	Market share (%)
35mm cameras	84
Video recorders	84
Watches	82
Calculators	77
Microwave ovens	71
Motor cycles	55
Colour TV	53
Zip fasteners	> 50
Pianos	> 50
Robotics	> 50

Source: PA Technology

by earlier investors. They tended to locate component supplies in lower-income countries to create two-way trade with Japan; they did not replace the trade in finished products (Kojima, 1978).[6] The Japanese moves cannot be explained in the defensive product-cycle terms; they were *offensive* in the sense that they were designed to establish positions that permitted new world-scale advantages to be created by subsequent expansion. Japan's success, shown in table 3.1, has provided the inspiration for other newcomers, described in chapter 5, to follow suit.

Japanese market domination in such products does not indicate exports from Japan; the shares are held by firms that use both exports from home and, increasingly, overseas production. High shares are increasingly important in industries where the economies of 'scope' are most apparent. They allow leading firms continuously to adjust to the collapse of the timescales for the diffusion of products around the world; people all over the world are increasingly aware of what others are buying. In addition, the precipitous decline in the real price of many products has made them accessible to many more people in the developing world.

Such adjustments, however, can only be made if firms invest in their internal capabilities. They have to build systems capable of integrating the knowledge of diverse trends in national markets with the management of flexible supply. Firms such as Kodak and Fuji in consumer film are able to launch new products simultaneously in multiple markets. Only the largest and most experienced firms can make such moves; others with lesser resources have to phase their market entry moves sequentially (Kogut, 1983). But a sequential approach runs the risk of entering some markets too late to catch the wave of fashion or of meeting already entrenched opposition from the more fleet of foot.

As firms learn how to capture the full potential of such 'scope' advantages, they change, once again, the structure of many international industries. The emerging New Forms of Production demand ever higher levels of skill in the workforce at all levels in the hierarchy. They do not however, apply to all industries, for there are many obstacles that firms have to overcome. As with all the economic forces affecting firms' behaviour, the impact of change is uneven and defies generalisation. Thus, it is to sectoral differences that we now turn, to illustrate how change has been occurring at different rates and with different implications for governments.

INDUSTRY EFFECTS

The range of possibilities for the pace and form of change can be seen in a few specific industries in each of the three sectors: national resource processing, manufacturing and services. The experience in each suggests that there are many common features, but also many differences. Each has its own momentum that critically affects how much developing country governments can influence the outcomes.

Natural resource processing

Adding more value to commodities is one of the most common means developing countries employ to increase the value of their exports. Yet they are often inhibited from doing so by the structure of vertical integration imposed by resource-seeking investors from the consuming markets. The combination of high fixed costs, limited numbers of actors and thin trading markets usually creates verticality (Williamson, 1975, 1985). These barriers are amplified by the intangibles of market knowledge and the specific skills needed to operate effectively both at each stage of production and across the entire value-adding chain of production.

The *aluminium industry* illustrates an extreme form of multinational verticality. It has three distinct stages of processing – bauxite mining, alumina refining and ingot smelting. In 1976, 91 per cent of all bauxite trade was managed by multinationals (Hashimoto, 1983). High capital costs – an alumina plant can cost up to $1 billion – limit the number of buyers and sellers in the chain. Moreover, overcapacity reduced margins during the 1980s when the real costs of construction rose, thus creating higher barriers to entry. Further barriers come from the fact that alumina plants are highly specialised; switching among alternative sources of bauxite of varying chemical composition can add anywhere between 20–100 per cent to the operating costs (Stuckey, 1983: pp. 53–55). Consequently, the trading between the mine and the refinery resembles a bilateral monopoly. The operating conditions make short-term or spot contracts highly risky; stockpiling is uneconomic, because bauxite has few alternative uses. Occasionally long-term contracts have been used, but recent experience has shown them to be uncertain, given the volatility of currencies. Consequently, industry practice has been to reinforce policies of vertical ownership – the creation of an 'internal' market – as a more effective method of managing the uncertainties (UNCTC, 1981; Hennart, 1988).

The power of the international oligopoly has limited producer countries' abilities to capture a greater share of the total value of the sector. For example, one study showed that if all the bauxite and alumina currently exported were converted into aluminium, Australia's export value could be tripled (Australian Manufacturing Council, 1989). Yet Australian producers have not yet felt capable or willing to confront the historical legacy of capacity installed in the consuming markets. In other countries, where a smelter has been installed near the mine, as in Indonesia, it has typically been built in partnership with the buyers of the output. Even then there have been difficulties, in part from the problems of developing the skills required to operate the equipment efficiently, and in part from other national dilemmas of choice in allocating local resources against competing demands.

When these barriers are less pronounced, as in the *tin industry*, the degree of verticality is reduced. Local producers can, depending on transportation costs, more readily locate refining and smelting units near small mines. Indonesia, for example, has successfully operated its own producer, PT Timah, created by the nationalisation of the local operations of Billiton, a major Dutch operator later bought by Royal Dutch/Shell. Even so, PT Timah took many years to develop its own technical expertise and still depends to an important degree on technical assistance from multinationals, including Billiton. Malaysia went further by buying the parent company of many local mines, The London Tin Company, and later bought more mines from Charter Consolidated to emerge as a major producer in its own right, selling to world markets through the London Metal Exchange. Such success for

developing countries is not always the case, even in the same industry; Bolivia has had a sorry experience in trying to do the same as its
Eastern rivals, but has suffered from a critical lack of expertise.

Verticality and high barriers to the entry of local producers co-exist
in many other industries, even where the structural balance is quite
different. Sometimes these conditions have been only temporary, as
can be seen from the history of many agricultural industries. For
example, the advent of marine refrigeration allowed such firms as the
American firm, United Fruit, in bananas from Central America, and
the British meat firm, Union International, in Argentina, to build
powerful integrated systems. They owned extensive producing
acreage and developed strong brand names in consuming markets, all
linked together by processing units and captive fleets of ships. Their
power was eroded as producer governments applied tougher regulations or nationalised the plantations and ranches.

A contrasting example, where technology is acting to concentrate a
previously fragmented industry, is the Kenyan *flower industry*. Here,
the chain of adding value in this industry can be considered as:

Research → breeding (seeds) → cuttings → cultivation → market

The integration of research and breeding allows faster development of
new disease-resistant strains; information is more efficiently and
creatively managed within an 'internal' market, especially given the
advent of bio-technology.[7] In this case, however, unlike the aluminium industry, there are serious barriers that limit the extent of
profitable integration through the rest of the chain, even for the
multinationals.

One obstacle is the fragmentation of export markets. National
horticultural markets have wide variations in price, seasonal effects,
methods of selling and quality gradations. Buyers place great emphasis on the reliability of supply and the ability of the supplier to
maintain quality during transit: quality is judged in the market, not at
the time of despatch. Sellers, therefore, have to know in detail where
and when to sell and how to match their market intelligence with the
planting cycle. Because quality is hard to define with precision,
reputation has a great bearing on suppliers' ability to deal with agents
and to command premium prices in a volatile market with a considerable fashion element (for example, colours for festivals).

Although these conditions place a premium on the 'intangibles' of
technical and market knowledge, they have not led to full verticality in
the firms' fixed assets. Instead, some multinationals have invested in
knowledge systems that provide access to state-of-the art breeding,

81

disease control and cultivation techniques in a form that allows them to control much of the total chain without investing directly in all stages. They can thus avoid the costs of variety and added risk in a volatile market. They have also invested in superior packaging materials, storage and transport systems and market knowledge. In short, they have used the advantages of 'scope' economies to limit their asset exposure while retaining control of the critical factors. For example, Sulmac, the Kenyan subsidiary of Unilever, controls about one third of Kenya's exports of carnations to Europe and has limited its integration to combining cultivation with warehousing and agency operations in the buying markets.[8]

Kenya faces a dilemma in its search for further growth, for a favourable climate is clearly not enough for success. Kenya could encourage further 'dependent' exports, or it could provide assistance for local producers to gain the necessary skills. But more 'dependent' exports would raise the import bill: the multinationals are reckoned to import proportionately more than local producers. But local producers have lesser reputations and command lower export prices. Besides, many of the locals will have to improve the management of their complex supply arrangements before they can develop the reputation for reliability needed for export growth. The dilemma is that Kenyan companies cannot export effectively until they command the volumes needed to justify investments in both knowledge and quality, but they cannot obtain those volumes without investment. Government assistance can overcome the financial barrier, but cannot deal with the managerial obstacles. For example, the government-owned warehouse that was built to provide another means of reducing the entry barriers seldom operates efficiently because of uneven supply from the farms. For Kenya, the issue therefore becomes one of judging how long it will take to build the necessary skills and whether the costs of delaying export growth outweigh the perceived longer-term gains from 'independent' exporting.

Manufacturing industries

For the manufacturing industries, skills and technology assume even greater importance than in the natural resource industries. In the petrochemicals industry, the advent of non-traditional exporters – Saudi Arabia, Brazil, Canada – has done little to disturb existing structures. Despite the power many potentially exercise by virtue of their oil resources, developing countries as a whole could only increase their share of exports from 4.6 per cent in 1970 to 7.1 per cent in 1983, leaving many as dumping grounds for the surplus capacity in OECD countries (UNIDO, 1985). Growth has been inhibited by lack of access to many of the critical technologies, despite the use of plant construction firms as intermediaries. Moreover, producer countries are having to resort to countertrade, with all its accompanying inefficiencies, to circumvent the shortage of foreign exchange for imports, which are allocated to develop other sectors (Vergara and Brown, 1988).

Two other manufacturing industries illustrate how market-seeking investors have been shifting attention to efficiency-seeking investments as competition has intensified. Automobiles point to the importance of investment in novel NFP structures to enhance design and production capability, product quality and the linkage between the factory and the market. The semi-conductor industry illustrates how quickly technology can both create and destroy competitive advantages and profits.

Global competition in the *automobile industry* has been driving out many of the smaller firms. As the minimum economic scale of production in the assembly plant has been decreasing, it has been increasing at the level of the firm for engineering, design and marketing. Success is increasingly determined by quality, the breadth of the model range and low total system costs. Global-scale investments in new skills and production approaches that can readily be transferred across borders have replaced much of the trade; few can keep up with the pace of change. The British firms were forced into defensive mergers and have now almost disappeared. Many other European firms are in trouble and some, like Volvo and Renault in 1990, began to consider merging as the prospects for protection continuing beyond 1992 seem dim.

These unfolding events are best explained by a close look at factory economics. The International Motor Vehicle Program of the Massachusetts Institute of Technology, which has studied eighty assembly plants around the world, provides hard evidence of what has been happening (Krafcik, 1988; Krafcik and MacDuffie, 1989). The central finding is that the rising superiority of the Japanese is based, not on scale or factor costs, but on the creation of what has been dubbed a 'lean' system of production. This allows them to proliferate their model ranges faster to cater for the growing demand for variety in each sector of the market. Critical in the workings of the system is the management of time. New models can be developed and introduced much faster and with fewer disturbances to the production flow than in the more conventional systems used by the Americans and the

83

Table 3.2. *Time management affects competitiveness*

	Japan	USA	Europe
Design time per model (months)	46	60	57
Design effort per model (million man hours)	1.7	3.1	2.9
Ratio of delayed products	1 in 6	1 in 2	1 in 3
Return to normal quality after new model introduction (months)	1.4	11	12
Return to normal productivity after new model introduction (months)	4	5	12

Source: Womack et al. (1990: figure 5.1)

Europeans. Table 3.2 shows some of the telling performance indices of these systems.

The advantages of the 'lean' Japanese system go further to affect both productivity and quality. Even more telling for the issues discussed in this book, is the fact that the system is capable of transfer across borders to provide new local advantages. Figure 3.3 shows that the Japanese 'transplants' in the USA have significantly better productivity and quality than their local rivals, despite using roughly the same wage rates for US labour. They have also been able to drive down costs faster than the locals and so create new export possibilities, even back to Japan; a feat that has eluded Detroit for decades. Figure 3.3 shows the same effects in Europe, though to a lesser degree. The MIT authors concluded that the Japanese had established world best practice, not simply in terms of more automation, but more critically in terms of combining design and production approaches in an integrated system that is highly dependent on the contributions from a skilled, flexible and motivated workforce. Only in those countries where they are able to adopt uniform work practice can the Japanese deploy these advantages. They are thus to some extent limited in where they can invest, as we discuss further in chapter 6.

As the gap widens between the Japanese and the locals in their own backyard, so the assumptions in many of the economic models discussed earlier are being challenged. For instance, Porter's model implies that national infrastructure and other factors determine national performance. For automobiles, this is clearly no longer the case. The power of a NFP structure that can successfully be transferred

84

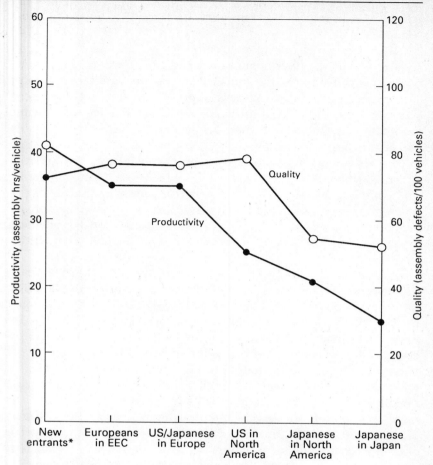

* Includes thirteen plants in Brazil, Mexico, S. Korea, Taiwan

Figure 3.3 Regional productivity and quality differences (automobile assembly, volume producers, 1989; weighted averages). Adapted from Womak et al. (1990), and industry estimates.

across borders is that it can begin to divorce the firm's performance from national factors and thus reinforce the advantages of global scope. There are, however, few other examples of this effect so far, so the implications are necessarily tentative. They are none the less important, for other industries are moving in the same direction. Kodak, for example, is beginning to reap the same sorts of advantage as it carefully allocates supply among all its producing units. But even Kodak is finding that differences in local union structures and local

85

demand needs impede the full implementation of a uniform system (Harris et al., 1990).

The implications for developing countries are obvious. Even though scale requirements have come down and thus open up new possibilities in small markets, the gains will not be great until the assembly plants are backed by world-class support structures. The thirteen plants in 'new entrant' countries in figure 3.3 are mainly owned by the multinationals, but even so there are severe productivity and quality penalties to be overcome. The alternatives are to find protection, either from government (as in Malaysia) or from alliances, as in Latin America, where Ford combined with VW in 1986 to form Autolatina, the world's tenth largest producer. Both have their disadvantages, unless they can be combined with a dynamic of continuous improvement: the present state of development of the global systems is capable of much future improvement and further competitive challenge.

More promising for developing countries, perhaps, are the possibilities of expanding the supply of components. They supplied $3.4 billion of exports in a total trade of about $60 billion in 1987, notably from Brazil, Mexico and Taiwan, and have been increasing their share as better systems of production and reliable supply have been introduced. The difficulty, however, is that competition for components has made them increasingly price-elastic and thus sensitive to exchange rate movements. Brazil's component exports increased rapidly in the late 1980s, only to fall sharply as buyers shifted their purchases to other developing countries in 1990 when the Cruzado became overvalued (Karmokolias, 1990). As we show for the export of electronic components in chapter 4, such seemingly independent exporting has its hazards. The winners are those who can keep up with best standards of quality and reliable supply and still maintain low international prices in a cut-throat business.

A wholly different dynamic of change can be seen in the *semiconductor industry*. This is a classic example of how competition can erode profits: rising barriers to entry and high growth do not necessarily make an industry profitable, even for the leaders. Over the forty years of its existence, the entire industry has produced returns close to zero. In part this is because of the cyclical nature of demand – high profits in boom years are offset by high losses during recessions (about $6 billion of losses worldwide during the mid-1980s) – and in part because of plummeting prices. Faced with these forces, governments have found they can support their national producers for only limited periods.

86

The US government originally supported its infant local industry by buying integrated circuits (ICs) for defence purposes before the commercial market emerged. The early US lead was eroded by countervailing Japanese and later the South Korean moves. They supported their local firms by providing direct research subsidies and trade barriers, forcing many US producers to go offshore to regain cost competitiveness. More importantly for long-run, strategic competitiveness, US firms have emphasised technologies best suited to their home markets, not necessarily the global ones. They have excelled in leading-edge technologies for military and computer applications. By contrast, the Japanese focused on components needed in consumer applications. As consumer products have become more sophisticated, so too have their semi-conductors. The chip that goes into a state-of-the art VCR begins to approach the requirements for a computer. Now that Japan has the world's largest market for chips, it will be increasingly difficult for the US industry to regain its former leadership.

Global competition has pushed out many of the weaker firms, has excluded most Europeans from profitable operations, and has transformed the part developing countries can play in its evolution. It has also provoked extensive networks of defensive alliances, as we indicate later on. Many of the component technologies matured rapidly and could be transferred abroad without making undue demands on the technical capacity of the local workforce. Developing countries have taken advantage of their low labour costs and plentiful supply of 'busy fingers' (Lecraw, 1989) to provide high-productivity sources of supply, attractive especially to the Americans in their contest with the Japanese. The resultant exports are, however, dependent upon the multinationals; relatively few local suppliers have yet broken out to provide an independent, though necessarily volatile, supply capability. The price of such dependency is that local suppliers are vulnerable when each new generation of technology arrives to upset existing patterns of supply.

The service industries

Services are now being internationalised faster than other sectors. In large part, this has been caused by demand derived from earlier investors. Just as many component suppliers to the automobile industry have expanded abroad in order to provide worldwide supply to their large customers, so many service firms have followed suit. Banks, accountants, advertising agencies and many other providers of professional services are the camp followers of the multinational

87

army. The growth of tourism has spurred equivalent developments in the hotel and leisure-related sectors. Other sectors such as construction and trading houses have had different spurs to go abroad, but they too have been influenced by the earlier investors.

Accurate data on the growth are elusive, for services are often omitted from official statistics. Even so, GATT estimates that services have accounted for 17–20 per cent of world trade every year since the mid-1960s:[9] other estimates are that FDI in services has risen even faster.[10] The problem for measurement is that much depends on what type of service is involved. Some, like construction, require physical proximity for the service is consumed (literally so in restaurants) as it is produced. Others like reinsurance and the design portion of a construction contract, can be produced at a distance. The former type is the most common, though even here there are further distinctions to be made. The consumer of the service can be immobile, as in the case of the construction site, but others are mobile, as for heart surgery patients. Improved communications have increased the ability of firms in some sectors to provide a service at a distance, as for mail-order shopping and database management. The more this develops, the more the service is 'disembodied' and difficult both to measure and to regulate.

A further difficulty with both definition and measurement has been created as manufacturers have extended their reach into services, such as warehousing and financial operations. They have done so as technology has altered the source of profits in the total system of supply. For example, to run a computer system in the 1960s, hardware accounted for 80 per cent of total costs. By 1990, many systems had changed to the extent that 80 per cent of the costs came from services – software, engineering support and applications consultancy – many of which were being provided by the hardware suppliers. The 'boundaries' separating manufacturing from service have thus been blurred, even though each has its dynamic affecting cross-border transactions (Hirsch, 1989).

Unlike most manufactured goods, however, the real price of most services has *increased* over the last few decades. Reflecting the substantial barriers to international integration, prices have not come to an equilibrium across countries. Even where labour is cheap, services can be more expensive than in advanced countries. As Bhagwati put it, 'in underdeveloped countries, you go crazy making phone calls; in developed countries, receiving them' (Bhagwati, 1986: p. 13). But, the application of new technology is now acting to change that, even though services, unlike products, cannot be stored. The real cost of servicing insurance claims, for example, has been reduced by computerisation. Moreover, system investments have created economies of scale where few existed before and have begun to make it more possible to derive benefit from global 'scope'.

Declining costs of information have been of critical importance in spurring the international growth of service firms and the service functions within manufacturing firms. Mitsui & Co. and other Japanese *Sogo Shosha* are notable examples. These trading houses have invested heavily in global networks of information-gathering affiliates and extensive communications systems. Their superior intelligence capabilities have allowed them to exert considerable leverage in setting the terms of trade and the manner in which the separate stages of production in their customers' factories are linked together. Similarly, many banks and airlines are investing heavily in information management. For example, Air France is reported to have spent as much on its communication system as on aircraft during the late 1980s. CitiBank spent $1.5 billion in 1989 on information management, equivalent to $19,000 per staff member or 20 per cent of non-interest operating costs. Such expenditures create new barriers to competition and serve to concentrate service industries, just as many manufacturing sectors have experienced.

The 'intangible' advantages of large-scale information capability seem best exploited within 'internal markets' if they are to assume their full efficiency. With few exceptions, such as franchising in hotels and fast foods, where the service can be 'packaged' and transferred to a third party under stringent conditions of control, most service firms find that they require equity control to 'internalise' the gains and recoup the high costs of developing the network in the first place. Besides, there have been so many opportunities for growth in countries that do not require local equity sharing that they have had little incentive to try to build businesses in those countries that do. Such reasons provide just one set of limitations against the wider adoption of forms of NFI, an issue we discuss in chapter 5.

Regulatory barriers have been an especially important obstacle to the full development of internationally traded services. One reason, of particular salience in developing countries, is that services are regarded with considerable suspicion. In part, as the UNCTC considers, this is due to a 'widespread impression that service industries consist largely of technologically stagnant, small-scale personal services based on unskilled labour working with little capital in ways that have not changed for many years'. As the UN concludes, this is outdated, for the service multinationals bring in the 'soft technology' and skills required to run an efficient business. They train the labour they need rather than import it (but note the exceptions like the Korean expatriate workers) and often give these workers the sorts of skills that can usefully be hired by indigenous rivals (UNCTC, 1988a). Even so, many officials remain opposed to liberalisation of the regulations: they regard services as culturally corrosive (as in media) or politically important for national control (as in financial services and trans-border data flows).

There are now signs that the generally negative attitudes may be changing. Evidence is accumulating that an efficient service infrastructure increases the attractiveness of a location for potential investors (Marshall, 1985; Browne, 1983). Just as regional 'externalities' created dynamic growth points for electronics in Silicon Valley and for textiles in the Po Valley, so national advantages can be created. Recognising these benefits for its infrastructure, Singapore has set out actively to woo foreign service firms. A government report concluded in 1986 that

> we must move beyond being a production base, to being an international business centre. We cannot depend only on companies coming to Singapore solely to make or assemble products designed elsewhere. We need to attract companies ... to establish operational headquarters ... (to) ... do product development work, manage their treasury activities, and provide administrative, technical and management services to their subsidiaries. Then it becomes worthwhile for them to establish a plant in Singapore, to produce goods or services for export. (Singapore, 1986: p. 12)

Where Singapore leads others may soon follow.

ALTERNATIVE GLOBAL STRATEGIES

Just as the economic trends have affected industries differently, so they have affected the players within an industry in various, often quite contradictory ways. Managers have had to make difficult choices about where and how to compete with their limited resources. Some of the earlier investors have found they could not adjust quickly enough; others have been severely battered by innovative competitors but managed to fight back. Ford lost $3 billion during 1980–2 in its fight with the Japanese, but recovered. Others proved less resilient. Some major shippers of the 1970s, like Ocean Steam in the UK, could not hold their position against the onslaught of newcomers like Evergreen and left the business altogether. For everyone, the structural shifts have placed new demands on managers' abilities to be strategically innovative. Merely repeating policies that worked in the past was not enough. The new competition is not so much a contest among the strong and the weak all obeying Queensberry rules; it is now just as much a contest among competing strategies.

There are over 600 multinationals in a 'billion-dollar-club' and a host of smaller fry all competing for a share of the market. Twenty years ago, about sixty of them accounted for roughly half of all FDI, reflecting the oligopolistic forces discussed earlier. The same proportion still holds true, but the composition of the top sixty has changed. US firms have lost many of their leadership positions in major industries, producing a dispersion of economic power among the firms akin to the alleged dispersion of hegemonic power referred to in chapter 2.

To explore why there has been so much flux in the structures of competition, some basic distinctions are needed. A 'global' product is not the same thing as a 'global' firm or a 'global' industry. A global product is conventionally regarded as being the same in all markets. An industrial gas like oxygen is chemically identical in all markets, but the means of its delivery may vary among markets. Moreover, though the majors may all be global in reach, only some, like BOC, has been investing to create global interdependence for some of the key functions of the business. The others have preferred to compete on a local-for-local basis with many others whose limits are purely national.

All global firms are balancing two competing forces: those gaining advantage from *integration* of their systems; and those for becoming more *responsive* to differences in local demand. How they strike a balance between the two is at the heart of corporate strategy. The answer is shown in their choices of product policy, location of assets, and investments in building skills. Because there is always uncertainty about the direction of future change, it is not surprising that competitors with different resources and different perspectives take different gambles about what the best position will be in the next round of competition. For example, the Belgian firm, Bekaert, which has emerged as the world leader in steel cord for automobile tires, has deliberately eschewed the benefits of building large scale in its factories. Bekaert concluded that the potential gains in unit costs would be more than offset by losses in terms of lack of focus on customer service needs. Conventional economic analysis would have pointed to the opposite policy, but would have ignored the human factor in making a complete system work. This does not mean that the competitive arena has become less global. On the contrary, the requirements for massive investments in systems have reinforced the power of Bekaert's global perspective and global scale of total resources.

Firms can choose to concentrate their resources in a few countries and emphasise exports to other markets, or they can disperse their resources and emphasise FDI. This is the company version of the industry 'map' shown earlier in figure 3.1. Laid on top of this choice is that of determining the extent of the investment in co-ordination of the various operations. When the assets are dispersed, firms can rely on relatively little co-ordination, as in the 'local-for-local' strategies, or they can emphasise co-ordination, as in BOC's global strategy.[11] The difference is akin to that between a bag of marbles and a pillar of marble. Many early investors built a bag of marbles, each well polished and each managed by a local team jealous of its independence. But the very strength of local independence has often impeded the transition to a more globally integrated structure: past strength can prove to be a handicap when the competitive battle changes.

Two features of the new contest are providing further pressures for future change. One is the move towards creating alliances, as means of dealing with the problems of rising resource costs just to stay in the game. The other is the emergence of new, third world competitors that deploy their resources in innovative ways that sometimes can minimise the handicaps of being a late entrant into established markets.

Alliances

The spurs to create alliances are the rising costs of research, the quickening pace of technological change and the costs of entry to heavily regulated markets. All these mean that even large multinationals may not have sufficient resources to succeed on their own. Alliances provide the mix of scale and flexibility needed to generate sufficient revenues for next-generation product development. As one senior official in Olivetti put it recently,

> In the 1990s, competition will no longer be between individual companies but between new, complex corporate groupings. A company's competitive position no longer (solely) depends on its internal capabilities; it also depends on the type of relationships it has been able to establish with other firms and the scope of those relationships.[12]

Alliances include many forms of joint venture, outsourcing agreements, product licences and co-operative research. They differ from older forms of association in that they are two-way trades of complementary strengths among competitors. A one-way outsourcing arrangement, such as General Motors' purchases of cars and components from Daewoo in South Korea, is little more than a sophisticated version of familiar NFI agreements: they offer the supplier the opportunity to gain value-creating activities and obviate the buyer's need to invest. A two-way trade is illustrated by ICL's alliance with Fujitsu, without which ICL could not have developed its current range of mainframe computers and Fujitsu could not have expanded so quickly into European markets.

The problem for many that have entered alliances is that, though the alliance can strengthen both firms against outsiders, it can also weaken one partner relative to the other.[13] A recent study of alliances defined them as

> a constantly evolving bargain whose real terms go beyond the legal agreement or the aims of top management. What information gets traded is determined day-to-day, often by engineers and operating managers. Successful companies inform employees at all levels about what skills and technologies are off-limits to the partner and monitor what the partner requests and receives. (Hamel et al., 1989: p. 134)

The essence of the successful alliance is the extent of the mutual learning about the partner's skills and the extent to which that learning can be diffused throughout the organisation to provide future strengths. 'Companies that are confident about their ability to learn may even prefer some ambiguity in the alliance's legal structure. Ambiguity creates more potential to acquire skills and technologies' (p. 139).

The impact of these alliances can be seen clearly in the semi-conductor industry. It seems unlikely that the earlier experience of one country having an autonomous capability in the industry will be repeated, now that the web of alliances has permeated almost all sectors of the industry. In 1990 alone, IBM joined forces with Siemens for some segments, Siemens was negotiating with SGS-Thomson (the Italian-French group) to develop semi-conductors and four other US producers allied with Japanese competitors. Similar developments were taking place in pharmaceuticals, aerospace, construction and automobiles, where it was becoming increasingly difficult for firms to maintain capability in *all* the technology options for the future.

Producers in smaller countries now face even higher barriers to entry in such industries, if they want to develop beyond 'dependent' exporting; they have little to offer by way of an entry ticket to the two-way partnership. These developments are, quite naturally, producing fears in government circles that alliances are no more than cartels designed to restrain competition, albeit dressed up in new and more attractive clothes.

Third world multinationals

Increasingly firms from developing countries are extending abroad, for many of the same reasons that earlier prompted the moves of developed country multinationals.[14] No longer dependent on cheap labour for competitiveness, many are pushing abroad in even high-technology fields and are doing so, perhaps ironically, to exploit other countries' cheap labour (Cantwell and Tolentino, 1990). As they expand and gain in political significance, they may act to constrain the actions of their own host governments: reciprocity will be needed.

Wells (1983) estimated that there were as many as 8000 subsidiaries of firms from developing countries operating in other developing countries. Expansion has continued, though there are no comprehensive estimates of the extent of the growth to the end of the 1980s. Brazilian firms provide engineering and construction services in Africa. The Regent, Peninsular and Park Hotel groups operate throughout Asia. Taiwanese firms build steel mills in Nigeria and make furniture in Malaysia. Indeed, Taiwan became the largest foreign investor in Malaysia during 1988, in terms of the annual flows of investment. This was during a time when Taiwan's exports to Malaysia were increasing rapidly. Already it seems clear that the same forces that have acted to bind together trade and investment flows within the OECD are affecting South–South economic relations.

Some third world firms have extended further into the developed world. For example, the Brazilian firm Gradiente Electronica bought the (near bankrupt) British firm Garrard from Plessey for $2 million in 1979. The purpose was to use the brand name and, more importantly, the distribution network to increase exports from the Manaus EPZ (Lall, 1983). More recently, and for much the same reasons, Stelux, from Hong Kong, bought the Bulova Watch Company in the USA. The Malaysian government has gone further and purchased the parent companies of many British-owned Malaysian subsidiaries: Sime Darby, Guthrie and other trading companies. Sime Darby has foreign manufacturing, plantation, trading, transportation and financial interests in many developing and developed countries. With 1989 sales of $1.6 billion, it is already an established and important multinational in its own right.

Though similar in many respects to developed-country multinationals, these firms have important differences, both positive and negative for their home and host economies. Recent analyses have shown positive host-economy effects in terms of their greater adaptability to local conditions, greater use of labour-intensive technology, and greater skills to work profitably at small scale. Their overseas affiliates tend to be highly autonomous and to remit small proportions of their profits to the parent. As new entrants, most are open to accepting NFI requirements. Most prefer market-seeking investments and few have created new exports. For some, the spur to going abroad seems more of a push from frustration at bureaucratic regulations at home than a pull from market opportunity. There are, however, troubling reports that many are prone to bribe local officials and to use more home country nationals than their advanced rivals. Further, the very fact that they use more 'appropriate' technology means that they compete intensively with local firms and thus exacerbate rivalries among local ethnic groups. These characteristics pose difficult additional choices for host governments.

IMPLICATIONS FOR GOVERNMENT

Global competition is undoubtedly here to stay. As industries continue to concentrate at the world level, the forces described in this chapter raise two possibilities. One is that future change may be driven primarily by the firms, not by government. If more firms can overcome the internal obstacles to resemble the Japanese automobile producers, the world economy will become increasingly dominated by oligopolies with growing abilities to divorce themselves from local conditions and to create new types of enclaves within host states. The other, perhaps more likely, possibility is that, far from becoming the 'borderless world' that Ohmae (1990) foresees, these major industries may become more susceptible to government influence.

The reason why the latter seem more likely is that it is on these major industries that much of the future competition among states for wealth-creating resources will be focused. A key question is how the management of the market imperfections that have so strongly influenced investment behaviour in the past will be conducted in the future. Can the combination of both inward and outward investment be made complementary to rather than a substitute for domestic investment? Rather than regarding the relationship as essentially adversarial, as did many observers twenty years ago, the issue is now one of searching for ways to allow the two parties to co-operate to promote their mutual interests.

In the search for collaboration, states need to watch carefully both

95

the dynamics of industry-level competition and the position of individual firms. Competitive innovation has proved decisive in many industries over the last two decades in determining which firms assume leadership positions and which disappear. Governments choosing weaker competitors, precisely because they were more accommodating of local demands for, say, ceding some of the ownership of the venture, have later regretted the choice when the firm failed in the global contest. The British experience of a quasi-partnership with Chrysler, and Chrysler's failure and eventual withdrawal from Brazil in 1979 provide testimony that both developed as well as developing countries can be disappointed by failing to judge the strength of the partner by international criteria (Stopford and Turner, 1985: p. 230).

National policy must therefore be crafted and implemented in the clear knowledge of the *international* structures of particular industries and the strength of individual firms seeking market access. The growing use of alliances in strategic industries heightens this need to understand the world scene. No longer can the worth of an investment proposal be evaluated by looking at the immediate terms of the deal: the longer lasting impact of the structure of alliances must also be taken into account. The resilience of the investor is critical to ensure that the deal will not disappoint people on both sides of the bargain.

The scenario of growing state-firm collaboration seems possible, given the ways that so many states are moving towards liberalising their regulations. They are removing many of the distortions that have made investors look elsewhere in the past. But the liberalising trends are not blind moves towards laissez-faire, but the product of many countervailing forces in the local society. How policies are emerging in developing countries to deal with both the general issues of the international political economy discussed in the previous chapter and the more particular ones created by global competition is explored in the next chapter.

4 DILEMMAS FOR GOVERNMENTS

Export-led growth and increased autonomy have proved elusive goals for most developing countries. Most are constrained by limited resources and by intractable domestic agendas that impede their capability to implement policy. The grinding together of internationally mobile capital and intellectual resources against immobile labour has produced acute dilemmas for choosing policy and reconciling conflicting objectives. Where some have attempted to ignore international structural changes, others, perhaps grudgingly, have accepted the need for change and grasped the nettle of internal adjustment. Few have rivalled Singapore's enthusiasm for harnessing the multinationals as agents of growth and economic transformation.

In chapters 1 and 2, we laid out some of the broad lines of argument about how national choices are conditioned by the international political economy. Chapter 3 described how multinationals' strategies are similarly being shaped by the combination of external and internal forces. In this chapter we begin to assess how the changes can both bring together states and firms in partnership and also pull them apart. Figure 4.1 suggests one way of looking at the emerging relationships. National resources, combined with policy choice, affect both the appropriateness of various forms of firm strategy and the nation's attractiveness to existing and potential investors. Multinationals' resources and ambitions shape both their global strategies and choices of location. The lines of causality and interaction go both ways, affecting the performance of both players.

The focus of this chapter is on the government side of the equations. We aim to illuminate the nature of their dilemmas and to show how they affect the bargaining relationships with foreign investors. Our main concern is with those policies and issues we regard as being the most important in determining the achievement of national goals through partnership with the multinationals. How firms actually reacted to these policies and practices will be best seen when, in the next chapter, we review how corporate strategies made at the world

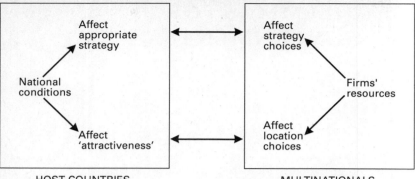

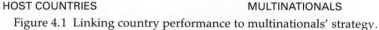

Figure 4.1 Linking country performance to multinationals' strategy.

headquarters have been adjusted at local levels to reflect national possibilities.

For governments, logic would suggest a simple sequence of thought and action. Starting from a recognition of the constraints and opportunities set by human and natural resource endowments, one might assume that they then define a broad set of goals for the future. These set the sights of ambition, often embodied in a series of national plans, what we called national *intent* in chapter 1. These goals form the basis of both macro-level policies for industry. National institutions and agencies, each responsible for one agenda, are charged with administering specific policies for each sector and each group of multinationals. Trouble arises at this point, for no country can ensure that all its ministries and agencies manage everything in a wholly coordinated way. There are dilemmas at every level of concern; different interest groups hold different priorities. Thus it is common for policies to be announced but not implemented fully or consistently. Where a country espouses outward-looking policies, it may continue to behave in many important respects as though it were still domestically focused. Dilemma is bred both by the interconnectedness of the various agendas and by dynamic environmental changes. The knock-on consequences of choice for one agenda are not always discernible in advance, nor are yesterday's choices necessarily appropriate for to-morrow. All too often, policies are introduced to solve particular problems of the day. Only later are unanticipated costs and benefits visible; hindsight can make them appear deliberate all along.

Disentangling all the connective strands and lines of causality is a task beyond our scope. Instead, we summarise the issues for the major policy agendas and illustrate the dilemmas with examples of particular choices of policy and administrative action. The data demonstrate how economic policy and political bargain interact and sometimes lead to unexpected outcomes. The reader can decide which of the possible explanations is the most plausible. For example, why did Malaysia initiate the Proton Project to develop its own car in 1982? Some claim that the spur came from a desire to raise the local content above the 20 per cent achieved by the multinationals' assembly plants. But, why in 1982? The situation had existed for many years. And why was the particular form of the deal chosen, with Mitsubishi as the minority partner granted a (seemingly lucrative) import licence for its own components? An alternative explanation lies in Dr Mahatir's 'look East' policy, designed to break away – finally and for ever – from the colonial past and to speed up the pace of change by harnessing the vitality of Japanese firms. The auto industry just happened to be a convenient sector in which to show his determination to change (Doner, 1987; Oman, 1989: pp. 164–166).

Before getting to such details, we first review the general considerations of policy regimes. The data in the appendix add details of the chronology of policy development in each of our three countries and the changes over recent years in trade and investment flows, sectoral composition of the economy and demographic indicators. These provide the backdrop for assessing more specific policy choices. The chapter ends with a discussion of how the growing problem of managing the additive agendas created by international developments affects governments' bargaining power and their behaviour towards the multinationals.

NATIONAL ECONOMIC POLICY

All countries possess an armoury of policy weapons that together add up to a policy regime. Drawing from his experience of Japan, Johnson (1984: p. 8) considered that this 'means the initiation and co-ordination of governmental activities to leverage upward the productivity and competitiveness of the whole economy and of particular industries in it ... positive industrial policy means the infusion of goal-oriented, strategic thinking into public economic policy'. That may well be the experience in Japan, but it is a far cry from practice in most developed and developing countries. None the less, this description serves as a useful goal to which countries can aspire.

Among developing countries, the difficulties of reconciling economic and social policies, and of ensuring adequate co-ordination

Table 4.1. *Incidence and direction of policy changes in 26 countries, 1977–1987*

Policy	Newly industrialising countries[1]		Developing countries[2]		Total	
	Liberal	Restrictive	Liberal	Restrictive	Liberal	Restrictive
Ownership	7	1	17	7	24	8
Taxes, tariffs	7	2	30	9	37	11
Currency	4	2	17	7	21	7
Price controls	3	2	16	7	19	9
Performance requirements	1	0	1	6	2	6
Sector-specific	5	2	16	2	21	4
Administrative procedures	4	3	21	9	25	12
Total	31	10	118	47	149	57

[1] Includes Brazil, Malaysia, Mexico, Singapore, South Korea.
[2] Includes Kenya and 20 others from Argentina to Venezuela.
Source: Adapted from Contractor (1990b): table 2.

among departments, is immense. Moreover, it is only recently that some have engaged in such strategic thinking at all. Brazil made a start when it set up its Grupo Interministerial in 1986, with representatives from Planning, Industry and Commerce, Finance, Science and Technology. Malaysia's Industrial Master Plan also represents such thinking, though many question whether the goals set for the twelve priority sectors of development strategy can be achieved. By comparison, Kenya's five-year plans are far behind in specifying a strategy. None the less, all countries have some form, whether or not it is spelled out and consistent. Just as a US Supreme Court Justice concluded for pornography, 'you know it when you see it, but you can't define it', so too with a development strategy.

These broad policy approaches take meaning for firms through a range of specific instruments.[1] Together, they indicate the direction of intended progress. A recent study provided a careful compilation of 206 policy changes in 26 developing countries between 1977 and 1987. Overwhelmingly, the data show how the general moves towards liberalisation, described in earlier chapters, can be seen in individual policies (Contractor, 1990b). This study classified policy into seven general categories: ownership policies, taxes (including subsidies, tariffs and transfer payments), currency (including exchange rate management, convertibility, and restrictions on remittances), price controls, performance requirements (such as local content regulations and exporting), sector-specific incentives and limitations, and administrative procedures for approvals.[2]

Table 4.1 shows the incidence of change in these seven categories. Though liberalisation is the dominant trend, there are important exceptions in every category. Performance requirements have commonly increased, indicating countries' determination to retain a degree of control over firms; liberalisation does not mean laissez-faire. Moreover, many poorer countries have increased restrictions, though some have felt forced by external shocks to begin to look outwards. Tanzania's 1990 investment promotion decree, promulgated after lengthy internal political debate, illustrates just how troublesome are the dilemmas for the poorest countries; a question to which we return in chapter 7.

Subsidise or regulate?

Part of the reason why cross-currents muddy the stream of liberalisation is the changing political approach to a general choice: to intervene in the affairs of enterprises directly or to provide general regulatory conditions? Intervention can be either negative for certain classes of asset holder or supportive by providing subsidies of varying magnitude. Regulation can vary from laissez-faire to the oppressive and capricious. The dual role of the state both to support business and provide finance on the one hand, and to be the guardian of social welfare and redistributor of resources on the other is exceedingly difficult to manage coherently (Steiner, 1975).

The choice indicates how much the state is willing to take on an active role of managing national resources for greater international competitiveness, and in what form. The choice is not solely a question of relative bargaining power, but also one of assumptions about the role of the state. Must states, as Evans (1979) argued, 'continually coerce or cajole the multinationals into undertaking roles they would otherwise abdicate' even as the pendulum swings towards liberalisation? How, in Schelling's terms (1979), a state manages the balance between voluntarism and coercion is a central key to understanding what its future investment climate might be like, and thus its attractiveness to potential investors.

The post-war history of South Korea shows how the balance of effect can change over time, driven by a coherently evolving logic for economic development, despite major changes of government and

101

military rule. Starting from near laissez-faire during the 1950s, when the main action of government was allocation of scarce dollars among importers, policy shifted during the 1960s to heavy subsidisation and limited regulation of key local enterprises (the *chaebol*), plus policies of excluding most foreigners. The determination to use private enterprises as key actors was later complemented by stronger regulation. As the *chaebol* gained in stature at home and abroad during the 1970s, the levels of subsidy for them were reduced and increased for smaller, export-oriented local firms (Jones and Sakong, 1981; Cho, 1984). Only during the 1980s did Korea begin to reduce its restrictions against foreign investment as an added means of linking more directly with the international system.

Similar changes can be discerned in the data in the appendix for our three countries. Though they have all faced more complex choices by virtue of having mixed policies towards foreign investors and internal interest groups, there has been some perceptible consistency in approach over time, even though that is at times obscured by administrative and political compromise.

MONETARY POLICIES

To illuminate the interlocking bargains that produce such compromises and contradictions, we focus first on monetary, then on trade policies, for these are the prime determinants of demand conditions. The choices governments face are conditioned by social constraints, as we discuss in chapter 6. Though these constraints can be decisive in some ways, we concentrate here on the economic policies and some of the more specific policies like price controls that affect the investment climate for multinationals.

Debt management

For many of the categories of indebted countries, identified in chapter 2, the continuing debt crisis is probably the greatest single influence on choices of monetary and financial policy and thus the ability to grow. Rescheduling the debt has merely deferred rather than solved the problems of increasing internal efficiencies and domestic savings rates. *How* states manage their debt thus becomes the point of departure for examining economic management.

Indebted countries' options depend on the magnitude of the debt, who lent the money in the first place, and on what terms. As the tables in the appendix show, all three countries have high debt (relative to

102

GNP), but of quite different composition. Their policies and perform-ance can thus illustrate a range of problems that many developing countries face.[3] Kenya, never able to borrow heavily from commercial banks, has relied on 'official' loans from aid 'donor' governments like Britain and from international organisations like the World Bank or the IMF. Consequently, the repayment terms are long, thus reducing the servicing costs below those required by commercial borrowing. Kenya's development has probably not been overly constrained by debt *per se*, though the strings tied to the loans have limited policy choice. One must look to their domestic policy dilemmas for more serious impediments to growth.

Malaysia's $20 billion debt, at 66 per cent of GNP, is proportionately almost as high as Kenya's. Though commercial banks have lent the majority of the capital, the debt-servicing burden is lower. The reason is that Malaysia's exports have been much stronger. Only for a short period in the mid-1980s, when commodity prices and demand for semi-conductors slumped, did Malaysia risk hitting its borrowing ceiling. In other words, borrowing can be a positive weapon for development when the borrower can provide the liquidity to service the debt.

Brazil provides the example *par excellence* of a country where borrowing during the 1970s seemed a sensible means of providing *liquidity* to finance industrialisation (Sachs, 1981: p. 39). Brazil also typifies the category of unsafe borrower, discussed in Chapter 2. Rising debt levels later provoked fears of a *solvency* crisis. The distinction between liquidity and solvency is important, for the lender must be confident that the borrower will invest wisely and eventually become able to repay both interest and capital. Though Brazil's massive debt of about $115 billion is only 30 per cent of GNP, its debt service ratio is over 50 per cent. Twice during the 1980s, Brazil effectively defaulted on its foreign debt and on many occasions has declared itself unable to carry out the promises made in its successive Letters of Intent to the IMF. Only its large size and large stock of FDI inhibited creditors from over-reacting to the crises.

Failing to do all the IMF wanted was one thing: escaping the exigencies of dependence on foreign credit, if only to continue financing of trade, was quite another. Rescheduling was deemed better than default. Once rescheduling had been agreed in 1987, Brazil could do more to capitalise its debt; that is to get creditors to exchange claims for interest and repayment on past loans for direct investments of some kind in the country.[4] Mechanisms to make this possible were first introduced in 1982, but only in 1988 was a debt/equity swap programme introduced.

Brazil's faith in debt/equity swaps as a means of easing the burden has been shared by many. Indeed, the whole market for secondary debt has boomed, reaching about $70 billion in 1989. Though officially endorsed in the 'Brady plan', there is considerable doubt about the wisdom of the approach, compared to the alternative of lending more.[5] Recent evidence suggests that buy-backs merely create banking commissions and do not stimulate growth. For example, in 1988 Bolivia bought back roughly half of its heavily discounted $670 million debt. Immediately afterwards, the market price of the remaining debt nearly doubled, leaving the total value virtually unchanged. General economic arguments, however, omit the spin-off benefits from the inventiveness of financial operators in search of bargains and easy profits. Moreover, some multinationals, such as the textile group Coats-Viyella, which had virtually stopped investing in Brazil, were lured by debt/equity swaps into putting new money into their subsidiaries at a very substantial discount – in that case, 41 per cent. With the discount moving down to about 20 per cent by mid-1990, others may be similarly tempted even though the discount rate reflects some measure of the depreciated economic value of the assets.

Responses to extreme forms of the debt crisis are also conditioned by who holds the debt, how much they are hurt and their power to take avoiding action. Frieden (1987) makes the crucial distinction between liquid and fixed asset holders – industrial firms being prominent in the latter category. In Mexico, liquid asset holders predominated. They could take their money to the USA: about $27 billion left the country between 1976 and 1984. The fixed asset holders, meanwhile, managed to get preferential help from the government to ease the pain. In Brazil, where fixed asset holders predominated, capital flight was much less serious. When industrial interest groups failed to get help, they took political action against the military. Postponing the necessary adjustment had, however, only made the ultimate adjustment harder, and the policy dilemmas sharper.

It is not, to be sure, only domestic social-political power structures that affect responses; it is also banks and creditor nations. As we illustrated in chapter 2, they had to choose between permitting default (and risk a banking panic) or insisting on repayment (risking cutbacks on trade with the debtor countries). They chose the second option, because their prime concern was for the safety of the international financial system. Consequently, none of the proposed remedies for the debt crisis has been fully implemented, allowing the creditors to continue muddling through.

Controls on capital and profit remittances

Debt problems, at the extreme, cause capital flight. Less obvious are their effects on the more 'normal' policies for controlling legitimate capital transfers and the remission of dividends and investors' other financial transactions. In some cases, the two become connected in ways that defy control, as Brazil has discovered.

Capital flight has as much to do with political structures as with a loss of confidence. Indeed, some of the worst cases have been associated with autocratic and corrupt governments like the Shah's Iran or Marcos' Philippines, where capital flight helped precipitate a debt crisis. Naylor (1987) tells some hair-raising tales of how politicians have often been the chief culprits, stashing away government revenues and foreign aid funds in numbered accounts. Brazil had no such push factors at work: when capital fled it was more because of the debt crisis than its cause. Brazil's controls on transfers date back to 1962, when the Profit Remittance Law was introduced to limit dividend remittances to 10 per cent of the value of the capital invested, excluding reinvestments. Later amendments made remittances over 12 per cent of registered capital subject to heavy taxes. By the late 1980s, Brazilian inflation had created such a thriving (and openly tolerated) black market in foreign currency that some multinationals found it worthwhile to exceed the 12 per cent limit. They could repatriate profits at the official exchange rate and then reinvest them at favourable black-market rates that more than offset their tax liabilities. The ultimate paradox of profit remittance policies came in mid-1989, when the debt crisis caused the government to freeze *all* profit transfers. The result, as shown in figure 4.2, was a catastrophic fall in capital inflow and an inability to control all outflows. A year later, the new government, having learnt the lesson the hard way, lifted the freeze on profit remittances.

By contrast, Malaysia has been able to be much more liberal; there have been no restrictions on the remittance of profits abroad or on the withdrawal of capital through divestment. The government has only insisted that fees and royalties charged to Malaysian affiliates should be 'reasonable'. We found, however, some cases where the definition of reasonableness had become a bone of contention and subject to tense renegotiation, especially by Japanese investors. So much so, that attempts were made – unsuccessfully – to make the 1988 package of expanded capital availability offered by the Bank of Japan conditional on an easing of the perceived unreasonableness of the Malaysian authorities. In other words, controls can be exercised indirectly by

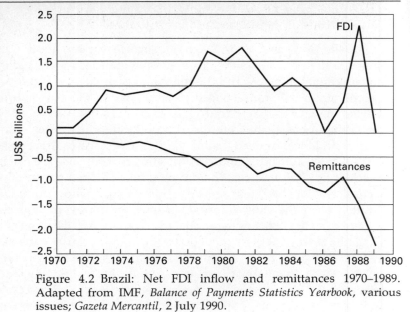

Figure 4.2 Brazil: Net FDI inflow and remittances 1970–1989. Adapted from IMF, *Balance of Payments Statistics Yearbook*, various issues; *Gazeta Mercantil*, 2 July 1990.

negotiation over what amounts to a question of how much can be charged against local tax.

Kenya, despite the fact that it has twice suffered massive haemorrhages of foreign capital, has been equally moderate. It has, however, sought other ways to stop earnings from leaving the country. For example, the government 'Africanised' the insurance business. The problem was inherited from colonial days when insurance, like banking, was British controlled. Premiums collected in Kenya were transferred to London for reinvestment. But, as other African countries have discovered, African insurance companies were too small to carry major risks and had to lay them off with foreign re-insurers. The government, therefore, established the Kenya Reinsurance Corporation in 1971 and decreed that all underwriters reinsure part of their business with Kenya Re. Kenya's success in increasing the proportion of the income retained at home has, however, been only modest. Market forces there, as in other developing countries that have similar local rules, cannot be wholly restrained (UNCTAD, 1987).

Exchange rates

Many developing countries attempt to manage their exchange rates. Past policies favouring over-valued currencies have proved

106

unsustainable. They had the effect of encouraging imports of capital-intensive producer goods for import-substitution and industrialisation and imports of luxury items for the elites. Prodded by the IMF and the drive for exports, combined with market forces, devaluations have been steep during the 1980s.[6] The average real exchange rate (trade-weighted and adjusted for inflation) fell by 40 per cent between 1980 and 1988 in the 80-odd developing countries monitored by the World Bank. Excepting internationally priced commodities, this meant that all developing countries had to export more in order to import the same amount of goods and services. A recent evaluation concluded, depressingly, that the devaluations by themselves did little to improve trade balances and tended to reduce investments (Faini and de Mello, 1990).

The link between exchange rates and debt is impossible to establish with clarity. None the less, Brazil's debt had an important role to play in creating downward pressure on the currency. Similarly, Kenya was obliged by the IMF to devalue its Shilling as part of the price of gaining stand-by credits (Delamaide, 1984: p. 61). Many other developing countries fared similarly. Between 1980 and 1987, the IMF and the World Bank provided $43 billion of 'adjustment loans'. The recipients had to agree to devaluation among other provisions. The links between foreign debt and domestic monetary and fiscal policies are equally obscure. None the less, the central importance of interest rates is widely recognised. Thus, many highly-indebted countries are now experimenting with novel mechanisms, such as currency options, interest swaps and caps and commodity-linked facilities, to reduce their exposure to adverse movements in international interest rates. The market for raising new finance by this form of risk management has grown to about $4 billion in 1989. Further growth, however, seems limited: it is expensive, very complicated and designing appropriate control mechanisms that limit the potential for losses in hedged positions has proved difficult (Mathieson, 1989).

Rather than attempt to review all the conflicting theories about such issues and about how exchange rates affect adjustment and growth, we focus on two factors that have a direct impact on the relationships with foreign investors. The first concerns how investors assess the various measures and the second concerns how governments manage the administrative mechanisms they use to influence exchange rates.

Investors watch exchange rates closely, because they calculate their profits in their home currency, and because they must assess how changes might affect the future international competitiveness of local output. If firms believe devaluation is likely in the near future, they typically defer investment until after the event, to avoid writing down the asset value. A prime indicator of future trends in many countries that attempt to manage the rates is the black market rate. For example, unlike Brazil, Myanmar insists that all multinationals' currency dealings are at the official rate. With the black market standing at roughly one-tenth of the official rate in mid-1990, many investors who might otherwise have wanted to invest were holding back, betting that the official rate could not indefinitely be propped up.

The second factor is *how* the government intervenes to affect the exchange rate. Kenya's practices illustrate the problem. By mid-1982, when Kenya's reserves were barely sufficient to cover a month's imports, plans to get rid of complex and arbitrary quantitative import controls came to a halt, 'because the Central Bank was unable to authorise release of foreign exchange [needed] for licences issued' (Commonwealth Secretariat, 1985). The administration was desperately overloaded with applications for import licences. The Foreign Exchange Allocation Committee operated on a case-by-case basis. The consequential uncertainties about both the outcome and the timing of its decisions were just as important to investors as the actual rate. Where efficiency and speed are of the essence, investors will look elsewhere. Small wonder that Kenya's plans to establish an Export Processing Zone (see later section) have yet to come to fruition, despite recent improvements in the exchange-management procedures.

Credit allocation

The three financial ingredients necessary for successful economic development – to judge from the experience of some Asian NICs – are an undervalued exchange rate, a high domestic savings rate, and a system of allocating cheap credit to industrial enterprises, either generally or on a discriminatory but competition-inducing basis.[7] Both South Korea and Taiwan have enjoyed all three, sometimes assisted by social policies that raise liberal eyebrows, such as the absence of public welfare spending. To compensate, Asian families were prepared to cut current consumption drastically, thus raising the ratio of savings to GDP to heights (such as 39 per cent) unheard of in developed countries. To that extent, the early economists' stress on the importance of local capital accumulation for development was not mistaken (Clark, 1984; Singer, 1989). What they mostly overlooked was the possibility of using state power to allocate credit to specific sectors – shipbuilding in Korea, for example, or steel in Taiwan – or for special groups of borrowers – the *chaebol* and more recently the smaller, export-oriented Korean firms.

Of these three ingredients, the first is seldom possible for open-market economies, given market forces. The second has more to do with society and cannot be changed readily. Only the third is open to specific administration. Among our three countries, only Malaysia has enjoyed the effects of the first: during the latter half of the 1980s, its real effective exchange rate dropped by 36 per cent. They have not enjoyed the second, nor have they set out to use credit allocation mechanisms as a means of promoting sectoral competition. Even when, as we show later, Brazil had an opportunity to do so when it invited the multinationals to establish its automobile industry, it chose not to exercise its power for fear of discouraging potential entrants.

None the less, some attempts were made to provide local, preferential credit. Malaysia set up its New Investment Fund in 1985. It was designed to use preferential interest rates to encourage investment in manufacturing, tourism, mining and agriculture. But it seems doubtful if it was big enough to have much impact. Brazil set up the National Bank for Economic and Social Development (BNDES) in the 1950s. Though its original statute forbad lending to foreign-controlled firms, a 1986 policy statement softened this policy by implying inclusion of local firms with minority shares held by multinationals (Brazilian Government, 1986). A new industrial policy decree went further in 1988, reflecting the growing opinion among Brazilian industrialists that some form of partnership with a foreign company was often the *essential condition* of attaining competitiveness abroad and even at home (Fritsch and Franco, 1988: pp. 82–4). Consequently, some Brazilians now regard BNDES as a relic of the 1950s, useful in its day but no longer a major instrument of development policy.

Lacking a high domestic savings rate, Kenya went further than most. Since the mid-1970s, Kenya has restricted the multinationals' access to the local capital market. Kenya feared they would 'crowd out' local borrowers and that scarce domestic savings would leak abroad through dividends. Kenya's dilemma then became that of finding how to make foreigners welcome whilst forcing them to bring their own capital. Thanks to what the Chinese call 'connectology', however, some have found ways round this and other restrictions. A favourite and well-tried one is to appoint a Kenyan director with good political connections and capable of finding ways to smooth the flow of import licenses and local credit. If successful, he will add another dimension to the problem. Discriminatory policies merely encourage established foreigners to employ marginally corrupt locals, thus adding a further disincentive to new entrants by conspiring to maintain the unsatisfactory status quo.

Domestic price and wage controls

Finally, there is the fraught issue of fighting inflation. There are significant negative relationships between inflation and growth, between inflation and investment ratios (Gylfason, 1989; Dornbusch and Reynoso, 1989), and among inflation, devaluation and export potential. In addition to fiscal measures, price controls have sometimes been used as a weapon. These have sometimes been effective in wartime: almost never in peacetime. They have been tried and abandoned in Eastern Europe, Britain and other developed countries. All found it one of the hardest forms of market intervention. Of our three countries, Kenya stands out as the only one which has tried to manage economic development and contain inflation by selective price controls on individual items. The result, predictably, was shortages of goods, the emergence of black markets (an additional incentive for corruption), as well as general aggravation and frustration for business, whether local or foreign. Meanwhile, real wages declined, despite attempts to fix minimum real wages, at least around Nairobi. Bowing to the inevitable, Kenya started to remove the controls in 1988 and had eliminated them all by 1990, except for a few agricultural products like maize.

Brazil tried draconian, general intervention at the height of its debt crisis. The 1986 Cruzado Plan introduced a mandatory anti-inflationary wage and price freeze. Unaccompanied by cuts in government spending or the money supply, the result was a predictable failure. Growth continued to create shortages that expanded the black market. The OECD (1988: p. 61) concluded that, because these conditions also hindered exports and cut the trade surplus, the policy proved self-defeating. By 1989, in the so-called Summer Plan, the Sarney government was still trying to control prices with a promise that inflation would be kept to 28 per cent/month. But the resignation in August 1989 of the Justice Minister on the grounds that a failed promise would bring social unrest showed how ineffective the controls still were. In June 1990, the controls were ruled unconstitutional. The new government, perhaps not knowing what else to do, took the drastic step of freezing all savings, while abandoning wage indexing even though inflation was still running at about 8 per cent a month. A consequent strike by outraged Ford workers ended in the entire plant being wrecked. Not only was administration of controls difficult; their abolition was politically risky.

110

TRADE POLICIES

Many developing countries try to liberalise their trade regimes by revising their policies of intervention and by reducing or eliminating tariff and non-tariff barriers. Free trade, however, is not a panacea. Drastic, unprepared liberalisation can lead to economic chaos, as in the Ivory Coast in 1988. The problems are most evident when tariffs have been cut without adjusting other macro-economic policies. If the budget worsens after revenue-yielding tariffs have been reduced, governments may not be able to wait for the longer term trade gains to emerge to replace the lost revenue. They may then feel obliged to reimpose taxes. By doing so, they signal to the private sector that outward-looking policies do not 'work'.

Such difficulties of determining the impact and the timing of adjustment make generalisations about trade policies elusive. These difficulties are compounded by the fact that industrialisation policies have their own dynamic in each sector and by foreign lenders' intervention in domestic policy. Trade theory seems of little help, for the advances in recent years of understanding how trade might affect national welfare are offset by limits to the theories in their capacity to yield policy advice that can work in practice (see, for example, Baldwin, 1988; Helpman and Krugman, 1989). The issues for trade policy are none the less clear. In the sections below we divide them into policies affecting imports, exports and countertrade. We also consider the use of export processing zones (EPZ) and commercial diplomacy in regional trading blocs.

Import controls

The problem with 'infant industry' and other import controls is that they protect the domestic producer, whether foreign or local. By removing the incentive to become or to stay competitive, countries risk losing in the longer term the benefits they sought in the first place. Perhaps recognising the risk, Malaysia has used tariffs only as a temporary form of protection for the first-comer investor in certain sectors, like television sets.

Before World War II, Brazil introduced high rates of effective protection for local manufacturers against imports (up to nearly 70 per cent during the 1960s) and thus created a strong and enduring anti-export bias (Balassa, 1985: p. 27).[8] This policy, known as the 'Law of Similars', was, until recently, administered by CACEX,[9] sometimes on the advice of business associations like ABINEE (electronics) or ABIMAQ (machinery). Where many import requests were combined

111

in one project, CACEX negotiated a 'national content' proportion for the project as a whole, leaving the enterprise to decide which imports were vital and which replaceable. CACEX licences have been much more effective in controlling imports than the high tariffs, which in practice affected only about 6 per cent by value of total imports.

By the late 1980s, however, the system came under increasing criticism from domestic and foreign-owned exporters. They complained that the Law of Similars often obliged them to use overpriced components, handicapping their products in world markets. In May 1988, the government responded to these complaints (prodded no doubt by criticism from the IMF as the debtors' watchdog) with a series of new decrees, labelled the New Industrial Policy. This promised to replace the opaque and often arbitrary protection offered by the licensing system with a transparent set of tariffs. Implementation, however, was slow – not so much from a lack of conviction as from the constraints of the chronic debt and adverse balance of payments situation. There was also resistance in the National Assembly and from protected vested interests. The new trade policy might act to reduce the power and corporatist influence of the powerful business associations (Fritsch and Franco, 1988).

Eventually, however, trade reform came as part of an apparent deal with Brazil's major creditor, the United States. On taking office, Collor replaced the CACEX list of banned imports with high but declining tariffs. But by June 1990, the country's economic situation had become so desperate that it had really run out of options. Collor announced that both import licences *and* tariffs would be abolished in exchange for the USA abandoning its threatened action under the notorious Section 301 of the US Trade Act. Brazil would also stop subsidising its coffee producers and would accept foreign property rights on pharmaceuticals, as demanded by Washington from the start of the Uruguay Round of trade negotiations. The impact on Brazil's informatics policies was equally drastic, as we show later on. Whether Washington was wise to use such coercive tactics is uncertain, because of the difficulties Brazil faces in adjusting other policies. Besides, whoever suffers the pain of adjustment will blame the United States, whether justly or not.

Kenya has made most use of import licensing, causing, some would say, most of the investors' problems there. But Kenya, being far more dependent on world commodity markets for its earnings of foreign exchange, always had fewer options. Just occasionally, however, the commodity price movements provided a window of opportunity to

112

relax the highly protectionist policies. One such chance came in 1986 when coffee prices (exports) went up and oil prices (imports) went down. The government's dilemma was whether to risk liberalisation, hoping prices would stabilise, or to play safe and keep the controls. Delays within the bureaucratic maze eventually allowed the opportunity to slip by.

Kenya's dilemmas were worsened by the very complexity of its protectionist policies. These included high tariffs – up to 100 per cent *ad valorem*, import duty drawbacks and rebates, combined with duty-free entry for some specific capital goods. The effective rate of protection for steel, vehicles and electrical goods, however, went much higher, up to 300 per cent. The latitude for administrative discretion in individual cases surely encouraged rather than checked official corruption. In principle, therefore, the World Bank's demand that all imports (except for some excluded on grounds of health or safety) should be free of controls by June 1991 seemed a step in the right direction. In May 1988, the Kenyan government, dependent on the World Bank for a structural adjustment loan, agreed to this as part of the approved Industrial Sector Adjustment Programme. But whether the balance of payments will allow the agreement to be carried out remains uncertain. In the meanwhile, it appears that the over-elaborate Kenyan system of import licensing has had a more dampening effect on the animal spirits of entrepreneurs than the more selective Brazilian CACEX system. And the longer reform remains on the sidelines, the harder it becomes to change: bad habits, like barnacles, encrust the ship of state.

Export promotion

Ever since the early 1970s, Kenya has used subsidies to encourage exports. These offset the extra cost of using either uncompetitive domestically produced inputs, or imported inputs on which high tariffs had been paid (Bradford and Branson, 1987). But deteriorating internal conditions forced them to increase the subsidy in 1985 to 20 per cent, and to promise prompt payment (Kenya, 1986, p. 96). In other words, the costs of the 'shadow price' can be considerable and the results indifferent. Consequently, many countries prefer alternative policies.

For manufactured goods, Malaysia has relied heavily on attracting foreigners to its Export Processing Zones (see below) and letting them fight it out in the exports markets with the minimum of intervention. There are considerable risks inherent in this policy, for export compe-

113

Table 4.2. *Asian exports of assembled semi-conductor components to the USA, 1969–1983 (under US Tariff Items 806.30 and 807) (per cent of total)*

Country	1969	1975	1980	1983
Hong Kong	49	12	5	1
South Korea	23	17	10	17
Malaysia[1]	0	30	34	37
Philippines[1]	0	5	16	21
Singapore	10	26	25	13
Taiwan	15	8	5	5
Others	3	2	5	6

[1] Started exporting under the programme in 1973.
Source: calculated from Grunwald and Flamm (1985): table 3.7.

titiveness can shift rapidly among countries, almost irrespective of relative changes in domestic costs. An extreme form of export volatility is shown in table 4.2 for semi-conductors made by US firms. The workings of the US tariff code have particular importance. Under Items 806.30 and 807 in the code, US firms can gain tariff exemptions for products exported from the USA, processed abroad and re-imported to the USA.[10]

Brazil, on the other hand, has combined export subsidies with other regulations to force firms to develop exports and add a greater net contribution to the balance-of-payments as the price for being able to sell in the huge internal market. Brazil's size gave it bargaining power not equally enjoyed by either Kenya or Malaysia. Under the BEFIEX system, set up in 1972 to consolidate earlier policies, firms promising to export a set portion of their production were allowed to bypass the 'Law of Similars' and also get soft loans for financing exports. Surprisingly perhaps, this programme was initiated at the suggestion of the local Ford affiliate (Baumann and Moreira, 1987: p. 2).

The success of BEFIEX can be judged by the fact that by 1985 it covered 40 per cent of all manufactures, with a significant increase of the net trade generated (Fritsch and Franco, 1988: p. 116). Much of the success was fuelled by the multinationals responding to the combination of carrot and stick. By 1986, they accounted for one-third of total exports of manufactured goods, mainly in transport equipment, machinery and chemicals.[11] Even though local firms were also permitted to use the BEFIEX rules, the multinationals increased their export propensities four times faster. But here, too, there was a dilemma. The BEFIEX programme affected both export prices and margins. For

114

much of the 1980s, internal price controls and market reserve policies combined to make margins on the domestic market much more attractive than for exports. Many multinationals told us they had switched supply accordingly, thus reducing the full extent of the export growth. In other words, Brazil found it hard to balance domestic and export intervention policies simultaneously.

For most developing countries the gains in trade from all such policies have been made primarily in price-sensitive goods. Especially in South–South trade, the evidence is that older notions of comparative advantage based on price elasticities still hold sway (Thomas, 1988). The implication is that a new 'sub-economy' is emerging alongside the world of global competition. This appears to be a zero-sum game, because what one developing country gains is at the expense of another. Only where the multinationals' power has been harnessed have substantial gains in income-elastic goods been achieved.

Export processing zones

Creating new export possibilities by establishing an EPZ in which exporting-only enterprises can be set up free of most local laws has appealed to many developing countries from the 1970s onwards.[12] Kenya's problems of being unable to adjust policies elsewhere to ensure efficiency, an essential requirement, have already been discussed. Brazil's only special economic zone is a rather different case, as we show below. Thus, our attention is focused on Malaysia, one of the pioneers of the idea in 1971.

For Malaysia, the New Economic Policy aimed, among other things, at employment-creating industrialisation, in which foreign capital, already prominent in the economy, would play a part in enhancing exports. But to make the location sufficiently attractive, the government decided to follow Singapore's lead and create an EPZ. A promotional drive in California was directed at specific industrial sectors – like electronics – where officials thought their best chance of success would lie. National Semiconductor became the first of a stream of US and later Japanese electronics investors to take the bait. Other EPZs were later established in many parts of the country. The range of investors widened, but mainly within electronics and some textiles. Together these two industries account for over 90 per cent of the exports generated.

Though the net gains to Malaysia's balance of payments and employment[13] have been valuable, the hoped-for transfers of tech-

115

nology to local suppliers have been disappointing. Some technological capabilities have been enhanced, but the main benefits have been restricted to the simpler parts of the industry.[14] Even so, Malaysia has become one of the world's largest exporters of semi-conductors. Excluding the minimal spillover benefits, one cost-benefit study concluded that the net benefits of the EPZs, in terms of jobs, trade and local purchases, had grown to the point where by 1982 they exceeded the costs of providing infrastructure and of foregone tax revenue (Warr, 1987: pp. 52–3). Such a conclusion has not, as we describe in Chapter 5, stopped Malaysia from continuing to press for even greater benefits in the form of enhanced linkages with local producers.[15]

More generally, the competition created as more countries have established EPZs has eroded their effectiveness (Basile and Germidis, 1984). Instead of considering them in purely 'enclave' terms (UNIDO, 1980a: p. 39), they must now be considered as a kind of magnetic field, reinforcing a country's existing attractiveness as a site for more foreign investment (Lütkenhorst, 1988). This changing role affects ability to stimulate local 'linkages', for other obstacles come into play and lead to mixed outcomes.

EPZ regulations must become much more flexible if countries are to retain the vitality of the original investors. Typically, firms have been required to export all their output to attract the full set of incentives. In Malaysian electronics, this 'has sometimes led to the ridiculous situation whereby a company based near a factory producing ICs places an order with the manufacturer's parent company or regional marketing office. Components that were made in and shipped from Malaysia a few days earlier are then shipped back'.[16] Malaysia has subsequently become more flexible in the application of its procedures. So too has Mexico, where *maquiladora* enterprises are now permitted to sell up to 20 per cent locally under some conditions. Other adjustments include those in Sri Lanka, where enterprises can, where costs suggest location close to a supply of raw materials, get the benefits without being physically in the zone. Some countries have lifted restrictions on nationality and now allow local nationals to set up in the zones. Further, South Korea is experimenting with the conversion of EPZs into science parks. All these developments suggest that the phenomenon of EPZs has its own life cycle and that policy must adjust accordingly, however difficult that may prove in practice.

Brazil's Free Zone of Manaus (ZFM) provides a good illustration of the difficulties of adjustment, even though it was set up for quite different purposes. Because ZFM was set up in 1967 at the insistence of the military, who argued that economic development in the Amazon

116

basin was necessary for national security, its managing authority, SUFRAMA (Superintendencia da Zona Franca de Manaus) is responsible to Defence rather than Trade. Consequently, the original policy of allowing tariff-free imports into the zone had little coherence with other national policies. Foreign firms found ZFM to be an excellent way of avoiding the import bans from the Law of Similars, especially in electronics. Only in 1987 did SUFRAMA begin to promote exports. The relative lack of success was due in large part to the lack of consistency with other policies – a fact that became apparent in 1990, when Collor abolished national import quotas, and threatened to cut tariffs too.

Countertrade

Countertrade is a means of escaping from the straitjacket of the world system when it pinches too tightly. Such evasion is, naturally, the subject of considerable controversy. Gilpin (1987), like many liberal economists, regards it as contrary to consumer interests, whereas others describe it as 'a ray of hope in a dismal world'. Whatever the merits of either argument, it is an option used widely throughout the world as the earlier example from petrochemicals showed. One recent study listed over 1,300 such deals concluded by developing countries between 1980 and 1987 (Jones and Jagoe, 1988) and concluded that most had been due to the instability of the financial system. Others echo this view, regarding countertrade as 'the symptom, not the disease' (Hammond, 1989: p. 252; Welt, 1985).

Brazil has been one of its greatest exponents. Many estimate that countertrade accounts for as much as 10 per cent of Brazil's exports of both raw materials and manufactured goods. Just as many third-world deals have involved oil so as to escape the OPEC output quotas, so Brazil exchanged $630 million worth of locally-made Volkswagens for Iraqi oil in 1984. With Nigeria, Brazil exchanged promises to trade $4 billion of sugar and some sugar-processing equipment in return for oil. Malaysia, too, has been active since 1983. Government-negotiated deals have included the exchange of tin and rubber for Yugoslav manufactures, textiles and electric goods for Korean patrol boats, oil for Brazilian iron ore.

Where Brazil and Malaysia have felt free to manoeuvre, Kenya has been constrained. The difference lies not in ideology, nor in what they have to offer for exchange, but in their unequal vulnerability to the disapproval of the United States, the IMF and the World Bank. Kenya has been so dependent on official aid and structural adjustment loans

117

that its government dared not go in for countertrading – despite the fact that, like Brazil, it was surrounded by poor, debt-ridden neighbours. Some major companies now seem, however, capable of finding ways around the obstacles. Recognising that Uganda permits barter deals, General Motors Trading Corporation in Kenya, for example, negotiated the export of Isuzu buses (assembled in bond in Kenya) in exchange for hides and skins which it then sold on to third parties.

Though most developed countries deplore such practices, most either practice them from time to time – as Britain did in its arms dealing with Saudi Arabia – or else turn a blind eye when it suits them. For example, Israel has since 1967 followed the general rule that all government purchases – including, of course, arms – should be paid for by offsets. The US Congress has never uttered a word of criticism against the Israelis. With such examples in mind, it is small wonder that developing countries feel equally free to use countertrade when short-term necessity over-rides any sense of the longer term and less certain consequences.

Regional trade blocs

Rather than act independently, many developing countries have tried to increase their competitiveness by forming regional trade blocs. They have typically had two motivations. One is to increase inter-regional trade and gain scale advantages by specialisation. All too often, however, the gains have proved illusory, for member states have had either competing, not complementary, products or have failed to agree on 'rules' for determining who gets what share of the newly specialised output. The other and perhaps stronger motive for regional bloc-building is the hope of increasing collective bargaining power.[17] In the case of ASEAN, there is some evidence of success. For instance, in 1977, Australia backed down on proposed cuts on Asian footwear imports after ASEAN threatened to buy food elsewhere (Gill and Law, 1988).

The severity of the obstacles against realising regional gains are shown in the dismal history of such policies. From the Central American Common Market in the 1960s onwards, almost everywhere hope has been followed by disillusionment. The collapse of the East African Economic Community in 1976 had damaging effects on foreign investors by cutting off important local markets. The 1983 agreement by eighteen countries to set up a regional preferential trading area (PTA) in East and Southern Africa has been little more successful in overcoming three familiar problems. One was imbalance in trade advantage. As the more industrially developed countries in the region, Kenya and Zimbabwe stood to benefit most from the association. Kenya gained a (largely unpaid) surplus and was there-fore reluctant to increase unrequited exports. The second was the rules-of-origin clause which excluded exports by firms not majority-owned by Africans. The third was the dependence of poor govern-ments on trade tax revenues – 70 per cent of total revenues for Uganda, 25 to 30 per cent for Kenya – and their consequent unwillingness to cut tariffs even to other African states. GATT's general disapproval of such trade-distorting initiatives is, by comparison, a gnat bite.

Latin American efforts to exercise collective bargaining power against multinationals have equally flopped. The Andean Pact's much publicised Decision 24 of 1970 progressively to exclude multinationals was reversed – the official euphemism was 'replaced' – by Decision 220 of May 1987, effectively leaving the bargaining up to the individual states (Bolivia, Peru, Ecuador and Venezuela). The original fade-out provisions that called for progressive expropriation of foreign firms have gone; and the attempt to create cooperative 'regional multi-nationals' on the basis of a division of labour and specialisation was abandoned in 1982.[18] The broader-based Latin American Free Trade Area appeared to increase intra-industry trade but had few other perceptible consequences. One reason was that it incorporated a most-favoured-nation rule that precluded bilateral deals and thus limited collective agreements to the willingness of the least cooper-ative member. It was effectively superseded in 1980 by the Latin American Integration Association (LAIA), which allowed bilateral deals and has since been an umbrella under which they have prolifer-ated (Tussie 1987: p. 129).

Equally questionable has been ASEAN's development. Though inter-industry trade is higher within the region than among developed countries (Erzan, 1984), this could be merely the result of good communications and cheap transport (Grimwade, 1989). The record of negotiating – and sticking to – regional specialisation in basic indus-tries has not been impressive. A recent example of how plans have come unstuck is the fate of the Japan-backed ASEAN plan for automo-bile components, where Indonesia's intransigency has put plans for regional specialisation back on the drawing board.

Bilateral agreements may hold out more promise, if only because they are easier to administer. For example, Brazil and Argentina are developing a free trade agreement, due to be completed by 1994. The initial agreement covers many capital goods (excluding informatics) and has led to an increase in trade and specialisation. Argentina's

119

exports emphasise goods where batch production is effective, whereas Brazil's emphasise products for which long runs and economies of scale are important. Future agreements are intended to cover a wider range of industries. Already complementary technology agreements have been made among local firms to support these ambitions.

Meanwhile, among economists, the jury is still out on whether regional trade blocs and bilateral trade agreements are any more than a second-best strategy. Yet the Canadian decision to join the USA in a free-trade area means that weaker partners think the risks of *not* joining are greater and the benefits, however marginal, worthwhile. The point is not lost on developing countries: if the rich countries think the strategy beneficial, there must be something in it for them too.

OWNERSHIP CONTROLS

States' policies towards the ownership of assets can be considered in four categories, depending on their priorities for state ownership and their attitudes to foreign firms. They can choose to insist on state ownership, as is common for public utilities, post and telecoms. Where state ownership is not at issue, they can be neutral, leaving the sector free to respond to market forces and to the general, national policies. For the rest, they can choose either to give preferential treatment to foreign firms (by means of incentives not available to local firms), or to discriminate against them by such means as Brazil's market reserve policies.

State-owned enterprises

Though they have existed in some countries for centuries, only after the 1940s did state-owned enterprises (SOEs) come to prominence in most developing countries. Either by nationalisation or by the creation of new industries, SOEs were widely regarded as an essential feature of managing the 'commanding heights' of the economy. In Brazil, President Vargas started creating SOEs during the 1930s. By 1960, their number had grown to 150 in 1960 and to over 600 by 1980. Some of these were mixed, in the sense that investment in some sectors like chemicals was created under the 'tri-pé' policy whereby ownership was shared among state enterprises, local firms and multinationals. SOEs multiplied in Malaysia with the desired roles, as explained by one official as 'patron, trustee, joint venture partner, complementer and inducer of expanded bumiputra participation in the commercial and industrial sectors' (Leeds, 1989: p. 743).

Over 100 industrial SOEs were formed in Kenya in most sectors, often in partnership with foreigners.

Because SOEs were created for multiple reasons, most faced conflicting pressures from various constituencies and could not reconcile multiple, and conflicting, objectives. The problems were worsened by corruption, as in the notorious Malaysian case when a major highway contract was awarded to a construction company of limited experience, but owned by the ruling political party. The inherent conflicts embodied in their creation has subsequently led to their demise in many countries.

Targets for output and employment often conflict with targets for profitability. Measures of contribution to government revenue could not be matched, as in Sierra Leone's petroleum SOE, with price controls designed to keep energy prices low (World Bank Staff, 1989: p. 225). With notable exceptions, SOEs have proved disappointing. Far from delivering priority goods and services efficiently, most have been shambling giants draining funds out of national coffers. In countries like Brazil, the original financing had come so heavily from foreign loans that by the mid-1980s, SOE debt was over half of the total foreign commercial debt. The position was even worse in countries like Tanzania, where SOEs were set up primarily to replace imports but worsened the trade balance. Moreover, Tanzanian SOEs became massive net consumers of state revenues with consequently negative impact on development (World Bank, 1989: pp. 11–13).

Expropriation of multinationals has created a good many SOEs. The history goes back to 1938, when Mexico took over US and British oil interests and reached a peak in 1975; eighty-three acts of expropriation of foreign firms in twenty-eight countries (UNCTC, 1988a: table XIX–I). Since then the tide has turned. In the first half of the 1980s, there were only fifteen expropriations compared with 336 in the first half of the 1970s. As the UNCTC commented, 'The mood today is very different ... Not many developing countries would now see the activities of TNCs as impinging on their sovereignty ... there are clear indications of a new pragmatic approach which comes from the growing belief that developing countries can negotiate agreements with TNCs in which the benefits of foreign investments are not necessarily outweighed by the cost' (UNCTC, 1988a: p. 314).

Privatisation

Failure, whether because of internal inefficiencies or because of the need to create new international partnerships, has led many

121

governments to consider privatisation as part of the cure. Broadly defined, privatisation ranges from sale of all or part of the equity to their transformation to management contracts or leasing agreements with private firms. It may also involve, as in banking, a degree of deregulation of markets.[19] Whatever the mechanism of the sale and to whom, the intention of privatisation is to increase economic efficiency (Commander and Killick, 1988) and to increase the degree to which the country can become part of the global economy (Vernon, 1988).

That intention has, so far, seldom been realised. By the mid-1980s, relatively few of the SOEs targeted for sale had actually been privatised. Moreover, the privatised firms had seldom showed the expected gains. The numbers show that in Africa and in Latin America, excluding Chile, only about 17 per cent of targets for privatisation had actually been sold and in Asia only about 30 per cent. In Brazil, where the total net assets of state enterprises amount to about $40 billion, the assets of those privatised amounted to only $27 million (Pfeffermann, 1988: p. 15). That is at least better than Nigeria or Turkey where despite much fanfare and expensive feasibility studies, nothing at all has happened.

Severe administrative obstacles and problems over valuation of the assets are prime obstacles to action. Chile has been far more successful than most, precisely because of the simplicity of its administrative procedures and considerable pragmatism in assessing values: features largely absent elsewhere. Valuation problems are exacerbated when privatisation has been undertaken as part of a wider adjustment to outward-looking policies. Often the World Bank and the IMF have required the hardest pressed countries to adopt both 'structural adjustment' and 'policy reform' (a euphemism for privatisation) before new financing is made available. Structural adjustment can make the internal market less profitable and thus less attractive to those prospective buyers seeking to exploit the local market. Perversely, this reduces the value of the assets for sale and thus the fiscal benefit to the treasury.

Further obstacles come from the short-term costs of re-construction and from a lack of local buyers. A Brazilian estimate was $1 billion for the physical rehabilitation of rundown, inefficient state enterprises. Thus, the 1985 proclamation of privatisation had largely stalled by 1989 for lack of buyers. A growing backlash of nationalist sentiment further impeded Brazil's programme. When debating their new Constitution in 1988, Congress passed a provision to force foreign companies to divest their controlling interests in mineral extraction over a four-year period. Though, as we discuss below, this provision has been modified, the nationalistic sentiment was clearly registered by prospective buyers. Brazil's pro-privatisation rhetoric needs to be supported by much further change in policy and practice to turn it into more than a minor curiosity in its history.

Progress has been less hindered in Malaysia since 1983, when the government began a new policy, led by the Prime Minister, of co-operation between government and the private sector in which multinationals could participate as minority partners or with management contracts. Yet Malaysia has not always gained greatly from the sales of assets, such as shares in its airline and the container terminal at Port Klang. Political control could still override commercial consideration (Nankani, 1988). In Kenya, the sparse results of the 1983 Task Force on Divestiture of Government Investment reflect less the unwillingness of the government to press on with privatisation – as demanded by the IMF and World Bank – than the absence of willing African – not Asian – buyers; most foreign private enterprise have been uninterested. All that happened was a marked decline in the preferential finance made available by parastatal Kenyan banks (Commonwealth Secretariat, 1985: p. 26). Government has also been reluctant to act, as we illustrate later on for textiles, for fear of loss of jobs.

As in Eastern Europe, where privatisation has been accomplished, the full longer term benefits will not be achieved until the enterprises gain greater competitiveness. The obstacles are considerable when one considers how much has to change in managerial attitudes, skills and in the internal control systems. Managers long cushioned by state intervention become driven by production targets, not by the test of the market. Their failures can all too readily be excused and even hidden by further infusions of state funds. Few are likely to be enthusiastic about taking up the burdens of having to compete. This problem is especially acute in smaller countries like Kenya and Tanzania, where there are now fears that state capitalism will merely be replaced by 'crony capitalism'. All too often, newly privatised enterprises remain dependent on political connections for a wide range of monopolistic privileges to cushion the full force of competition. Unless adequate attention is paid to building robust institutions that promote internal competition and offset the lack of commercial experience or knowledge in the political system, privatisation will merely transfer privilege and feather-bedding from one group to another.

123

Controls over private ownership

Controls over private ownership go beyond state ownership or policies towards foreign investors; they can also affect racial or tribal groups in the local society. In Kenya, it sometimes seems as though the main issues regarding ownership have not really been foreign vs. African so much as African vs. Asian[20] and state vs. private. The low savings rate and the low literacy rate among Africans left the economy heavily dependent for growth on either Asian enterprise or foreign investment and expertise. Given the policy of explicit discrimination against Asians and constraints on foreign ownership, SOEs had to fill the gap. Even recent liberalisation has failed to dispel deep-seated suspicions that discrimination still lurks beneath the surface.

Malaysia has been primarily concerned to secure the economy against too much Chinese ownership. Spurred by severe racial riots in 1969, the New Economic Policy (NEP) was introduced in 1970 with the primary objective of forcing a change of ownership to reflect the ethnic composition of the country. Thus Malaysian, or bumiputra, shares of corporate ownership were targeted to rise from about 2 per cent to 30 per cent. The foreign investors' share was to reduce from 60 to 30 per cent by 1990 (Malaysia, 1973: table 4.9). Chinese interests were also forced to restructure their equity holdings as the government became more directly involved in the redistribution of national resources and enacted restrictive legislation such as the 1975 Industrial Co-ordination Act. Moreover, anti-Chinese discrimination extended into the educational field and employment in public service, with a high percentage of places reserved for bumiputras. One response was to create both an exodus of talent from the country and capital flight. Ironically, this capital flight has been rumoured to have fuelled some of the growth of inward investment from ASEAN countries. Capital fleeing the country has been recycled through family connections abroad to reappear as fresh capital imports capable of attracting the more recently relaxed rules for foreign investors, regardless of national or ethnic origin. Though such rumours cannot be proved, they are so endemic that they suggest something of the sort has been occurring.

The general climate of gradual relaxation of constraints against foreign ownership that prevailed at the end of the decade has probably extended to the Chinese and the smaller Indian local population. The fact that bumiputra ownership had increased dramatically, no doubt helped smooth the way. By 1986, the bumiputra share of equity among the 173 members of the Malaysian Chamber of Commerce and Industry, which broadly represented the international business community, had grown to 21 per cent. Yet it must be noted that much of the growing Bumiputra ownership was held in a series of trusts and pension funds. By attenuating the link between ownership and control, the benefits have not been widely distributed among local entrepreneurs and individuals (Sieh and Chew, 1985).

Controls on foreign firms

Just as firms have to modify what they want in strategic terms with what they can get, so too for government. Attempts at privatisation, designed to push SOEs on to the global bandwagon, have often been accompanied by an easing of equity limitations in other sectors. For example, the first constitution of independent India in 1947 laid down that foreign ownership should be limited to less than half in oil, and in certain other restricted sectors. Only where the foreigner brought in technology that could not otherwise be obtained or where the firm exported the great bulk of its output were these constraints relaxed. Today, such exemptions have been extended as governments understand more fully just how much of a deterrent ownership restriction is to certain types of investor, especially those pursuing some form of global strategy.

Liberalisation of ownership is seldom a matter of states retreating to a policy of indifference. Most wish to retain or promote some form of local participation. This preference is shown up in growing governmental preference for the many variants of NFI, in which a local enterprise associates with a foreign partner (or sometimes with two as in Brazil where Tintas Renas teamed up with both ICI and Dupont to produce paint for the local market). Just how sensitive is the issue can be seen in US firms' responses when ownership controls have been relaxed. Where they could, they increased the proportion of their wholly or majority owned foreign affiliates between 1977 and 1982 (Contractor, 1990a). American preference for equity control remains, it would seem, undiminished. Others can be more flexible, depending on their competitive strength and strategy of expansion. A full discussion of the issues is therefore deferred to the next chapter, when local strategy is matched against local regulation.

Incentives

The question naturally arises as to whether liberalisation of policy leads to greater inflows of direct investment. With so many weapons to hand, some cancel out others in a tangled web of incentives and disincentives. Thus, while Korea found that inflows rapidly increased after their liberalisations in 1981–2, Pakistan found a decline in investor interest after introducing a new policy of welcome in 1984.

Part of the reason for such seemingly irrational behaviour is the suspicion among many managers that incentives rise as governments try to offset inherent economic disadvantages or protect restrictive domestic policies. Besides, the forms of the incentives themselves come in a bewildering array. Guisinger (1985) lists 59 varieties of incentive and obstacle that governments use. The effectiveness of each depends on many other factors. For instance, US investors are not swayed by tax holidays as tax policy in the USA offsets much of the benefit. Most importantly, effectiveness cannot be measured in the generality; it has to be seen in the context of what each firm is trying to achieve. As we have repeatedly observed, the critical distinction is between whether a firm is seeking to exploit the local market or to create exports. Internal price controls may be important for the former (IFC, 1986), but not for the latter. As Wells (1986) pointed out, failure to recognise this distinction leads to confusion.

Effectiveness is also a function of the efficiency of the agency or agencies responsible. In many countries, a single agency deals with assessing investors' proposals; in others the investor has to negotiate with several ministries, with all the attendant delays and possible inconsistency of messages received. Given the sensitivity of time, it is not surprising that there has been a trend towards countries adopting 'one-stop-shopping' approaches.[21] Many, like the BKPM in Indonesia, are also simplifying the procedures so that smaller projects can go through without screening, or adopting procedures that allow automatic approval (unless subject to official objection) within thirty days. The record for ambition to be speedy seems to be held by the Selangor State government in Malaysia, which announced in 1988 that it was now 'possible for applications to be approved in one day'.[22]

Admirable though they are, the benefit of these moves are eroded by administrative inefficiencies and distrust. For example, when Kodak wished to set up a regional distribution centre in Nairobi, it failed to gain permission for 'green channel' facilities for the re-exports. The Kenyan government could not believe the duty-free photographic chain would not somehow leak out into the economy. In addition, Kodak found so much administrative hassle was to be involved in serving the regional market via Kenya that it was more cost-effective to fly in the chemicals direct to each country. When Malaysia turned attention to export promotion, local manufacturers eligible for export incentives 'did not avail themselves of the facility either because of ignorance or owing to the cumbersome procedures' (Ariff and Hill, 1985). Besides, the subsidies implicit in the incentives were insufficient to offset the anti-export bias created by the NEP 'padding' and protectionism and were aimed at only the largest enterprises.

Such obstacles apart, all these facets of ownership policy and incentives to change behaviour, taken together, have led to a 'new pragmatism'. Flexible arrangements for decision making on projects in which having a bare majority in equity ownership is not the deciding factor are now becoming more common (UNCTC, 1988a: p. 326). Because the needs of governments – for technology, for foreign exchange earned through exports, for managerial experience – differ from sector to sector, as does the prospect for profits for the investor, the sectoral differences among bargains are likely to be even greater than national differences.

SECTORAL POLICIES

So far, the discussion has concerned general policies that affect all industries, but in varying ways. Firms in global industries tend to be much more concerned with exchange rate questions, for example, than those in domestically oriented ones. To deal with such problems, governments can choose to adopt a specific sectoral policy. They have the same four basic options we described for general ownership policy: state ownership; specific support for or discrimination against locals or foreigners; or neutrality. At the sectoral level, however, these choices can be more difficult, especially when powerful interest groups are directly affected, or when specific sub-sectors of industries have been designated as flagships of industrialisation. Political deals can add confusion about the implementation of a particular policy.

The balance of effect varies widely among the three parties shown in figure 4.3. Brazil's military government, according to Evans (1979), envisaged a 'triple alliance'. Local firms were to provide the skills in political manoeuvring, multinationals the technology and the state to supply the institutions and the arena in which to forge a common set of goals to unite the alliance and manage the national economy. In practice, in Brazil and elsewhere, the alliance within sectors is always unstable, because coalitions form to oppose the status quo. Privatisation moves may initially favour a strengthening of links with foreigners, but later give way to greater support for local firms when

127

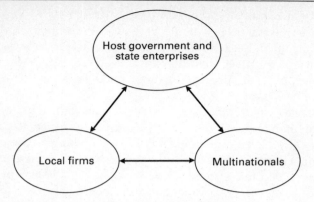

Figure 4.3 Balancing competing interests.

their objections to being excluded are heard. Inherent competitive weakness in a state/local sector coalition may break down as some local firms seek advantage by alliance with foreigners. Sectoral policy that favours foreigners may, as in Malaysia's electronics, provoke calls for greater linkage with and support for local firms.

These shifting balances and the accompanying administrative muddle and dilemma are illustrated by experience in five national industries. These indicate the pressure for change, the dilemmas of choice and the difficulties of implementation when different parts of government take opposing views. More detailed consideration of the human and political aspects of these issues is given in chapter 6.

Informatics is a prime example. Spurred originally by demands from the Navy (for special performance requirements, not well catered for by the US suppliers) and by internal security needs for faster information, Brazil had determined to go for a policy of self-sufficiency in the underlying technologies. In the terms of our matrix in chapter 1, this was a move in intent from left to right for a global industry, with all the attendant risks of such high ambition. Most imports were banned and foreign investors forced to renegotiate their position. Some, like Honeywell, chose to leave, while others chose to commute equity into licence agreements. This policy approach was, however, overtaken by the events of 1990, when the new Collor government agreed the plan, described earlier, to reduce trade friction with the USA. Rather than immediately repealing the existing Informatics Law of 1984, however, the government decided to abolish it when it expires in 1992. The reasons for the delay were explained by the Minister for Science and Technology:

We had no choice. The Informatics Law must be changed by Congress, which is clearly opposed. I'm caught in the cross-fire between on one side the US which wants to export computers, the motor and textile industries which complain they cannot modernise and thus compete without a change in the law, and on the other side the Brazilian computer industry which argues we are leading them into bankruptcy.[23]

To add further confusion to an already muddled picture, the SEI (Secretaria Especial de Informatica) is reported to have maintained the similarity examination and placed bureaucratic obstacles in the path of importers. They seem likely to continue to do so even after the reserve policy has been replaced by an interim policy of providing maintained protection for a list of specific products with the *potential* to compete with foreign products. Under these circumstances, it is unlikely that foreign computer firms will scramble to take advantage of the new policy under which they can subscribe for 30 per cent of equity in a local producer.[24]

The Brazilian *arms industry* provides a second example, but in this case change came more from the workings of market forces, not, as one might suppose, from the continuing strong influence of the military in Brazilian politics (C. Evans, 1990). Here local firms have been pre-eminent, though some have used selective technical agreements with foreign enterprises, like that between Embraer and British Aerospace, to keep up technologically. Their export success was, for a time, phenomenal. They rose to fifth place among arms exporters, helped perhaps by the embargoes constraining some competitor nations.

According to Carol Evans' detailed analysis (1991), the land-based arms industry was not planned: it emerged after a slump in demand for machine tools and other capital goods. Producers desperately needed to find new outlets for the capacity they had installed in the boom times. As most of their expansion had been in transport sectors, it was a natural step for them to try switching production from trucks to tanks. The timing seemed fortuitous, for they expanded just as demand was booming in the Middle East. But the end of the Iran–Iraq war led to a precipitous decline in exports and to the bankruptcy of two major firms: Avibras and Engesa. A narrow export base was inadequate to protect the sector from the boom-to-bust cycle.

The origins of Brazil's export success in military trainers and small civilian aircraft were quite different. Here, government discrimination against foreign firms, combined with preferential protection for Embraer,[25] broke the earlier US stranglehold on the industry. During

129

the 1950s the US light aircraft company, Cessna, dominated the Brazilian market. When the government initiated a preferred partner strategy to force import-substitution, it offered Cessna a deal. Protection would be granted if Cessna produced aircraft in Brazil and modified its US designs to suit local conditions. Cessna refused. Its smaller rival, Piper, agreed to a joint-venture, and for a while enjoyed Cessna's position, before being displaced when Embraer took over complete control. By the end of the 1980s, the sector had developed, with the aid of foreign partners and technology, to the point where Embraer claimed nearly 40 per cent of the world regional airliner market. Exports to the USA had, however, been impeded during the late 1980s by US obstacles, placed in retaliation against 'unfair practices'. Only after the market reserves for imported planes were dropped in 1990 did the export position improve. In this instance, it is notable that the domestic monopoly did not create inefficiency. Embraer had long adopted policies of aiming for international competitiveness; the domestic market was too small to support its ambition.

The Brazilian *automobile assembly* industry was created in the 1950s to replace imports by using investment allowances and protection as inducements to foreigners to invest. Though the policy of according preference to foreigners has been retained, its application has changed dramatically. Originally, under the Law of Similars, investors were offered a protected place, one foreign firm in each segment of the sector, just as in aircraft. This created quasi-monopolies, marked by inefficiency and lack of export potential (Fritsch and Franco, 1988). This strategy changed in 1972 when BEFIEX was introduced. The large size of the internal market gave Brazil the power to insist on the transition, despite objections from the firms about the cost of the reinvestment needed. Further fuel to the drive for competitiveness was added at about the same time by inter-provincial rivalry. Minas Gerais, for example, wanted to gain some of the job-creating benefits of playing host to foreigners that had previously been concentrated around Sao Paolo, and did a deal with Fiat; Parana acted similarly with Volvo. But the sector suffered like chemicals and shipping from cyclical downturns in world demand which thinned the ranks. Two major producers – General Motors and Autolatina[26] – came to dominate the sector while minimising their risks by building closer links with local component suppliers. Though some, like Dahlman (1984), consider this industry to be a 'success story of infant industry development', the reality is much more complex. It is a sector where the multinationals dominated, but had to be coerced into action that produced export gains but at the price of deepening the dependence not just in the main products, but also in key component suppliers. Besides, the Japanese presence in the industry is limited. Some argue this is because of the decision to adopt sugar-derived alcohol, not solely to reduce oil imports, but also to add a further barrier against new foreigners.

Policies designed to increase the added-value content of *natural resource* exports have taken different forms, depending on the nature of the world market. As discussed in chapter 3, open, competitive markets confer greater power on the government when the sophistication of the technology and the scale in advancing downstream are slight. But when there are advantages from vertical integration, as in aluminium, the multinationals can defeat government policy. For example, Brazil's 1988 resolution to prohibit foreign controlling interests in natural resource ventures was circumvented by the exemptions granted to those who 'industrialised' their operations by building refineries and the like. Though many in Brazil feel that this softening in the law was due to lobby pressure from the multinationals, others take a different view. One authority in the Brazilian Mineral Institute claimed that 'Congress felt that foreign mining companies that had already made huge investments here should be differentiated from newly arrived companies'. The new provisions hit hardest at the exploration stages of minerals projects, where there is the greatest risk. Shell has stated that it 'no longer wants to invest in exploratory mining in Brazil. None the less, as 95 per cent of Shell's (minerals) investments in Brazil are in aluminium, we will still be a strong presence here'.[27]

Policy shifts and administrative compromise are common experiences. The Kenyan textile sector shows clearly how dilemmas and conflicts of policy can multiply over the years.

Textiles were one of the earliest modern manufacturing industries to be established in Kenya. By independence, seven mills were in operation, all owned, wholly or partly, by local Asians. In the decade following independence, a number of vertically integrated companies were founded as joint ventures with foreign partners, some with minority government participation. Up to 1972, these ventures were modestly successful, due mainly to high rates of effective protection (Langdon, 1986: p. 186). Such protection, however, bred inherent inefficiency by encouraging excessively wide product ranges, short production runs and costs at least 40 per cent above world prices.

In the early 1970s, government policy shifted towards promoting manufactured exports. Textile exports were targeted in the 1974–8 Development Plan, and four new projects were negotiated by the government with foreign partners. In each, a complex consortium of development finance institutions held majority equity positions. Promises of export earnings failed to materialise: most of the projects had bought overpriced and sometimes obsolete equipment from the shrinking European textile industry. By 1983, all the ventures involving government development finance institutions were nationalised after defaulting on loans. Even in public ownership, most were seriously undercapitalised. Most were also inefficient: irregular supplies of raw materials encouraged over-stocking (UNCTC, 1988b). The only remaining profitable joint venture textile company was the private venture between local Asians and the Japanese, Nomura.

In effect, the government became trapped by its original, but incomplete, logic. The planners held the conventional view that textiles was an attractive industry, because it was labour-intensive and could compete on world markets by virtue of low local wages. What the planners ignored was the effect of competition on profitability. High effective rates of tariff protection (up to 93 per cent) (World Bank, 1987: p. 283), were no defence against competition from local Asian producers and from smuggled goods. Even when the industry persuaded the authorities to introduce *and* enforce bans on imports, it did not change the operation of the highly concentrated domestic wholesale textile market. This remained largely controlled by Asians who also owned most of the garment manufacturers. Naturally, they exerted as much downward pressure on ex-mill prices as they could.[28]

Low profitability meant the textile ventures could not finance their substantial foreign borrowings when Kenya began a series of devaluations in the 1980s.[29] At the same time, although the government did not have the resources to finance adequate re-capitalisation, it was unwilling to close mills for fear of creating unemployment. The situation was so bad in one company – it had started life as a joint venture with Lonrho – that the losses from 1985 to 1988 were substantially greater than its aggregate wage costs. The state-owned textile companies now operating with insufficient working capital are even more vulnerable to price gouging by Asian wholesalers (Coughlin, 1987). Moreover, while upper management may be reliable political appointees, Asians (and a few Europeans) still dominate the ranks of senior textile engineers.

Sectoral policy can also lead to unexpected problems as protected national entities themselves attempt to compete in international markets. These attempts represent a shift in 'intent' from left to right in the matrix of agendas shown earlier in figure 1.7. Whereas a few, like Embraer in Brazil, have succeeded in creating the resources and abilities to become global players, many others have stumbled. Kenya Re, mentioned earlier, illustrates the problem. Once established to control domestic reinsurance flows, Kenya Re attempted to grow further by taking on risks from such countries as their African neighbours and Bangladesh. These risks had been previously rejected by the more experienced majors. The perhaps inevitable consequences were accumulating losses and a withdrawal back to the protected home market. What started with high hopes for mutual support among poor countries was confounded by market forces. In other words, the limits to South–South collaboration at national levels, described in chapter 2, are also visible at the sectoral level.

All these examples show the wide range of forces – economic, competitive and political – that together shape both the balance of sectoral bargaining power and the basis of government choice about the form of desired control. The chances of being treated preferentially or even of being treated on a left-alone basis also depend critically on the level and pace of change of the technology involved and on the degree of concentration and competition in the sector (Mytelka, 1979; Milner, 1988; Grosse, 1989). Often, as in household products or industrial chemicals, hot competition among affiliates of big multinationals ensures both growth and cost-competitiveness.

But global competition, by itself, is not necessarily enough. Multinationals can use their market power to fiddle transfer prices. Though rare, such abuses do happen.[30] Kenya Canners (now renamed Delmonte Kenya) was subjected to an Interpol investigation in 1978, prompted by the fact that it persistently showed local losses while continuing to export 96 per cent of its output. The investigation revealed wide discrepancies in the invoices shown to the Kenyan authorities and those submitted to foreign buyers. Subsequently, the company agreed to independent auditing and has returned to profitability. Given that the company received about 20 per cent of its profits from the government's 'export compensation', such acquiescence was not surprising. In pharmaceuticals, firms can use the power of their technological oligopoly so blatantly that there has been a policy reaction by many governments. Sri Lanka, for example, once adopted a national reserve policy to switch supply to generic drugs, mainly from Eastern Europe. Though designed both to save foreign exchange and for social welfare reasons, this policy had later to be modified as problems of quality and unreliable supply multiplied.

WHERE THEORIES FAIL

This brief look at sectoral differences raises some much broader questions about the adequacy of academic theories to explain how the emerging state–firm relationships affect bargaining. Bargaining theory is common to the study of both international relations and international business management. Indeed, there is a growing consensus among writers on transnational corporations in developing countries that the relationship between the parties is the product of bargaining, whether explicit or implicit. (Grosse, 1989; Kobrin, 1987; Dunning, 1989; Doz and Prahalad, 1987; Safarian, 1983; Wells, 1977; Encarnation and Wells, 1986; Austin, 1990). There is also consensus that there are certain common factors, negative and positive, that affect a country's ability to bargain successfully with transnational corporations (Katzenstein, 1978). Yet, even the theoretical models that underpin the relationships sketched in figure 4.1 do not constitute a general explanatory theory of why and when the balance of bargaining power shifts, nor why outcomes differ, nor yet why and how the bargaining process (involving more than narrowly defined one firm-one state conditions) gets started.

The much wider social sciences literature concerning bargaining offers little more help. At best, it merely clarifies some aspects of the processes by which parties with different, even mutually conflicting, objectives manage to reach agreement both can live with. In political science and international relations, from Schelling's seminal book (1960) onwards, much of the literature started from positivist, realist assumptions and focused almost exclusively on the behaviour of states (Rapoport, 1960; Iklé, 1964). The further assumption of public choice theory, that states are rational actors and interact rationally with each other, has led many scholars in this field to follow the lead of the economists – who in turn were following the mathematicians – to use game theory and to make limiting assumptions about the nature and duration of the game. Logical coherence has been gained at the expense of empirical relevance. At the extreme are international lawyers like Falk and the conflict resolution school of writers like Galtung whose purpose is explicitly normative, seeking to use game and bargaining theory to change the behaviour of the protagonists. Only a few writers in international relations (notably Jervis, 1976; Steinbruner, 1974) have seriously questioned the assumption of rationality in state policy making and some more recent works have distinguished bargaining in which the parties are not consciously conflictual but are searching for a point of convergence (Raiffa, 1982; Rangarajan, 1985).

134

Why bargaining theory helps so little should be clear enough from our evidence. A state has objectives that are multiple, often conflicting, always shifting. It cannot in reality be a rational actor in the game-theory sense of having a fixed order of priorities in its policy goals. It always wants incompatible, conflicting values. It wants to be efficient and competitive *and* to preserve social peace and the cohesion of the state with society. It wants autonomy and the freedom to choose its own path to economic development *and* access to advanced technology and overseas markets. It is playing a trade-off game in which the variables are never constant.

Policy-making dilemmas, we repeat, have been increased in number and difficulty by the necessity of partnership with multi-nationals in the hunt for world market shares. States must choose, in industrial policy as in corporate strategy, between diversification and specialisation. Specialisation may improve the chances of successful exporting as with Korean and Malaysian electronics, Taiwanese containerships, or banking in Hong Kong. But the risks from new competitors and from changing technology or market demand will also be greater. Korea's choice of shipbuilding shortly before the shipbuilding and especially the tanker market virtually collapsed in the mid-1970s could have been disastrous. And in textiles, Kenya's experience shows that cheap and plentiful labour was insufficient to overcome increased import quotas and Voluntary Export Restrains, or to compete against new, still cheaper competitors. States must also choose which policy approach should apply to which sectors, and when and how to move a sector from one category to another.

The politically optimal policy toward the foreigner may be precluded by the inequality of factors affecting the balance of bargaining. There has never been a time in economic history when comparative advantage was less static. Understandably, governments have difficulty reconciling their macro-policies towards foreigners with the need for discriminatory policies among sectors, and still more with the specific bargains they may be tempted to make with particular firms. Foreign investors typically call loudly for clear, unambiguous rules by which to play the game. They want continuity of policy, not capricious or arbitrary decisions. But each enterprise also wants government to be flexible, to discriminate in its favour; and for itself wants to be free to take advantage of any shifts in the factors which improve its own bargaining power.

The dilemmas are often more acute for the government with a small economy like Kenya's than one with a large domestic market like Brazil or India. Both, however, have difficulty in choosing among

135

firms in the same sector. In the final analysis, much of the success or otherwise of a policy will depend on which firms carry out the operations. But this introduces a further dilemma. Should the state favour a leading multinational that will likely insist on tougher terms? Or should it seek weaker competitors or new entrants who are often more accommodating to local policy, but may lack the resources to keep up with the pace of change? These questions are addressed in the next chapter. For now, it is important to remember that the bargaining relationship is never static.

Rational, economic analysis is far too static to capture this dynamic; governments are left to choose their policies on political grounds. It is they, not international advisors, who have to suffer the consequences of wrong political decisions. This is why they often consider advice from the IMF or the World Bank to be hopelessly abstract and unrealistic. These organisations have to give – or at least be seen to give – the same advice to all their members, regardless of politics. Backed by a combination of sticks and carrots, the advice often gains credibility only because it is taken. But it is not always or necessarily the best advice. Their experts are not infallible, as when the World Bank boosted tourism in the 1960s as a sure-fire multiplier of development.[31] Their advice, even today when it is more flexible and politically sensitive, consequently often falls on deaf ears, not because the economic logic is at fault but because the political factors in the equation are both unquantifiable and subjective for the decision takers.

A final weakness of bargaining theories in this context arises from the complexity of interlocking relationships in the real world. Government policy must be seen as a whole, not in parts. There are bargains between ministers within government; there are bargains between political parties supporting government; there are bargains with labour unions, with business associations, with religious groups and ethnic minorities. There are also bargains which interlock all these with foreign corporations, foreign governments and the international organisations. In all these, over-generosity with one partner can cost dearly in relations with another. Conversely, being too hard in one set of negotiations – as the Chinese government was in the Bloody Summer of 1989 with its Peking students – proves enormously costly in terms of lost credibility and lost confidence in another set of negotiations – in that case, with the foreign banks, corporations and governments who were due to help with credit, technology and market access.

5 LOCAL DECISIONS FOR FIRMS

In earlier chapters, we painted broad pictures of the issues in the world system, in multinationals' headquarters and in national government. By standing back far enough from the action, we could see some patterns in recent behaviour. But, as when looking at an impressionist painting, the image blurs as one approaches the canvas. So, too, when observing activity at the grass-roots level, the sense of order dissipates. Local managers are pulled in different directions by the multiple forces acting on them. Their behaviour is conditioned by the demands of their corporate masters and of the local bureaucracy; and by the need to build robust human systems capable of harnessing and developing local skills and resources. What patterns of behaviour as exist are to be seen more at the level of the individual firm than within industries. In this chapter, we examine the interplay of the first two influences, leaving the human side of the argument to the next chapter.

Among the many ways by which corporate strategy affects local managers, two stand out as being of prime importance. The first arises from the shifts towards global strategy that raise the costs of staying in the business. Because, as we showed in chapter 3, seemingly similar firms hold contrasting views on how risks and opportunities are measured, they respond differently to the growing need to focus on 'core' activities. Many industry leaders are now finding they have to shed activities that made sense in earlier years of expansive diversification. When managers at headquarters judge that a developing country has become marginal to new international priorities, the firm is likely to divest or to adopt other policies that minimise its asset exposure, irrespective of change in local circumstance. The second is that local and central managers do not always share a common vision for the future of the enterprise. We found that local managers were increasingly contesting these hard and supposedly 'rational' decisions as they attempted to adapt international strategy to local needs. These two trends are beginning to be further affected by the more recent developments of New Forms of Production (NFP). The stronger the bonds among national units and the greater the standardisation of production techniques, the less the possibilities for local adaptability.

Equally difficult for local managers are their dealings with the local governments. National policy can be interpreted inconsistently by those departmental officials who deal directly with the firms. Because private and public interests often diverge, officials feel obliged to screen projects. Yet, despite advice from bodies like the World Bank to adopt 'outward-looking' policies to increase efficiency, officials typically find they have to adopt 'second-best' approaches. The cabinet or similar bodies may determine the menu, but it is the many officials, each reflecting departmental interests, who cook and may spoil the meal. How either side determines the attractiveness of a particular investment thus assumes great importance in the negotiations both for entry and for retention of investments in a particular country.

In this chapter, we also examine the impact on different types of firm of demands for some form of NFI to 'unbundle' the equity package and for the creation of greater linkages and adaptability to local needs. Where established, leading firms may resist or react defensively to these demands, newcomers may embrace them enthusiastically as they attempt to break into the market. Throughout, we focus on individual firms, for it is not always the firm most accommodating to local demands that provides the best deal in either the short or the long run. Governments thus need to choose carefully their partners for realising ambitions for development.

MAKING GLOBAL STRATEGY LOCAL

The national strategies firms adopt to implement a given global strategy are not homogeneous. Firms must choose which markets to contest and *how* they will do so. Separate choices must be made about the location of each of the activities that together make up the local operation. Should firms locate R & D activities abroad or concentrate the laboratories at home? Should advertising copy be produced locally, or should it, as in Coca-Cola, be based on a common worldwide image? Should some of the production be located near to customers and consumers to increase the level of service? Further choices are needed about how much each activity should be adapted to local needs or standardised to global requirements. Governments must understand that firms' choices of local activities are determined as much by internal politics as by rational economics.

Multinationals have had to build elaborate structures of organisation that allow them to balance the tensions these choices create. These structures reflect both the economics of the industry and the strategy of the firm. At one extreme, firms delegate responsibility entirely to local managers, who act autonomously, much as did Roman Pro-Consuls. At the other extreme, firms permit their subsidiaries little or no local freedom of action. In between, lies a vast range of structures that balance local with central authority and expertise.[1]

One of the world's most complex forms of such balance in a 'matrix' structure has been developed by Royal Dutch/Shell. Figure 5.1. sketches the different lines of reporting for Shell's wholly-owned subsidiaries and its 1,000-plus joint ventures that operate in over 100 countries. Central service companies provide expert advice and guidelines on specialist functions, from finance to technology; business sector organisations look at the global implications of the various businesses and help with strategic thinking; and regional organisations provide shareholder representation. The balance of effect varies by business and over time. For example, central initiatives in the 'upstream' sector of oil exploration dominate decisions to explore new areas, but once oil has been found control is gradually delegated to a newly formed production company in the country concerned. This elaborate structure allows profit responsibility to be delegated to the operating companies, but in a form that permits the Group to gain advantage from its world stature.

Such organisations can only be built slowly over the years. Managers have to learn how to cope with the complexities of operating across borders and managing in different cultures. When Alcatel, the French electronics group, was starting to develop its business in China, the manager in charge is reputed to have said at the first meeting, 'Mr Fong, time is money'. To which Mr Fong replied, 'time is eternity' (Kupfer, 1988). Our interviews repeated many times such vignettes of the need to learn about local conditions. Because most managers in multinationals work in their country of origin, the need is to find ways of transferring and accumulating experience. For example, of Shell's 135,000 employees worldwide, only about 5,000 are international staff, though they represent seventy nationalities. Shell has spent a great deal of money over decades building human systems that allow their managers to work effectively at local levels without losing a global perspective. Few others can rival that depth of experience. Its value has many dimensions. One is in the ability to find ways through the corridors of power more speedily and effectively than newcomers. Yet that advantage does not always translate into superior performance (Grosse, 1989:

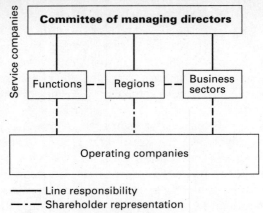

Figure 5.1 The matrix organisation for Royal Dutch/Shell.

p. 171). Superior organisational capability needs to be matched with superior products and strategies.

The challenge for firms is to maintain the vitality necessary to respond to the dynamics of the market at both global and local levels. That vitality is greatly affected by two features of how managers see the world around them. One is the time scale for strategy. The other concerns the balance between consistency and flexibility firms strike in their operations in any one country.

Most major multinationals try to take the long view on strategy and are not therefore as foot-loose as they are often depicted. One of the authors, when joining Shell as a junior engineer, remembers having it drummed into him that Shell's perspective was *fifty* years, and that decisions to build new facilities had to be calculated with that in mind and not be overly influenced by current events and current costs and prices. Though Shell is at an extreme end of a continuum, most have to look far ahead in order to develop competitive products and market positions. A long forward-orientation also affects the value of incentives offered by government: those, such as capital grants, that have only short-term impact seldom sway firms' location decisions.

It is one thing to decide to stay in a global business for the long-haul, it is quite another to manage local operations consistently and to change appropriately as local advantages shift. The penalties for losing the momentum that consistency brings are well illustrated by the erosion of GE's once strong position in electrical appliances (Bartlett and Ghoshal, 1990).

140

> Over a period of 20 years and under successive CEOs, the ... international strategy never stayed the same for long. From building locally responsive and self-sufficient 'mini-GEs' in each market, the company turned to a policy of developing low-cost, off-shore sources, which eventually evolved into a de facto strategy of international outsourcing (buying in from others). Finally, following its acquisition of RCA, GE's consumer electronics strategy made another about face and focused on building centralised scale to defend domestic share.[2] Meanwhile, the product strategy within this shifting business emphasis was unstable. The Brazilian subsidiary ... built its TV business in the 1960s until it was told to stop; in the early 1970s, it emphasised large appliances until it was denied funding; then it focused on housewares until the parent company sold off that business. In two decades, GE utterly dissipated its dominant franchise in Brazil's electrical products market.

In that instance, efforts by local managers to respond to changing local circumstance were overridden by other priorities at headquarters. Indeed, GE's Brazilian managers had no idea, from year to year, what was really expected of them.

At the local level, inconsistencies can also arise when managers are transferred among subsidiaries. For example, the Malaysian operations of one European firm with world brand leadership in many products suffered from a succession of managers, none of whom stayed for more than two years. As the subsidiary was held on only a light rein from head office, the local bosses could each in turn determine priorities for products and processes, based on personal experience from other countries. The result was confusion and a severe loss of market position and morale. Improvement had to wait until headquarters asserted more consistent controls and direction.

By contrast, Unilever has had a long commitment to Brazil, despite the volatile swings of fortune that have caused competitors like the German firm, Henkel, to leave and discouraged entry, as in the case of Unilever's great rival Proctor and Gamble. As one director colourfully put it, 'in those parts of the world you take your management cues from the way they dance. The samba method of management requires you to take two steps forward, then one step back. Companies with a short-term perspective are unable to adopt this perspective.'[3]

Firms need to combine flexibility with persistence to overcome local obstacles and with the maintenance of consistency over time. Successfully balancing these factors helps a firm to remain competitive in local markets and to maintain a viable bargaining status with government (Poynter, 1985). Just as we argue elsewhere that firms and governments need to invest in building mutual understanding as the basis for sustainable co-operation, so firms have to do the same inside their own organisations. This is not always easy or possible, for the sorts of reasons we describe below.

Choosing a location

Before investing, managers must be confident that the project will provide an adequate return on the investment. How they interpret the financial calculations (described later on) depends on several key aspects of all international investments. One is the incremental nature of the decision. The firm's interest is not just in the return from the local operation, but also in the marginal impact of the investment on the enterprise as a whole. Multinationals can draw on resources located in other countries and at prices or costs that differ from those prevailing locally. Thus, their optimal location decisions differ from those made by national firms. National firms use national factor costs and import resources at prevailing world prices: multinationals use the best prices they can find anywhere in the world and transfer resources within their own systems at marginal costs. The difference between full cost and marginal cost can be enormous when considering such factors as commercial and technical information, brand names, and credit guarantees.

A second factor is that of risk, both economic and political. Economic risk involves both local factors and consideration of competitors' reactions. World-wide risk is usually regarded as more important than local risk. Measuring risk is, however, a subjective business. It is manager's *perceptions* that count. Nestlé, for example, announced in 1980 that it was slowing down its investments in developing countries even though they were highly profitable. The company considered that having 35 per cent of its sales in such areas was too risky. Such perceptions heighten the risk for local suppliers, for they are seldom capable of influencing the outcomes.

Perceptions of risk also depend on personal position, experience and knowledge. In one major chemical company, managers at headquarters had long avoided investing in ASEAN countries, because they thought them riskier than the developed countries with which they were familiar. Only after many briefings from corporate planners, who were concerned about missing growth opportunities, did the board members begin to realise that their perceptions were based more on ignorance or prejudice than reality. The consequence was the announcement in 1989 of ambitious goals for establishing a large share of their worldwide assets in the region by 1995.

A third factor has been introduced by the NFP developments. These decidedly limit the degree of latitude open to local managers and constrain the choice of country. The integrated managerial and operating systems deployed by the Japanese automobile manufactureres, for example, are successful because everyone in the organisation is singing from the same score. To assure interchangeability of parts and standard levels of quality and service, there is little room for adjustment even to local work practices. Shop-floor workers have to be trained to conform to group practice. In other words, the benefits can be reaped at the cost of limiting the range of countries where such practices are acceptable.

Many attempts have been made to determine which of the many influences on location choice are rated as most important by managers.[4] In the main, the results consistently point to the overwhelming priority managers attach to market size and market growth, offset by concerns about political instability. Political and administrative concerns, such as limits on profit remittance and price controls, are commonly rated as more important than the offer of incentives (Kobrin, 1982). For example, a MITI survey in 1988 of Japanese motivations for investment in ASEAN and other Newly Industrialising Countries showed that only 20 per cent of the firms considered incentives to have some bearing on their choices and only 10 per cent paid regard to trade regulations. Yet, as we pointed out in the previous chapter, such evidence does not mean that incentives are *necessarily* weak: much depends on what the individual firm is trying to achieve.

Most attempts to match such statements of priority with actual investment behaviour have been disappointing, mainly because of severe methodological problems of measurement. Schneider and Frey (1985) provide a good summary of the literature and of these problems as a prelude to their own attempt to provide a 'predictive' model. They studied FDI flows into eighty developing countries during the later 1970s and found some reasonable degree of 'fit with managers' political and economic priorities. Perhaps surprisingly, they found little impact from such variables as the ideological position of the government, the rate of inflation, wage levels or skills.

Firms' difficulties of reaching a common perspective on risk and opportunity are compounded for reinvestment decisions: there is the added presence of local managers whose careers may be at stake. They do not necessarily share the same perspectives as their remote and perhaps more dispassionate bosses (Boddewyn, 1983). We found numerous examples where local managers acted as advocates for greater local investment than was considered wise by headquarters.

143

For example, one European firm expanded in Malaysia only after the local manager had put his career on the line to insist that greater funds should be made available. In other cases, we found that headquarters remained unimpressed by such arguments. Some local managers of German chemical firms in Brazil were forced to give in, despite remaining convinced the decisions were, as in the GE case, disastrous for the local business.

Like the armed forces where operational commanders disagree with staff officers, or within government itself, multinationals are not monolithic in their internal behaviour. There can be considerable tension in the debates about how to reach an acceptable common perception of risk and return. Government negotiators do well to know the state of play within the firm and not judge the proposals simply by the *pro forma* statement of intention. They may have unexpected allies within the firm.

The problem of marginality

These problems of differential expectation have been compounded by global competition. Firms are finding that increased competition limits the number of businesses and local markets they can finance and manage adequately. Consequently, many have been shedding product lines deemed to be of minor importance; what is sometimes called 'slimming the corporate portfolio'. Earlier policies of product diversification that were thought to reduce risk, were fashionable in the 1960s and 1970s. In the 1980s, they largely gave way to policies of focusing on a limited set of businesses to which the centre of the corporation could add value.[5]

Similarly, many firms now limit the geographical spread of their 'global' businesses. Some countries are so small that the cost of management time in exercising control exceeds the returns. Goodman (1987) cites many managers who said in the early 1970s much of what we heard in the late 1980s. One regional manager, responsible for a small Caribbean plant that contributed 0.02 per cent to the divisions earnings said that the 'political turmoil [means] I am spending one fourth of my time holding on to that 0.02 per cent, and I have taken the time away from ... [overseeing] operations in Brazil and Canada' (p. 114). Not surprisingly the plant was sold even though it was earning more than 20 per cent on the capital invested. Another, responsible for the Peruvian subsidiary, said 'making huge profits is not my bottom line. Even doubling or tripling last year's profits would have little impact at headquarters. My bottom line is ... not to waste

PRODUCTS

	'Core'	Peripheral
'Core'	Insist on control; develop stronger international links	'Defensive' use of NFI to reduce exposure and re-investment
Peripheral	'Defensive' use of NFI to reduce exposure and re-investment	Divest, where possible

COUNTRIES

Figure 5.2 Global competition forces new choices of priority.

my boss's time' (p. 1). Assessment of a multinational's strength at the world level needs revision when one looks at its tiny subsidiaries.

Among multinationals with established global positions, the combination of product and territorial marginality can lead to new choices of where and how to focus resources. Figure 5.2 lays out some of the possible considerations. Managers typically insist on control and often on complete or at least majority ownership of those products and territories considered central to the firm's future. They are most resistant to government demands for local adaptation, particularly when they are growing by extending their cross-border linkages. In these 'core-core' areas, traditional forms of bargaining persist. At the other extreme, multinationals may try to exit from marginal product lines in marginal countries, but can be constrained by exit barriers. In between are two possibilities where firms attempt to limit their exposure by adopting some of the forms of NFI. They do so 'defensively', as they consider reinvestments to protect existing operations.

Exit barriers

Firms will stay, even in marginal territories, when the costs of exit exceed the benefits. The exit barriers they face come in both negative and positive forms, depending on the available alternatives. Only overwhelmingly strong reasons, including total business failure or a central decision to quit the line of business altogether, will cause the firm to leave (Grunberg, 1981). The initial investment can thus act to lock the firm into the country.

Negative exit barriers make the firm stay on when they would prefer to go. The cash costs of exit can be greater than the alternative uses of the assets recovered and remitted abroad. These costs include redundancy payments and other regulations affecting the handling of liabilities and responsibilities. One cannot simply walk away from the subsidiary. Another barrier can be the effect on competitors. In industries of the 'local-for-local' variety (e.g. detergents) the firm might not want to cede local market share for fear that competitors might gain future cash flows which could be deployed later on for an attack in other markets.

Barriers also exist when firms wish to retain a presence in the market, just in case conditions might improve. Some Kenyan investments have been maintained primarily to keep 'a window on Africa', even when they were unprofitable. Many drug and chemical companies like Glaxo, Hoechst and ICI run simple 'mix-and-stir' facilities in Kenya as a way of providing a platform for other operations, such as the import of high-tech drugs made in large plants and not therefore suitable for local production. To help spread local overhead, Glaxo also manufactures other products on contract for competitors. But such 'wait-and-see' policies often mean that firms may not maintain their assets in as efficient a form as in more strategically important territories. The host country thus ultimately suffers from the growing inefficiency.

A further motivation to stay is when a local presence helps to build close liaison with the government in a form that permits a joint lobby to aid-giving bodies. For example, when Chancellor Kohl visited Kenya in 1988, executives of the German business association lobbied him to provide funds for German pharmaceuticals and chemicals to 'help Kenyan development'. They were outraged by what they saw as Germany's 'neutral' aid policy. In other words, investment and trade assistance can become interlocked to reduce the incentive to leave.

For General Motors, the commitment in Kenya came in the rather more complex form of what we call the 'Sullivan effect'. The Reverend Leon Sullivan is both a prominent black activist against apartheid and also a main board member of GM. Many consider that a disproportionate amount of board time was devoted to their Kenyan affiliate, precisely because it was their most significant investment in Black Africa. Kenya thus provided a form of protection for their South African operations against anti-apartheid protestors until GM

146

decided to quit. Ironically, most of GM's Kenyan sales were made by Isuzu, in which GM holds a minority 42 per cent share.

Positive forms of exit barrier exist when the 'sunk costs' of investments in human capital make it cheaper to stay than to build afresh elsewhere. For example, by 1988, when nineteen of the twenty-six foreign-owned electronics firms in Malaysia had exhausted their tax holidays, none had relocated. One manager stated: 'We came here for cheap labour and the tax advantages, but we are staying because of the expertise we have built up here. As far as assembly and test are concerned we have more expertise here than we have in the US. We sometimes have to send our Malaysian engineers to the States to solve their problems.' Intel has also had to use Malaysian experts to solve chip assembly problems in the USA, because they had stopped that kind of work there some years earlier.[6]

More generally, NFP systems are extremely costly to relocate, because of the high costs of training on a new site and realigning the complex cross-border administrative system. Faced with such barriers, established firms have a strong motivation to find new ways of harnessing existing resources. In Brazil, for example, VW has extended the idea of exploiting local niches of demand by linking them to niches elsewhere. Its Fox model has been exported to ethnic communities in the USA. Innovative responses like this go far towards explaining why the 'obsolescing bargain' hypothesis discussed in chapter 1 does not apply so strongly to manufacturing as to minerals extraction (Kobrin, 1987). In other words, host countries can reap, perhaps unexpected, advantage by not pressing for greater local linkages.

States may have little positive power over such decisions, but the forces in inertia can work to their advantage. Nonetheless, multinationals on occasion use the *threat* of exit to extract a better bargain from the host nation. Ford has used this tactic many times publicly in its dealings with the British government, but has stayed. Though many new projects have been located in other parts of Europe, despite the offer of generous incentives, British negotiators have become sceptical of the threat to quit altogether. They can see that Ford faces high exit barriers. So too in developing countries. The threat may be potent before initial entry is made; thereafter, the sabre can rattle ineffectually.

A new form of divestment?

Where leaders may use some form of NFI to defend existing, but marginal, operations, newcomers may aggressively exploit them to compensate for their relative competitive weakness. The contest for

147

leadership of global industries and its effect on policies towards NFI is illustrated by the long-running battle for leadership of the earth-moving equipment industry. During the 1970s, Komatsu, the Japanese newcomer, created manufacturing joint ventures in many developing countries that demanded local participation. The established leader, Caterpillar, generally insisted on complete ownership. For Komatsu, the joint ventures helped to build volume and experience that could later be leveraged into cost advantages. As it gained strength, Komatsu established its own wholly owned units, though mainly in OECD countries. Meanwhile, Caterpillar, defensively, modified its ownership policy.

Because leaders have more pressing agendas on other fronts, they may be prepared to relax previous policies and 'unbundle' the equity 'package' in some countries and for some products. Such moves may be regarded as a new form of divestment. Whether they confer advantage on the host nation is a matter of great debate. One example makes the point.

In 1972, Firestone opened a tyre plant in Kenya, with a minority interest divided between the government and a European development finance agency. The original agreement paid a royalty fee of 2 per cent of net sales, free from restrictions on profit remittances. This had been negotiated directly with President Kenyatta, who also ruled that Firestone was to be exempted from the general price and foreign exchange controls. After a protracted row with the Central Bank, this agreement was terminated in 1979, on the grounds that the original intention had been to allow only temporary exemptions. This dispute led headquarters to cancel plans for expansion and require the affiliate to repatriate all its profits. When the Kenyan government objected, Firestone filed a claim against the Kenyan government through OPIC.[7] A compromise was reached whereby Firestone funded money to Kenya under a bilateral treaty, but no additional investments were made thereafter.

Firestone's weakening global position overtook events in Kenya. Smaller, non-core, operations were earmarked for sale. The Kenyan operation was eventually sold to a local consortium in 1985, after protracted negotiations to find a politically acceptable deal. Firestone retained 19 per cent of the equity and was allowed to repatriate its capital proceeds free of exchange controls. In addition, Firestone negotiated a 3 per cent royalty plus a 1 per cent management fee on net sales: twice the previous level of fees. Further gains came from the fact that the new consortium could borrow locally once it had become a majority locally owned, and could also raise prices. The consortium has expanded aggressively to command a near monopoly of the local market, but remains dependent on Firestone for critical raw materials, on which Firestone collects a handling fee. Moreover, Firestone has a monopoly of importing those types of tyre not made locally. In short, Firestone increased its profit flow from Kenya with reduced asset exposure and risk.

Achieving majority local ownership was trumpeted in the domestic media as an advance for Kenya. But at what price? The drain of foreign exchange has increased, local prices have risen and no compensating gains in local efficiencies achieved. Moreover, now that Firestone has been bought by the Japanese firm, Bridgestone, it is unclear what future transfers of technology will take place under a deal made by previous owners.

Defensive actions are common in 'mature' industries, where the leaders' abilities to control all the critical inputs, such as technology, are waning. Partial divestment offers an attractive means of producing additional, marginal returns and cash flows that can be used to fight battles in 'core' territories. There are, however, limits.[8] Both Fiat and Pirelli have issued licences in small territories, though both consider them trivial within the scope of their overall strategies. Pirelli, in its tyre business, has licensees in Eastern Europe (though its policies there may now be changing), in Iraq and a few other markets that are small and uncertain. A common attitude was summed up by one manager who stated, 'we do not fear competition from LDC licensees; their scale is too low'. Others may not be so sanguine, fearing that licensees will turn out to be future competitors, as Glaxo found in Australia. Its licensee found ways to work around Glaxo's patents and created a rival product for the Australian market. When this firm was later acquired by Nestlé, the international consequences for Glaxo were serious (Davenport-Hines, 1986).

Such fears provoke firms to restrict their licensees to selling only locally, and to prohibit exporting. These attempts have attracted much criticism from developing countries and are specifically barred by regulation in many countries. Given these problems, it is no surprise that most of the firms we talked to limited their licences to their older technologies. They insisted on retaining complete ownership and control over those newer technologies which they thought might produce world-class products.

Similar limitations apply to contracts. Major problems are created by uncertainty, technical change and imperfect information that can seldom be adequately captured and managed within the framework of a legal agreement. One US multinational had such success with a

Chinese supply contract for a standard product for which it was the world leader that it repeated the approach in an ASEAN country for an electronic component. In the second instance, however, technology changed so rapidly that the agreement had to be abandoned within a year.[9] Accordingly, many multinationals strongly prefer some form of equity control when they expect changes that cannot be managed without conflict with their partners.

PROJECT ASSESSMENT

Assessing how firms have reacted to changes in government policy requires an understanding of how both firms and governments measure the worth of a project. The differences in approach provide clues to government officials about why firms do not always react as might be hoped.

Firms measure worth by the rate of return on the investment. The return is calculated in terms of the total cash flows generated. These are generated by dividends, *plus* royalties, management fees, trade-mark fees and the effects on the profitability of operations in other countries. They invest when the project is deemed likely to yield a return greater than the risk-adjusted cost of capital for the enterprise as a whole. The riskier the project, the higher is the required return. Firms' estimations are called the *financial* rate of return; the minimum rate they require is the *hurdle* rate.

Firms have to deal with two major problems in making these calculations. One is the difficulty of valuing all the benefits and costs in financial terms. One German manager in Brazil said, 'we run out all the numbers, but then we have to use our judgement about whether we really want the investment. Sometimes we will invest in projects that seem at first sight to be unprofitable. When we believe that the strategic gains for the company as a whole are real, even though the finance department cannot quantify them, we will go ahead'. Such difficulties are compounded for NFP-type projects, for which most of the returns are reaped outside the country of investment.

The second problem is that of calculating the appropriate risk premium. The perceived risk of investing in a country is not the same as the risk for the particular project. Some projects can more easily be protected from general risks (e.g. devaluation and regulation) than others, depending on the business in question.[10] Moreover, where exchange controls limit profit repatriation, the 'real' cost of capital is indeterminate. One manager went so far as to say that under such circumstances, his company conducted no post-investment audits of the returns, because 'once the money is invested, it is locked into the economy and has virtually no value; there is no point in finding out whether it is actually being deployed efficiently'. Though few would take such an extreme, long-term view, all are conscious of the problems.

Governments' measures differ, because they value the worth of a project to the country, based on the *economic* or *social* rate of return.[11] Both prices and costs used in the firms' projections may be distorted by government intervention and by imperfect markets. For example, prices may be high in relation to world prices, because of tariff protection. Costs are distorted by subsidies and the lack of local competition. To allow for these distortions, 'shadow prices' are used to assess prices and costs in terms of the most efficient alternative use. Though these are hard to calculate with confidence, they are increasingly being used to provide an alternative benchmark of worth. Governments also use a hurdle rate, calculated on the basis of the opportunity cost of national capital resources.

Today, all projects using World Bank or IFC funding must be evaluated according to these principles. The importance of this requirement is shown by the fact that in fiscal 1989, the IFC invested $1.3 billion in 90 projects and mobilised $8.4 billion of others' funding. But even the experts have their problems. A recent internal study showed that most of the IFC's forecasted rates of return were higher than those realised in practice (IFC, 1989). The greatest errors arose in the agricultural and agricultural processing industries, where the difficulties of assessing all the developmental impacts of the project – the so-called 'externalities' – are most acute. Volatile commodity prices add particular problems of prior estimation for such projects. In one Kenyan export project for vegetable oils, the international price dropped by 80 per cent within two years. However, the IFC's initial over-optimism does not necessarily mean that it accepts 'bad' projects. The IFC claims that by weeding out about two-thirds of the proposals it receives and by providing advice, it contributes to the wide development process.

What seems good for the firm is not necessarily good for the country. The firm makes calculations in terms of the global return; the government looks only at the local effects. One careful review of 183 projects in more than 30 developing countries showed that 25–45 per cent of the projects had negative economic outcomes, even though they were profitable for the multinationals (Encarnation and Wells, 1986). These results were roughly in line with earlier studies conducted under the auspices of the OECD (Reuber, 1973) and UNCTAD

(Lall and Streeten, 1977). The 'bad' projects were sanctioned where government offered high rates of tariff protection for import-substituting projects: no export-oriented projects had negative public consequences. This analysis reveals the dilemma for government. If it wants import-substitution, it often has to pay a high price. Yet, on occasion, the government may feel it has no other option, especially in the early stages of industrialisation or when highly indebted. There are, to be sure, instances where strong political figures will sanction a 'bad' project for reasons of prestige or even personal gain.

Both measures of worth can be combined to show how different relative valuations can lead to different kinds of bargaining. In figure 5.3 we show four different possibilities. The hurdle rates are drawn notionally, for both firms and states have varying requirements. A real (i.e., inflation-adjusted) social rate of 10 per cent is indicated, following the IFC's estimations for the average opportunity cost of capital for developing countries during the early 1980s. A private real rate of 15 per cent is used, as this is a commonly required risk premium in many developing countries. Projects below both rates are normally unacceptable to both sides. Projects below either of the hurdle rates are also unlikely, unless special circumstances can be found to offset the financial calculations. For example, because the distribution of risks among local and foreign partners is uneven, the risk premium each seeks will differ. Thus, as in the Firestone case, 'unbundling' the project can turn a financially unattractive project into a politically acceptable one.

Almost all the bargaining we observed has been in the area of joint financial acceptability. Here the bargaining is over the distribution of the gains and the exercise of relative power to insist or accede to demands to alter the project. Part of the sense of relative power comes from the mastery of the data that lie behind the numbers used for calculation. Does the firm really know its business better than government? Many officials to whom we spoke took the view that the firm's figures had to be accepted. 'Who am I to tell General Motors that its forecasts are wrong?' was a common attitude. Yet the trail of mistakes and abandoned projects tells another story. Consider Alcan, the major Canadian aluminium multinational, with a long and distinguished history of third-world operations. Alcan established a fabrication facility in the Ivory Coast during the 1970s, only to find that it persistently lost money. Eventually they sold out to the East African group, Comcraft, who understood how to manage a small-scale local business and made money almost from the first week. Alcan had originally resisted pressure from a large British bank that they should

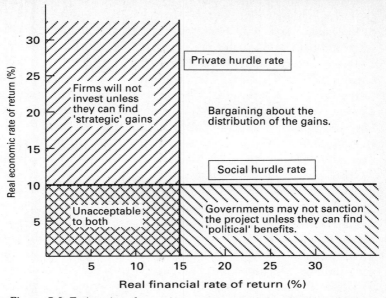

Figure 5.3 Estimating the project returns precedes the bargaining.

provide a parent company guarantee as part of the 'price' for loan financing, but broke its normal no-guarantee policy and had to pay up. One Alcan manager concluded, 'the bank's insistence on a guarantee told us we should not have been there in the first place'. Because managers can exaggerate their own understanding of the business when expanding in an unfamiliar country, government officials should not automatically assume that the firm always knows best.

One particularly troublesome issue is that of calculating a project's environmental impact. Shell's recent experience in developing the Rabi-Kounga oil field in partnership with the Gabonese government is a good example of what has now come to be standard practice in the oil industry. Shell commissioned an environmental impact study of the $330 million project, conducted by independent experts from the Dutch university of Wereningen, and made important modifications as a result. Similarly, BAT's Kenyan subsidiary supports only those local tobacco suppliers who grow sufficient trees for the timber they need to cure the tobacco. BAT's extension service has led both to better yields on trees and better designs for the kilns, enabling local farmers to enjoy a surplus of wood to sell as timber or fuel for others. Such work is not philanthropy, but good commercial sense.

Though such practice is now routine for many, others are less

153

careful (Shaikh, 1986). Increasing cost pressures and the rush to industrialise have led some countries to accept less than the best international standards for pollution control. The bill to clean up past mistakes is escalating, not just in Eastern Europe, but also in such cities as Cubato in Brazil, where many petrochemical plants, both foreign and local, have created what is known locally as the 'Valley of Death'. Another type of pressure is illustrated by the deal concluded between the Myanmar government and Thai interests in exploiting the dwindling teak forests. Myanmar's pressing need for foreign exchange seems to have over-ridden long-run environmental concerns.

Good practice can only be established in partnership between firms, governments and international regulatory bodies. As the former head of the Massachusetts Institute of Technology put it recently, we are caught in a 'paradox of technology': industry causes environmental damage, but also offers the main way to repair its own damage (Ausubel and Sladovich, 1990). Both firms and governments thus have a strong incentive to work together to find solutions, otherwise what purpose is there in a world devoid of citizens and customers?

FIRMS' RESPONSES TO PRESSURE

No matter how sophisticated the project assessment before the event, many issues remain outside the realm of financial calculation. Despite the general liberalising trend, many governments have felt obliged to intervene on specific aspects of performance to coerce multinationals into greater local responsiveness. They want greater local 'linkages', both to reduce import costs and to create local entrepreneurial capability. Concerned about the impact of other aspects of the firms' behaviour, many also press for some form of NFI rather than traditional FDI, considering NFI to be a better bet for the future. Faced with such pressures, multinationals have three basic options. They can resist any change in the status quo; they can accede to the demands; or they can positively embrace the new rules as a way of aggressively creating new advantages over others who may find the changes difficult and expensive to accommodate. Much depends on two factors: the characteristics of the industry (as we discussed in chapter 4) and the firm's position in the industry – whether it is a leader, defending an established position, or a weak competitor or a newcomer. The firm's position and its attitudes and values explain much of the seemingly disparate bargaining outcomes.

154

Creating more local linkages

During the 1970s, most would have agreed with the ILO that 'without . . . government intervention . . . it is likely that, despite some market pressure, local MNE linkages would be much less developed than they are today' (ILO, 1981: p. 94). Such linkages were to go far beyond merely consideration of local content regulations, to include local supplier and buyer relationships. Today, that general conclusion is more suspect. There seems little doubt, however, that, without the maintenance of such pressure, leading firms that are defending their costly investments in the NFP prefer to minimise the local linkages for fear of losing international efficiency. Referring back to figure 1.7, new tensions are created when policies of allowing 'dependent' exporting in global industries are later modified by government requirements for foreigners to buy more locally.

The extent of the linkage that can efficiently be created is constrained by many factors, including limited local availability of materials and efficient suppliers and inefficient infrastructure. Though better alternatives may be created over time, the costs and delays can deter investors from assuming the burden when they have other options. As Parry (1980: p. 151) put it, 'absorptive capacity really determines the extent to which *potential* linkages take the form of *actual* linkages between the MNC and the host economy. Very often . . . minimal impacts . . . [result from] the lack of absorptive capacity in the host economy rather than the unwillingness or inability of the MNC to link up with it'. We found many examples of this constraint. For instance, Delmonte claims that its exports of canned pineapples from Kenya are impeded by the poor quality of local packaging materials. In this case, another multinational, Metal Box, is the supplier with a local monopoly of metal cans. Metal Box has been unwilling to make some of the needed investment in new equipment for lack of other customers to make the project profitable. Delmonte also asserts that its exports of fresh pineapples are well below achievable levels for lack of rapid transport from the estates to the port of Mombasa.

Governments want more linkages in a form that promotes greater local entrepreneurial capacity. They fear that local competitors will be 'crowded out' by powerful foreigners.[12] How firms have actually behaved on this issue is open to considerable debate. Lall (1979), for example, concluded that foreign investors in Malaysia had little concern for local entrepreneurship and had acted to increase industry concentration by introducing new processes and products that were not available to local firms. Lall's data, however, were from the early

155

stage of Malaysia's industrialisation, Besides, his averages obscure wide sectoral variation (Lim, 1976). At more advanced stages, as in Mexico today, Blomström (1989) shows that concentration has *not* been increased by the foreigners, though he leaves open the possibility that the causality runs the other way around; namely that it is the higher concentration that attracts the foreigners. Moreover, Blomström and Wolff (1990) have shown that over the period 1965–1984, the gap between locals and foreigners had diminished most in those sectors where the multinationals were most prevalent. At first sight, this evidence might be taken to mean that there is a strong 'spillover' effect; a form of transfer of technology and managerial competence that obviates governments' fears.

Such contradictory evidence reflects the complexity of individuals firms' actual responses. Matsushita's actions in Malaysia illustrates what can happen. When it transferred all its production of window-type air-conditioners out of Japan Matsushita agreed to aim for a 70 per cent local content, as required by the government's incentive deal. But Matsushita created few of the hoped-for linkages. The company decided to build half of the local components itself; the other half was divided among local firms and Japanese suppliers. One local director explained why. 'We have to make the complicated fan casings in-house for better quality control. We let the local suppliers make the simpler and less sophisticated polystyrene parts'. For other parts, managers looked to suppliers they already knew at home. 'Developing suppliers by ourselves is not enough. We have brought in more supporting companies to make more in Malaysia and buy less from Japan. We do have good suppliers in Japan and we are arranging for these suppliers to transfer their know-how and management techniques to companies here'. Some of this has required local investment rather than licensing. 'We encouraged them to come to Malaysia and now they are supplying us here'.[13]

More generally, the Japanese seem to be less willing than American and European investors to develop linkages with local suppliers. They are the most prone to use suppliers with whom they were familiar at home; reflecting perhaps the ways in which they have established long-lasting and close relationships with suppliers in Japan. Where the economics justified it, these suppliers were 'pulled' into the local territory to create a foreign 'enclave' with little connection with the locals. Such enclaves are most prevalent when firms have developed patterns of international specialisation and so become locked into their NFP structures. For example, the South-East Asian electronics industry has heavily concentrated the production of semi-conductor chips in

156

Malaysia, disk-drives in Singapore, etc. These patterns reflect differ-ent national factor advantages of labour costs, technical skills and the liberal trade regime in the region.

Whether multinationals enhance or inhibit the host country's inno-vative capacity is the subject of much debate. One side of the argument is given by Ernst (1987), who argues that local develop-ment is speeded up by investors transferring 'integrated' units of production using the very latest technology and methods of pro-duction control. Yet, though local output is enhanced, very little if anything is transferred in terms of the *'know-why'* rather than the *'know-how'* embodied in the engineering drawings.[14] Dunning's (1990) recent authoritative review of the evidence led him to conclude that there was no basis for resolving the argument: so much depended on the particular form of cross-border linkages, the reactions of local firms and the role government played in shaping a climate for innovation. Inman and Burton (1990) argued that impact could only be measured by firms' contributions to local upgrading over time. Such evidence raises questions about the relevance of considering nationality, rather than individual firm activity, as the issue: a question to which we return in chapter 7.

These arguments apply to firms with strong bargaining power. For others, especially in the 'local-for-local' industries and those selling non-essential items, the need to accede to local demands is much greater. This thinking applied to Pepsi-Cola in India (Austin, 1990: p. 170). Wanting aggressively to expand, the company agreed to India's foreign exchange requirements by promising to export tomato paste and fruit juices to five times the value of its imports of Pepsi ingredients. It also acceded to requests to carry out research to develop export crops. Similarly, in Kenya, Booker McConnell which at one time was involved with a sugar plantation, later expanded into contract poultry production. And Brooke Bond, before it was bought by Unilever, was tempted to put some of the profits it made from the 1976/7 coffee boom into growing chrysanthemums.

Compliance with government demands on some issues can gener-ate goodwill that provides possible future benefits on others to offset the initial costs. This is evident from some of the reactions to calls for ownership changes, as we show below. Yet, even where firms are willing to create new linkages, they may be constrained by a lack of suitable skills and manpower resources, as we discuss in the next chapter.

Preference for market forces

All our evidence supports the age-old contention that most, if not all, firms naturally prefer to be free to exploit their international strengths in local firms without intervention. There are thus important trade-offs to be managed. Multinationals' behaviour to expoit their strengths in marketing, research and trade can indicate some of the dimensions of the adjustments that have, perhaps grudgingly, been made in response to local pressure.

In marketing, the adjustment is limited. Multinationals clearly dominate the advertising spending in developing countries. They accounted for 80 per cent of Kenya's spending (Jouet, 1984) and over 75 per cent in Mexico (Bernal, 1976). In this they have no doubt been helped by local preferences for foreign brand names, because of the connotations with an international life-style. How else can one explain the effectiveness of Malboro's cowboy image in tropical countries? Superior advertising muscle clearly helps 'crowd out' the locals, as it did in the Malaysian tobacco industry. Twenty years ago, Malaysia had about 100 firms: today it is the exclusive preserve of the multi-nationals.

Yet, advertising-intensive multinationals can adjust other parts of their operations. BAT's Malaysian subsidiary has developed new acreage that was previously considered unfit for growing tobacco. The displacement of competitors has been offset by the creation of new employment for local farmers. In addition, though much of the Malaysian output is not considered technically appropriate for world markets, some tobacco is exported in a fashion that would be impossible without the multinationals' supply chains. Because policies to constrain the foreigners can lessen the achievement of other goals, many governments have not attempted to impose discriminatory regulations.

Besides, it is not always the case that locals spend less on advertising. In Brazil, the evidence is mixed (Willmore, 1986), but in Argentina, local drug firms spent more during the 1970s and gained back share previously lost to the multinationals (Chudnovsky, 1979). In Malaysia, we observed several cases where locals had seen the need to match the foreigners' spending and were succeeding in holding onto share. Some, like Zaitun Industries, were also successful in developing new niche markets based on their superior knowledge of local, ethnic demand. Zaitun has, however, had a minority bought by Colgate Palmolive and may lose its independence.

The arguments about advertising are frequently tied to concerns

158

that multinationals promote inappropriate products that distort the process of development. But how should appropriateness be determined? It is rather like beauty – in the beholder's eye. Multinationals promote products for which they believe there is a local demand. Are local consumers not to help judge the question? In addition to such troublesome issues as those raised by Nestlé's selling processed milk to mothers who do not understand the basics of hygiene, the fact of local demand poses awkward dilemmas for policy. Some goods may be regarded as unnecessary luxuries for developing countries, but demand for them reflects the 'rising expectations' of consumers around the world. There are limits to how much governments feel able to deny voters what they want.

The advantages of superior research capability are limited only by the issues on licensing, discussed earlier. Where they have been free to act without constraint, multinationals have indeed dominated local industries, as in the Brazilian drug industry. By the late 1960s, many local firms were spending more on research than the subsidiaries of the international majors and were considered to be technically progressive. They could not, however, match the spending of the parent companies. The most progressive local firms were later acquired by the multinationals, reducing the number of locals in the top thirty-five from eleven in 1957 to one by 1974. As Evans (1979: p. 128) stated, 'companies that talked of developing their own products in 1969 had given up these aspirations by 1974'. Brazil attempted to reverse this trend by using its discriminatory market reserve policy and by not signing the international patent agreement. The attempt ultimately failed as a result of the agreement with the USA, described in chapter 4.

Many observers have concluded that multinationals also try to impose their own trading patterns on host countries according to the needs of their international networks, and not always in the best interests of developing countries. This assertion needs to be examined carefully, for it is all too easy to be misled by aggregate statistics. For exporting, the position of individual firms is so diverse that few general conclusions can usefully be drawn. In theory, the multinationals' development of global networks of distribution suggest that they should export more than local firms. At the national aggregate level, early statistical studies suggested that this expectation was false: local firms had higher export propensities (see, for example, Cohen, 1975; Lall and Streeten, 1977; Fajnzylber and Tarragó, 1976). Yet, a later study suggested the multinationals were beginning to export more than local firms (UNCTC, 1988a: table X.1). Such general figures, however, obscure industry effects. Many studies have concluded that

159

there is no statistical significance between foreign and local firms in the same industry.[15] One reason for this is that many multinationals limit exports from some locations in order to balance the workings of the system as a whole. Another is that NFI developments mean that some local firms can increase their 'dependent' exports without being considered foreign-owned. The implication is that the mere presence of multinationals (outside the EPZs) neither helps nor hinders the export performance of the country as a whole.

Importing is another matter. Theory suggests that multinationals have a higher import propensity than locals, because of the effects of economies of scale on the marginal costs of components transferred and the opportunities for transfer price gains on the imports. Evidence from the 1970s provides some support for the theory even at the industry level (see, for example, Riedel, 1975; Vaitsos, 1978; Jenkins, 1979; Newfarmer and Marsh, 1981; Newfarmer, 1985). Yet, there are significant exceptions, as in the case of the soap industry in Kenya (Langdon, 1981). Nonetheless, such studies fuel governments' belief that the multinationals', even the export-oriented ones, must be coerced to form greater local linkages.

Local ownership requirements

How firms react to calls for greater local ownership depends largely on the costs of compliance. Much depends on the form in which the equity is to be shared. If it is a question of listing the shares on the local exchange, the foreigner's control is seldom eroded. But if there are powerful local partners or the partner is a state-owned enterprise, then the issue of control can become acute.

Consider Malaysia's experience with implementing its NEP requirements for Bumiputra shareholding. These were brought into force during the 1970s, with varying provisions about the timescale for implementation. Where the change involved a listing on the Kuala Lumpur exchange, the bargaining was over valuation, not control. This proved especially difficult in banking. Plans to restructure Chartered Bank and Hongkong and Shanghai Banking Corp. were delayed by valuation disputes.[16] The resulting delays were lengthened by the problems of finding sufficient local funds and setting precedents for other banks at a time when the government was starting to think about privatising its state-owned financial institutions. In other sectors, however, these problems have not been so severe. BAT floated part of its equity in its Malaysian subsidiary, MTC, on the Kuala Lumpur Exchange, on an agreed timetable.

160

In some cases, the veiled threat of discrimination should the firm not comply with the NEP guidelines spurred actions that might not otherwise have been taken. Some investors sold part of their holdings to Bumiputra investors to generate 'goodwill'. ICI's restructuring in 1987 was reported to have been motivated in part by plans to accelerate divestment of the fertilizer subsidiary to Bumiputra interests (the government is a major customer) and also to help with local acquisitions. In other cases, however, the threat was quite explicit. One US investor found that permission to build a new facility was refused until it had complied with the NEP. In this case, there was a conflict of policy. The firm wanted the investment to increase its exports, arguing that their export potential was constrained by having to buy locally at high price and low quality. Though this met the government's desire for greater local linkages, it conflicted with policies of supporting local entrepreneurs. Compliance with the NEP was exacted as a means of escaping the dilemma.

More recently, even though the NEP requirements have officially been relaxed, some feel the threat remains. In mid-1990, R.J. Reynolds Tobacco found an innovative, but seemingly risky way to comply. It announced its intentions to take over Juara Perkasa, a troubled local textile group. Technically, the deal called for Juara to take over all of RJR's Malaysian operations, for RJR to assume liability of the debts and the combined group to be floated on the stock exchange. 'RJR's foreign status, having no local partners until now, has affected its opportunities for expansion in a market sensitive to official corporate equity guidelines'.[17] Expansion opportunities were purchased by diversification into unfamiliar businesses, implying a difficult trade-off for management.

In all these cases, established market-seeking investors complied with the equity-shedding requirements. It did not cost them much to comply: some even benefitted financially from the deal. But in the great majority of the cases, little had changed as far as future development prospects for the country were concerned. Where the costs of compliance would be high, as for the exporters in the EPZs, the government did not even attempt to enforce the policy.

Officials need to recognise the further problem that firms can sometimes mitigate the impact of regulatory change by adjusting the form of their legal ownership. For example, in Nigeria, when the indigenisation decrees were implemented in the 1970s for manufacturing, one brewery split its operations in two. The brewery became a joint venture with local interests, but the sales company remained wholly owned. Because the sales company had an exclusive contract

161

for all the output and controlled both the brand and the prices, it could control the brewery in all important respects. For it, too, the cost of compliance was low.

Responding to NFI requirements

Malaysia's temporary use of the ownership weapon to force the pace of change is part of the wider movement among governments to insist on greater use of non-equity routes to local expansion. Indeed, they have official encouragement to do so in the form of the 'Cheysson facility'. This *ad hoc* financial instrument was introduced by the European Community in 1988 with the aim of promoting joint ventures between European firms and firms from Asia, Latin America and Mediterranean countries. But NFI goes beyond simply sharing equity; it involves licensing and contracts as well. How firms have responded and what states have gained are questions to which we now turn.

Though rising overall, the incidence of NFI has varied considerably, depending upon the importance of control over efficiency and quality and the extent to which the 'investor' can exercise control without equity. Licensing agreements and joint ventures (often locally financed) have been commonly used in automobile components, petrochemicals and some sectors of electronics. NFI has been less evident in very high-tech fields like biogenetic engineering, where the needs for internalising control within the equity 'package' have remained predominant for the reasons we suggested in chapter 3. Despite such limits to the effectiveness of NFI compared to the alternatives, many agencies have persisted in making blanket recommendations for their greater adoption. What is needed, in our view, is a greater appreciation of the need to tailor the solution to the needs of the specific project. Frank (1980: p. 57) concluded that firms' opinions 'on unbundling depend largely on the individual company's philosophy and its subsidiaries' experiences in particular host countries'. Our evidence supports this view.

None the less, some patterns of behaviour are discernible, depending on whether firms are defending an established position or attacking another's stronghold. The defenders' reactions have been discussed in terms of resisting the change or accommodating it within a revised local strategy. What needs to be added is that even the majors can find the resource-limiting aspects of NFI advantageous in parts of the world they had previously ignored. One major oil company told us that 'we now accept joint venture position in South-East Asia, where we have been a late entrant. We found that in our marketing and non-oil investments particularly, our previous policies of insisting on total ownership were too expensive and too slow'. They and others like it have found that, though joint ventures can create tensions and interfere with the development of integrated global strategies, few serious problems had so far arisen. Yet, if such new ventures succeed, investors may be tempted to revert to their more 'normal' policy and buy out the licensee and establish conventional forms of FDI ownership and control.

Oman (1989) provides plentiful examples of contrasting, aggressive moves by newcomers and late entrants in metals, synthetic fibres, textiles, clothing, petrochemicals and foods. There are many similar examples in Malaysia. Reflecting the Malaysian government's 'Look East' policy, most of the recent joint ventures with SOEs have been with Japanese firms. It is perhaps no accident that the partner in Malaysia's Proton car, Mitsubishi, was a latecomer and weak relative to other Japanese car producers. In sectors where Malaysia has natural resource advantage it has sometimes been able to insist on joint ventures, even for export projects. For example, the German Everts company has invested in a factory to make toy and meteorological balloons from local rubber in partnership with Platt Malaysia (owned mostly by the Malaysian Rubber Development Corporation) and the West German state-owned investment bank that promotes such ventures. But there are limits: Malaysia has failed so far to translate its supply advantage into significant tyre exports, as we discuss below.

Aggressive newcomers can force established leaders to change their policies, just as in the Komatsu/Caterpillar contest or in the sectoral contests discussed in chapter 4. Much the same effects can be seen in investors' initial responses to Decision 24 by the Andean Pact (refer back to chapter 4). US investors, the largest group with the most to defend, opposed the move to impose fade-out provisions and forecast a sharp drop in FDI. This did not materialise as new investors, perhaps spurred by the newcomers' success softened their opposition (Koopman, 1979: p. 116); some even increased their investments (Mytelka, 1979: p. 100). Yet, the fact that Decision 24 was abandoned in 1987 suggests that the countries involved realised the costs of excluding the foreigners altogether.

LIMITS TO NFI BENEFITS

The success of many countries in promoting NFI begs the question of whether they really create benefits to the host country, and in what form. There can be two opposing outcomes. The positive outcome happens where the country gains greater control of its ability to accumulate competitive resources without significantly reducing the multinational's control over the issues which most concern them. The negative occurs when the local elites or host government are unable to take advantage of the control they have wrested from foreign investors (Evans, 1977). Franko (1989) studied US investments in developing countries during the 1970s and concluded that the NFI gains were greatest for import-substitution, not exporting. He also concluded that little benefit accrues to the host country when the firm is an 'also-ran' in its industry, lacking the technical dynamism or experience of the majors. We found no evidence to suggest that much has changed.

There seems little doubt that newcomers provide positive initial gains. It is perhaps too early to tell whether countries continue to reap rewards as these firms gain strength and change their strategies. There are possibilities that the gains may be only temporary. If Japanese investors are any guide, governments need to be on their guard. Their initial preference for joint ventures is giving way to wholly owned facilities in countries like Singapore that do not regulate the form of investment (Lim and Fong, 1988: p. 68). Equal shifts in behaviour are visible among some of the new breed of third-world multinationals described in chapter 3.

The most questionable or illusory gains, however, arise when existing facilities have been transformed. The example of Firestone in Kenya is only the tip of the iceberg; there are others of even more dubious gain to the country. Where some firms have exchanged their entire equity for a management contract, the expatriate managers have continued to run the local enterprise as though nothing had changed: a common complaint in Africa.

The issues involved in the assessment of the efficiency or effectiveness of NFI as an alternative to traditional FDI can be grouped into three separate, but linked, categories. First, the added costs and efficiencies affecting the international transactions may inhibit further development. Second, the added costs of simply maintaining the existing operation may unduly depress profitability to the point where one or more of the partners may wish to withdraw. Third, there is the question of whether NFI structures enhance or impede the creation of extra exports.

The problem of added costs

The first category has two parts. The first concerns the nature of the international transactions. As we showed in chapter 3, these may need to be 'internalised' within the firm if they are to be managed

164

efficiently. The greater the volatility of the markets, the greater is this need. The second arises in many newly established consortium projects, where none of the partners is sufficiently motivated to ensure that all the pieces fit properly together, and on time. The result can be the wrong choice of technology or a complete misreading of the supply chain or the market. The literature of development is littered with stories of such failures. An example from Kenya can illustrate the extent of the problem.

In the late 1970s, a consortium was established to process corn cobs into furfural, acetic acid and formic acid, chemicals that are actively traded internationally. The basic idea was to add value to a waste product and produce an additional stream of export earnings. Three foreign partners shared 45 per cent of the equity, the rest held by Kenyan government agencies and a local investor. Equity represented only 33 per cent of the total finance. The European Investment Bank and the Bank of Scotland put up the foreign loans, mainly in $-denominated notes. From the start, a combination of mistakes led to bankruptcy in the early 1980s. The project managers failed to recognise the risks of using an untried technology: they could not licence the proven process, which was held by Quaker Oats of the USA, who also held a dominant position in the world market. As the project only ever managed to produce at 8 per cent of the design capacity, the expected exports never materialised. Moreover, with break-even calculated at 82 per cent of capacity, cash flow problems rapidly became serious. Further problems came from considering corn cobs as a waste product. Local farmers had many other uses for them, for cattle feed or fuel. Supply was therefore uncertain and far more expensive than originally thought. The receiver later estimated the supply cost at more than double the cost used to justify the investment in the first place. Furthermore, construction was delayed when the ship carrying the equipment sank in the English Channel. The delay meant that production started in the early 1980s, just as recession hit, prices collapsed and the Kenya Shilling was devalued. The loans could not be serviced and the project collapsed.

This story is instructive on many counts. First, the high level of debt meant that none of the equity holders had much at stake: they could therefore afford to take risks. Second, the project was managed by firms that were not first-division players in the market. Perforce, they had to use second-best technology and second-best export routes. Third, the denomination of the debt in dollars reflected undue confidence in the project's ability to export. Fourth, one can ask why the Kenyan authorities had sanctioned the project on the terms

165

agreed. Surely, someone could have alerted the managers at least to the supply risk. Fifth, one can ask whether Kenya might have been better off working in partnership with the established leader, assuming Quaker Oats was interested.

The second category of concern is that of the additional cost burden that partnership can entail. In one Kenyan agricultural project, ownership was shared among a subsidiary of Unilever, the IFC and the Commonwealth Development Corporation. Each partner rigorously implemented its own audit procedures, even in a small £1 million venture. To prepare three separate statements meant that about 30 of a total office staff of 40 were accounts clerks. Precisely the same sorts of extra costs affect larger projects and can lead to a severe erosion of profits. These inefficiencies are compounded when the partners disagree about strategic priorities for the venture. Conflicts among local and foreign partners, each with quite different perspectives, different time horizons and, often, different sources of profit from the venture can severely delay or distort investments.

Limits to export development

The third category, export development, goes beyond the effect of applying NFI conditions to include the general issue of the difficulties of transforming existing import-substituting facilities into export-competitive ones. NFI success has been primarily limited to the older technologies. This creates the old dilemma that employment may be gained but, as in Kenyan textiles, export competitiveness diminished. Moreover, the value added locally may increase locally in absolute terms, but yet diminish as a proportion of the total added value in the international chain of production. Forces of globalisation can mean that more of the total value is created in upstream activities such as research and design. For example, exports of textiles from Mauritius have increased, but their share of the total value has steadily dropped over the last ten years. Mauritius' ability to control and adjust to future shifts is therefore declining.

Government policies to encourage the transition to exporting run up against a variety of constraints. Existing facilities, often cushioned by protection, are usually inefficient by world standards. They therefore need considerable modernisation, whether or not they remain majority owned by multinationals. Much of the problem stems from the fact that managers and the work force are incapable or unwilling to meet the new tests, just as in post-privatisation moves. NFI conditions can worsen an already difficult task, as we discuss in the next chapter, when we consider the effect of different kinds of export development on human systems.

Above all, NFI can do little to alleviate the problems of transition when they are impeded either by the reluctance of governments to adjust other policies or by market forces. Malaysian production of monosodium glutamate (MSG), which is used in food seasoning, illustrates the first of these two factors. MSG is made from molasses or starch, derived either from corn or tapioca. Ajinomoto, from Japan, is the world leader with an estimated 40 per cent share of the world market (UNCTC, 1987). They and other Japanese and Taiwanese competitors established plants in Thailand and have developed exports to varying degrees. Akinomoto set up a local plant in Malaysia with the same aim in mind. Its factory is of world standard, but the input price of tapioca is maintained by government regulation at levels well above world prices. Exports, consequently, are negligible. In this case, it was not the firm but the government that was unable or unwilling to adjust policy to allow the transition to be achieved.

The constraints of market forces are illustrated by the Malaysian tyre industry. Tyres were targeted in the Industrial Master Plan for rapid export expansion: from M$20 million in 1986 to M$1 billion by 1995. Yet various investigations have shown that, irrespective of Malaysia's technical skills, local producers would have to use heavy price discounts to offset the lack of any brand presence in the major markets. These would more than offset raw material advantages and make the returns to the investment highly negative in both social and financial terms. Lacking any independent options, Malaysia could work in partnership with one of the majors, such as Goodyear, that has an existing Malaysian operation. But the costs of adjustment to Goodyear's existing international network of supply would be high and would require major subsidies to make the investment attractive. As it happens, Goodyear and others have shown little interest in taking on the new risks (other than in some small-scale, niche products). Consequently, little progress has yet been achieved.

Exactly the same sorts of constraints from market forces were faced by Grenada when, in 1982, it wished to add value to its exports of cocoa beans. A study of the possibilities, concluded that all but one of the possible projects had a negative rate of return. The problem was that Grenada's beans were especially suited to some types of chocolate, notably Rowntree's 'After Eight' mints, and commanded a premium of 20–25 per cent in the commodity market. The country could not replace a premium based on the buyer's brand strength with its own resources. Instead, the experts advised that Grenada should concentrate on improving supply efficiency and not attempt, as a small player, to change the existing market structure (Commonwealth Secretariat, 1984).

Conclusions

The national behaviour and performance of multinationals depends upon their strategies at global and local levels and upon the position of the firm within its industry. The interaction between governments wanting to change firms' behaviour and firms resisting or acceding to pressure throws up a kaleidoscope of responses. The tussles between headquarters and subsidiaries can lead to unexpected outcomes that sometimes help and sometimes hinder host states. We found enormous variation in behaviour on all the issues we have raised among the projects we reviewed, even within an industry. Industry averages thus provide poor guides for how sectoral policy should be implemented in firm-specific bargaining. The questions can only be answered at the level of the enterprise.

Fully to understand how the bargaining works and how the desired ends might be achieved requires a deeper investigation of what really conditions the behaviour of both states and firms. Policy requirements are formed, not just by economic considerations, but also by political and social forces. But policies can be distorted by the way they are implemented as different departments jockey for position. Thus, it is to the real grass roots of behaviour at the human and social level that we turn in the next chapter.

6 SOCIAL CAUSE AND CON-SEQUENCE

by John Henley

It should be clear by now that the issues of partnership in development go far beyond economics and industrial competition. The dilemmas we noted in chapter 4 for states seeking equally desirable but mutually exclusive goals can only be resolved over time and with political choices of priority at each step on the way. But political choice inextricably involves society. Who benefits? Who wins? Who loses? Who takes on new risks or sheds old ones? Whose opportunities to make choices are enlarged, or restricted? These are always key issues in political relationships. Bargaining between multinationals and their host governments is no different. For our purposes it is necessary to try to sort out which consequences for different social groups have resulted *primarily* from the state–firm relationship rather than from other factors. That is what we attempt in this chapter, focusing particularly on the issues that affect organised labour and the development of skills.

An example shows the analytical problems that come with the question 'who benefits?'. Recall Firestone's moves to reduce its exposure to risk in Kenya. The controlling interest in the tyre factory was bought by a small group of local investors sufficiently influential to be able to persuade the authorities to make a special case. The 'concessionary' negotiations were limited to a chosen few: the state development finance institution was not permitted by the authorities to increase its holding though this would have required a smaller equity transfer to achieve local majority control. Kenya increased output and workers got new jobs. Local investors were awarded a rich 'prize'. But there was a price. Firestone's monopoly was strengthened and consumers got less competitively priced products. More seriously, the apparent increase in Kenya's autonomy was offset by greater *vulnerability* to corporate decisions. The parent's shift from majority to minority holding, from a profit-driven to a fee-driven interest in the operations, placed the local affiliate in a weaker position: as for most NFI arrangements, the fees have to be negotiated case by case, in intracompany bargaining. Only over the long haul will the question of 'who benefits?' be answered.

THE IMPACT OF DOMESTIC POLITICS

By the 1960s, it had become difficult to maintain that the transfers of modern capital and technology were part of a benign process of modernisation, as originally conceived by the early development theorists. Many like Prebisch (1963) regarded the third world as the victim of 'unequal exchange' with the advanced industrial economies and argued the case for policies of import-substitution as a means of disengagement from world markets. Others were more concerned with the dislocations that the process of modernisation inevitably creates. Huntington (1968) considered political development as a function of the growth of institutions competent to deal with the stresses and strains of social and economic development and to adapt to crisis. The notion of the 'strong state' emerged to reflect that competence. Binder (1971) suggested that the multinationals' social impact should be measured in terms of their contribution to political stability and regime maintenance. Many today would regard that measure as unduly limited. For example, De Soto (1989), concluded from his investigation in Peru, that the state and its officials were more concerned with the distribution of the economic 'cake' amongst political supporters and clients than with economic development.

Where the state becomes both the engine of development and the arbiter of social relations, benefits are distributed by 'concessionary' bargaining with local and foreign groups. Over time, state-controlled dispensation of 'favours' becomes important for maintaining the regime. In this, multinationals are rarely innocent bystanders, particularly where they were oriented towards the domestic market. Concession bargaining, however, does not exempt them from sometimes cut-throat competition with domestic and other foreign firms for monopolistic privileges.

One can see the consequences of this approach in Kenya, where members of the elite can use the rhetoric of economic nationalism to advance their own positions. The domestic insurance business (recall, from chapter 4, the developments of the international part) was critically affected by the Insurance Act of 1984. This Act was more notable for the form of its implementation than for its technical provisions, which included a minimum level of local equity participation. Equity in two major companies was bought by syndicates said to represent interests including those of the President, the Minister for

Finance and the then Governor of the Central Bank.[1] While most reputable insurance companies accepted the need for an improved regulatory environment, forced alliance with those with 'connections' was resented.[2]

Brazil's period of military rule illustrates the point we make throughout this book: new policies are *additive*, even when a regime proclaims it is making a 'fresh start'. O'Donnell (1988) argues that Brazilian politics have almost always been based on patronage and clientelism, irrespective of the type of regime. This, he suggests, is symptomatic of the persistence of the political style of an oligarchic republic in a primarily agrarian society, where conflicting urban and rural political interests have been resolved by distinctly authoritarian means. An industrialisation has gathered pace, the persistence of structural dualism – the coexistence of a traditional rural sector and an unintegrated modern urban sector – has inhibited the formation of state institutions capable of developing policy priorities that receive widespread support. Though Brazil's agricultural development policies have stimulated output, they have greatly favoured the rich elite and the corporations, but 'have reduced labour demand and have made it impossible for a poor person to buy land and become a farmer' (World Bank, 1990: p. 59). Moreover, past use of the state apparatus to distribute jobs for political patronage has left an inflated bureaucracy and a plethora of vested interests. The multiplicity of different administrative and bureaucratic organisations that exists today in Brazil, both at central and state levels, in part, represents the residue of successive efforts to develop national policy. Their inflexibility was shown by their entrenched opposition to President Collor's commitment to sack 360,000 civil servants.

Ethnic divisions

Such problems are greatly exacerbated in countries bedeviled by ethnic divisions. Evans' (1979) 'triple alliance' model of industrial policy formation in Brazil assumes industrialisation policy emerges from bargaining among horizontally-organised, class-based coalitions. However, where there are strong vertical divisions, as in Malaysia and Kenya, conflict is often as fierce or fiercer over which ethnic group commands economic activities. Horowitz (1985) suggests that the primary struggle in ethnically divided societies is the struggle over relative group capability and economic worth.

The main contest is usually between a 'backward' group and a more 'advanced' group, often an economically successful immigrant group.

In Kenya, the situation is especially complex because of political power being transferred from a more numerous and 'advanced' indigenous group – the Kikuyu – to a less advanced and smaller indigenous group – the Kalenjin – when the presidency passed to Moi in 1978 on the death of Kenyatta.

One might wish to attribute the behaviour of political leaders from relatively 'backward' ethnic groups, who use their superior position in the state apparatus to advance their supporters' interests, to a sense of inferiority.[3] It is equally plausible, however, to interpret this behaviour in terms of the rational calculations implicit in patron–client relations, albeit defined within the parameters of ethnic competition. Over time, the redistributed resources provide the basis for legitimating the erstwhile 'backward' group, since some recipients will be successful and thereby 'justify' the policy and enhance the status of their group. Clearly, the objective of consolidating one group's economic and political control at the expense of others constrains the pursuit of 'rational' economic policies.

A key question arises where one group predominates economically, but another dominates the political sphere: how to achieve a stable division of power and economic commitment (Jesudason, 1989: p. 12)? The economically advanced group is unlikely to take a long-term view of the benefits to be obtained from a more equitable distribution of national wealth. Instead, their members will probably restrict reinvestment, export its capital and/or switch to short-term trading activities. Such behaviour, of course, merely reinforces the negative stereotypes held by the political elite and provokes accusations of 'economic sabotage' and 'racketeering'.

Politically powerful, but economically insecure, groups are equally inclined to a short-term view. Their members without business experience are most interested in concessions that offer the chance of quick returns. State-orchestrated economic redistribution is thus constrained by the availability of acceptable, 'loyal' management willing or able to take a long-term professional view of their responsibilities. Few authorities openly acknowledge this constraint, because to do so would bring into sharp focus the wider social costs of economic discrimination. Yet, one can see the costs in, for example, Kenya's textile industry. As we showed in chapter 4, even joint-venture arrangements could not compensate for shortages of entrepreneurial skills among the 'right' ethnic group. Political pressures obscured the need to address commercial priorities. When the inevitable crisis arose, the Kenyan bureaucracy, far from being flexible, proved to be timid and procrastinated interminably. For example, one parastatal textile company failed to get any governmental help and, for five years, was forced to rely on non-collection of sales tax to fund its working capital.

Deep ethnic divisions have meant that, though multinationals may sometimes be vilified for 'imperialism' by populist politicians, they are generally preferred to domestic immigrant-owned firms. Evidence from Malaysia suggests why this is so. When the government introduced the Industrial Co-ordination Act in 1975 to increase Malay shares in urban employment and equity ownership, the Chinese business community protested vigorously against the discriminatory nature of the legislation. By contrast, as discussed in chapter 5, multinationals were much more relaxed about selling off equity if the price was right. It was relatively easy for them to accommodate increased Malay participation in their managerial cadres. Chinese business, typically smaller and family-owned, could not be equally accommodating because of the disruption to the personal relationships amongst a closed group of relatives. As a defensive measure, some resorted to what the press called 'Ali-Babaism'; they employed prominent Malays as window dressing. Kenyan-Asian firms have responded similarly to government redistribution policies. They have been able to survive and even prosper, thanks to the administration's weak implementation capacity.

These are conditions that accord great autonomy to foreigners, who can often continue as 'dominant partners', even after losing equity control. Some recent reports have been highly critical of the supervisory capacity of Kenyan investment agencies and their ability to enforce adequate financial reporting standards (see, for example, Henley and Maynard, 1991). By failing effectively to harness multinationals as partners in development, these agencies have allowed firms to resist change and to preserve their vested interest in the 'sweet deal' negotiated with government-appointed directors.

THE STONY PATH TOWARDS LIBERALISATION

If concessions provide a poor response to today's economic challenges, the question arises as to how a state is to break out of the trap and create a virtuous circle that aligns private and public interests for sustainable nation-building. How can an interventionist administration orchestrate a policy switch to foster competition and exporting, while at the same time maintaining its political base of support? To radical populists, the new-found emphasis on global competition is but thinly disguised rhetoric aimed at returning developing countries to a 'colonial' economic function: sources of cheap labour, raw materials and places in which to locate environmentally hazardous industries. Much of the export success, for example, of Brazil's local auto components manufacturers is due to their ability to 'informalise', by employing cheap labour from the *favelas* of the major conurbations under sub-standard working conditions and largely outside the tax system.

The challenge is to build both administrative competence and an effective infrastructure. Actions are, clearly, constrained by the exigencies of domestic politics, among which ethnic divisions are only one. Political leaders need to sustain a minimal level of legitimacy with *all* their important supporters. The dilemmas can be exacerbated by rural problems, the drift to the towns and rapid population growth. Where there are likely to be too many losers among the favoured elites, the logic for change can be resisted.

These dilemmas can be seen in the aftermath of the Brazilian 'miracle' of the late 1960s and early 1970s. The growth was not sustainable, because it was socially divisive. As the poor got poorer, the rich got much richer and domestic opposition increased. Change, when it came, did so only slowly. When General Geisel took over control in 1974, he favoured *distensao*, a gradual move towards civilian rule. But economic problems, combined with reports of corruption beginning to appear after years of censorship, offset many of the gains from local elections. The middle classes became restive; the students demonstrated; the unions struck, despite laws forbidding strikes; and President Carter condemned Brazil for serious breaches of human rights. At one point, Geisel even temporarily closed the civilian congress when it opposed his proposals. When power was transferred to President Figuerado in 1979, the government started a process of liberalisation, called *arbetura* (opening), culminating eventually in the election of a civilian president in 1985.

With hindsight, it is not so clear now that the military commanded adequate administrative skills to run an efficient centrally-planned economy. The Council for Industrial Development (CDI) made 'decisions . . . on a case-by-case basis . . . [this] made the system potentially corruptible and highly dependent upon the common sense, fairness and personal integrity of those government officials making decisions on the granting of the so-called incentives' (Tyler, 1981: p. 42). Entrepreneurs soon recognised that authoritarianism was no more than 'concessional capitalism' with rather grander pretensions; business profitability depended more upon relations with the government than upon productive efficiency. Inadequate administrative competence has been troublesome elsewhere. For example, when the Andean Decision 24 imposed much more specific assessment require-ments on the member states, 'many of the problems encountered in the implementation . . . have been due to a lack of preparedness in the member countries' (Mytelka, 1979: p. 64).

Kenya's dilemmas, though equally severe, have quite different causes. Its relatively equitable distribution of agricultural land after Independence has been a source of political stability. But this benefit is being undermined by rapid population growth – nearly two million new people will enter the labour market before the year 2000. So far, the expanding labour force has mostly been absorbed in the rural areas and in the informal sector. The small number of new formal-sector jobs that are created each year are allocated, as in Brazil, through a fiercely competitive patronage system based on personal recommen-dation.[4]

Liberalisation needs to be accompanied by a growing ability to *accumulate* financial and human resources over time. Financial resources are needed to fund the appropriate infrastructure and industries to complement private investment. Indigenous technical resources are needed if local firms are to adapt the imported tech-nology and start generating their own. But how to allocate resources efficiently among many competing needs? To some, sponsoring investment with state funds, alone or on a joint venture basis, may seem a straightforward policy option. However, state development finance institutions will be new to the sector concerned. They need to spend time and resources *learning* how to assess the viability of projects. We found many instances where local officials were unable to take a view on the appropriateness of the technology being proposed, or indeed whether it was already obsolete. Many could not judge whether the level of management fees being demanded was reason-able by international standards. Few were clear about either the real priorities implied in the national plans or how interdepartmental disputes might best be resolved. These are circumstances where the chances of making mistakes are high. That the record of project management by state agencies has been poor is not surprising given the limitations of the local management pool available. Even more debilitating can be the lack of direct accountability for project success; officials are measured on how they disperse the funds, not on the performance of the project.

The dilemmas are worsened by the vested interests of both existing national elites and foreign investors. Liberalisation can act to pull them apart on some issues and create temporary alliances on others: neither group is necessarily in favour of reform. National elites, formed from shifting coalitions of interest groups, are rarely, if ever, passive in their reaction to the prospect of inward foreign investment, for any net addition to national resources offers possibilities for patronage and extending political power. For their part, multinationals that have prospered under protectionism may welcome relaxation of import controls on essential inputs, but may oppose liberalisation of controls over finished products, for this can often increase smuggling.[5] They may be equally ambivalent about other measures, such as the introduction of 'realistic' exchange and interest rate policies. The effects feed through rapidly in increased packaging, transportation and financing costs and can cancel out any longer term potential gains in export markets. As wage costs rarely amount to more than 20 per cent, and often less than 10 per cent, of factory gate prices, firms have only limited scope for increasing labour productivity and competitiveness.[6] Capacity utilisation and thus overall operational efficiency, however, is much more likely to be adversely affected by depression of domestic demand. Furthermore, structural adjustment tends to ignore the problems of local producers, who may unite with market-seeking multinationals in opposing some or all of the changes.

Faced with such socially and politically disruptive dilemmas, the political leadership typically splits. One faction with its power base in the finance ministry, recognises the consequences of a rapidly expanding government budget deficit and deterioration in the balance of payments and accepts the need to improve domestic resource utilisation and to expand exports. The other faction, consisting of an alliance of radical nationalists and conservative beneficiaries of the old regime, resists the ensuing cuts in welfare programmes and public sector lay-offs, usually singling out the multinationals as the main culprits. Such factional struggles, evident in Brazil ever since the return to civilian rule in the 1980s, add yet further blocks on the road to liberalisation.

HUMAN RESOURCE DEVELOPMENT

International competition and the erosion of protective barriers expose weaknesses in the local human resource base. Where previously inefficiency could be tolerated in import–substituting investments, exporting demands much more of local capability. No amount of political and institutional liberalisation suffices to meet the new challenges without growing indigenous capability to accumulate new technical skills and efficiency-enhancing procedures. Human resource development is a necessary pre-condition for development.

How this affects relationships with the multinationals depends critically on what type of exports are to be created. With some degree of simplification, one can see differences between the 'dependent' and 'independent' exports we identified in chapter 1 in terms of their demands on local capability. 'Dependent' exporting requires either the use of EPZ-type arrangements or the transformation of previously market-seeking investments. Despite the obstacles, transformation is possible when the enterprise is limited to one or a few stages of production and highly reliant on continuing transfers of technology and procedure from other parts of the multinationals' corporate structures. The demands on society at large are modest, for the upgrading of skills is managed largely within the firm.

'Independent', or at least semi-autonomous, exporting incurs much more far-reaching demands. As local firms develop their own ability to compete internationally, they become increasingly exposed to the need to change continuously if they are to keep up. The difference from 'dependent' exporting is essentially one of a progression along a 'learning curve'. Though exporting from an EPZ exposes the local affiliate to international pressures, the extent of the learning is bounded by the reliance on technologies and designs produced elsewhere. To move towards greater independence firms, whether local sub-contractors or affiliates of multinationals, must increasingly develop their own human resources to enhance knowledge, self-reliance and flexibility. They become more dependent on other local sources of advantage from the infrastructure and from local suppliers; few can go far along the curve without help from others.

To enable a full flowering of 'independent' exporting, the political and administrative regime needs to foster both labour efficiency and firm competitiveness. This is seldom possible within a repressive, authoritarian regime that trusts neither its workers nor its managers. Given the uncertainties of change, sources of future competitiveness cannot be planned fully in advance; they have to emerge within a general climate of competition in which devolution of political power features largely.

Moves towards 'independent' exporting, thus, introduce new tensions between the development of far-reaching 'self-reliance' and open-door liberalism. Previously authoritarian regimes have to concede that, in the interests of spreading the responsibility for creating wealth-creating resources, they must devolve political power. One of the most visible signs of these tensions appears most clearly at the enterprise level in the system of labour relations and the role that governments assign to organised labour.

LABOUR RELATIONS POLICY

Policies of protecting import-substituting industries have generally been supported by extensive state intervention to maintain docile unions. Ostensibly, the state's interest in maintaining harmonious labour relations has been a function of its concern to foster an attractive investment climate. Ruling elites, however, have an additional security interest in labour relations; large concentrations of labour offer potential rallying points for disaffected opposition groups. Politicians, not unreasonably, tend to fear the disruptive power of the 'urban mob'. Indeed, many leaders in developing countries have come to power on a surge of labour unrest. Thus, corporatist rhetoric has been marshalled, when needed, to justify coercive action against labour unrest.

To maintain harmony, trade unionists are officially enjoined to accept that they must restrict their activities in the 'national interest'. For example, an account of the right-to-strike prepared by officials of the Malaysian Ministry of Labour for the ILO states: 'To achieve the objectives of development as outlined in the Fifth Malaysia Plan 1986–1990, antagonistic relationships must give way to the creation of a harmonious industrial relations climate. This is essential for growth and also to encourage greater foreign and local investments to solve the unemployment problems that have hit the country since 1985' (Alagandram and Rahim, 1988: p. 11). Clearly, the Malaysian government regards an over-assertive labour movement as a deterrent to investment. Similar pronouncements have been made by the Brazilian and Kenyan governments.[7]

The implication is that industrial relations are too important to be left to voluntary bargaining between employers and employees: the state feels it must intervene, if only to curb a potential political threat to regime stability. Most states therefore tend to oscillate between exclusionary, repressive policies and attempts to incorporate the labour movement in the official political and administrative structure (De Villiers, 1989). They try to pre-empt pressure from labour organisations by co-opting them into restricted participatory roles, using a mixture of inducements and constraints (Collier and Collier, 1979). Inducements include systems of registration; the right to form a union; allowing monopoly of representation, compulsory membership and/or subsidisation of unions. The constraints include provisions regulating wage determination and strikes; controls on political activities; on the appointment of the leadership; and state monitoring and intervention in the internal affairs of unions. The constraints are, however, now being challenged by rising demands for increased political participation.

Procedures for wage-bargaining and dispute-settlement

Industrial relations in our three countries are based on the principles of 'tripartism'. This is the notion that trade unions and employers, either individually or as members of an association, should participate in state-sponsored and regulated institutions that exist to resolve issues of mutual concern. In theory, tripartism is meant to foster co-operation between management and workers, to discourage confrontation and to broaden the focus of industrial relations away from solely wage-related issues to include the enhancement of productivity. In practice, however, it can be unstable: the state's political overlords have their own views on the desired economic and public-order outcomes. In theory, the nation's rulers should be able to identify the national interest and discredit any opposition groups such as trade unions (or employers) trying to damage it. Hence, the legitimacy of the system depends very heavily on the nature of any political intervention and whether it is perceived as partisan by either of the other two parties. The history of violence in the development of national systems of industrial relations in all three countries suggests severe limits to that theory. At various times, trade union organisations have been associated with subversive opposition to the established regimes.

Kenya and Malaysia inherited the British Colonial Office 'voluntary' industrial relations system based on enterprise unionism and collective bargaining. Shortly after independence, both found it expedient to move towards tripartism. They added an extensive government conciliation service and a labour court to provide binding arbitration on collective and individual disputes. At the same time, legal restrictions on the right to strike were extended. The role of the registrar of trade unions was also strengthened by adding responsibility for overseeing the unions' internal affairs and the power to settle recognition and jurisdictional disputes.

The Malaysian registrar's actions have, over time, increased the number of registered trade unions, while decreasing their average size. This is because the registrar has chosen to interpret changes in industrial structure as implying the need for new unions, including in-house ones, rather than merely an extension of the scope and power of existing ones. The level of unionisation has never exceeded 20 per cent in manufacturing since the 1960s (Wad, 1988: p. 213) and in 1988 was only 10 per cent of the total work force. Meanwhile, strike activity declined gradually from around 60–80 strikes a year in the 1960s to only 9 in 1988.

That some foreign investors take advantage of Malaysia's anti-union laws in the EPZs is beyond doubt. For example, 1,003 workers employed by Hitachi Consumer Products went on strike during 1990 to demand recognition for the Malaysian Electrical Industry Workers Union (EIWU). The strike was illegal, because only unionised workers were allowed to strike, and because government guidelines disallow industry-wide unions in companies producing electronic (rather than electrical) components. After negotiations, the company agreed to reinstate all but twenty-one of the strikers accused by the company of being 'union leaders', and an in-house union was recognised.[8] Judging from its actions, Hitachi seemed to adopt a narrow legalistic definition of its 'product' in order to avail itself of the Malaysian government's restrictive legislation. This stands in contrast to other Japanese investors who have recognised the EIWU. As an additional side-light, Charles Gray (1990) of the American AFL-CIO asserts that US and other foreigners forced the Malaysian Ministry of Labour in 1988 to continue its policy prohibiting unionisation in the electronic industry. Yet, from what evidence there is, union activities do not seem significantly more difficult in export processing zones than in other industries (UNCTC/ILO, 1988: pp. 96–100).

The Kenyan government has extended its power over the labour movement more directly. Nearly all strikes since 1967 have been deemed illegal. The Minister of Labour prohibits arbitrary strikes, that is, those that fail to exhaust all conciliation and arbitration procedures. Moreover, the government is represented on the Central Organisation of Trade Unions (COTU) and the President has the right to veto the appointment of its top officials. Further, since 1988, COTU has been affiliated to the ruling party and therefore, in theory, is bound as a subsidiary organ of the party to follow government policy.

In the attempt to keep wage increases below the rate of inflation, the Kenyan government, through the Ministry of Finance, issues wage guidelines to the Judge of the Industrial Court. These guidelines are followed when determining wage awards and other terms and conditions of employment or when the Court accepts voluntarily negotiated collective agreements for registration – some 384 in 1988. Those currently in operation limit all wage increases to 75 per cent of the rate of inflation. In exchange for union acceptance of this limitation, the government has at irregular intervals exhorted employers to increase their labour force by 10 per cent.

Data on current union membership is far from complete in Kenya, but is estimated at one-half of the permanent labour of large-scale manufacturing. Union membership levels have held up, despite real average wages declining by 3.8 per cent per annum between 1972–83 (World Bank, 1987: p. 172). Strike activity declined steadily from the highs of the early independence period, but rose again as the economy began to recover from recession and drought in the late 1980s. Most of the recent strikes were, however, short wild-cat actions over local issues, such as dismissals and the use of temporary workers, and did little harm.

Brazilian industry has, until recently, operated under a labour code, *Consolidaco das Leis do Trabalho* (CLT), consolidated in 1943 during the dictatorship of Vargas. The code was corporatist in character and based on the Italian fascist 'Carta del Lavoro'. It sought to incorporate both the entrepreneurial and working classes in the political system through a structure of parallel trade union and employer organisations (Erickson, 1979). Brazil's Labour Ministry has set and enforced labour relations policy much more extensively than in Kenya and Malaysia. The CLT required terms and conditions of employment to be established through tripartite, binding arbitration in the local *municipio* or local labour court on an industry-wide basis. A 1965 law gave the government powers to set wage levels for both the private and the public sectors. This was to be achieved through a complicated formula for adjusting a benchmark minimum wage. Adjustments were simply imposed. Ever since, wages have been computed as multiples of the minimum wage. Semi-annual indexation was introduced in 1979.

Trade unions were licensed by the Ministry on a geographic basis corresponding to a *municipio*. The Ministry determined to which industry a particular enterprise belonged and, therefore, to which union its employees could belong. All employees in the formal sector were covered by CLT guarantees over minimum standards of pay, working conditions and terms of employment. All workers, regardless of union membership, had to pay the *imposto sindical*, equivalent of one day's pay per year. The Ministry then channelled 60 per cent of the funds to the union concerned.[9] The Ministry could and did withhold funding from unions held to be in violation of the CLT, dismiss the leadership and appoint a new leadership (Pastore and Skidmore, 1985). Additional legislation, aimed at controlling the poli-

181

tical activities of unions, included issuing 'ideological certificates' to approved leaders (Roesch, 1987).

Because the state had assumed prime responsibility for keeping industrial peace, there was little incentive for employers to take collective action to resist trade union encroachment. Individual employers usually dealt with disputes by sending the company lawyers to the labour courts. Indeed, the CLT was used by government-appointed labour court judges systematically to limit the scope of cases brought by trade unions: once an issue was ruled to be outside the jurisdiction of the CLT, any attempt at strike action was declared illegal. Between 1964–70, the government intervened in union affairs on 536 occasions: labour militancy was limited to brief work-to-rule actions.

Matters changed in the late 1980s with the advent of an elected civilian government. Unions learned rapidly how to deploy the political leverage of their 25 million members. They lobbied successfully for the inclusion of many new labour rights in the 1988 National Constitution, thus substantially modifying the CLT. In particular, Article 90 removed the restrictions imposed by Law 4,330 of 1964 on the right to strike. In the public sector, much unrest was provoked by the government's policy of limiting wage increases to less than the rate of inflation. Many private-sector employers, by contrast, opted for regular pay increases at or near inflation rates. Where strikes started without union support, internal competition between political factions often obliged union leaders to support unofficial action. Most such actions, however, were short-lived: workers were too worried about job security to take protracted action.[10]

Writers such as Scoville (1973) might have argued that these developments were merely a catching-up process. Yet, even though the 1988 Constitution conferred new legal rights on unions, many union leaders have remained reluctant to negotiate directly with employers, being well aware of their weak bargaining position in recessionary conditions. Besides, the labour courts retained some utility by continuing to index wage awards: a little was better than nothing. Even though the Collor administration has resolved to abolish all forms of wage indexation, it seems unlikely that the labour courts will go: as Kenyan unions have found, they confer official recognition of the union's representative functions.

Job security

Though most governments in developing countries curb labour unions, few compromise job security. Some managers in multinationals feel that this places them at a disadvantage, for local employers find informal ways around job security laws; they are unable to do likewise, for fear of the political repercussions. For example, the Malaysian government has consistently defended the right of employers to lay off workers without hindrance, always provided the legally stipulated severance payments are made (Islam, 1989). But, as Salih and Mei Ling (1988) describe, some non-unionised employers in the electronics industry have approached workers individually and persuaded them to agree to retrenchment on less favourable terms than those provided by law. This is despite the fact that the Ministry of Labour's conciliation service is active in protecting workers from wrongful dismissal.

The Kenyan Ministry of Labour has been more strongly protective of jobs. The *1982 Annual Report of the Labour Department* records that at the bottom of the 1982 slump, it rejected 40 per cent of the applications for redundancies. The Industrial Court also regards itself as a guardian of 'security of employment': this means that after 90 days a casual worker must be hired on a full-time basis. The Kenya Industrial Court judge observed, 'If a worker is doing his job nicely if not very well . . . then through the Industrial Court we have granted him security of employment . . . I have made it clear to employers that it is no use for them to come and tell me that they have given the workers one or two months' notice and therefore not a wrongful dismissal . . . I say no, that is not on [sic] because that notice is colourable [sic] if you have no real reason' (ILO, 1985). Nonetheless, many employers increasingly employ temporary workers or 'casuals'. Casual jobs accounted for about 14 per cent of employment in 1988, and a rising proportion of new jobs – up to 39 per cent in 1988 (FLT-Kenya, 1989).[11]

Emerging practice

Brazil has changed radically in the last twenty-five years. On the one hand, the erosion of state powers and the decline of corporatist institutions suggests new sources of instability in Brazilian labour relations. On the other hand, the emerging situation offers opportunities for building new alliances between labour and management, with multinationals in the van. The challenge from an increasingly sophisticated trade union movement has spurred employers' associations to develop their capacity to assist members in their dealings with unions. Clearly, if Brazil is going to increase the competitiveness of its high value-added engineering and other manufacturing industries, there must be a new deal with labour: a much broader social infrastructure and greater trust has been recognised as essential if the new technologies are to be harnessed effectively (CEAM/SEI, 1983).

The new possibilities for union/firm alliances can be seen among the 'dependent' exporters, who are already beginning to move away from wage-setting through the labour courts and towards company-based collective bargaining. The Ford plant in Sao Paulo was one of the first to establish a workplace labour-management committee in the early 1980s. More dramatically, Autolatina challenged a government price freeze in the courts in November 1987. The CUT-affiliated metalworkers leader, Vicente Paulo da Silva, came out in public support of the company, calling the government's pricing policy 'incomprehensible'. Another metalworker leader, Luiz Antonio de Madeiros, criticised Brazilian 'bias' against multinationals and warned against what he called the 'Argentine' phenomenon of foreigners' disinvestment. In early 1988, another CUT-affiliated union reopened dialogue with General Motors, broken off after a bitter dispute in 1985 (FLT-Brazil, 1989).

In Kenya, labour relations policy has oscillated between fixed extremes, as the government has mixed cooption with coercion. It has encouraged tractable unions with state patronage, but harassed radical unions through strict enforcement of laws relating to the conduct of union affairs. The labour leaders have in many ways become 'hostages' of the sole political party. In theory, this close relationship should provide access to the highest political levels and help promote a favourable legislative climate: in practice, the political elite seems unwilling to assign priority to labour interests in a predominantly agricultural economy. The disadvantages of accepting party discipline are, by contrast, immediate. Dependence has reduced the ability of labour organisations to respond to the needs of rank-and-file members and has caused increased factionalism and instability as the interests of the leadership and membership diverge. The recent increase in wildcat strikes may be symptomatic of the membership's view of the leadership's political involvements.

The Malaysian government has continued to remain suspicious of the political motives of union leaders. For example, the MTUC Secretary General and Transport Workers Union General Secretary, V. David, was detained in October, 1987 in a widespread crackdown on politicians and prominent government critics.[12] Because of such constraints, nearly one-third of members are represented by in-house unions. The decentralised structure and small size of individual unions disperses the total resources of the labour movement and hinders the development of a strong unified labour movement (O'Brien, 1988: pp. 164–5). Malaysian unions therefore remain susceptible to employer interference and pressure and, because they are not permitted to organise temporary workers or support political activity, they tend, as in Kenya, to be inward looking.

Accompanying these internal moves has been a rise in international pressure, affecting most particularly Malaysia's reluctance to change. The outcry over V. David's detention was used by the international labour movement to put pressure on the government to modify the amendments it was proposing to labour law. In 1988, the AFL-CIO submitted a petition to the US Trade Representative (USTR) urging that Malaysia's tariff preferences under the US Generalised System of Preferences (GSP) be withdrawn on the grounds that Malaysia did not respect internationally recognised workers rights (FLT-Malaysia, 1989). Shortly afterwards, the government released David from eight months' detention and changed the law in favour of organised labour. In particular, it became easier to organise workers and awards of the Industrial Court became enforceable by the regular courts. In 1989, the USTR determined that the Malaysian government was taking steps to recognise workers' rights and should therefore retain its GSP benefits.

International concern for human rights, including the freedom of association, seems likely to be increasingly mobilised to restrain host governments' more authoritarian actions against organised labour and thus to change the balance of power within the tripartite structures. For example, in 1990, the US Government sought to establish a GATT working party to study the possibility of including 'social clause' rules in trade agreements. These rules would cover a limited number of internationally recognised worker rights.[13] It seems unlikely, however, that a code would stop governments from ensuring regime maintenance at the expense of freedom of association during periods of political and social unrest. The resulting cross-fire between organised labour and government would place managers in an awkward dilemma. However, when peace returns it is not inevitable that enterprise/labour relations or productivity will suffer irreparable damage, provided management is not seen to have taken sides.

INVESTMENT IN HUMAN CAPITAL FOR EXPORTING

The extra demands on labour from a move towards exporting cannot be merely 'bolted on' to multinationals' systems of production: they require greater awareness, understanding, motivation and commitment of employees at all levels in the enterprise. And they are heightened by moves towards 'independent' exporting. Thus it becomes important to reconsider how multinationals manage their subsidiaries in developing countries to provide a platform for further development. There are some basic questions to be asked first. Do they create or displace employment? Do they pay inflationary wages and crowd out local employers? Do they enhance domestic labour productivity? Finally, do they provide adequate training and skills enhancement? Most of the answers are necessarily blurred, because of the inescapable methodological problem of assessing what would have happened if the investment had not occurred. Much of the literature on the subject amounts to little more than burning of straw men. What follows is thus more a listing of the issues than a complete assessment of how multinationals affect local labour markets.

Employment

Measures of the employment attributable to foreign investment are notoriously unreliable, not least because of an absence of common definitions of the underlying investment. In Kenya, the Central Bureau of Statistics distinguishes between firms with some government participation, local private companies and majority foreign-owned enterprises with no government participation. Yet most of the larger manufacturing firms have both government and foreign equity. Malaysian statistics relate to majority foreign ownership. On these variable bases, the multinationals' shares of employment in industry and commerce are estimated at roughly 23 per cent in Kenya; in Malaysia 29 per cent and in Brazil less than 20 per cent.

The problem with such figures is that they hide as much as they reveal, particularly as regards the dynamic aspects of employment: the labour/capital relationship is variable. For instance, when foreign exchange is in short supply, firms cannot freely indulge their preference for what Wells (1984) calls 'engineering man'. Given a free choice, managers in oligopolistic industries prefer capital-intensive technology as a way of insuring against risk and uncertainty in product markets, of reducing operational problems to those of managing machines rather than people and of producing the highest possible quality. For local firms, a broad technological perspective that includes an appreciation of the financial implications of the alternatives is difficult to acquire in a developing country when only limited information about production technologies is available (Austin, 1990: p. 246).

Foreign exchange shortage also constrains the supply of spare parts, leading engineers to eschew state-of-the-art technology. They are more inclined to direct their energies towards extending the life of existing equipment, investing in the 'fix-it' skills of local craftsmen and nurturing the repair and replication capacities of local parts suppliers. But shortage can provoke innovation, such as that of the managing director of a can-making subsidiary who reported that he usually spent part of his visits to the parent company checking through any machinery being scrapped in case it might be useful in his own operation.

Such adaptation and deepening of skills is conspicuously absent in the initial development of export-processing operations where the emphasis is on simple standardised production systems and de-skilling. Skills, such as they are, are firm-specific. Reliability and quality is engineered into the headquarters-defined 'system'. However, Malaysia's experience suggests that with maturity there is a gradual deepening of the skills transferred. This trend has been driven by the logic of cross-border sourcing of parts and components in the SE Asian region in tandem with increased employer confidence in the quality and productivity of local labour. Matsushita, discussed in chapter 5, has, for example, announced plans to specialise its overseas production centres in the manufacture of specific components. To this end, it will up-grade them 'to a level comparable to that of the headquarters company in Japan, particularly focusing on the aspects of operations related to design technology, purchasing, marketing and system-wide integrated management' (UNIDO, 1989: p. 111). Clearly, to be in a position to reap employment benefits from this trend towards rationalisation and consolidation of component production, host countries need to be able to offer both a positive investment environment *and* a highly skilled labour force.

Wage rates and productivity

Many surveys have shown that multinationals pay more than local firms. Because wages account for very low proportions of total costs, many firms are more sensitive to operating efficiently at full capacity than to minor variations in wage rates. Besides, few can afford to alienate their overseas customers by cavalier treatment of compatriot employees. They usually employ their resources more efficiently than local firms, even though they import very little technology (Kunio, 1988). A rough proxy for comparing productivity might be the average wages prevailing in foreign and locally owned-firms but, of course, it is extremely difficult to compare like with like. Foreign-owned companies tend to be disproportionately represented in the high value-added sectors. For example, in Kenya in the mid-1980s, wholly foreign-owned industrial companies paid their employees 30 per cent more than the average for manufacturing, but were overwhelmingly concentrated in the pharmaceutical, paints, plastics and related industries (UNCTC, 1988b: p. 26). In the services sector, the differential was 55 per cent.

There are further reasons for such differentials. Though multi-nationals possess considerable power in setting wages, they do not always use it when seeking long-term advantage. The local management, in part, embodies the supranational decision-making powers of the parent in matters such as investment, and transfer of product and process technology; it confronts a comparatively poorly organised labour movement whose members are mostly preoccupied with job security. However, the 'efficiency wage' hypothesis suggests that a high-wage policy can be economically rational where a low-wage policy discourages worker motivation, increases labour turnover and reduces labour productivity (Ackerlof and Yellen, 1986; Lindbeck and Snower, 1987). Managers are thus reluctant to cut nominal wages when they believe that doing so would adversely affect future productivity and unit costs.

Demands on workers' incomes from the extended family are also rising. Partly as a result of population growth and the consequent increase in the number of young dependents, and partly as a result of declining employment opportunities in Brazil and Kenya, many workers are subject to cash demands they cannot meet in full. This encourages pilferage, particularly in Kenya, even though the threat of dismissal should be a powerful disincentive. The challenge for human resource development policy is to work out ways of encouraging employees to take pride in high quality and productivity, even though income differentials between management and workers may be substantial – as high as 40 to 1 in Kenya and Brazil.

Above-average wages and work of low intensity usually indicate high effective rates of protection. Heavily protected firms may be inclined to share any monopoly 'rent' with their employees. In large, heavily protected economies, many local enterprises are quite capable of defending themselves against competition by mobilising government protection, so that it is sometimes they – and not the multinationals – that displace employment. Locally-owned, Kenyan 'manufacturers' who assemble a small number of mostly imported, subcomponents into finished car components such as sparkplugs and wiring harnesses, sometimes with negative value-added, create a small number of semi-skilled jobs but displace employment by wasting resources (World Bank, 1987: p. 310–11).

Training and skill enhancement

The real issues for long-term development of 'independent' exporting are not whether or not multinationals pay inflationary wages or create jobs, but whether they enhance the accumulation of skills that permit greater international competitiveness. When low domestic growth depresses reinvestment levels, manufacturing processes remain relatively skill-intensive: a forced substitution of labour for capital equipment. When there are also chronic shortages of equipment and spare parts, one priority is to create as much self-sufficiency as possible, particularly in machine maintenance. This can be accomplished by building up a core of employees with practical experience of the specific machines in the factory. Because these skills are acquired primarily on-the-job, not by formal off-the-job training, there is widespread use of screening of peripheral, casual workers for the requisite practical skills (Mikkelsen, 1986). Even in Brazil, various attempts by the government since the 1940s to encourage formal in-company training has met with limited success (Roesch, 1987). In Malaysia, the promotion of training schemes is part of the government's strategy to increase participation rates of Malays in skilled occupations, previously the exclusive domain of the Chinese and to a lesser extent Indians.

Elite skilled workers with extensive 'fix-it' knowledge, however, are sharply differentiated in terms of status and terms of employment from their unskilled and semi-skilled assistants. A comparative industry study of Egypt and West Germany illustrates the way in which technology dependency encourages 'over maintenance'. In Egypt, the exhaustive maintenance programme went 'far beyond the programme stipulated by the manufacturer', and was justified by management on the grounds that it was preferable to the risk of breakdowns and the problems of obtaining spare parts (Malsch, 1984: p. 16). The assistants worked to a highly specialised and rigid form of labour deployment under very close supervision by the skilled men.

189

With some exceptions, multinationals are reluctant to invest in *general* skills training (Castro and Carneiro, 1981). By paying above-average wages, they can normally meet specific company needs by internal training. Any shortfall can be met by poaching from less prosperous local firms with the offer of higher wages. Much of our evidence suggests that market-seeking multinationals employ a stable, mostly male, core of self-sufficient managers and skilled workers supported by a numerically flexible, unskilled casual wing. Efficiency-seeking global players, like the Japanese auto assemblers, prefer a stable workforce with highly developed firm-specific skills. The significance of any wider social benefit from the superior training capacity of multinationals must therefore be in doubt. After all, no rational management would set out to train manpower for another's benefit without some expectation of gain. Spinoffs to the wider economy through labour mobility are limited in all three countries.

National manpower advisers, usually concerned about the overall skills equilibrium in national labour markets, miss the point that it is the pattern of demand from existing employers that largely determines the accumulation of skills. Where companies overwhelmingly concentrate on manufacturing mature, standardised products, as in Kenya, the skills required of the labour force are limited, inhibiting progression to more sophisticated activities. This in turn has a knock-on effect on the 'graduate unemployment' problem which is of much current concern in both Malaysia and Kenya. The structural problem poses a dilemma. Should governments invest ahead of demand in expensive general technical training in the hopes of attracting more sophisticated investments?

Malaysia attempted to resolve the dilemma by promoting export-oriented industries. Because the government had an industrially-inexperienced (Malay) labour force it wished to have employed, and because the domestic market was small and already saturated with import-substitutes, it had little choice but to encourage 'dependent' exports. An industrial monoculture was created, based on foreign electronics companies and reliant primarily on the comparative advantage that the availability of low-cost, high productivity and disciplined labour confers. The gains in terms of accumulating new skills have therefore been modest. Moreover, because as much as 80–90 per cent of the labour force created were new female entrants, there has been little impact on male unemployment.

One way to start the process of building greater national capacity is to promote 'linkages', as we discussed generally in chapter 5. The Japanese have been particularly successful in harnessing the potential of intimate, vertically (dis)integrated networks of sub-contractors centred on a large firm and numerous satellite smaller firms (Odaka et al., 1988). The evidence, however, suggests that such a policy works to encourage substantial backward linkages with local firms only when industrialisation has reached a considerable level of sophistication and minimum scale economies reached. For example, Hill (1985) reports that a Philippine government programme introduced to force the pace of backward integration and technology diffusion had little impact on the propensity of foreign-owned assembly firms to sub-contract part of their operations to local suppliers. Studies of Korea (Koo, 1985) and Taiwan (Ranis and Schive, 1985; Schive, 1990) indicate how and why it is that the successful development of greater local linkages depends on substantial prior investments in education and infrastructure before they can become a source of dynamism.

The limited pay-offs from linkages in Malaysia and Brazil have been discussed earlier. In both countries, however, there are some signs of lasting gain coming in some sectors, Malaysian electronics and Brazilian aircraft for example. Such exceptions serve to highlight the extent of the investments needed over long periods of time. There are no quick fixes.

In Kenya, where there have been no such investments for industry, a promising alternative has been to develop agriculture by means of subcontracting. As in manufacturing, the 'intensity' of the agricultural contract – the extent to which the company exercises constant supervision over the production process – varies according to nature of the product market (Glover, 1984). For example, BAT sources its tobacco leaf from 10,000 local Kenyan outgrowers. The company's extension service provides advice on cultivation, curing and storage, seedlings and fertilizers. Cured leaf is purchased cash-on-delivery at collection points in the growing areas which helps to make sure outgrowers do not switch to other crops where payment is less reliable. The importance of prompt payment is shown by the record of the government's crop marketing boards, whose payments are often delayed by six months or more. These delays led to cotton production collapsing from over 20,000 tonnes to no more than 2,000 tonnes in two years in the 1980s.

Enduser-financed extension schemes rely heavily on the practicalities of enforcing the contracting. In the case of tobacco, BAT was the only buyer.[14] By contrast, a joint venture established in 1985 between Unilever, the Commonwealth Development Corporation and the IFC to encourage contract farming of oilseed rape and sunflower was a disaster. The company failed to allow for the possibility that farmers would be tempted to cheat on their loans and to sell oilseed direct to existing local processing firms. Consequently, the company was faced with the fairly common problem of having many unenforceable contracts.

Successful contract arrangements provide substantial benefits for both parties and distribute risk between them in an interdependent relationship. The 'intensity' of the relationship varies according to the extent to which the buyer exercises control over production. For example, as we discussed in chapter 3, commercially exploitable proprietary biotechnological 'design' and marketing knowledge is relatively difficult for the local producer to appropriate.[15] Without market access, such knowledge is impossible to exploit. However, a major long-term advantage is the opportunity for building up a reputation for meeting the stringent quality and delivery schedules required by international markets in partnership with the buyer.

Similar benefits have been gained by transfers of technology and skills to local entities under programmes of 'good citizenship'. Unilever, for example, has an Indian Integrated Rural Development programme. This was motivated by the need to help local farmers improve their lot so as to promote greater prosperity that would in turn build a better business climate and stimulate demand for the firm's products. In Chile, it has successfully transferred its salmon farming technology in partnership with the government to create a new source of exports. In Kenya, Unilever and other multinationals are active in the Management Assistance Programme that provides advice and other forms of help to small business. The Bata Shoe Organisation has a similar philosophy in its 'Partnerships in Progress' schemes in many developing countries. Though small in scale, all these initiatives show how beneficial 'externalities' can be established by the presence of responsible foreigners.

There is no necessary conflict of objectives between foreigners and local producers for large scale projects. Indeed local firms may act as a supplement or substitute for company production, as is common in the sugar industry. Kenya, for example, has a highly successful state-owned enterprise, the Kenya Tea Development Authority, which has fostered smallholder tea-growing for export through the provision of an outgrower service and processing factories. Its finished tea competes alongside foreign-owned, estate-produced tea in the London tea market and commands premium prices. The Tea Authority owes much of its success to its ability to resist political interference, a point we make many times in this book.

WOMEN AT WORK

The UNCTC/ILO (1985) study of women workers in developing countries draws attention to the fact that women account for a small, but growing, minority of employees of multinationals. Where women are employed, most are employed in unskilled and semi-skilled production jobs by 'light' export-oriented multinationals, and associated local companies manufacturing for export under contract. Most of these firms are located in some form of export processing zone (EPZ). It is doubtful if anyone ever 'anticipated that the main employment effect of EPZs would be to draw into the labour forces hundreds of thousands of young women who, in other circumstances, would not have sought a job in industry because there was no such job available to them, nor indeed to anyone else' (p. 149). As for example in Malaysia, 85 per cent of employees in EPZs are young women. In the rest of manufacturing, women's share of employment is under one-third (p. 60). By contrast, the creation of skilled, technical, professional and managerial jobs has been relatively few and largely dominated by men (Maex, 1983: p. 53; UN, 1986: pp. 79–80).

The obstacles as well as the opportunities for greater employment of women are shaped by national cultural factors as well as industrial needs. Many Muslim countries, such as Egypt, resist female employment (Henley and Ereisha, 1989). Yet no such problems seem to arise in Malaysia, another Muslim country. In Kenya, many factories discriminate against female production workers on the grounds that formal sector employment opportunities are so limited that they should be reserved for men even in the textile and food processing industries. In export-oriented agribusiness there are no such barriers to female employment.

Female employment is concentrated in a few industries, notably the garment, electrical and electronic industries. Hirata's (1989) study of the French and Brazilian plants of a French electronics firm highlights four of the superior qualities male managers believe female workers possess: physical ability, particularly nimble fingers; endurance in carrying out monotonous and repetitive tasks; the patience and concentration needed for visual inspection work; and speed. Other studies also mention employers' belief in the submissiveness and docility of women workers (Elson and Pearson, 1981).

Generally, women are employed in jobs requiring little investment in training but high intensity of work. Kergoat (1982) explains this in terms of the interconnection between the skills learned at home and those required in the factory. She argues that the availability of women

193

with these 'natural' skills acquired in the home and at school save employers from heavy investment in training. Thus, seemingly 'unskilled' women bring valuable skills to the enterprise.

Multinationals, perhaps predictably, prefer to employ young, usually unmarried women – on average more than 70 per cent below the age of twenty-five (UNCTC/ILO, 1988: table 8). With few domestic commitments they are more flexible, are more readily available for shiftwork and overtime, and generally have better health, eyesight and physical reflexes than older women. They are also less likely to come to work exhausted as a result of combining factory and unpaid domestic work at home. In Ruth Pearson's (1986) telling observation, multinationals target daughters rather than wives for employment. By doing so, the firms maintain the semblance of 'socially responsible' working conditions, while at the same time allowing opportunities for numerical flexibility: the majority leave when they marry in their mid-twenties. Whether these practices are exploitative is the subject of endless controversy. Our limited observations on the issue leads us to agree with the, admittedly tentative, data cited by Lim and Fong (1988) to the effect that working conditions for the young women are at least as good and often better than those prevailing for the unemployed in their villages.

The youthful age structure of developing countries and the prospect of abundant supplies of this type of labour has been a powerful incentive for relocating labour intensive manufacturing industry from developed countries with their rapidly aging population. As a UNIDO report (1980b: p. 5) concluded, 'female intensity of employment in an industry in the developed country is usually a strong predictor of this industry's propensity to redeployment. In the USA, for example, women form over 90 per cent of all production workers and operators in the two industries which have been most heavily redeployed to developing countries – electronics assembly and wearing apparel.'

As might be expected from our earlier discussion, multinationals in EPZs are likely to be no worse, and in many cases considerably better employers than local firms, in terms of the wages and conditions of work they offer women (and male) employees. In a study of Malaysian textiles, electronics and wood-based exporting industries, Fong (1987) found that women workers earned significantly less than their male counterparts but that the differentials were narrowing as women gained seniority and skill. Addison and Demery (1988) found no significant influence of a firm's market orientation on wage rates in East Asia. While hours of working are not very different from what prevails in other domestic industries, a number of countries, including

194

Malaysia, have not ratified ILO Convention No. 89 that prohibits women from working at night. This obviously substantially enhances the competitive advantage of firms located in those countries that break the Convention.[16]

The opportunities for women in 'new' industries can be seen in the rapid expansion of the cut-flower and floriculture exporting agribusiness in Kenya. Whereas traditional plantation agriculture has relied on a primarily male, rural proletariat, formed originally from migrant and indentured labour, modern export-oriented floriculture depends heavily on the 'natural' skills of women. Female labour is in abundance, because of limited alternative wage employment opportunities in rural areas. Labour intensity is essential for high productivity commercial crops to create the necessary homogeneous growing conditions. Successful operations therefore rely on a high level of control, so a first priority is to inculcate endlessly routinised work practices and obsessive attention to detail. One success in Kenya is Yoder Brothers. Its corporate slogan, 'something to grow on', indicates its particular niche in floriculture, namely the production of planting materials for sale to ornamental plant growers and retailers. The Kenyan subsidiary exclusively supplies the European market with chrysanthemum cuttings. Two-thirds of the fieldworkers were young women, 90 per cent of whom lived in the company compound where only single status was allowed. Even though the farm was located in a relatively remote area, Yoder could recruit a literate labour force with at least primary education and capable of keeping planting records of the 230 varieties cultivated.

By creating a whole new generation of 'target workers', the social impact of increased female employment mirrors many earlier patterns of social change induced by industrialisation. Instead of male workers migrating to the towns to seek higher paid industrial employment before returning to subsistence agriculture, we now have young women workers seeking to enhance their living standards and savings before exiting from the labour force to marry and rear children. As with the earlier male migrants, the women workers remit a substantial portion, typically about half, of their wages to their extended families. This 'trickle-down' effect has made an appreciable impact on local communities close to export-processing enterprises and more widely (Ackerman, 1984).

In terms of family relationships, the evidence suggests that an enhanced economic role strengthens the woman's position within the family. With the weakening of male labour markets, this erodes traditional male authority. Inevitably, there have been allegations

195

about the social conduct of young single women factory workers from some quarters. Yet it seems fair to conclude that it is not the employment of women *per se* that leads to social tensions, but rather the general social impact of the more independent behaviour wage work engenders. For example, Ackerman (1984) describes the increased tendency of rural female migrants to marry other male factory workers and to become permanent urban residents. That said, there is no evidence that the new emerging generation of urbanised women factory workers believes less strongly in marriage, the family and the importance of having children (UNCTC/ILO, 1985: p. 89).

The competitiveness of much 'dependent', export-oriented production depends heavily on the intensive use of low-cost, 'unskilled' female labour. Whether or not a host government has recognised this and created an enabling environment clearly has an influence on the development of the sector. Most of the new women entrants to the labour force typically spend no more than ten years in employment and learn few new skills. Those they learn are highly company-specific. While there may be some long-term social benefits from the spread of an appreciation of industrial-type employment and increased earnings amongst a wider cross-section of the population, such employment of itself does not enhance the accumulation of the kinds of skills required to progress towards self-sustainable industrialisation. For that to happen, women will need to be given a far greater role in the learning required.

MANAGEMENT DEVELOPMENT AND CULTURAL COMPLEXITY

Managers of multinationals' subsidiaries in many developing countries feel a keen sense of remoteness – technically – from industrial markets, advanced production systems and supply lines, and – psychologically – from great uncertainty about the basic parameters of social and economic activity. The contradictory pulls on them from headquarters, from local officials and from their employees can seldom be resolved by rationality alone. For example, in the run up to the 1989 election, many managers in Brazil deferred employment-relations initiatives for fear of reprisals in the event of a left-wing candidate being returned as president.[17] To deal with the uncertainties, managers rely on what Triandis (1984, p. 88) calls the culture of 'personalissimo', defined as 'the social process of knowing somebody, who knows somebody, who knows the person from whom you need a service'. Under these conditions, new managers, especially expatriates, experience a sense of powerlessness, even though their formal status leads others to expect authority and expertise. Without good understanding of the local organisational climate, managers can make expensive mistakes.

Organisational culture in developing countries is significantly different from countries with a longer history of industrialisation. The main differences revolve around the inseparability of authority and obligation. While senior managers have considerably more direct power at their disposal in relationships with subordinates than would be the case in a mature industrial economy, they are also embedded in a parallel network of social obligations which requires them to assist relatives and friends. Often, these obligations came from the support people need during the process of adjustment from rural migrant to a fully 'captured' member of urban capitalist society. Social networks and obligations inevitably penetrate organisations because employees cannot insulate themselves from their wider social commitments.

All organisations must, therefore, decide whether to accept such traits or attempt to create new ones. Family and other social networks can be harnessed to form an important basis for maintaining the cohesion of formal organisations and thereby reducing the probability of transactional failure. It is clearly more effective if the formal system of rewards and sanctions used to manage organisational relationships is underpinned by a degree of moral obligation. Even better, if traditional communal values can be coopted to this end. Blunt (1980), in a study of two private security organisations in Kenya, for example, claimed that when they were recruited largely along kinship lines, individuals felt that they exercised a greater degree of control over their lives. Such practice served to reduce labour turnover and damage to company property, and to increase service to clients.

This strategy of syncretism or harnessing aspects of traditional culture for essentially modern managerial ends has been one of the major factors contributing to the success of industrialisation in Japan since the end of the nineteenth century (Dore, 1973) and in Hong Kong, Singapore, South Korea and Taiwan since the 1950s (Hamilton and Biggart, 1988; Clegg, 1990). All of these states, however, have a relatively homogeneous cultural milieu. By contrast, most developing countries in Asia and Africa are multi-ethnic societies. Unfortunately, the very feature that is characteristic of traditional social structures and gives them their coherence and strength – exclusiveness – translated into a modern organisational setting in a multi-ethnic society can lead to severe inefficiency. Thus, for example, while the traditional imperative of mutual self-help may allow flexibility for the in-group, bureaucratic standards tend to be enforced with an exacting thoroughness on the out-group. Such behaviour is liable to set in train a process which convinces most people (the out-group) that the organisation considers them to be untrustworthy. Before long, behaviour conforms to expectations and it becomes necessary for a simple act, such as signing a cheque, to require three people where one would otherwise suffice.

Elitist Latin American cultures have also tended to encourage the development of groups with strong vested interests, none more so than in Brazil. As in government, so in business. Wallender (1979: p. 195) reported that 'the Brazilian business firm and its management are closely intertwined with family relationships and politics. The primary reason for this is the traditional dominance of the relatively small number of wealthy and powerful family groups in the various commercial sectors. Too often, management positions are filled by members of these elite families and who have only marginal management experience and ability.' Brazilian executives therefore tend not to delegate to managers with operational experience. Instead, a 'live-for-today' attitude is adopted with emphasis placed on the attainment of immediate objectives and the neglect of management development. This lack of trust of subordinate managers makes it difficult to establish joint ventures with multinationals.

Great subtlety is needed on the part of managers in multinationals if they are to avoid the dangers of severe efficiency losses inherent in tight administrative controls. The most subtle way of achieving integration, of allowing managerial autonomy without compromising overall control, is through management training, socialisation and development. In general, 'hard' mechanisms such as management information systems and 'soft' mechanisms such as manager management seem to go hand in hand (Paul Evans, 1988). Without soft integrative mechanisms leading to organisational commitment, the hard systems are unlikely to function well. Obviously, barriers to management integration are greatest in a multi-ethnic society and where traditional obligations remain strong. Somehow, multinationals have to forge loyalty to shared goals and visions of corporate strategy. As we illustrated in chapter 5, those firms embarked on developing more integrated forms of global integration need to push the global 'mentality' down to low levels in the organisation. In a business environment of increasing diversity, complexity and change, managers' ability to work together regardless of nationality or culture to achieve a common corporate mission is essential.

A serious challenge to traditional headquarters-driven thinking about management development is the need to take greater account of the availability of local management. In the past, many firms assumed they could make up shortages of local management talent with expatriates. Today, host government restrictions on work permits and the rising costs of expatriation from OECD countries are forcing multinationals to review their international personnel policies. Virtually all our informants reported that the proportion of expatriate managers employed had dropped dramatically since 1980.

Market-seeking multinationals in mature industries face great obstacles to making continuous improvements in standards. If they promote local managers, they find the consequent training expensive and often discouraged by local regulations. One company in Kenya reported that the Central Bank would permit a *per diem* allowance that covered only very basic accommodation. The company felt this undermined one of the purposes of overseas training, namely boosting the status of local managers so they felt they were members of a global elite and not made to feel like 'poor country cousins'. If they rely solely on regular infusions of expatriate managers, they do little to ensure that the entire subsidiary is less isolated from corporate thinking.

Even greater obstacles face multinationals in knowledge-based industries. Purely in-house training may be so expensive for the higher grades of skill that firms give priority in their location decisions to those countries where such skills are already available. Clearly, this puts an onus on those governments eager to attract foreign investment to develop national higher technical education and management training capacity.

Accumulating new human resources

In theory, governments can contribute substantially towards improving the productive capacity of employees through investment in formal educational and training institutions. In practice, there are real political and fiscal limits to what many can do. We started this chapter by showing how conflicting political interests weaken the will and the ability of the state's administrative system to promote economic efficiency. In particular, we pointed to the inefficiency introduced by concession bargaining among powerful vested interests. Added to this, is the limit to the amount of resources that can usefully be directed into training. Even so, the generally low status of ministries of labour and manpower development, combined with poor coordination with ministries of industry and commerce, suggests that these fiscal limits are rarely reached – except in rhetoric.[18]

Governments also have a relatively poor record of being able to anticipate the training needs of industry through institutional provision.

Empirical evidence demonstrates that the large, well-established firms benefit disproportionately from government training levies; small firms treat them as taxes (Mikkelsen, 1986; Roesch, 1987). Yet, when left to their own devices, small local firms tend to underinvest in training, for fear of losing skilled employees to richer poachers. It is a sad reflection of political priorities that 'tripartism' is only fully developed in the industrial relations sphere, while 'joint venture' training arrangements organised by government agencies and groups of private local and foreign-owned firms are assigned much lower priority. Host governments might well be more vigorous in their efforts to persuade multinationals to share their superior training capacity with locals, but many fear this would discourage new entrants.

Governments could also do more to promote a motivational environment that encourages productivity, quality and reliability. Regrettably, the traditionally instrumental approach to employee relations, embodied in the labour codes of Brazil, Kenya and Malaysia, is incompatible with the development of a highly skilled and committed labour force. These codes assume low, even recalcitrant, worker commitment and aim to achieve stability in union relations by (restrictive) recognition agreements and grievance handling procedures. They fall far short of the requirements seen clearly in developed countries. Walton (1985), for example, argues that, while control-oriented employee relations may achieve reliable, if not outstanding performance, they are unlikely to foster the standards of excellence set by world-class competitors.

Accounts of attempts to introduce Japanese management methods such as Total Quality Control and Just-in-Time inventory management systems into American and European enterprises all suggest that these techniques are most successful when they are linked with broader changes in the organisation. Unfortunately, there are few signs that multinationals engaged in 'dependent' exporting are investing in building up indigenous technological capabilities. For example, despite Malaysia being a major world 'producer' of DRAM memory chips, only SGS-Thomson, a relatively minor producer, has chosen to locate the high technology diffusion stage of production in Malaysia.[19] Japanese electronics companies in South-East Asia seem to adopt as instrumental and short-term a view of human resource development in developing countries as do their US and European counterparts.

The importance individuals accord to wage employment affects the ability of management to 'capture' the commitment of its work force. In any newly industrialising economy, experience of formal employment is by definition a recent phenomenon. Extra-organisational commitments and obligations of employees are bound to be of some significance and render psychological commitment to an organisation ambiguous. The persistence of ethnic, kinship and family ties also acts to limit the ability of trade unions to organise workers into coherent groups that can challenge and also cooperate with management. While the employment relationship may lack moral content, the cash nexus exerts a much greater influence than in high-wage industrialised economies.

Another limitation to managerial effort to strengthen and deepen employee commitment is the extent of local management influence on global corporate strategy. Because the locus of decision making for a foreign-owned or foreign-managed enterprise is, in part, located overseas, employees of a local subsidiary would be foolish to ignore the extra-territorial commitments and obligations of senior executives. And the more marginal the subsidiary, the more marginal is the commitment of corporate headquarters. Policy oscillations can be severe, unpredictable, and unrelated to subsidiary performance. When local perceptions are that strategy is no more than 'short-termism', employees are likely to be equally tenuous in their commitment.

If abundant supplies of low-cost, unskilled labour are of declining interest to multinationals, what are the human resources strengths of developing countries? To build up autonomy and therefore defence against 'short-termism', local subsidiaries need to develop their indigenous technological capability. Some already do so, though more from necessity than by design. Katz (1987) points to a number of strengths of import-substituting firms in developing countries that are often neglected. First, because they are designed to supply limited domestic markets, they begin their operations on the basis of discontinuous 'batch-like' technologies, and at a relatively low level of automation. Over time, however, many have to acquire skill in adapting the imported technologies the better to fit local conditions. Second, because of shortages of competent subcontractors, firms tend to carry out far more operations 'in-house' than they would in a developed economy. Third, scarcities and distortions in supplies force firms to learn to make substitutes for imported technology.

In other words, despite all the obstacles, many local firms, even those making mature products, possess considerable human resources. With notable exceptions, however, most allow these resources to remain latent and do not direct them towards export markets. Governments could help greatly by funding the transitions and thus reducing the risk for the individual firm. The problem is that this process of adaption can take decades before the pay-off is earned. Faced with the more pressing demands of structural adjustment programmes, most governments feel unable to do more than bow to the tyranny of the immediate.

7   THE WAY FORWARD

We now draw together the strands of argument in preceding chapters to indicate the types of new questions we believe should be asked both by those who study international relations or international political economy and by those whose main concern is with corporate strategy and management. All our findings suggest that many of the conventional frameworks of analysis fail to deal adequately with the contemporary dynamism of change. The most common reason why they fail is that they do not take sufficiently into account either the broad structural changes in the global political economy, nor the highly differentiated conditions of individual states, where social, cultural and political forces often clash with economic imperatives. In looking at host-state/foreign firm relations we see governments typically perceiving themselves as caught between the upper millstone of structural change that forces them to compete for world market shares and the nether millstone of their dependence for survival both on foreign investors and on local political support. We also see foreign investors feeling caught between the same upper millstone of structural change and the nether one of the rooted resistance of third world governments to more accommodating policies.[1]

In suggesting new questions to be asked, we also attempt to provide some advice for both governments and managers. That task is extraordinarily difficult, for there are few generalisations that hold up to scrutiny in particular circumstances. Advice that might be appropriate for Brazil may be wholly inappropriate for Kenya. Moreover, changing circumstance means that specific lines of policy appropriate for any one country will inevitably have to be altered over time. The same is evidently true for firms. How then to draw together the strands of the argument? We approach the task with a healthy dose of humility, yet we believe that there are some basic policy approaches of general validity.

Central to the whole argument are the propositions we stated in chapter 1. The evidence, however partial, strongly suggests that there is a growing possibility for new forms of collaboration between states and firms in the pursuit of shares of world markets. We recognise that this hope for a world of less adversarial bargaining will not be realised as a generality: mutual suspicion remains strong. None the less, our conclusions reflect the belief that dilemmas can be resolved, but only over time and in a series of small steps, not giant leaps. They can and will be embraced by the more forward-looking states and firms. As that happens, many of the conventional frameworks of analysis will need substantial adjustment to deal adequately with the dynamism of change. New research issues that require perspectives much broader than in the conventional literatures are being thrown up and followed the whole time.

BASIC PREMISES

Our initial propositions can be re-stated as three basic premises. The first is that the primary influences on the behaviour of firms and states are found within the international political economy. Changes in the world system are, to be sure, the product of a myriad of actions by all actors, whether individuals, firms, states or inter-governmental bodies. Taken together, their actions have limited the independent options for states during the last two decades or so.

The second is that most states have become more directly engaged in the competition for shares of the world's wealth, and not solely concerned in their foreign policy with power. They have therefore adjusted their frameworks of thought and priority for allocating national resources in ways that promote the accumulation of wealth-creating resources. These shifts suggest the basis of possible co-operation and partnership in production.

The third premise concerns the means to achieving the desired ends, namely that there are growing interactions between national strategies designed to achieve rising levels of social and economic aspiration and the global strategies of the firms. The policy inter-actions sketched in figure 4.1 are influenced, not solely by the specific regulations for dealing with foreign investors, but also by the actions taken to achieve other policy goals. Creating a climate for competition within the state as a means to manage these interactions has thus become an important agenda item.

It is only recently that some states have tried to link their nego-tiations with foreign firms to their other policy agendas. The reasons for the past behaviour are not hard to find. Foreign investment, particularly in the inward component, was of small consequence for many nations such as the USA. In others, such as Brazil, the dominant attitude has been that the impact of the foreigners could be handled without reference to other policies. Only as the magnitude of FDI has grown to the point where it assumed significance in national decisions have governments learned that multinationals' actions directly affect the outcomes of their economic policy choices. Malaysia's drive for growth in the export of manufactured goods to diversify away from undue reliance on commodities could not have been accomplished in such industries as electronics without the active participation of the multinationals. Moreover, many states have been learning that the multinationals also affect the outcomes of social policy: for example, by contributing to or detracting from the innovatory capacity of the country, or by their practices in the labour market.

These three premises are fundamental to the conclusions we draw. For readers who may not be convinced, we offer some further amplification of all three.

Global shifts

The crucial structural changes in the international political economy have been both political and economic. The most dramatic of the political changes occurred in the latter half of the 1980s: the melting of the Cold War between the superpowers; the liberation of Eastern and Central Europe from the Soviet Union; the drive for multiparty democracy and national self-determination not only in Europe but in many developing countries. Less dramatic, but equally important, have been the drives towards deregulation in developed countries and towards privatisation in most countries around the world. Such economic changes were primarily in the financial structure, where the mobility of capital increased, and in the production structure, where the diffusion of existing technologies also increased. In turn, these changes fuelled the exponential growth of FDI during the later 1980s and affected the forms of global competition among firms.

Taken together, these structural changes have often been loosely lumped together under the generic label of 'Interdependence'. But this is too vague and value-laden a label to tell either policy makers in government or corporate strategists how best to respond. Each has its own impact.

No political change was confined within a single nation state. The collapse of the Berlin Wall in 1989 reverberated throughout the world. The lack of any Western consensus, akin to the Marshall Plan, about how to assist the reforms in the East sent a clear message to firms; it would be each for himself. Firms, in the West and in the East, would have to use corporate diplomacy to get the best possible deal from their home and potential host governments. Where appropriate, they would have to seek corporate allies among banks at home and the formerly state-owned enterprises in the East.[2]

The reverberations also served to put economic concerns more centrally on states' international agendas. All developing countries now face the advent of new competitors for government aid, bank credit and FDI. Many fear that reconstruction aid for central Europe will divert scarce development funds from other areas. As Noordin Sopiee, the director-general of Malaysia's Institute for Strategic and International Studies and a former editor of the *Straits Times*, succinctly put it, 'In the long run, more for Eastern Europe must mean less for everyone else' (*World Link*, 1990: p. 87). Vehemently though donor governments have denied it, the conviction remains in the developing countries that for them, too, political change in the Soviet bloc will sharpen the competition among them for market shares and for the multinationals' capital and technology.

Growing economic interdependence, however simplistically it is defined, creates other limits to national options. The proportion of the economy that is subject to external influence has been growing for almost all nations, except perhaps the smallest, poorest states. Failure to manage the external account constrains domestic policy, for balance-of-payments deficits can seldom be financed for long. The classic example in recent times has been the effect on the French government of such deficits in 1983. Mitterand's socialist government was forced by the external deficits and the exhaustion of foreign credit into a major U-turn in policy away from state-owned enterprises and organised labour and toward productivity in export industries.

When combined with internal pressures induced by individuals' knowledge of events in Eastern Europe, external economic pressures can have an even more far-reaching local impact. An extreme example was the almost complete U-turn attempted by the former communist (since 1975) state of Laos in 1989. Laos allowed private trade to take over from state-controlled enterprises by abolishing all currency controls and removing all import controls on consumer goods. Past ideology was set aside. Elections were planned and foreign investment – most of it from Thailand – welcomed. Quite clearly, the role model was Thailand, not its other neighbour, Myanmar (Burma). But even Myanmar, as discussed in chapter 4, has also now begun to reverse its former policies of economic isolationism, if not its politics.

More generally, the shifts in the global system have linked together

206

agendas that were previously kept separate. The debate over the future of GATT illustrates the problems that have been created. Though the debate had not been resolved at the time of writing, the agenda was clear. Trade issues are increasingly and inextricably bound up with FDI and the behaviour of the multinationals. The use of the so-called trade-related investment measures (TRIMs) that tie government incentives to a broad range of trade, investment and financial policies provides one contested agenda.

Our evidence suggests strongly that, when linked to policies of import-substitution, TRIMs can be self-defeating by requiring the ineffective use of second-best local resources and so inhibiting the exports the policies are designed to create. They can cause the foreign firm great aggravation, especially when the local supplies are substandard so that the firm has to lower the quality of its product, risking the loss of market shares. With import substitution, it did not matter too much if, say, Filipino-made pencils were lower in quality than imported American ones. But if they are designed for export, it matters both to the firm and the host government. The moral is that policy should be directed to helping local suppliers to upgrade the quality of their inputs, rather than forcing inferior inputs on the manufacturer. And to give the suppliers time *and* incentive to do so, an advertised timetable of reducing proportions of required local content can be an effective compromise – as in the case of Nissan-built cars in Britain.

Similarly, the debate over trade-related intellectual property measures (TRIPs), muddied by polemics over 'theft' and 'piracy', fails to recognise that there are perfectly valid reasons for different calculations of the socially optimal length of time for protecting a patent. These differences are important, for they affect investors' perceptions of likely project returns and trading possibilities. Italy, for example, corrected many of its deficiencies in patent protection about a decade ago. The consequence has been a growing inflow of FDI, stimulating local creativity, employment and exports. By contrast, India, under pressure from its local producers, has opposed inclusion of intellectual property rights in GATT. Like Brazil until recently, India does not officially recognise the impact of such policies on future flows of technical transfers and exports.

Without resolution of the TRIPs and TRIMs debates for all sectors, including services, the multinationals' full potential for assisting export-led growth will not be harnessed. All too many developing countries hide behind Clause XVIII (b) that allows them to use balance-of-payments difficulties as an excuse to deny firms access to their markets. Equally, developed countries undermine the discipline of international competition by limiting market access in agriculture and textiles and by invoking Voluntary Exports Restraints for their troubled industries. As we showed in chapter 4, these devices are largely self-defeating in the face of long-run shifts in the international economy. Gradual moves to eliminate both sets of constraint would greatly facilitate the development of a more equitable and dynamic set of relationships fostering sustainable growth.

That multinationals' interests are directly concerned by the outcomes of such debates seems incontrovertible. Yet few of them speak out on the issues. One exception is British Petroleum, which has issued a series of policy statements. In 1990, BP came out with unequivocal support for GATT: 'as an international company, BP's commercial success is crucially dependent on the health of the world's economy, which in turn is based on the maintenance and enhancement of the GATT-based multilateral trading system'. BP's statement recognised that progress on each of the specific issues depends on progress on the others. Multinationals need to become more directly concerned with the public debates about how progress might be achieved in practice and how the corrosive influence of unwise side payments may be avoided.

The issue of side payments, or 'concessionary capitalism' as we called it in the previous chapter, stems from the worry many officials have that the new competition makes management of the trade agenda less effective as a means of controlling the externalities of a national economy. Managing for export-led growth is much harder than managing import-substitution. Caves (1982: p. 295) stated that

> national policies consistent with maximum global welfare from MNEs' activities diverge from those that appear to maximise national welfare. This proposition holds if countries fail to recognise the interdependent effects of their policies, and there is no guarantee in the theory of bargaining and retaliation that recognition will bring consensus on policies that maximise joint (global) welfare.

He went on to argue that, unlike assumptions made in trade theory, there is 'no comparable balance condition for a country's interests as source and host of MNEs. Therefore, no globally efficient change in policy that is not neutral between source and host can claim to spread its benefits equitably without side payments being made'.

The problem is that a government's policy agendas can affect each dimension of a firm's activities in contradictory ways. Is it possible, given how the public policy process is typically managed in most countries, that officials can see the whole rather than merely the limited agendas of their own ministries? More likely, most will see only a part and will act accordingly. The resulting inconsistencies can create problems and encourage firms to negotiate for special deals.

We repeat: an obvious but vital lesson from all these changes is that the global trends for change now set the context within which national changes are attempted. Purely national frameworks of analysis, for political risk analysts as much as for sociologists, are outgrown. The dominant structural changes in the world of today and tomorrow are likely to be global, perhaps regional, but not national or local. These changes directly affect national options and the feasible forms of adjustment within states. They have heightened the importance of the two new dimensions of diplomacy – the bargaining between governments and firms, especially multinationals, and bargaining among firms. The importance of the new 'triangular' diplomacy has been revealed in almost every project we reviewed.

The pursuit of wealth

Our second premise is that among their multiple goals, governments now accord greater priority to the accumulation of wealth-creating resources. This has direct implications for the study of international relations. Hitherto, students of international politics started from the presumption that, in an anarchical, Hobbesian international society, in which each state claims sovereignty and there is no superior ruling authority over them, the over-riding concern of every state was for its security (Bull, 1978; or, for a shorter and clearer statement of the realist view, Miller, 1982). This view assumed that governments, as guardians of the national interest, pursued power as a means of securing their independence from interference by others. International relations was therefore about the pursuit of power as a means of self-defence; wealth was needed primarily to provide that state with the revenue with which to match the offensive military capability of predatory neighbours. Now, many argue, wealth is needed to preserve the state more from internal rather than external threats to its cohesion and survival. Without wealth or the prospect of future sources of wealth, even if there is no external security threat, the state begins to fall apart.

Of course, this pursuit of wealth is part of a long, secular change that began in the Middle Ages with the spreading concern for raising the conditions of material life. It is still not finished. For decades to come, there will still be reversions to the old form of inter-state conflict. States will continue to be threatened by their neighbours with coercive

209

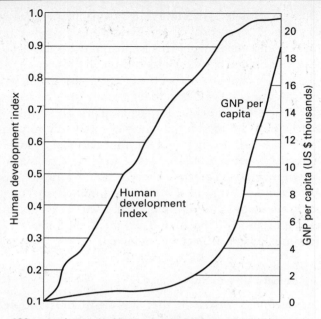

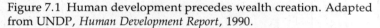
130 countries ranked by human development index and by
GNP per capita

Figure 7.1 Human development precedes wealth creation. Adapted
from UNDP, *Human Development Report*, 1990.

violence, especially when there are scarce resources such as access to
water at stake (Myers, 1989). The recent invasion of Kuwait by Sadam
Hussein, after it had already been coerced into cutting back its oil
output in order to try to keep prices up, is evidence enough that there
are, and will continue to be, instances of the older power game of
international relations hitting the headlines.

Many states, however, now appear to regard security more broadly,
as meaning more than defending territory against invasion. Wealth,
too is needed for political stability; and wealth can demonstrably be
achieved by success in the new contest for world market shares. A
helpful analogy might be to envisage governments as gardeners, each
with his patch of ground. The gardener's prime concern used to be the
fencing: to protect the plants, it had to be secure enough to keep
marauders out. Even today, fences are not totally obsolete; many
gardens still need them. But most gardeners now pay more attention
to husbandry, to improving the water supply, to enhancing the
fertility of the soil, and to keeping a proper balance of sun and shade
so that small plants grow bigger and established plants produce more

and better flowers and heavier crops. Forward-looking gardeners are now learning about becoming good husbandmen rather than effective fence-keepers.

The need for good husbandry has vividly been demonstrated by a recent report by the UNDP (1990). This developed a complex formula to measure 'human development', based on indices of life expectancy, literacy and wealth. For 130 countries, this indicator was matched against the real per capita GDP to produce the chart shown in figure 7.1. If one considers this relationship over time, one cannot escape the conclusion that human development *precedes* economic development. The problem is a shortage not just of capital resources but of human resources to make effective use of what capital is available.

More advanced developing countries need to extend the base of human resources to tertiary education if they are to compete in the increasingly knowledge-intensive industries. As we showed in chapter 6, exporting income-elastic products cannot be accomplished until countries close the skills gap that separates them from OECD countries. Malaysia's ability to start upgrading the technological content of the electronics output of the multinationals has been greatly enhanced by its supply of low-cost, but well trained engineers and technicians. As the salaries of such employees can amount to as much as 15 per cent of the firms' variable costs, such local supply can act powerfully to motivate investors to climb the technology ladder that rises from mere adoption of others' ideas to the creation of entirely new possibilities.

Partners of a kind

The third of our premises is that politicians are already acutely aware of the high stakes for which the game is being played. By wooing multinationals into their territory, they are learning that the firms demand more than simple accommodation within the existing policy framework: that framework often needs major adjustment if the benefits of the investments are fully to be captured. This premise challenges the conventions of international relations. In most text-books, discussion of the multinationals comes as an afterthought at the end. They are described as 'non-state actors' in a secondary category behind states as the main players.

All our evidence shows clearly that the multinationals are not secondary at all. They are increasingly indispensable allies, whether liked or not. They too are competing for world market shares as a means to wealth and survival. But whereas the state needs the

211

production for the world market to be located on its territory, no matter who is organising it, the firm needs the production for the world market to be under its ultimate control no matter where it is located – and in many cases, no matter who possesses title to ownership.[3]

These are conditions that lead to both co-operation and conflict. There is a complementarity of interest when the state can secure the location and the firm can establish the control. There is conflict when the firm decides that it prefers another location (and can overcome the exit barriers) or when the state seeks to restrict how the firm exercises its control.

The qualities and assets needed to succeed in the new competition among states differ from what it was assumed, until recently, they were. In the traditional International Relations conception, it was the foreign policy of the state, and its defence policy, that was crucial for survival and success. Belgium failed and was occupied in 1940 at least partly because, clinging to neutrality, it had refused to join France in extending the Maginot Line to the coast. Sweden succeeded in surviving the same war at least partly by being 'neutral' in favour of Germany at the start and 'neutral' in favour of the Allies after Stalingrad. And so one could go on, drawing on the interpretation of the past experience of states by historians and scholars in international relations. Nowadays, however, traditionally defined foreign policy is relatively less important. Ministries of Finance, Trade or Economic Development offer more interesting and ultimately more rewarding careers. These and related ministries are where decisions will be taken about making the country a more or a less attractive location for multinationals and where new alliances will be fashioned between the state as host and the multinational as a welcome, though perhaps temporary, guest.

The multinationals' growing role in shaping internal policy has become a central issue in understanding the dynamics of the inter-actions between states and firms. As investment has matched or overtaken trade as the driving force in international economic relations, so the nature of the external policies and the appropriate weapons to be used by states have changed. Much of the recent analysis in International Relations and in its growing use of game theory has, as discussed in chapters 2 and 4, depicted the bargaining as inherently adversarial. In the interests of both sides, it is equally important to stress the co-operative aspects of the relationship as the conflictual ones. The evidence from our three countries suggests strongly that policymakers have often made concessions, adjusting to the needs of the foreign investors, even when there have been political costs.

Such conditions make it increasingly difficult for states explicitly to manage all the interrelationships among general policies as they apply to the specifics for building new sources of wealth-creating assets. Rather than attempt to forecast the outcomes when forming policy, some states are now turning to the possibility of ensuring progress by choosing partners that are capable of providing a stream of future benefits. In other words, forming alliances with particular firms is one way of dealing with the problem of enforcing the side payments. It is the choice of partner that can prove decisive.

The importance of choosing the 'right' partner is indeed one of the lessons of international history. The choice may be as crucial to survival as skill in bargaining. History is littered with examples of foreign policy-makers who made choices of other states as partners that proved unreliable, or who bargained too hard and lost a potential partner. Poland in 1939 refused to give the French and British bases in Poland and turned to the Soviet Union for a non-aggression pact. In the 1960s, Tanzania chose the People's Republic of China; South Yemen chose the Soviet Union. The same issues affect the choice of corporate partner, though here the choice is more complex.

A central question is whether the firm that is permitted to invest in the country really will deliver the future benefits promised and prove capable of enhancing its own competitiveness worldwide to ensure survival. Related to this question is the problem that stronger, established firms may be less accommodating to host country demands for adaptation in accordance with local policy than the newcomers we described in chapter 5.

Until recently, perhaps impressed by the size of the multinational, few officials asked questions or even considered the relative strength of the investor in its international industry. Yet, as we showed earlier, the experience of Brazil and the UK with Chrysler was unfortunate; Chrysler's international weakness meant that it could never honour its promises. The same story has been repeated in the many cases where yesterday's leaders have failed to keep up with emerging global competition. Such problems can be disguised when attention is caught, as it was in Malaysia, by general enthusiasm for imitating the 'Japanese model'. State support for key industries has been given to joint ventures with Japanese investors. Lacking any rigorous examination of the individual investors, some joint ventures in steel and cement have suffered from serious technical and financial problems (Bowie, 1988). One implication is that much greater care and attention should be paid to examining the specific strengths of the prospective investor, and that greater preference should be accorded to the strong, even if that means lesser short-term accommodation to local demands. Another is that wholesale importation of ideas from abroad seldom, if ever, works unless it is tied quite explicitly to local capabilities for future adaptation and enhancement.

There can be no general 'rules' for making these judgments. There are simply too many variables to be handled. For instance, there is the question of whether preference should be given to new entrants from other developing countries. They may have technologies and product ranges more suitable to local conditions. But there is considerable evidence that their operating practices are no more accommodating to local needs than those of others. To deal with such issues, developing countries need to build much better intelligence systems that are capable of evaluating the project and the investor in the international context. The resources and skills required for this task are formidable; an issue to which we return later.

The partnership implied by such deliberate choices is not necessarily permanent. On the contrary, it may be even less durable than most of the old-type alliances between states in the international political system. And, as in inter-state alliances, the relationship will be one of conflict at the same time as it is one of co-operation. Allies have always quarrelled over who was to do what; over the circumstances in which the mutual commitment was binding; over who was to pay the bills; over what weapons system was preferred and who was to 'press the button'. It takes only a little imagination to see what benefit the managers of large global companies might derive from a bedtime reading of international history from Thucydides to Giuccardini or more recently, of Liddell Hart and Michael Howard, not to mention the perhaps more familiar Machiavelli.

So who has gained power?

Before we go on to offer some advice to either side in these partnerships, we cannot pass over this crucial question. For a partnership between equals in power is obviously very different from a partnership of unequals. And the outcome of bargaining in the real world – as distinct from bargaining in game theory models – depends on who holds the whip hand, on who has the balance of bargaining power. We cannot dodge the question, how has the intensified competition between states and between firms for world market shares affected the balance of bargaining power between states *as a group* and multinationals *as a group*? Are governments now less able to influence outcomes including their own economic growth and development, while firms have more influence? Is that why, in the 1990s, 'Welcome' is written on the mat in so many more developing countries than it was in 1975? Not because of any great love that developing country governments have for the foreign firm, but because they fear their growing power to help or hinder national economic development?

Our conclusion is that governments *as a group* have indeed lost bargaining power to the multinationals as the possibilities for collective action have diminished. Intensifying competition among states seems to have been a more important force for weakening their bargaining power than have the changes in global competition among firms. This is not to deny that governments can maintain considerable power in their dealings with any one foreign firm. The reasons lie in the nature of the competition for world market shares.

That competition is of two kinds. One is for access to the factors of production: whoever commands the critical factors has advantage for import-substituting investment. The other is for command of the profits and rents to be derived from selling the product or service on the world market. Command over *both* factors is a necessary condition for participation in export-led competition.

It seems to us that the changes in the production structure described in chapters 2 and 3 have altered the relative importance of those factors over which states had most control, as compared with those over which firms had most control. States control access to land and to labour living on that land. Firms control capital and technology, or at least have better access to both. They can raise both debt and equity capital on international markets, whereas through most of the 1980s governments had severely limited access to capital. Firms' control of technology has increased as the accelerated pace of technological change has reduced the power of the patent system. Despite, or perhaps because of, the TRIPs debates, many firms increasingly rely on unpatented 'know-how'. Moreover, as we showed in chapter 5, many are also reluctant to issue licences in key territories for fear of creating new competition.

Given that the relative importance of labour and the raw materials derived from land has fallen dramatically in determining competitiveness, while that of capital and technology has risen, does it follow that firms *as a group* have increased their bargaining power over the factors of production? Here the argument becomes complex, for the power of the individual firm may be regarded as having also fallen as

215

competition has intensified. New entrants have altered the rules and offer governments new bargaining advantage.

One needs to separate the power to influence general policy from the power to insist on specific bargains. Multinationals can act collectively to exercise considerable influence over government choices. The role of big business in spurring Brussels towards the 1992 objective by pointing out the costs of 'non-Europe' is one example. Through such representative bodies as the International Chamber of Commerce, firms also play a central role in shaping international standards on a wide range of issues, from bilateral tax treaties to environmental standards. Equally important in many sectors is the control developed by firms in some sectors over transnational advertising and marketing networks. Or, in other sectors, the global networks of communications and access to data which, with the aid of new technologies, have made them independent of governments while linking up their own managers scattered across the globe.[4]

Another variable factor in the power relationship that has impressed us is the time factor. Often we see a state constrained by social or political factors it cannot ignore to slow the pace of adjustment. A government may be convinced for instance that its autonomy requires public ownership of natural resources. Yet state-ownership may make it more difficult to market the country's oil or copper or bauxite on the world market than if it were privately owned by a transnational corporation with its own internalised access to foreign markets. Similarly, a state monopoly of power-generation may over-invest in new capacity, or be inefficiently managed, so that energy costs for users are raised above that of their competitors. In labour relations, the welfare concerns of government may give rise to policies that protect workers against summary dismissal. But when policy is directed to winning world market shares, manufacturers, whether national or foreign, may need to have more flexibility in employing labour, increasing output to take advantage of rising demand or cutting back when orders slacken.

Quite clearly these dilemmas cannot be resolved in one giant leap forward: they can only be resolved over time. Indeed, we have shown repeatedly that change in one agenda without change in others is ineffective and that simultaneous change on all agendas is beyond the capacity of either a firm or a state to manage properly. As Kant wrote long ago when glorying in the pluralism and variety of civilisation, 'out of timber so crooked as that from which man is made, nothing entirely straight can be carved' (quoted in Berlin, 1990). The path of progress much be recognised as a historical process, where prescriptions for change are in keeping with the stage that the society has reached in that process (Galbraith, 1983).

In Malaysia and Kenya, the ruling elite has clear political reasons for their policies of ethnic discrimination. When dealing with import substitution, such policies may actually be mutually reinforcing, since intervention to improve the living standards of bumiputras will tend to raise demand for home-produced goods and services. It is when the state decides to direct policy to increasing production of manufactures for export that the conflict emerges: the preferred ethnic group – the bumiputras in Malaysia – may not be as good as other groups at discovering and exploiting the capital and technology necessary for exporting. Similarly, in Brazil, the rapid growth of the late 1960s and early 1970s was socially divisive and not sustainable. Yet, it was not until the mid-1980s that President Sarney declared that social concerns were on the national agenda. By then the delays had proved so costly that Brazil is still trying to find ways of resolving the dilemmas in its national agenda.

Policies of import-substitution combined with central, authoritarian power focused attention on what went on inside the garden fence, to return to the earlier analogy. A politically 'strong' state could push through its policies against opposition, and ensure that its decisions were carried out by government agencies and state-owned enterprises. Thus, many theorists have supposed that strong states were inherently better able to compete than politically weaker, more democratically responsive ones. But if the strong state now has to resolve the new dilemmas that come with an export-orientation, its political power does not necessarily give it the same advantage. In fact, rather the reverse, for all the corporatist devices by which strong states reinforced their authority are apt to become hindrances. They make it more difficult to achieve the flexibility required to fashion appropriate policies for different sectors of the economy. For export-orientation, 'soft' controls are usually more effective than edicts and bans: building trust within the society and with foreign firms gets better results than political muscle-flexing. In short, the strong state is less effective in international competition than the *shrewd* state; it is good judgment and a clear vision of priorities that counts.

It is to those priorities, the do's and don'ts suggested by our research, that we now turn, first for governments then for firms. Both have much to learn about managing more effectively the complexities of the markets in the 1990s. For governments, we are not presuming to advise on the whole range of economic policy-making: there are too many geopolitical, social and cultural variables involved. Our concern is only with how best to deal with foreign-owned or controlled firms, in order that they should become effective allies in the competition with other states. We assume that governments want – as almost all now say they do – to attract foreign investors. How best should they go about it?

ADVICE TO GOVERNMENTS

1   *Go for growth* – but *sustainable* growth. This means avoiding a dash for growth based on excessive borrowing, landing the economy in a debt trap. It also means avoiding growth that only worsens social divisions, undermining the cohesion of civil society, or that destroys and poisons the natural environment for future generations. That is the clear message from the 1980s. Yet governments must go for growth, making clear their determination to change old ways, to overcome obstacles and set the economy firmly on an upward path with clear longterm goals in view. The evidence from the 1980s also shows that sustainable growth can be and has been achieved by even poor countries. Those that achieved annual real growth rates above 4 per cent have maintained a balance among the needs for economic discipline and control of inflation, for outward-looking policies and attention to building internal capabilities. The notion that economic discipline and growth are mutually exclusive is as demonstrably false as is the notion that heavy investments in building internal resources and social consensus impedes growth. Yet, there are serious questions about how to establish such a balance for states that have been protected and are now trying to face outwards. Some countries in dire straits may have no option but to do as they are told by the IMF and the World Bank, even though their advice sometimes overemphasises the value of fiscal constraint. But others will be aware that both institutions have different, system-preserving priorities and can beg to differ, noting that the multinationals are less likely to be put off by a degree of inflation than by the signs of economic stagnation. The success of Poland in 1989/90 in making a dash for economic freedom, abolishing controls and floating the zloty, despite high inflation, was more encouragement to foreign, especially German, firms than the more cautious policies of the Czechoslovac government.

2   *Concentrate on essentials* that define the priorities for accumulating future resources. These clearly include attention to health, education, building an efficient infrastructure, legal and bureaucratic reform and the elimination of personal patronage and corruption.

These priorities are not easy to manage; they all incur short-term

218

risks. With education, for example, new dilemmas arise when resources are devoted to education in order to raise the standard of the local workforce as a means of attracting potential foreign employers. Every firm, every observer of development, knows the importance of upgrading the education system and training a skilled workforce. But educated workers will be more aware than unskilled workers of job opportunities elsewhere, and better able to move away, or to stay away if they have been helped to go abroad to study. The Malaysian government for example has trained Malaysian Chinese engineers, but has lost many of them to Singapore where there is no pro-bumiputra discrimination within firms. One of the striking features of the global competition for factors of production, indeed, is the rising numbers of third world workers in industrialised countries: Turks and Tamils in Norway; Filipinos in Japan and Taiwan; Moroccans and Algerians in France; Tunisians and Senegalese in Italy; Mexicans and other Hispanics in the USA. The growing mobility of labour despite the most strenuous efforts of immigration officials to stop them is a matter of concern to their home states as well as to their (often unwelcoming) hosts. There is also the risk that political opposition will grow in the new universities to threaten the political stability that foreign investors prefer. But neither that risk, nor the risk of losing trained people, is as great as the risk of being overtaken by other countries – Taiwan or Singapore for example – where education has been a long-term priority.

3   *Enforce competition* among manufacturers and producers of services, whether local or foreign. Authorised feather-bedding has been demonstrably ineffective. A foreign monopolist is as bad as a local one. If there are no local firms able to compete, don't let the foreign firm have a monopoly. Or if there is more than one foreign firm, make sure they do not get together among themselves to share the market, keep up prices and operate a covert cartel. If you have to depend on one firm, the state should require the maintenance of international standards and should regularly monitor performance.

This approach can create a policy dilemma for smaller countries in that many multinationals will only invest if offered a field clear of competition. Or, they will threaten to leave if the government allows in a competitive product, whether imported or locally made. In a country with severe economic problems like Egypt, for example, foreign firms have gone to the extreme of demanding *new* protection – against allegedly dumped Japanese imports – as the price of staying in the country. Without good international intelligence, how is the government to know whether the assertion that

219

otherwise their local operations would be unprofitable to them is true or not?

Another obstacle to promoting competitiveness is shown by the weaknesses of the Brazilian government engendered by the political influence of the big sectoral business associations in which foreign owned firms have been allied with strong domestic interests. In Malaysia, the problem has been of foreign firms 'crowding-out' local competitors. The answer is not to exclude the competition but to find some means of giving help – but only temporarily – to the locals.

4   *Give up national champions.* At first sight, this piece of advice will seem to fly in the face of the aspirations of those states seeking 'independent exporting' as the source of future development possibility. The issue, however, is not so much to do with aspirations for independence, but with the feasibility of realising it through the mechanism of a favoured and protected national entity. The dismal record of the state-owned enterprises, described in chapter 4, is testimony to the paucity of the gains governments have reaped from their distortions of competition.

Within Europe, where national champions have been nurtured both with and without state ownership, the record has been equally poor (see, for example, Sharp and Holmes, 1989: chapter 8). Consider the British computer champion, ICL. The Japanese firm, Fujitsu, eventually bought 80 per cent of ICL in mid-1990 amidst a furore about Britain once again selling off its 'family silver'. Yet the facts were that, though profitable, ICL was dependent upon Fujitsu's chip technology and could not hope to survive independently. Many plans were canvassed to create a European solution, but all these failed because possible partners were unwilling to cede their own control into a consortium with others of similar skills and resources. Whether the UK has benefited from according ICL a long-standing status as the preferred supplier to government can be answered in part by the fact that ICL's local content was lower than IBM's alternative supplies. IBM's investments in the UK had made it a more local 'presence' than the national champion.

If the European experience shows that reliance on national champions is apt to be both too costly and too risky, developing countries face even greater risks and costs. Their indigenous firms have further ground to cover before they can catch up with the leaders. In Japan and South Korea, where national firms have been more successful than in Europe, strong protection was needed for at least one or two decades. But neither country protected a single 'national champion'. Both were careful to preserve a strong sense of internal competition as one of the primary forces conditioning how the competitiveness of each enterprise developed. The successes of champions like Embraer in Brazil are likely to remain the exceptions to the rule.

5   *Liberalise in stages.* The risks of trying to do everything at once are clear. Attention should be paid to the *sequencing* of reforms.[5] There is growing awareness that the external challenges for all developing countries have added such complexity that forecasting short-term outcomes from the reforms is virtually impossible. The risks can, however, be limited by allowing time to gain experience of the new-found capabilities. All the available evidence suggests that the transition from protectionism to international competitiveness is more difficult and takes longer than economists typically believe. Opposition from entrenched elites can only be eroded slowly; it cannot be eliminated by administrative *fiat.*

A related issue is the management of demands for some form of NFI to replace traditional equity investments. The evidence we showed in chapter 5 has strong implications for how governments calculate the expected benefits. All too often, these prove to be illusory, because of a failure properly to anticipate the full set of consequences. Considerable learning over time is needed before officials can avoid the more obvious pitfalls.

6   *Use both sticks and carrots.* Governments deploy a large armoury of controls to try and get the best out of foreign firms and a large store of incentives to offer them as inducements. The choice is bewildering. The sticks of such performance requirements as TRIPs and TRIMs are best used sparingly and selectively, for they can be counterproductive. Carrots too should be sparingly dispensed. Firms will never refuse tax holidays, cheap subsidised credit and other kinds of incentives to come into a country. But all recent research suggests that they are seldom swayed, one way or another, by such carrots. By failing to understand fully how firms behave, many developing countries give them away quite unnecessarily. It is the long-term prospect that counts.

7   *Modernise the administration.* Officials of many developing countries do not realise the very real costs that bureaucratic delays and uncertainties create for managers. To them, time is no object and, as explained in chapter 6, the claims of family relationships can take precedence over the efficient despatch of business. Thus, an official may not realise the costs *to the country* of spending two weeks processing a bundle of trivial licensing applications, thus holding up more important applications. Family connections also make it difficult for local politicians to enforce bureaucratic reform.

221

Instead of expensive feasibility studies by visiting experts sent by international agencies, the employment of administrative mercenaries – Swiss, perhaps – on a long-term basis might be more cost-effective. Appropriate monitoring of existing investments is necessary, for many firms will, given half a chance, find the temptation to bend the local rules irresistible. Equally, training officials in the analytical techniques would reduce the problems we noted in chapter 6 about misunderstanding how social and economic returns differ and where the priority issues and risks lie in any project.

Training them abroad would pay dividends in the long run. It is false economy to insist – as some developing countries do – that local managers and skilled workers must be trained *in situ* rather than spend foreign exchange on their education. There seems little doubt that Indonesia's recent progress owes much to the fact that President Suharto has insisted that his top officials all received extensive training abroad and could consequently command a world view of priorities. More generally, an international perspective shared among many officials would help to reduce the wide divergence of views held in different ministries and the consequent inconsistencies of policy and implementation. Only by sustained investments in such education can the needed learning begin to permeate the administrative structure.

8   *Set clear rules* is a corollary of the advice above. The less adminis-trative *discretion* the better, both for firms and for development prospects. In many developing countries, legal systems are anti-quated, contradictory and impenetrably obscure. Firms need to know the extent of their legal obligations and of their legal rights. Although it is reasonable for a government to reserve the right to change the rules, the changes should be consistent, pointed in the same direction, and transparently clear. Arbitrary decisions provide one of the biggest disincentives to investors.

Small, poor states may find this advice especially difficult to accept. They may feel it imperative to continue to intervene, even if it is to start the process of reform. They should, however, recognise the costs of prolonged intervention and lay the ground work for later change as early as possible. A major dilemma for them is that they are 'marginal' to most multinationals' interests (in the sense described in chapter 5) and can find that persistent intervention can serve to discourage new entrants and established players alike. Similarly, states that begin to achieve high rates of growth may be tempted, as Grosse (1989: p. 251) noted, to intervene more on the grounds that their bargaining advan-tage had increased. Such thinking is, in our view, a dangerous, though perhaps outdated, illusion: the data explored in chapter 4 show how strongly the tide of liberalisation is running in both high- and low-growth countries.

9 *Watch the competition.* Do what firms have always done – watch what the competitors are up to, and learn from their successes and failures. Some governments have plainly been stimulated to act by the example of other states. One such instance was when Tunisia emulated the King of Morocco in ending delays in dealing with licensing applications from foreign investors. A royal decree in 1989 allowed any firm that had heard nothing from the bureaucracy within two months to assume that its licence was granted. In the same year, Tunisia followed suit by reinterpreting the provisions of an existing law. Another was Malaysia copying the example of Singapore in privatisation and in moving to build Kuala Lumpur as a financial market and banking centre. But, just as in corporate competition, mere imitation is not sufficient; distinctive local advantages must also be created.

Watching the competition between firms in world markets may be important too. When military power was the key to survival, states spent – some still do – large amounts on gathering information – intelligence – about enemies or rivals. Today, attention paid to monitoring the costs and benefits, the risks and opportunities of different policies, and of particular deals with foreign firms in specific sectors is equally in the national interest. The difficulties arising from a switch to export-oriented development are compounded by greatly increased uncertainty and a dearth of information on which governments can make considered judgments. Added to the uncertainties about how international markets will evolve, which partners to choose and which markets to attack are uncertainties about how firms will react to evolving government policies. It will pay to devote more resources to finding out. In addition, officials can benefit from engaging the firms in dialogue to help build the basis of confidence and lasting trust.

ADVICE TO MULTINATIONALS

Our advice to the multinationals is largely the mirror image of what we say to governments. It is similarly limited, in the sense that we do not attempt to cover all the complexities of global strategy. Instead, our focus is on firms' behaviour as it applies in developing countries. We are conscious that many leading multinationals are already well versed in what we have to say. Yet we have found that practice, especially among the new entrants, often falls short of the standards of behaviour we imply.

1 *Watch global trends.* In almost every sector of international business, managers today must take a world view, carefully watching structural change in politics and security matters, in finance and in the climate of ideas no less than the details of their own business. Many could make better use of corporate research departments, making them collect and interpret statistical and other information as new trends affect the firm. Some firms would be well advised to ensure that their managers, scattered around the world, meet or at least communicate regularly to pool their information. How change is perceived depends largely on where one sits in the organisation. As illustrated in chapter 5, managers at headquarters in even experienced multinationals can formulate policy more out of ignorance than knowledge of new conditions or new opportunities. A common base of knowledge and understanding is imperative if the decentralised organisation is to act in a co-ordinated and consistent way over the long haul.

2 *Recognise the political role* that firms increasingly have with their host governments. World-class firms almost need a kind of foreign ministry and a cadre of corporate diplomats that combine local expertise and broad experience of dealing with governments in other countries. If firms only rotate managers among their foreign subsidiaries on a two-year cycle, they will tend to lack local *savoir-faire*. Most of the experienced investors to whom we talked in Brazil had established central departments for managing political and administrative relationships with governments and its labyrinth of agencies. Staffed largely by locals, these departments provided the political expertise and knowledge that could be tapped by the decentralised divisions. In business, as in diplomacy, personal rapport and intimate knowledge of the 'corridors of power' helps to build trust and a lasting relationship.

Like good diplomats, managers must be able to work positively with local politicians and officials and understand how their kinds work and whence they derive their power. Nor dare they neglect the political opposition. Only in this way can the firm realise the ambition of most managers to be truly agents of development and progress. Like their opposite numbers in government, managers must have the perspective and tolerance needed to search continuously for areas of common ground and mutual interest and not to retreat to assumptions of an adversarial relationship.

As 'diplomats', managers must be on their guard against, perhaps unwittingly, falling into the trap of conspiring to exploit local corrup-

224

tion or behave in other ways that are not acceptable. This is only good business sense; sooner or later the failure to recognise the firm's lasting political role will catch up with the firm as administrations change, as many have found to their cost.

3   *Look for sustainable growth* when choosing where the firm should expand its operations. Managers must be able to look through the short-term economic numbers to relate them to the social and political conditions of the country. Failure to analyse the local investment 'climate' in broad terms can prove expensive, as we have illustrated. Lacking good understanding of how a state may wish to shift its 'development intent', firms will remain blind to the new risks created as negotiating priority slips from one cell to another in our matrix of agendas. Moreover, dealing with events *ad hoc* as they occur often means that policy is inconsistent and the long-term strategic objectives for the firm forgotten.

A corollary of the above is that managers need to set themselves an agenda for assisting the states where they invest. If the growth is truly to become sustainable, then firms must become part of the process of accumulating the necessary local resources. Just as we argued earlier for environmental issues, it is the firms that possess many of the crucial resources that need to be deployed if the constraints to growth are to be harnessed.

4   *Good citizenship* becomes critical for profitable survival in each territory. Not only must managers be culturally aware and able to deal with local issues effectively, they must also avoid tying their futures to a single elite group. Given the dynamics of change, it is vital that firms cultivate many local allies, not front stooges or oligopoly cronies, but among social groups like unions, farmers' co-operatives, women, environmentalists. Such behaviour should not be restricted to a few favoured territories, but should become a matter of standard practice. As IBM's president said recently, 'IBM cannot be a net exporter from every nation in which it does business; we have to be a good citizen everywhere' (quoted by Reich, 1990: p. 58). We heard many similar statements from experienced multinationals that had learned the hard way.

To be turned into the social legitimacy now demanded in many countries, good citizenship must be seen as involving more than building up contacts in the local society; it means taking actions that help fuel development in the ways we described in chapter 6. It also means disclosing more than profits and losses in their annual reports. These should report contributions to local social and economic goals, while signalling to government at least their broad future strategies.

225

Of course, there are limits to such policies. Firms must always reserve the right to move elsewhere if circumstances so dictate. There is thus inherent tension in the relationship. Like ambassadors, local managers must on occasion dissemble so as to protect the firm's options. Both sides need to recognise that reality. Yet, both also should recognise that some multinationals have a superb record of 'transparency' in their dealings with states and delivering on their promises. Such firms provide role models for others to emulate.

5 *Train up the locals* – both in the workforce and in the managerial cadre. Because change is such a fundamental factor in contemporary management, building greater capability in ways that permit greater future adaptation in the subsidiaries has become an imperative. In addition to providing training of all kinds, the firms need to ensure that local employees fully understand the global strategy and the purposes of the local investments. What has already become a cliché – 'think globally: act locally' – remains an imperative if firms are to weather the storms of future change. This is merely putting into practice the long-term perspective we advocated and defined in chapter 5.

6 *Capitalise on local inefficiencies* may seem at first sight to be strange advice, but it means that managers should seek advantage from helping to remove inefficiencies rather than regard them as immutable constraints. For example, where many firms have resisted regulations for increasing the local content of their operations, others have found innovative and profitable ways of complying with and even exceeding the regulations (UNIDO, 1986). This attitude can become a powerful tool for harnessing the energy and enthusiasm of local employees, by giving them a purpose that transcends the guilt many feel when working in privileged circumstances for a foreigner.

Many of the attitudes and practices we espouse can only be sustained within the firm by changes in conventional management. Traditional notions of a command hierarchy need to give way to an organisation where 'soft' controls and mutual learning up and down the chain of command become a source of continuing vitality. All our evidence convinces us that building a stronger sense of partnership between headquarters and its foreign operations must *precede* the building of partnership with local governments. This is a large topic in its own right and one that deserves separate treatment. Our purpose is not to spell out all the conditions and managerial difficulties, but rather to point to the fact that those firms most vociferous in calling for greater 'responsibility' and 'consistency' in government are often those least able to practice what they preach. Lasting partnership demands that both parties develop their internal capabilities of patience, learning and persistence as preconditions for managing the crooked path of progress in the future.

CONTINUING THE INQUIRY

We have only scratched the surface of what might be called the micro-political economy of government–enterprise relations. We never did manage to collect as many micro-case studies of bargaining at the grassroots, plant or enterprise level as we had hoped for and would have liked. In many cases, the individuals most directly concerned had moved on and their successors were unable to give us more than generalised accounts of what had really happened and why. Government records were also incomplete for our purposes, requiring in some cases extensive but inconclusive detective work. But we found enough to realise what a rich seam of gold was there for the mining, and to appreciate the value of the nuggets accumulated by others we have cited. What we have written will, we hope, spur others to improve on our start. We learned from our labours that the perspective of a single discipline is inadequate to comprehend what is happening in the changing world. We therefore believe that there is urgency for broadening the base of the thinking of students of international economics and political economy.

There are two sets of reasons for this belief. One concerns the liberating effect that attention to the reality of contemporary government–firm relations can have on our fellow social scientists – liberating because it can free them from some of the constricting, but increasingly obsolescent, concepts on which much current theory is founded. The other concerns two major areas which we find have been illuminated by this micro-political economy, but which call loudly for more systematic exploration and investigation.

The two constricting concepts most called into question by our evidence are Class and Dependency. There are plenty of others but for present purposes these are the most significant. The concept of Class dominates much of sociology and some political science, especially comparative political science. The basic assumptions are that indus-trialisation/capitalism creates two main classes – capitalists and their employees – and that there is inherent conflict between them, which is apt to be reflected in political associations and policy decisions. Capitalists are characterised by their ownership and control of the means of production, and by the form of their reward – profit. Employees – workers – are characterised by their limited control over

227

the sale – in marxist lingo, the 'commodification' – of their own labour, and by the form of their reward for it: wages. These characterisations imply the inevitability of conflict between the classes and the probability that members of each class will share common interests.

These assumptions are seriously challenged by the internationalisation of production, and the consequent competition among 'capitals' – to use once more the marxist phraseology – for world market shares. They are challenged more seriously still by the conflicting interests among employees. For example, there is inherent conflict over job opportunities and relative wage scales, and over job security and welfare benefits between the Brazilian employees of General Motors or Volkswagen and their employees in Detroit or Wolfsburg. As change in the production structure of the world system demotes labour as a quantitatively insignificant input and promotes capital (in the form of money, technology and human skills), it becomes increasingly unclear as to whether there is such a thing as a class war, or who is on whose side in it – and indeed whether there are any firm rules about the coincidence of interest between elements of government, elements of business and any specific social or economic grouping (Weiss, 1988). The affiliations of individual people on the basis of interest have become much too complex to fit into this antique procrustean bed.

The other antique bed we consider due for the junkyard is the concept of Dependency. It always was rather shaky and is now showing signs of imminent collapse. Perhaps it never was a genuine antique anyway; only a poor modern reproduction of older models that distinguished Christian from heretic, civilized from savage, mandatory states from the peoples judged by the victorious allies in both world wars to be 'not yet ready for independence'. At any rate, the underlying assumptions were that developing countries were poor because of their common dependence on industrialised countries both to buy their primary products and to sell them manufactured goods and services. Now it has been shown that there is nothing inherent in the system that makes it impossible to escape the role of primary producer. Moreover, the structural changes we described in chapter 2 make it impossible for *any* national economy to stay outside the world market economy and thus avoid being dependent on it both as buyer and seller (the concept of Dependency as a predestined quality pertaining to all developing countries). Moreover, Dependency, as a quality exclusive to them, no longer carries conviction. The rise of government measures in the 1980s to attract foreign firms to come to them and not to the neighbours suggests that there is little left of South–South solidarity, as proclaimed in the 1970s.

With the development of trade blocs in the North and the growing divergence of trade interests in the South – the world of *sauve qu peut* we described earlier – one has to question whether the rhetoric of the North–South dialogue has any meaning any longer. The divergence we have repeatedly noted pulls developing countries further apart. Where Mexico may want to join the US–Canada free-trade area, Brazil may want other forms of alliance. Where states that are relatively latecomers to exporting manufactured goods want liberal trade regimes, poor states in Africa may want special forms of assistance. Lacking solidarity in the South, global-level policy needs to recognise explicitly the plurality of states' interests.

This is not to say that there is no asymmetry in dependency – of course there is. But it is not the simple asymmetry between the OECD countries and the Group of 77 developing countries supposed by the UNCTAD rhetoric of the 1970s. According to that interpretation of dependency, the OECD governments determined the rules and set up the international regime, whether for shipping or air transport, for example, and the latecoming developing country governments have had no choice but to accept it. But there is also another more complex kind of dependency. Both developed and developing country governments may have their choices constrained by the decisions of the dominant firms in a particular sector of world business. In oil, in advertising, in banking and in some sectors of manufacturing, the major firms, though based in the rich countries, will decide to locate production, to decentralise research away from home, and will design products and choose between alternative technologies independently of both rich and poor governments. The dependency on firms therefore is one shared by the governments of developed and developing countries alike.

Asymmetry of risks

There are two dark (or at least partly shadowed) areas of enquiry in which some significant beginnings have been already made, but which call for much more investigative and/or analytical light to be shed upon them if the field of international political economy is to be developed to the full. In each of them we find writers from a variety of disparate disciplines – economists, political scientists and specialists in management – groping sometimes in clear patches, sometimes totally in the dark, for some epistemological *terra firma* on which to build new theory. Their efforts suggest that the shadowed areas are probably those where, in future, most innovative and interesting work will be done.

The first concerns the nature of the foreigners' involvement in a national economy. This subject is worthy of attention, most emphatically *not* because this is a measure of dependency. We have already argued that this is a red herring. Rather, such involvement can be seen as an indicator of success for the host country, just as much as a full order book is an indicator of a successful business or a multitude of invitations is an indicator of social acceptance. But our research suggests that there are many different forms of foreign involvement so that it will be important to government policymakers to know more about the pros and cons of all these forms than they do at present. For social scientists it is also important because it appears to be the source of certain major changes in the working of the world economy.

This much is evident from the work that has already been done (Oman, 1984, 1989; Julius, 1990). That work has established, first, that this is an area of great ignorance on which existing statistical data shed little light.[6] Secondly, that FDI or NFI involvement, however measured, is growing very fast. And thirdly, that its growth throws serious doubt on conventional theories on international trade, international exchange rates between currencies, and on the practicality of international policy coordination (Julius, 1990: pp. 71–92).

The measurement problem seems more or less insoluble. In the first place, who is to say what is a foreign-owned firm? In 1982, the OECD agreed on a rule-of-thumb that if 10 per cent of the voting stock of a firm was owned by a foreign enterprise, it was a foreign-owned firm. But this was simply in order to have a standard definition for the collection of data. Most multinationals prefer a majority equity interest. But in a growing number of sectors, where franchising is customary (hotels, food and drink, retailing), the foreign firm may have control without owning any shares at all. The IMF – again for its own statistical purposes – insists that foreign involvement be limited to cases where the 'owner' has a 'lasting interest' in the enterprise. But very large involvements in foreign countries – for example, by construction companies directing a turnkey or a build-operate-transfer (BOT) operation – cannot be said to have a lasting interest. As Oman has explained (1984: p. 23), there are plenty of instances where what looks like a sale is really an investment, the test being whether the seller continues to derive profit – in the shape of licensing fees, royalties or buy back output – from the machinery, plant, or know-how sold to the foreign buyer.

While, therefore, we know that the rate of increase of foreign direct investment as conventionally defined – which is clearly just the tip of the iceberg – has gone up rapidly, we have no comparably precise knowledge of the rate of increase of NFI, nor of its significance in different sectors of the economy. From the circumstantial evidence of reports in the financial press, we can only guess that it has been at least as great and has contributed quite substantially to the overtaking of the total value of international trade by the total (estimated) value of international production noted in chapter 2. Thus, in view of the difficulties both of collection and definition – we will probably never know the precise extent of the involvement of foreign-owned firms in any particular country, developing or developed.

The material that could be collected, therefore, and which would be of interest both to governments and to firms, is disaggregated information concerning such involvement in a variety of specific sectors of the national economy of one or of a group of countries. We have repeatedly made the point that the experience of developing countries has been highly divergent and so has the experience of multinationals in different sectors. It would help both sides if there were more studies done of the almost infinite variety of negotiated arrangements set up in particular kinds of business in developing countries. If success in the competitive game depends so much on watching what the competitors are up to, there will be no lack of interest in such research.

One change on which it could throw useful light is in the incidence and distribution of risk in international production. For when a firm embarks on a direct investment abroad it risks its capital – and/or that of its financial creditors. They may lose if the venture fails or if a devaluation depreciates the value of the profit in terms of the home currency in which the corporate balance sheet is calculated. But when a firm makes a franchise arrangement with a foreign partner, the risk of loss through failure or devaluation is much less. It is transferred in the first place to the franchisee who raises capital to build the hotel or equip the industrial plant in return for the opportunity to gain access to the foreign firm's technology, its brand name and thus its better market access. While the balance of cost and benefit can be estimated for the direct investment, it is much more difficult to do so for the NFI arrangement, simply because it is so hard to quantify the degree of risk or to evaluate the opportunity.

231

The nationality of the firm

This is the second important question for further research, more perhaps for the study of international relations than for international business. For the dominant realist paradigm in international relations theory assumes that the international system consists essentially of states as the dominant units; that we know what we mean by 'a state'; and that all states share 'functional sameness' – that is, they all perform the same functions with regard to society and economy (Waltz, 1979). Thus, when people refer to 'the United States' or 'Britain' or 'Japan', these words are a comprehensive short-hand meaning both government, territory, people and economic enterprises. The pluralist, or liberal, paradigm in international relations does not fundamentally challenge this characterisation of the international system. It merely adds that there are transnational actors like multinationals who play a part in the system, but do not fundamentally alter the state-based nature of authority in the international system. These are thus extras in the scenario, supercargo in the ship. They do not change the name of the game. It is tacitly assumed in both paradigms that US multinationals 'belong' to the United States. French ones to France and so on. If they are not actually an additional instrument of foreign policy, a 'tool of American imperialism', their fundamental association with the United States government is not seriously questioned.

By contrast, marxist, structural or radical paradigms – and, implicitly, much management literature – do however question the closeness of the association of state and enterprise. A common explanation sums it up by saying that the logic of accumulation is different for the nation, and for the firm. The nationalist logic of accumulation demands that value-adding operations be conducted and the profits retained, within the territory of the state. The global logic of accumulation demands that the firm manages and locates its value-adding operations wherever it decides this will maximise profit and minimise risk. It would therefore be illogical, according to this interpretation, to assume that the interest of the firm and the state – even its home state – will always and necessarily coincide. If they do, the theory would claim that it is merely coincidental.

A recent policy-oriented exposition of this logic by Robert Reich of the Harvard Business School has suggested that countries like the United States that ignore its practical implications do so at the risk of losing, instead of gaining, competitiveness to others (Reich, 1990: pp. 59, 64).

232

> Because the American-owned corporation is coming to have no
> special relationship with Americans, it makes no sense for Americans
> to entrust our national competitiveness to it. The interests of
> American-owned corporations may or may not coincide with those of
> the American people ... Corporations that invest in the United
> states, that build the value of the American work force, are more
> critical to our future standard of living than are American-owned
> corporations investing abroad.

But while Reich argues that Sony, Thomson, Philips and Honda
contribute more to the US than do IBM, Motorola, Whirlpool or
General Motors, popular – and indeed, political – opinion in the
United States and in other developed countries is not so sure.
Although governments have generally decided to take a more liberal
attitude to foreign firms, most of them still reserve the right to forbid
them to make some acquisitions. The German government refused
permission to Kuwaiti interest to buy Krupp; the British government
would not let a Hong Kong bank take over the Royal Bank of Scotland.
There was an outcry in the United States when Japanese interests
bought the freehold of the Rockefeller Center in New York.

Xenophobic emotion apart, there are two kinds of reasons for such
reactions. One is that the foreign interest will be less responsive to or
considerate of local social *mores* or national interests than a native
owner. This is patently weak in logic, precisely because the rights
which government keep in reserve inevitably put the foreign firm
more at risk of being thrown out than the local one, and therefore more
strongly motivated to avoid giving offence to local national susceptibi-
lities.

The second reason is more substantial. It is that, however great the
global reach of their operations, the national firm does, psychologically and sociologically, 'belong' to its home base. In the last resort, its
directors will always heed the wishes and commands of the government which has issued their passports and those of their families. A
recent study of the boards of directors of the top 1,000 US firms, for
example, shows that only 12 per cent included a non-American –
rather fewer, in fact, than in 1982 when there were 17 per cent
(*Economist*, August 11, 1990). The Japanese firm with even one token
foreign director would be hard to find. Even in Europe, with the
exception of bi-national firms like Unilever, you do not find the top
management reflecting by their nationality the geographical distribution of its operations.

It is precisely on this point concerning the relation of national
identity and corporate identity that conflict has arisen in international

relations concerning the management of international trade and investment. For there is a clear perception that this relation is closer in some states than in others, and that this affects the competition between states for market shares, both at home and abroad. It is felt in America that US firms, perhaps because they are 'older' multinationals, having anticipated the Japanese in moving production offshore, are somehow more truly 'multinational' than the Japanese – and suffer for it.[7]

This has led to confrontation between governments, especially those of the US and Japan. The Americans argue that if the competitive game between states is to be played fairly, with everyone observing the same rules of the game, then there should be a measure of symmetry in the relations of each home government towards its nationally-based firms. And there should be a measure of reciprocity in each government's treatment of foreign firms, whether banks, stockbrokers or manufacturers. 'If you won't let ours in, we won't let in yours!' has been said to the Japanese by both the Americans and the Europeans. Both are convinced that not merely are some Japanese companies more efficient and better managed, but that, in addition, they enjoy significantly closer relations to their government and to government-influenced banks. Moreover, there is a conviction that the relationship is symbiotic; in return for state support, the firm more readily adapts its strategies to accommodate national political (including economic security) goals. It is on the basis of such conviction that pressures are put – especially by Washington and the USTR's office – on Tokyo to open up on a more level playing field as the American say, to foreign firms as well as to foreign goods – or else to face even greater barriers to Japanese exports to the American market.

Yet American policy has not been without its own kind of bias. Ever since the passing of the Buy American Act in the 1950s, the government has been statutorily obliged to give preference to US firms when it came to defence and other government procurement. Its trade agreements, with the USSR, for instance, habitually insisted on the preferential use of US-owned shipping. A provision of the US–Canadian Free Trade Agreement gives preference to cars produced in North America with a high minimum local content. If there is a 'special relationship' between the government of Japan and Japanese firms, so is there between the government of the United States and US-owned firms. One way, however, in which US policies are more visibly even-handed as between domestic and foreign firms is that the US, as compared to some European and developing countries, has relatively few state-owned enterprises under its direct control; and its financial and commercial intermediaries are less suspect than either German or Japanese banks and *sogo shosha* (trading companies) of favouring their home teams (Spindler, 1984). These are the two grounds on which, although the evidence is contested by Japanese scholars, retaliatory US trade measures have been justified.[8]

The other major difference between the US and other industrialised countries including Japan arises from its special role in the international security structure. While other states – the USSR and China excepted – have to accept the dependence of their defence forces in whole or in part on foreign suppliers, the Americans see their security at risk if US forces are dependent for militarily vital weapons or parts of weapons on firms based in other countries, especially those which could conceivably be neutral or enemies in time of war. This has led to proposals for elaborate new statutory rules to prevent any such vulnerability. For instance, it was suggested that security is threatened if supply comes from only four countries or from four firms producing more than half total world supply.[9] But the American experience with the Strategic Defense Initiative suggests that no rules can entirely avoid technological dependence of foreign firms. The question is only how to manage the dependence. Moran (1990) concluded that the choice lies between relying on sub-optimally efficient US producers or recognising the inevitability of reciprocal security dependence. The latter would mean working towards a multilateral code by which all states would give up the right to claim extraterritorial jurisdiction over the use by others of military or other technology. Just what sanctions might be contemplated to give credibility to such a code is one of many unanswered questions.

The political debate has generated quite a substantial literature on Japanese corporate management practices, and on the political economy of Japanese trade and industry.[10] It has also given rise to much discussion, especially in the United States, of what is called strategic trade policy.[11] Yet the empirical evidence for the allegation of asymmetry in state-firm relations is patchy at best. More detailed firm-level and plant-level data need to be collected. It is all very well for Cohen to say that economists need to broaden their horizons from industrial organisation theories and 'help to build a formal structure to the interactions between market and politics' so that the nature of functional relationships between political authority and economic enterprise can 'be modeled in ways that are theoretically robust and empirically generalizable' (Cohen, 1990). That is a lot easier said than done and the bricks for building such formal structures and making such models are just not available at present.

We have said enough on these two shadowed areas of foreign involvement in national economies and, conversely, of the degree to which multinationals by remaining national at heart can affect the economic relations of states, to show that we shall make little progress on the vaster issues until we have collected and analysed much more data on the relations of firms to governments and governments to firms. We shall certainly not be able to make more sense of general theories of bargaining power between states and firms, nor make intelligent guesses about the long-term consequences for the world economy of even more internationalisation of production. We can only hope that our joint efforts have indicated to other scholars at least some pointers for the future.

APPENDIX
Brazil, Kenya, Malaysia

Nothing could demonstrate more clearly the dangers of using 'developing country' as a generic term than the statistical tables which follow. Our three exemplars of developing countries could hardly be more different from one another. Equal differences would emerge from any other randomly chosen group.

Brazil is obviously much larger than the other two, both in area and in population. The disparity in GNP very roughly matches the difference in physical size. Brazil's GNP in 1988 was estimated at $323 billion; Malaysia's at about a tenth of that at $35 billion; and Kenya's barely $8 billion. In wealth per head, there's not much to choose between Brazil and Malaysia – an average of $2,160 per head against $1,940 – while Kenyan poverty is striking. And the gap widens. Where Kenya has grown annually since 1965 at barely 2 per cent, Malaysia has achieved 4 per cent. The disparity, however, is not as sharply reflected in life expectancy at birth as one might have expected or as it probably was earlier this century. One possible reason is that, though poor, fewer Kenyans live in towns – 22 per cent compared with 41 per cent in Malaysia and 75 per cent in Brazil – where urban infant mortality is known to be very high.

In terms of economic growth, Malaysia is unquestionably the star performer of the three. It has the highest savings rate proportionate to GNP, and the highest growth throughout the 1980s of its exports, of which 45 per cent are now manufactures. Contrast Kenya's continued dependence on commodity exports, which account for as much as 83 per cent of the total.

All three countries are in debt to foreigners – most of all, Brazil with a massive $115 billion foreign debt. But though small, Kenya's $6 billion debt is predominantly 'official', that is, owed to foreign governments and international agencies, while Brazil's is predominantly owed to foreign banks. The difference is not due to divergent choices by the debtors so much as it is to unequal opportunities for borrowing. But the availability of foreign bank credit brought with it added

237

vulnerability to structural change in the international financial system that created the credit famine of the 1980s. The cutting off of foreign credit and the loss of confidence in the future was reflected in four years of stagnation up to 1984.

Tables A1–A3 provide some broadly comparable social and economic data to highlight these differences. These indicate just how rapidly change has occurred in many salient features of the economies and societies up to 1988.

Though much has been made in the Latin American literature of the close politico-economic connection between undemocratic, authoritarian systems of government with the world capitalist or market system, the statistical comparisons hardly bear out the implicit hypothesis. Kenya is the least democratic – and also the economy that has been least well integrated into the world market economy. Internal political factors seem to have far less influence over the country's options for development than have external economic factors of a general, global nature. Differences in national history, culture and social structure seem to affect the choice of strategy at home and abroad more strongly than economics or comparative politics.

The data that follow for each country are divided into two sections: a chronology of the major political and economic developments that have had a bearing on the subjects discussed in the main text; and selected statistical data that amplify the aggregate figures shown above. The statistical material varies somewhat among the countries, due to the unequal detail available. It is arranged, for each country, as follows:

> Growth and inflation
> Currency and balance-of-payments
> Foreign debt
> Foreign trade
> Employment
> Foreign investment

The combination of the two sets of data suggests the context within which relationships with multinationals have emerged over time.

Table A1. *Basic social and economic data*

		Brazil	Kenya	Malaysia
Area ('000 square km)		8,512	583	330
Population (mid-1988, mn)		144.4	22.4	16.9
Population growth (%/yr)	1980–88	2.2	3.8	2.6
	1988–2000	1.8	3.4	2.2
GDP (US$ bn)	1965	19.45	0.92	3.13
	1988	323.61	7.38	34.68
GDP growth (%/yr)	1965–80	8.8	6.4	7.3
	1980–88	2.9	4.2	4.6
GNP per capita (US$ 1988)		2,160	370	1,940
GNP per capita growth (%/yr)	1965–88	3.6	1.9	4.0
Inflation[1] (%/yr)	1965–80	31.5	7.3	4.9
	1980–88	188.7	9.6	1.3
Life expectancy at birth (yrs, 1988)		65	59	70
Age structure (%) 0–14	1988	35.7	50.9	37.2
15–64	1988	59.8	46.1	58.9
0–14	2025	22.8	31.9	23.4
15–64	2025	66.9	64.7	67.2
Education (% of cohorts)[2] Primary		105	94	101
Secondary		39	20	54
Tertiary[3]		18	47	27
Urban population (% of total)	1965	50	9	26
	1988	75	22	41

[1] Change in GDP deflator.
[2] Figures over 100 per cent reflect numbers of mature students enrolled.
[3] The tertiary figure relates to the estimated percentage of all tertiary students enrolled in science and engineering.

Sources: World Bank, United Nations.

Table A2. *Dimensions of the economy*

	Brazil		Kenya		Malaysia	
	1965	1988	1965	1988	1965	1988
Distribution of GDP by sector (%)						
Agriculture	19	9	35	31	28	∷
Industry[1]	33	43	18	20	25	∷
Manufacturing[2]	26	29	11	12	9	∷
Services	48	49	47	49	47	∷
Manufacturing value added	1970	1987	1970	1987	1970	1987
(US$bn)	10.43	78.99	0.17	0.84	0.50	∷
Share of (%)						
Food, Bev., Tobac.	16	15	31	38	26	21
Textiles[3]	13	10	9	11	3	6
Machinery, transport equipm.	22	21	18	13	8	22
Chemicals	10	12	7	11	9	15
Other	39	42	35	27	54	37
Investment rate	1965	1988	1965	1988	1965	1988
(% of GDP)	20	23	14	26	20	26
Savings rate	1970	1988	1970	1988	1970	1988
(% of GDP)	22	28	15	22	24	36
Foreign debt	1970	1988	1970	1988	1970	1988
(US$ mn)						
Total[4]	5,127	114,592	407	5,888	440	20,541
Public[5]	3,421	89,841	319	4,241	390	16,101

Private	1,706	11,514	88	627	50	2,340
IMF	0	3,333	0	455	0	0
Short-term[6]	..	9,903	..	564	..	2,100
debt ratios[6]						
Debt/GNP	12.2	29.6	26.3	58.5	10.8	56.3
Debt service/GNP	1.6	4.5	3.0	5.7	2.0	16.5
Debt service/exports	21.8	42.0	9.1	25.3	4.5	22.3

[1] Mining, manufacturing, construction, electricity, water, and gas.
[2] Manufacturing only.
[3] Including clothing.
[4] 1965 figures are calculated from incomplete data and are probably underestimated.
[5] Public and publicly guaranteed.
[6] Excludes short-term debt.

Source: World Bank.

Table A3. *Trade and trade composition*

	Brazil		Kenya		Malaysia	
Trade	Exports	Imports	Exports	Imports	Exports	Imports
(US$ bn, 1988)	33.69	14.69	1.03	1.99	20.85	16.58
Growth (%/yr.)						
1965–80	9.3	8.2	0.3	1.7	4.4	2.9
1980–88	6.0	−2.9	0.1	−0.6	9.4	0.4
Import composition	1965	1988	1965	1988	1965	1988
(% of total)						
Food	20	14	10	11	25	15
Fuels	21	28	11	22	12	6
Other primary	9	7	3	4	10	5
Machinery, trans. equip.	22	25	34	31	22	47
Other manufactures	28	26	42	31	32	28
Export composition						
(% of total)						
Fuels, minerals,						
metals	9	21	13	20	35	18
Other primary	83	31	81	63	59	37
Machinery, trans. equip.	2	18	0	2	2	26
Other manufactures	7	30	6	15	4	19

Source: World Bank.

BRAZIL – CHRONOLOGY

1944–64	Government based on liberal constitution and free elections.
1964	Government overthrown by the military and indirect election of a new president. Price and wage freezes abandoned. Taxes increased and public spending cut.
1969–74	Medici government adopts import-substituting development plan, with heavy emphasis on state-owned enterprises as the engine of growth.
1974	First oil price rise. Geisel government combines a strategy of import substitution with measures to promote exports while financing the improvement of the infrastructure with foreign bank loans. A policy of *distencao* is adopted to permit local elections.

| 1979 | Figueiredo government continues import-substitution and export development strategy and subsidises public sector projects. Geisel's policies are extended in the form of *arbetura*, a gradual move towards civilian, democratic rule. |

| 1982 | Expecting to continue its heavy Eurocurrency borrowing, Brazil is badly hit by Mexican debt crisis. |

| 1984 | Political reform allows formation of separate liberal and radical opposition parties. Informatics law 7232 reserves market for computers and other information technologies to Brazilian (that is, 70 per cent Brazilian owned and controlled) companies. |

| 1985 | Tancredo de Neves from PMDB opposition party wins indirect presidential elections. But on his death is succeeded by Vice President Jose Sarney. Social issues begin to feature prominently on the government agenda. |

| 1986 | Sarney brings in Cruzado Plan to change the old inflated cruzeiro with a new hard currency, sustained by price and wage freezes and de-indexation. At first, inflation rates fell, growth rates rose. But rising imports and lagging exports cut trade surplus. Corrective measures are delayed until after Congressional elections in November. Cruzado II plan raises taxes and controlled prices and allows crawling peg devaluations. |

| 1987 | Sarney suspends payment of debt interest on foreign loans. Prices rise steeply when controls are lifted. Cruzado III, or Bresser Plan, again tries a price/wage freeze to check inflation, plus tax reforms and monetary stringency to check public investment. It lasts even less than its predecessors. |

| 1988 | Summer Plan in January brings in the 'new cruzado' (= 1,000 old ones), more price and wage controls and a 17 per cent devaluation. Indexed Treasury bonds, which had financed public spending, are abolished and promises made of privatisation and cuts in public employment. |

Rescheduling agreements with official creditors and with private creditor banks ends debt moratorium of 1987.

After nearly two years of debate Congress approves Brazil's new Constitution. Some of its provisions on welfare benefits, limits on foreign ownership and interest rate ceilings are clearly unrealistic. Reforms of labour regulations started.

1989   US puts Brazil on its Super-301 list of unfair trading countries, jeopardising the country's access to a major export market.

1990   Two prominent multinationals, Shell and Nestlé, publicly postpone investment plans while economic uncertainty persists. In March the new president Collor de Mello proposes an economic reform package of tax reform, trade liberalisation, a floating currency and privatisation of SOEs. The latter to be financed by forcing banks and pension funds to subscribe to non-negotiable interest-bearing privatisation certificates. Collor also proposes phasing out of SEI's market reserve policy for informatics, cuts in regional and coffee subsidies.

In June, after nine months of arm-twisting, the US drops Brazil from Super-301 list as part of an implicit deal on trade policy; property rights and the releasing of multinationals 'remitted' profits, frozen for twelve months.

Bush's proposal of closer economic cooperation between the US and Latin America leading to a W. Hemisphere free-trade zone, and including cancellation of official bilateral debts, paves the way for September negotiations on rescheduling private bank debts.

Some selected sources

Coffey, P. and Corrêa do Lago, L.A. (eds.) (1988), *The EEC and Brazil*, London: Pinter.
Evans, P. (1979), *Dependent Development: The Alliance of Multinational. State and Local Capital in Brazil*, Princeton, NJ: Princeton University Press.

Fritsch, W. and Franco, G.H.B. (1988), 'Foreign Direct Investment and Industrial Restructuring in Brazil: Trends and Emerging Issues', unpublished paper for OECD Development Centre, December.

Hollerman, L. (1988), *Japan's Economic Strategy in Brazil: Challenge for the United States*, Lexington, MA: Lexington Books.

Robock, S. H. (1975), *Brazil: A Study in Development Progress*, Lexington, MA: Lexington Books.

Table A4. *Brazil: growth and inflation, 1980–1989*

	GDP[1]	Real growth rate	Per capita GNP (1985 US$)	Consumer price inflation
1980	11,412	9.6	2715	82.9
1981	10,895	−4.5	2414	105.6
1982	10,966	0.7	2274	97.8
1983	10,597	−3.4	1955	142.1
1984	11,128	5.0	1770	197.0
1985	12,056	8.3	1670	226.9
1986	12,957	7.5	1796	145.0
1987	13,436	3.7	1873	259.2
1988	13,410	−0.2	1965	618.8
1989	13,893	3.6	2001	1764.9

[1] Calculated in 1980 New Cruzados (millions)

Growth during most of the 1980s has been well below the rates achieved during the 'Brazilian miracle' (1968–73), when it averaged over 10 per cent. Indexation has been a feature of economic management. Inflation has risen sharply, peaking in 1989 at the highest level in Brazilian history. Living standards, in terms of per capita GNP, fell steadily, but recovered somewhat in the past few years. This is a result of both increased external constraints and the austerity programs implemented since the onset of the debt crisis.

Sources: World Bank, *World Tables, 1989–90*; IMF, *International Financial Statistics*, various issues; *Gazeta Mercantil*, various issues.

Table A5. *Brazil: currency and the balance of payments, 1980–1989 (Current US$, millions)*

	Exports	Imports[1]	Trade balance	Current account[2]	Nominal exchange rate[3]	Percent real exchange rate change[4]
1980	20,132	22,955	−2,823	−12,806	0.00005	14.3
1981	23,293	22,091	1,202	−11,751	0.00009	−3.5
1982	20,175	19,395	780	−16,312	0.00018	−4.2
1983	21,899	15,429	6,470	−6,837	0.00058	89.6
1984	27,005	13,916	13,089	42	0.00185	−3.5
1985	25,639	13,153	12,486	−273	0.00620	1.8
1986	22,349	14,044	8,305	−4,477	0.01366	−42.5
1987	26,213	15,061	11,152	−1,450	0.03923	59.5
1988	33,789	14,605	19,184	4,448	0.26238	38.5
1989	34,392	18,281	16,111	..	2.83400	11.5

[1]   c.i.f.
[2]   After official transfers.
[3]   Period average.
[4]   Calculated using the end of period exchange rate, the Brazilian consumer price index and the US producer price index. A positive number indicates a real *devaluation*, negative number a real revaluation.

The largest revaluation occurred in 1986, the year of the Cruzado Plan. The government held the nominal exchange rate fixed from February until after the November Congressional elections.

Sources: Banco Central do Brasil, *Boletim Mensal*, various issues; IMF, *International Financial Statistics*.

Table A6.1. *Brazil: foreign debt, 1980–1988, (US$ billions)*

	1980	1981	1982	1983	1984	1985	1986	1987	1988
Total external debt	70.8	80.6	92.2	97.5	104.3	104.6	112.0	123.9	114.6
Short-term debt	13.5	15.3	17.5	14.2	10.9	9.3	9.3	13.9	9.9
Use of IMF Credit	0.0	0.0	0.6	2.6	4.2	4.6	4.5	4.0	3.3
Private nonguaranteed									
disbursed	16.6	19.8	23.1	21.5	19.3	17.2	14.6	14.4	11.5
Public/Public guaranteed									
disbursed	40.7	45.5	51.1	59.1	69.9	73.5	83.6	91.6	89.8
of which:									
Official credits	7.0	7.8	8.6	10.0	12.4	15.4	20.5	25.3	24.6
Private Credits	33.7	37.7	42.5	49.1	57.5	58.1	63.1	66.3	65.3
Debt service	14.7	17.8	19.1	13.1	13.6	12.8	11.7	12.1	18.3
of which:									
Principal	6.8	7.4	7.5	3.7	4.5	3.7	3.9	4.6	5.1
Interest	7.9	10.3	11.5	9.4	9.0	9.0	7.7	7.5	13.2
Debt service ratio[1] (%)	63.1	65.9	81.3	53.8	44.9	43.5	46.5	42.6	50.1
Total external debt/									
GNP (%)	30.6	31.9	35.8	50.1	52.3	48.2	41.7	39.4	30.7
Average terms of new commitments									
Official Creditors									
Interest rate	9.2	10.7	10.8	10.5	10.0	9.0	8.3	8.3	7.5
Maturity (years)	13.3	13.0	14.0	13.0	10.5	12.9	13.5	13.6	15.2
Private Creditors									
Interest rate	13.3	16.2	13.1	11.3	13.1	9.3	9.2	7.8	9.9
Maturity (years)	9.2	9.1	10.2	8.9	9.4	9.1	8.1	8.1	10.4

[1] Total interest payments as a percentage of total exports of goods and services.

Source: World Bank, *World Debt Tables, 1989–90*.

Table A6.2. *Brazil: foreign debt: the sectoral use of debt/equity swaps by auction, 1988[1] (US$, millions; percentages of total in parentheses)*

Manufacturing	787.2	(53.2)
Electronics	157.4	(10.7)
Paper cellulose	105.6	(7.2)
Machinery/capital goods	99.9	(6.8)
Chemicals/petrochemicals	93.8	(6.4)
Other	330.5	(22.4)
Service industries	517.9	(35.2)
Equity participation	207.8	(14.1)
Commerce	135.4	(9.2)
Other	174.7	(11.9)
Other	167.0	(11.3)
Total	1,472.1	

[1] Matured debt only.

Debt-equity swaps were introduced in 1982. The present programme, introduced in 1988, allows debt swaps by multinationals that had purchased Brazilian foreign debt at a discount on the secondary market: the earlier programme was restricted to the original creditor banks. Monthly auctions were held from March through December 1988, but were suspended in early 1989. Official swaps without the auction process continue in small volumes. The largest swaps of matured debt at the first ten auctions went to the USA ($435.9m), followed by Japan ($223.6m) and France ($130.3m).

Source: Rubin, S. M., *Debt Equity Swaps in the 1990s, Volume 1: Swaps under the Brady Umbrella* (London: The Economist Publications, 1989).

Table A7.1. *Brazil: foreign trade: major partners, 1975–1988 (US dollars, millions)*

	1975	1980	1985	1988
Imports				
USA	24.9	18.6	19.7	20.9
Japan	9.2	4.8	4.3	6.6
Canada	1.7	3.9	3.1	2.9
France	2.8	2.9	2.3	3.8
Germany	10.7	7.0	6.5	9.5
Switzerland	1.9	1.4	1.6	2.6
UK	2.7	1.9	1.9	2.7
Nigeria	0.0	0.4	9.9	0.9
Argentina	1.9	3.4	3.4	4.6
Chile	0.8	1.9	1.6	2.3
Mexico	0.9	1.9	2.9	0.8
Venezuela	0.9	2.4	1.9	1.0
Iraq	6.7	15.8	13.8	8.5
Saudi Arabia	8.3	8.7	7.2	6.8
Exports				
USA	15.4	17.4	27.1	25.8
Japan	7.7	6.1	5.5	6.7
Canada	1.6	1.2	1.7	2.6
France	2.9	4.1	3.1	2.5
Germany	8.1	6.6	5.1	4.2
Italy	4.2	4.9	4.5	4.1
Netherlands	6.5	5.7	6.1	7.7
Spain	4.2	2.6	2.1	2.2
UK	3.9	2.7	2.5	3.2
PRC	1.0	0.4	3.2	2.1
Nigeria	0.7	1.4	3.6	0.4
Argentina	4.4	5.4	2.1	2.9
Chile	1.2	2.2	0.9	1.6
Mexico	1.5	2.3	0.9	0.8

Brazil has successfully diversified its export markets away from dependence on the USA – 40 per cent of exports in the 1950s. Exports to LAFTA countries grew very little proportionately until the early 1980s; after rising to 18 per cent in 1981, they declined to 8.6 per cent in 1985, the lowest share since the 1960s.

Source: IMF, *Direction of Trade Statistics Yearbook*, various years.

Table A7.2. *Brazil: foreign trade: composition by principal products, 1990 (percentages)*

Exports	
Automobiles and components	11.0
Iron and steel products	10.6
Iron Ore	8.2
Soybeans and derivatives	7.1
Orange juice	4.5
Coffee	4.1
Shoes	3.6
Textiles	3.3
Electrical machinery	3.1
Machinery	3.1
Chemical products	3.0
Beef	1.9
Imports	
Oil	17.5
Machinery	13.2
Chemical products	8.5
Electrical machinery	7.4
Iron and steel products	2.0
Plastics and artificial resins	1.6
Non-ferrous metals	1.6

The table shows the high dependence of Brazil on imported oil; and its low dependence today on exports of coffee – less than orange juice. Manufactured exports, if iron and steel products are included, amount to 37.7 per cent of total exports. Multinationals account for the majority of these exports.

Source: *Gazeta Mercantil*, August 6, 1990.

Table A8. *Employment*

We were unable to obtain reliable up-to-date statistics on the size and composition of the labour force. Of some relevance is the following table showing the great inequality of incomes.

Monthly family income (1988 US$)	Proportion of families (%)
Less than $100	17
100–200	19
200–500	31
500–1,000	17
1,000–2,000	10
Over 2,000	6

Source: United Nations, *Demographic Yearbook*, 1989.

Table A9.1. *Brazil: foreign direct investment flows, 1980–89 (Current US$ millions)*

	Inflows[1]	Reinvestments[2]	Remittances[3]
1980	1,913.2	411.3	544.0
1981	2,525.8	745.2	587.2
1982	2,922.3	1,572.1	864.4
1983	1,556.5	690.6	759.0
1984	1,598.0	473.6	799.5
1985	1,361.6	542.2	1,139.2
1986	445.8	447.0	1,272.9
1987	1,216.8	615.5	947.8
1988	..	..	1,540.0[4]
1989	..	..	2,400.0[4]

Inward FDI fluctuated between 10–15 per cent of the foreign loans that Brazil receives. The large drop in 1986 seems to be the result of the uncertainty associated with the election of a civilian government. In July 1989, the Brazilian government froze remittances, resulting in a fall in new investment (net of reinvestment) to almost zero. In July, 1990, the Collor government lifted this freeze and agreed to a plan of phased withdrawal of remittances.

[1] Inflows are reported on a net basis; includes reinvestments.
[2] Includes all earnings of foreign affiliates that are not remitted outside the host country.
[3] Includes all earnings of foreign affiliates that are identified as being remitted, in addition to dividends and interest.
[4] Estimate of Banco Central do Brasil (source: *Gazeta Mercantil*, 11 December 1989).

Sources: IMF, *Balance of Payments Statistics Yearbook*, various issues; UNCTC, *Transnational Corporations in World Development, Trends and Prospects*, 1988.

Table A9.2. *Brazil: foreign direct investment stock, by industry, 1988 (US$, millions)*

	Total	(%)	New investment	Reinvestment
Agriculture[1]	293	(1.0)	220	72
Mining	783	(2.6)	668	115
Manufacturing	22,710	(74.0)	14,887	7,823
of which:				
Metals[2]	2,296	(7.5)	1,711	584
Mechanical	2,637	(8.6)	1,891	745
Electronics[3]	2,444	(8.0)	1,670	774
Transport[4]	4,307	(14.0)	3,015	1,292
Chemicals	4,166	(13.6)	2,660	1,506
of which:				
Basic[5]	2,851	(9.3)	1,881	970
Pharm[6]	1,404	(4.6)	1,043	361
Textiles[7]	764	(2.5)	439	325
Food[8]	1,861	(6.1)	821	1,040
Services	6,315	(20.6)	4,616	1,699
of which:				
Banking and				
other fin.[9]	1,672	(5.4)	1,190	482
Commerce[9]	1,170	(3.8)	869	301
Administr.[11]	2,998	(9.8)	2,141	856
Total	30,703		20,843	9,860

Prior to World War II, inward FDI was concentrated in public utilities, trade, finance, and petroleum distribution. Since the beginning of the 1950s, however, foreign investments have shifted largely to the manufacturing sector. This was the result of various incentives given to import-substituting production. In 1988, manufacturing accounted for 74 per cent of the total, up from approximately 50 percent in the early 1950s.

[1] Includes fishing and livestock.
[2] Steel and metals processing.
[3] Includes electrical and communications goods.
[4] Including auto and auto parts manufacture.
[5] Basic chemical products, including petrochemicals.
[6] Pharmaceutical products, including medical and veterinary products.
[7] Includes clothing and footwear.
[8] Includes drink and tobacco.
[9] Commercial and investment banking, insurance, and other financial services. Excludes administration and real estate.
[10] Includes international trade.
[11] Includes local holding companies for equity participations in other countries, thus overestimating total FDI in services.

Source: Banco Central do Brasil: *Boletim Mensal*, Separata (March 1989), based on registered foreign capital.

Table A9.3. *Brazil: foreign direct investment stock, by country of origin and type of investment, 1988 (US$, millions)*

	Total		New investment	Reinvestment
US	8,900	(29.0)[1]	5,940	2,560
Germany	4,712	(15.4)	3,159	1,553
Japan	2,958	(9.6)	2,416	543
Switzerland	2,808	(9.2)[2]	1,666	1,142
UK	1,916	(6.2)	1,047	869
Total (incl. others)	30,703		20,843	9,860

[1] Numbers in parentheses indicate percentage of total FDI stock in Brazil.
[2] The international holding companies of firms from other European countries (most notably Germany) are located in Switzerland. Thus, Swiss FDI figures are greatly overstated.

At the end of World War II, the US dominated total FDI in Brazil, and in 1951, its share was still 44 percent. However, as American economic hegemony has declined, the US share has fallen steadily.

Source: Banco Central do Brasil: *Boletim Mensal*, Separata (March 1989), based on registered foreign capital.

Table A9.4. *Brazil: US foreign direct investment, by sector, 1988 (US$, millions)*

	Direct investment capital Stock[1]	Outflows	Equity capital reinvested Outflows	earnings	Intercompany debt Outflows	Income[2]
All Industries	11,810	1,403	318	1,019	66	1,641
Petroleum	244	21	**	-1	**	52
Manufacturing	9,004	1,044	146	828	70	1,304
Food and kindred products	506	-88	1	-23	-66	25
Chemicals and allied prods	1,739	202	13	167	22	259
Primary and fabricated metals	977	163	**	128	**	135
Machinery, exc electrical	1,733	143	25	119	-1	220
Electric and electronic equip.	477	130	**	26	**	50
Transportation equip.	1,308	317	43	279	-5	342
Other manufacturing	2,265	176	3	132	42	272
Wholesale Trade	55	-4	**	-6	**	*
Banking	661	226	103	123	0	137
Finance (exc. banking), real estate and insurance	1,272	78	64	25	-10	95
Services	470	32	**	46	**	50
Other industries	104	6	0	3	3	4

** Suppressed to avoid disclosure of data on individual companies.
* Less than $500,000.
1 Book value of equity capital, plus net outstanding loans to affiliates.
2 Parents' total return on debt and equity stock, less foreign withholding taxes on dividends, plus interest on intercompany accounts.

Source: US Department of Commerce, *Survey of Current Business,* August 1989.

254

Table A9.5. *Brazil: US foreign direct investment, all industries, 1980–88 (current US$, millions)*

	Direct Investment stock	Capital outflows	Equity capital outflows	Reinvested earnings	Intercompany debt outflows	Income
1980	7,703	..	..	337	..	499
1981	8,235	..	..	300	..	519
1982	9,290	1,036	623	330	83	760
1983	9,068	−150	194	−250	−94	134
1984	9,377	384	225	72	87	503
1985	9,480	106	56	101	27	681
1986	9,268	123	−74	−18	216	833
1987	10,288	572	89	463	20	988
1988	11,810	1,403	318	1,019	66	1,641

Source: US Department of Commerce, *Survey of Current Business*, August issues.

KENYA – CHRONOLOGY

1952–59   Mau-Mau troubles lead to major capital outflows from Kenya, only partly replaced by official aid.

1956   *Price Control Ordinance* (later the 1972 Price Control Act) places basic commodities under central control.

1962   The *Imports, Exports and Essential Supplies Act* introduces a licensing system to close the trade gap and to protect domestic production. The *Exchange Control Act* controls local borrowing by foreign-controlled firms.

1963   12 December: British rule ends.

1964   Republic of Kenya is established under President Jomo Kenyatta.

    The Foreign Investment Protection Act (FIPA) reiterates many of the provisions of the new Constitution, and rules that the government may not take over private property without good reason and must pay adequate compensation.

1965   *Sessional Paper No. 10: African Socialism and its Application to Planning in Kenya* proclaims the government's faith in state intervention in the economy. The main features are: the assertion of the need to transfer economic resources to the indigenous population; the prime role assigned to the development finance institutions; the introduction of work permits for foreigners and the overseeing of a planned indigenisation of high-level manpower; plans to Africanise distribution, by introducing controls over Asian traders; the establishment of the Ministry of Tourism to develop the hotel and tourist industry.

1966   The 1920 East African Currency Board is dissolved and exchange controls introduced.

1967   The East African Economic Community sets a common external tariff but allows Kenya, Uganda and Tanzania to raise trade barriers against each other and to be independent in monetary management. By now, reserves are half what they had been in 1963.

The *Trade Licensing Act* excludes Asians from trading in rural and non-central urban areas. The Ministry of Commerce puts pressure on foreign manufacturers to switch to African distributors.

The *Immigration Act* aims to regulate non-citizen employment by means of work permits.

1970   The *Second Development Plan (1970–4)* reaffirms the belief in import substitution and imposes tariff protection and quantitative restrictions on imports.

1971   In the 1970s various state regulations on the control of foreign investment came into force. The *Capital Issues Committee (CIC)* is set up to vet all capital issues, to reduce capital outflow and to promote greater local ownership of large corporations.

1972   The *Price Control Act* applies to consumer items, mainly basic foods and beverages, to protect the purchasing power of low income groups. The scope of the Act is gradually extended; by 1976, only fruit, vegetables, pulses, clothing, furniture and household equipment are explicitly exempt.

1973   The *New Projects Committee* is established to regulate the flow of foreign capital by evaluating industrial projects in terms of the 'national interest'.

1974   The *Export Compensation Act* introduces flat-rate duty drawbacks for *locally* manufactured goods

1976   Amendment to *FIPA*: foreign investors require a 'Certificate of Approved Enterprise', issued by the Minister of Finance in order to repatriate capital, profits or interest payments. The Certificate specifies the amount of foreign-currency-denominated assets invested, including loans. A coffee boom triples prices and boosts economic growth.

1978   The East African Community, established in colonial times between Kenya, Uganda and Tanzania, is finally dissolved.

Kenyatta dies and is succeeded by his vice-president, Daniel arap Moi.

257

1981   Under IMF and World Bank guidance, Kenya begins an 'active' exchange rate policy – the shilling is pegged to the SDR and the peg adjusted frequently to keep the real effective exchange rate constant.

1982   A coup attempt by Kenyan Air Force units fails.

1983   The *Fifth Development Plan (1984–8)* aims for 4.9 per cent/year growth; the local district as the focus of development; a reduction in reliance on external borrowing; and a shift away from import-substitution policies by encouraging exporting industries. The Plan reiterates the mixed-economy orientation, but calls for greater reliance on private investment and savings.

1984   *Preferential Trade Area Treaty (PTA)* becomes operational. There are currently fourteen signatories, mainly throughout East, Central and Southern Africa.

Kenya suffers its worst drought for fifty years.

1986   *Sessional Paper No. 1: Economic Management for Renewed Growth* calls for a 5.6 per cent annual growth rate for 1984–2000 and emphasises the development of the rural sector and manufacturing industry. Rather than state intervention, the growth in domestic demand generated by expanded agricultural production is now seen to provide the foundation for industrial growth. The Paper is the first major official reassessment of economic policy since 1965.

The *Investment Promotion Centre Act* establishes a 'one-stop' bureau for inward investors.

1988   An amendment to 1964 the *Foreign Investment Protection Act* permits repatriation of reinvested profits at the rate of exchange prevailing at the time of investment. A second amendment enables the investment of 'blocked funds' from sale of an investment in market-rate government bonds for five years instead of the previous punitive rate. The Finance Act allows tax relief on foreign exchange losses *realised* on approved external loans.

The *Restrictive Trade Practices, Monopolies and Price Control Act* makes all fixing of prices in trade agreements illegal and confers wide-ranging powers onto the Monopolies and Price Commissioner.

1989   The *Sixth Development Plan* (1989–93) aims for an annual growth rate of 5.4 per cent and calls for 'Participation for Progress', involving higher growth rates in agriculture, industrial diversification and increased emphasis on small-scale farming and the informal urban sector. Plans to establish a green channel system for exporters willing to purchase necessary inputs for processing for export are announced.

1990   Various Acts are introduced to develop and regulate the financial system, and to simplify the administration of imports.

A scheme to establish an *Export Processing Zone* with tax incentives comparable to those in SE Asia is announced.

The US government plans to suspend military assistance unless Kenya improves its practices on human rights, including the release or trial of political prisoners.

Some selected sources

Commonwealth Secretariat, *Foreign Investment Policy: Kenya's Experience*, SFIP/Com.Sec. (4), June 1985.
UNIDO, *Industrial Development Review Series: Kenya*, 1988.
World Bank, *Kenya: Industrial sector Policies for Investment and Export Growth*, 1987.
Various Kenya Government publications, including the annual *Economic Survey* and *Statistical Abstract*.

259

Table A10. *Kenya: Growth and inflation, 1980–1988*

	GDP[1]	Real growth rate	Real per capita GNP (1985 US$)	Consumer price inflation
1980	44,684	4.0	535	13.8
1981	47,600	6.5	497	11.8
1982	49,629	4.3	435	20.4
1983	50,758	2.3	367	11.5
1984	51,159	0.8	331	10.2
1985	54,634	6.8	310	13.0
1986	57,618	5.5	314	4.0
1987	60,355	4.8	323	5.2
1988	63,474	5.2	328	8.2
1989	66,330	4.5	..	10.4

[1] Calculated in 1985 Kenyan Shillings (millions).

Even from a low base, Kenyan growth rates in the 1980s have been well below those during the 'miracle' years (1964–73). A coffee book in 1986 combined with budget discipline helped restore growth after 1985. Rapid population growth, the third highest in the world during the period, offset much of the gains. Inflation remained stubbornly high until 1986 when oil prices fell, but have risen again, partly because of large public sector pay awards and the removal of price controls on some consumer items.

Sources: World Bank, *World Tables, 1989–90*, and IMF, *International Financial Statistics Yearbook*.

Table A11. *Kenya: Currency and balance of payments, 1980–1989 (current US$, millions)*

	Exports	Imports[1]	Trade balance	Current account	Nominal exchange rate[2]	Per cent real exchange rate change[3]
1980	1,389	2,590	−1,201	−887	7.5685	3.6
1981	1,183	2,081	−898	−560	10.2862	32.6
1982	1,045	1,603	−558	−305	12.7249	4.8
1983	979	1,390	−411	−48	13.7959	−1.6
1984	1,083	1,529	−446	−126	15.7813	6.3
1985	988	1,445	−458	−174	16.2843	−9.1
1986	1,217	1,649	−432	−69	16.0422	−8.0
1987	961	1,755	−794	−491	16.5149	
1988	1,071	1,975	−904	−454	18.5994	8.2
1989	1,150	2,100	−950	−535	20.5700	..

[1] c.i.f.
[2] Period average.
[3] Calculated with the end of period exchange rate, the consumer price index for Kenya, and the produced price index of the USA. A positive number indicates a real *devaluation*; a negative number a real revaluation.

Since 1981, Kenya has followed a 'crawling peg' exchange rate policy under which the shilling is periodically devalued by the Central Bank whenever the demand for foreign exchange exceeds the available supply.

Sources: IMF, *International Financial Statistics*, World Bank, *World Tables, 1989–90*.

261

Table A12. *Kenya: Foreign debt, 1980–1988 (current US$, billions)*

	1980	1981	1982	1983	1984	1985	1986	1987	1988
Total external debt	3.5	3.4	3.5	3.8	3.7	4.4	4.9	6.0	5.9
Short-term debt	0.6	0.5	0.3	0.4	0.4	0.5	0.4	0.6	0.6
Use of IMF Credit	0.0	0.0	0.0	0.0	0.0	0.0	0.0	0.0	0.0
Private nonguaranteed disbursed	0.4	0.4	0.4	0.5	0.4	0.5	0.5	0.5	0.6
Public/Public guaranteed disbursed	2.2	2.3	2.4	2.4	2.5	2.9	3.6	4.5	4.2
of which:									
Official credits	1.3	1.5	1.7	1.8	2.1	2.5	3.0	3.7	3.6
Private Credits	0.9	0.8	0.7	0.6	0.4	0.4	0.6	0.8	0.7
Debt service	0.4	0.4	0.4	0.4	0.5	0.5	0.6	0.6	0.5
of which:									
Principal	0.2	0.2	0.3	0.3	0.3	0.3	0.3	0.3	0.3
Interest	0.2	0.2	0.2	0.2	0.2	0.2	0.2	0.2	0.2
Debt service ratio[1] (%)	22.1	28.2	32.3	35.6	37.7	42.0	44.2	44.2	37.8
Total external debt/GNP (%)	51.2	52.3	57.8	65.9	63.7	75.2	71.2	77.8	71.3
Average terms of new commitments									
Official Creditors									
Interest rate	3.5	5.5	5.2	5.1	5.8	4.4	4.2	1.4	1.9
Maturity (years)	31.3	21.8	30.2	30.7	20.7	22.0	20.1	36.6	21.8
Private Creditors									
Interest rate	7.8	14.5	8.9	9.0	8.4	9.9	6.4	0.0	0.0
Maturity (years)	10.6	9.2	14.8	15.0	10.6	12.0	11.7	0.0	0.0

[1] Total interest payments as a percentage of total exports of goods and services.

Notes: Both the IMF and the World Bank have been supporting sustained efforts to implement policies of structural reform.

Source: World Bank, *World Debt Tables, 1989–90*.

Table 13.1. *Kenya: Foreign trade: major partners, 1975–1988*

	(Per cent of total)			
	1975	1980	1985	1988
Exports				
United Kingdom	10.1	11.4	16.7	17.0
West Germany	8.6	11.4	11.9	10.2
Uganda	12.2	11.4	8.5	11.1
Netherlands	3.4	3.6	6.7	2.9
United States	3.7	3.3	6.8	4.6
Italy	2.6	4.8	2.3	3.5
Rwanda	2.2	2.5	3.2	2.6
Sudan	0.8	1.7	3.3	3.4
Pakistan	1.4	1.4	6.8	1.8
France	0.7	1.3	3.5	2.9
Tanzania	9.4	0.7	2.0	2.0
Japan	2.0	0.8	0.8	1.2
Imports				
United Kingdom	20.1	16.9	15.2	17.9
West Germany	7.8	8.1	8.3	8.1
United States	7.2	6.4	7.1	4.6
Saudi Arabia	7.8	17.5	3.3	1.1
Japan	8.6	10.0	10.3	11.3
France	2.8	3.4	3.7	6.5
Iran	14.7	2.1	5.5	2.9
Netherlands	2.0	2.4	2.5	4.6
Italy	3.6	3.9	3.4	5.2
Singapore	0.4	0.7	4.5	2.5
United Arab Emirates	0.0	0.8	10.1	5.4

The EC is the most important destination for Kenya's exports, mainly due to the special trade and aid arrangements of the Lome Convention. Exports to Tanzania have revived somewhat after the re-opening of the border in 1983. Exports of manufactured goods to Uganda are particularly important but have not expanded as much as desired largely due to political instabilities.
Source: IMF, *Direction of Trade Statistics*, various issues.

Table A13.2. *Kenya: Foreign trade: composition by principal products, 1986–1989 (Kenya £, millions)*

	1986	1988	1989 (provisional)
Exports			
Coffee	388.3	244.5	203.8
Tea	172.7	185.2	271.9
Horticultural products	N/A	114.3	112.1
Petroleum products	99.0	110.3	101.9
Hides and skins	12.6	26.1	13.6
Pineapples (canned)	24.2	25.1	N/A
Soda ash	14.1	18.6	22.1
Sisal	10.9	11.9	16.3
Pyrethrum extract	11.5	11.5	16.7
Imports			
Industrial machinery	236.6	395.4	460.2
Crude petroleum	207.6	210.4	299.1
Motor vehicles and chassis	88.0	138.0	175.0
Iron and steel	64.4	120.6	152.0
Artificial resins, plastic materials, etc	41.4	80.9	75.7
Fertilisers	50.0	49.1	69.4
Pharmaceuticals	32.6	43.7	56.2
Petroleum products	27.9	30.0	40.1

Source: Ministry of Planning and National Development, *Economic Survey*, various issues

Table A14.1. *Kenya: Employment by main sectors, 1983–1989 (thousands of persons)*

	1983	1985	1987	1989 (provisional)
Agriculture and forestry	231.1	240.9	257.0	257.1
Mining and quarrying	3.5	4.8	4.4	4.1
Manufacturing	148.8	158.8	167.9	182.3
Electricity and water	17.2	17.7	19.2	22.4
Construction	60.2	49.9	58.2	67.4
Trade, restaurants and hotels	80.3	89.7	99.5	110.3
Transport and communications	55.0	55.7	58.1	69.4
Finance and business services	45.7	53.4	57.5	63.7
Community, personal and other services	451.5	503.5	540.9	582.3
Total wage employees of which:	1,093.3	1,174.4	1,262.7	1,359.0
Public sector	527.8	574.6	624.6	680.6
Private sector	565.5	599.8	638.1	678.4

The total work force was estimated at around 7.2 million in 1987 and was forecast to grow to 14 million by the end of the century. The figures given here are for the modern sector only and exclude, amongst others, the 'working poor'. The relative importance of agriculture and forestry and manufacturing has declined: that of community, personal and other services has increased, due mainly to the increased numbers of teachers.
Source: Ministry of Planning and National Development, *Economic Survey*, 1990.

Table A14.2. *Kenya: Ethnic composition of the population, 1969–1979 (thousands)*

	African	Asian	Non-African European	Other	Total
1969	10,733	139	40	45	10,967
1979	15,112	59	50	117	15,327

Source: *Kenya Statistical Digest*, September 1981

Table A14.3. *Kenya: employment: real wage trends, 1964–1985*

	Private total[1]	Private manu- facturing[2]	Large-scale manufacturing[3]	Contractual manufacturing[4]	Nairobi minimum wage[5]
1964	83.4	. .	. .	. .	106.7
1975	91.8	102.9	. .	106.0	111.4
1976	100.0	100.0	100.0	100.0	100.0
1977	97.3	97.3	103.3	95.9	87.1
1978	90.4	86.9	92.1	90.3	86.9
1979	92.1	83.7	92.6	90.3	80.4
1980	98.6	84.8	97.6	86.6	92.1
1981	98.1	85.3	94.1	85.6	82.4
1982	90.0	80.0	82.2	78.1	72.0
1983	86.7	78.6	78.6	77.1	64.6
1984	. .	76.8	84.2	77.8	58.6
1985	. .	71.3	90.3	76.2	62.2

1   Includes agricultural wage employment. All series deflated by the average annual rate of inflation (Mid Income CPI).
2   Excludes repair activities in manufacturing.
3   Refers to private manufacturing establishments with more than 50 employees.
4   Refers to contractual agreements in manufacturing registered with the industrial court.
5   Based on the General (unskilled) Minimum Wage for adult workers in May of each year. Real wages have declined significantly throughout the late 1970s and early 1980s, despite the presence of a minimum wage. That 30 per cent of households at the bottom end of the income distribution scale earned less than 9 per cent of total income in 1976 emphasises the highly unequal nature of Kenyan society.
Source: World Bank, *Kenya: Industrial Sector Policies for Investment and Export Growth*. 1987.

Table A15. *Kenya: US Foreign direct investment, 1985–1989 (US$, millions)*

	Direct investment stock	Capital outflows	Income
1985	97	−20	2
1986	106	12	11
1987	90	17	10
1988	98	12	17
1989	116	19	4

Notes: Reliable data on all FDI in Kenya are impossible to assemble from official sources. Even the USA does not provide details by sector.

Source: US Department of Commerce, *Survey of Current Business*, August issues.

MALAYSIA – CHRONOLOGY

1947	Malaysia and Singapore remain under British colonial rule when India, Pakistan and Burma become independent.
1948–1953	Britain sends troops to Malaya to resist Chinese-supported revolutionary attacks. Slowly, the civil war is brought to an end, but Malaya still looks to Britain for security.
1957	Malaya becomes independent under Tunku Abdul Rahman but agrees to stay in the sterling area in return for British military protection. This keeps Malaya in a dependent monetary role for another ten years, committed to a comparatively cautious and conservative style of economic management and to leaving capital transfers free of control. Foreign (mainly British) investors are lightly taxed and capital gains and profits are exceptionally high.
	Economic policies are ruled by Britain's need to support sterling. Exploitation of tin and rubber gets priority; industrialisation comes a poor second. This strategy is endorsed by the first Five Year plan in 1955 and by the World Bank, which urges that over half official development loans should go on infrastructure. Neither an infant-industry protection law – the Pioneer Industrial Ordinance of 1957 – nor a government report favouring industrial development have any marked effect.
1961	Malaya's second Five Year Plan stresses rural development, job creation, infrastructure improvement and diversification away from rubber and tin.
1963–65	Federation of Malaya, Singapore, Sarawak and Brunei, though favoured by Britain for military and economic reasons, fails to last. Lee Kuan Yew withdraws and Malaysia and Singapore both set up independent central banks.
1963–66	'Confrontation' (i.e. war) with Indonesia. Britain provides Malaya with military forces at undisclosed cost to the UK.

1966	First Malaysian Plan fixes employment targets and adopts import-substituting strategies to offset the falling export earnings from commodities.
8 August 1967	Malaysia, Indonesia, the Philippines, Singapore and Thailand form the Association of South East Asian Nations (ASEAN).
1968	*Investment Incentives Act* provides additional investment incentives for manufacturing. The Federal Industrial Development Authority – now known as the *Malaysian Industrial Development Authority* (MIDA) – is formed to promote and evaluate all industrial projects. 'Pioneer' status (extra incentives) is awarded to firms making the first import-substituting investment in each industrial sector.
13 May 1969	Race riots demonstrate Bumiputra frustration at their perceived exclusion from the benefits of economic growth.
	The Perbadanan Nasional (PERNAS) (the National Corporation) and various State Economic Development Corporations (SEDCs) are established to promote industrialisation.
1971	The *New Economic Policy* (NEP) is introduced with the Second Malaysia Plan (1971–75), concerned mainly with the eradication of poverty among Malays and the overall restructuring of society. This has two quantitative targets. First, employment by sector should reflect the ethnic composition of the population. Second, by 1990, 30 per cent of the corporate sector should be owned and managed by Bumiputras and the foreigners' share reduced to 30 per cent. In addition, various policies of positive discrimination for Bumiputras are introduced in housing, civil service recruitment, and education, among other areas. Public expenditure is set to rise sharply.
Early 1970s	Free Trade Zones (FTZs) are established.

1975	*Industrial Coordination Act* is introduced to ensure the NEP equity restructurings. The Act requires that manufacturing firms apply for licences to operate their production facilities and is strenuously opposed by the Chinese business community.
1976	The Third Malaysia Plan (1976–80) increases efforts to alleviate poverty, especially rural poverty. The NEP targets are seen to be impractical and are relaxed.
1981	Datuk Seri Dr Mahathir Mohamed is elected prime minister.
	The Fourth Malaysia Plan (1981–85) sets ambitious targets for further industrialisation and exports, but these are missed, due to the slowdown in the world economy.
1982	Dr Mahathir announces 'Look East' policy, aimed at introducing Japanese work ethics and managerial systems to improve economic performance and productivity.
1985	Malaysian Parliament approves privatisation of the Telecommunications Department and Malaysian Airlines System (MAS).
1986	The Fifth Malaysia Plan, representing the fourth and last segment of the twenty-year NEP, sets fresh growth targets. These are to be achieved by: (1) Privatisation and an increased role for the private sector. Rules and regulations that constrain growth will be phased out. (2) Policies to increase efficiency, especially in public agencies, and to mobilise domestic savings. (3) The *Industrial Master Plan* (IMP), which targets twelve industries for substantial export-led growth over the period 1986–1995.
	To stimulate sluggish inward FDI, the *Promotion of Investments Act* introduces new incentives and new flexibility in the guidelines for foreign equity participation.
1987	Dr Mahathir challenged for leadership of UMNO. He narrowly survives, but splits the political community.

269

1988   *Privatisation Master Plan* adopted.

1989   *Banking and Financial Institutions Act* limits foreign activities in domestic financial institutions, but implementation is delayed by confusion over the technical provisions.

1990   New investments in infrastructure are planned to assist rapid growth in manufacturing and inward FDI. Extra financial support for exporters is announced.

Some selected sources

Cho, G. (1990), *The Malaysian Economy: Spatial Perspectives*, London: Routledge.
Lim, D. (ed.) (1975), *Reading on Malaysian Economic Development*, Kuala Lumpur: Oxford University Press.
Rao, B. V. V. (1980), *Malaysian Development Pattern and Policy, 1947–1971*, Singapore: University of Singapore Press.
Strange, S. (1971), *Sterling and British Policy*, Oxford: Oxford University Press.
Wong, J. (1979), *ASEAN Economies in Perspective*, London: Macmillan.

Table A16. *Malaysia: Growth and inflation, 1980–1989*

	GDP[1]	Real growth rate	Real per capita GNP (1985 US$)	Consumer price inflation
1980	60,398	7.4	2,193	6.7
1981	64,591	6.9	2,237	9.7
1982	68,429	5.9	2,129	5.8
1983	72,706	6.3	2,052	3.7
1984	78,349	7.8	2,112	4.0
1985	77,547	−1.0	1,970	0.3
1986	78,509	1.2	1,816	0.7
1987	82,675	5.3	1,731	0.9
1988	89,906	8.7	1,765	2.0
1989	97,522	8.5	1,780	2.8

[1] Calculated in 1985 Malaysian ringits (millions).
Sources: IMF, *International Financial Statistics*, World Bank, *World Tables*, various issues.

Table A17. *Malaysia: currency and balance of payments, 1980–1989 (current US$, millions)*

	Exports	Imports[1]	Trade balance	Current account[2]	Nominal exchange rate[3]	Percent real exchange rate change[4]
1980	12,393	11,602	791	−285	2.1769	8.6
1981	11,734	13,052	−1,318	−2,486	2.3041	0.4
1982	12,027	14,042	−2,015	−3,061	2.3354	−0.2
1983	14,100	14,669	−569	−3,497	2.3213	−1.6
1984	16,484	14,849	1,635	−1,671	2.3436	2.2
1985	15,632	12,746	2,886	−613	2.4830	−0.7
1986	13,830	11,447	2,383	−122	2.5814	3.4
1987	17,911	12,506	5,405	2,633	2.5196	−2.5
1988	21,110	16,551	4,559	1,875	2.6188	11.1
1989				−145	2.7088	1.6

[1] c.i.f.
[2] After official transfers.
[3] Period average Ringgit per US$.
[4] Calculated using the end of period exchange rate, the Malaysian consumer price index and the US producer price index. A positive number indicates a real *devaluation*, a negative number a real revaluation.
Source: IMF, *International Financial Statistics Yearbook*.

Table A18. *Malaysia: foreign debt, 1980–1988 (current US$, billions)*

	1980	1981	1982	1983	1984	1985	1986	1987	1988
Total external debt	6.6	9.2	13.4	18.0	18.8	20.5	21.9	22.7	20.5
Short-term debt	1.4	1.6	1.7	3.0	2.5	2.7	2.4	2.0	2.1
Use of IMF Credit	0	0.2	0.3	0.3	0.3	0.1	0	0	0
Private nonguaranteed disbursed	1.2	1.6	3.2	2.7	2.8	3.0	2.9	2.6	2.3
Public/Public guaranteed disbursed	4.0	5.7	8.2	11.9	13.2	14.7	16.6	18.0	16.1
of which:									
Official credits	1.4	1.7	1.8	2.1	2.7	3.3	3.8	4.5	4.3
Private Credits	2.6	4.1	6.4	9.8	10.6	11.4	12.8	13.5	11.8
Debt Service	0.7	0.9	1.3	1.7	2.5	5.1	3.2	4.2	5.4
of which:									
Principal	0.3	0.4	0.6	0.7	1.1	3.7	1.8	2.7	3.9
Interest	0.3	0.5	0.7	0.9	1.3	1.5	1.4	1.5	1.5
Debt service ratio[1] (%)	4.0	5.1	6.5	7.1	8.1	9.7	9.8	7.9	6.8
Total external debt/GNP (%)	28.0	38.2	52.4	63.6	59.4	70.5	85.3	75.9	66.0
Average terms of new commitments									
Official Creditors									
Interest rate	6.7	7.6	8.0	7.1	7.4	8.3	8.3	8.2	5.1
Maturity (years)	13.8	13.8	11.4	11.1	14.7	21.5	14.1	14.8	14.9
Private Creditors									
Interest rate	14.1	13.6	12.4	9.6	9.9	8.8	6.3	5.9	6.8
Maturity (years)	10.9	12.7	10.1	10.0	13.6	22.1	13.5	14.2	9.8

[1] Total interest payments as a percentage of total exports of goods and services.
Source: World Bank, *World Debt Tables, 1989–90.*

Table A19.1. *Malaysia: Foreign trade: major partners, 1975–1988 (current US$, millions)*

	1975	1980	1985	1988
Imports				
United States	10.6	15.1	15.4	17.7
Japan	19.9	22.9	23.1	23.1
Australia	7.8	5.5	4.1	4.2
France	2.0	1.9	2.3	1.5
Germany	5.0	5.4	4.5	3.9
United Kingdom	10.0	5.4	4.0	4.9
PRC	4.2	2.3	2.0	2.9
Hong Kong	1.8	1.4	1.7	2.3
India	1.3	0.9	0.8	0.7
Indonesia	2.2	0.8	1.1	1.7
Korea	0.4	1.9	2.3	2.6
Singapore	8.5	11.7	15.9	13.2
Thailand	3.9	3.0	3.6	3.0
Taiwan	0.0	0.0	2.7	4.6
Exports				
United States	16.0	16.4	12.8	17.4
Japan	14.3	22.9	24.5	16.9
Australia	1.9	1.4	1.7	2.4
France	1.5	1.8	1.0	1.4
Germany	4.3	3.6	2.6	3.4
Norway	8.4	6.0	5.8	3.0
United Kingdom	6.0	2.8	2.6	3.5
PRC	1.4	1.7	1.0	2.0
Hong Kong	1.1	1.9	1.3	3.4
India	0.7	2.2	2.8	2.6
Indonesia	0.7	0.3	0.4	1.3
Korea	0.7	2.0	5.9	4.8
Singapore	20.2	19.2	19.4	19.3
Taiwan	0.0	0.0	2.2	3.0

Valuation in US dollars has a distorting effect on relative importance of trading partners. But the decline in imports from Britain and the importance of the US and Japanese market for Malaysian exports is striking. A good many exports to Singapore are for re-export.

Source: IMF, *Direction of Trade Yearbook*, various issues.

273

Table A19.2. *Malaysia: foreign trade: composition by principal products, 1987–1989 (current US$, millions)*

	1987	1988	1989
Exports			
Electronic components	2,740	3,325	3,758
Petroleum	2,496	2,399	2,899
Logs and Timber	2,396	2,233	2,678
Palm Oil	1,294	1,732	1,731
Rubber	1,554	2,006	1,457
Others	7,449	9,491	12,508
Total	17,929	21,186	25,031
Imports			
Manufacturing inputs	4,622	5,783	7,392
Machinery and Transport equipment	1,460	2,022	3,739
Consumer durables	669	1,293	1,704
Metal products	684	1,094	1,484
Food, beverages and tobacco	800	978	1,167
Others	4,461	5,407	6,986
Total	12,696	16,577	22,472

Source: Economist Intelligence Unit, *Country Profile*, 1989–90

Table A19.3. *Malaysia: Foreign trade: net invisibles accounts, 1986–88 (M$ million)*

	1986	1987	1988
Freight & insurance	−1,252	−1,437	−2,357
Travel	−1,357	−1,414	1,461
Invest. Income	−4,347	−4,828	−4,936
Other services	−1,831	−900	−1,346
Services balance	−8,787	−8,579	−10,100

Malaysia has a chronic invisibles deficit reflecting substantial freight and insurance payments and outgoing investment income (including debt interest payments). The largest component of the services deficit is investment income payments, due to the payment of interest on the national external debt and increased profits and dividends accruing on foreign investment.
Source: Bank Negara, *Annual Report, 1988*; Economist Intelligence Unit, *Malaysia, Brunei Country Profile, 1988–89*.

Table A20.1. *Malaysia: Employment, 1983–1988 (thousands and per cent)*

	Employment	Total labour force	Labour force growth rate	Unemployment rate
1983	5,413.8	5,735.0	3.1	5.6
1984	5,564.7	5,907.0	3.0	5.8
1985	5,624.6	6,039.1	2.2	6.9
1986	5,706.5	6,222.2	2.9	8.3
1987	5,880.8	6,408.9	3.0	8.2
1988	6,087.5	6,622.2	3.3	8.1

Source: Ministry of Finance, *Economic Report, 1989/90.*

Table A20.2. *Malaysia: Ethnic composition of the population, 1980–1988 (peninsular Malaysia only) (thousands, and percentages in parentheses)*

	1980	1988
Malay & other bumiputra	6,315 (55.3)	8,063 (57.7)
Chinese	3,865 (33.8)	4,439 (31.8)
Indian	1,171 (10.2)	1,388 (9.9)
Other	75 (0.7)	88 (0.6)
Total	11,426	13,978

The other Malaysian states, Sabah and Sarawak (both in East Malaysia, situated in northern Borneo) have their own distinctive racial compositions. In Sabah, of a total population of one million in 1980, 83 per cent are *Pribumi*, a general category that includes twenty-eight different ethnic groups. The Chinese make up 16 per cent and 'others' less than 1 per cent. The ethnic composition of the 1.3 million people of Sarawak is more diverse.

Source: Economist Intelligence Unit, *Malaysia, Brunei: Country Profile 1989–90.*

Table A21.1. *Malaysia: Foreign Direct Investment flows, 1982–88 (US$ millions)*

	Total inflow	Remittances
1982	1,398	1,009
1983	1,260	1,257
1984	797	1,333
1985	694	1,137
1986	489	802
1987	423	1,089
1988	649	1,231

Source: IMF, *Balance of Payments Statistics Yearbook,* various issues.

Table A21.2. *Malaysia: US Foreign Direct Investment by sector, 1988 (US$ millions)*

	Direct Investment stock[1]	Capital outflows	Equity capital outflows	Reinvested earnings	Intercompany debt outflows	Income[2]
All Industries	1363	316	-12	327	*	404
Petroleum	735	114	0	**	**	**
Manufacturing	521	190	**	143	**	148
Food and kindred products	5	-7	**	**	**	*
Chemicals and allied prods	20	*	0	**	*	3
Primary and fabricated metals	-1	-1	0	-1	0	-1
Machinery, exc electrical	16	**	0	*	**	*
Electric and electronic equip.	429	182	0	127	54	128
Transportation equip.	0	0	0	0	0	0
Other manufacturing	52	**	0	16	**	17
Wholesale Trade	63	8	-4	**	**	**
Banking	-10	-2	**	**	0	**
Finance (exc. banking), real estate and insurance	29	4	*	4	*	4
Services	0	0	0	0	0	0
Other industries	26	2	0	2	*	3

** Suppressed to avoid disclosure of data on individual companies.
* Less than $500,000.
[1] Book value of equity capital, plus net outstanding loans to affiliates.
[2] Parents' total return on debt and equity stock, less foreign withholding taxes on dividends, plus interest on intercompany accounts. Calculations of total value of past FDI can never be exact, as historic values may be much less than current market values. Unfortunately, other industrial countries do not collect as much information about their firms' foreign investments as the United States does.

Source: US Department of Commerce, *Survey of Current Business*, August 1989.

Table A21.3. *Malaysia: US Foreign Direct Investment, all industries, 1980–88 (US$ millions)*

	Direct investment stock	Capital outflows	Equity capital outflows	Reinvested earnings	Intercompany debt outflows	Income
1980	632	..	..	54	..	314
1981	849	..	..	52	..	265
1982	1221	1026	10	150	214	284
1983	1157	−81	−14	166	−233	381
1984	1101	−112	**	102	**	384
1985	1140	44	6	111	−52	333
1986	1021	−61	−9	−37	−14	157
1987	1019	20	−3	10	13	228
1988	1363	316	−12	327	*	404

** Data suppressed to avoid disclosure of data on individual companies.
* Less than $500,000.

Source: US Department of Commerce, *Survey of Current Business*, August issues.

Table A21.4. *Malaysia: approved manufacturing projects, 1983–88 (monetary units in US$ million)*

	1983	1984	1985	1986	1987	1988
Number	490	749	625	447	333	732
Potential employment	43,537	56,831	53,597	40,230	59,779	136,647
Proposed called up capital	1,022.5	1,213.4	1,823.7	1,878.8	1,529.4	3,469.7
Bumiputra equity	460.2	515.4	992.8	707.1	450.2	822.6
Non-bumiputra equity	266.1	422.6	506.1	647.3	329.2	636.6
Foreign equity	296.3	275.4	324.9	524.5	750.0	2,010.5
Loan	1,335.6	2,587.7	3,863.2	3,284.4	2,404.5	5,624.2
Total proposed capital investment	2,358.1	3,801.1	5,686.9	5,163.2	3,933.9	9,093.9

According to MIDA officials, approximately 70 per cent of foreign investment applications are approved, a slightly higher rate than for domestic applications.

Source: MIDA, *Statistics on the Manufacturing Sector, 1989.*

Table A21.5. *Malaysia: Projects approved with foreign participation, by country, 1989–90 (monetary units in US$ million)*

	1990, Jan.-June			1989, Jan.-Dec.		
	Number	Foreign equity	Estimated total foreign investment	Number	Foreign equity	Estimated total foreign investment
Taiwan	143	1,922.5	5,560.7	191	1,013.1	2,159.9
Japan	54	508.5	1,134.6	127	1,065.3	2,690.4
Indonesia	7	217.9	1,060.6	7	18.9	105.4
Iran	1	202.7	1,013.7	..	..	..
UK	6	202.5	492.9	16	255.6	764.1
Sweden	2	81.9	478.5	..	..	..
Hong Kong	32	105.0	298.1	40	112.5	352.1
Singapore	74	123.1	274.7	150	269.6	914.7
USA	6	24.2	144.1	30	126.8	320.8
South Korea	11	24.5	82.9	29	78.9	188.9
India	3	23.5	73.5	1	0.8	0.8
Total (incl others)		3,633.5	11,154.8		3,401.2	8,652.7

Source: MIDA.

NOTES

1 The new diplomacy

1 Some strands of Eastern thinking have recognised this for centuries. As Rimei Honda, a Tokugawa philosopher (1744–1821) said, 'foreign trade is a war in that each party seeks to extract wealth from the other'.

2 ICL, the British computer manufacturer, claims labour accounts for only 3 per cent of the final assembly, but this figure excludes the cost of labour in the (growing) sub-contracted component of total cost. Cited in the *Economist*, 3 March 1990.

3 For an excellent treatment of the general implications of new technology on the economics of supply and demand, see Piore and Sabel (1984). For an exploration of the specific impacts on developing countries of microelectronics, see Ernst and O'Connor (1989).

4 An example of the tone of the debate in the early 1970s is provided by Barnet and Müller (1974). This book, though extremely fashionable for a time, now seems dated and unhelpful.

5 For an analysis of these trends, see Deardorff (1987) and IMF (1988).

6 This opinion survey also reported that 85 per cent of multinationals' managers thought they were doing 'a good job' and 'behaving well'.

7 There is much economic literature debating this issue. See, for example, Ballance (1987), Aho and Bayard (1980), Cline (1982), Kindleberger (1973, 1990) and Holtfrerich (1990).

8 Among a burgeoning literature, we would draw attention to trade theorists such as Dixit and Norman (1980), Helpman and Krugman (1989) and Krugman (1979). In development theory, the 'new growth theory' of Romer (1986), Lucas (1988) and Murphy et al. (1989) has begun to ask the same questions.

9 Reported in the *Economist*, 23 June 1990.

10 The other side of the coin has been a much more rapid change in the cast list of major enterprises. New ones have appeared and grown more quickly than they did fifty years ago. Increasing risk for firms is a theme we pick up in later chapters.

11 Care should be taken to distinguish FDI from international portfolio investment. FDI measures the assets managed directly or indirectly by a foreign parent company, even if that company owns only a minority of the equity capital. Portfolio investments are purchases of equity or debt from the international capital markets that do not confer managerial responsi-

bility. Siemens' ownership of Siemens do Brasil is not the same thing as an individual British holder of 100 shares of Siemens on the Frankfurt market. Our focus throughout the book is on FDI with all its consequential powers and responsibilities.

12 The official figures are subject to enormous distortion because of the different national accounting procedures, most especially those affecting the treatment of corporate debt. They are, sadly, the only figures available and will remain unsatisfactory for so long as governments persist in measuring investment only by the financial flows that enter the balance-of-payments accounts. Furthermore, figures for the accumulated *stock* of FDI are further distorted by revaluations to account for fluctuations in exchange rates.

13 Robock and Simmonds (1989) estimated that multinationals' production and trade accounted for about 20 per cent of total world activity in 1985. Their figures depended on some complex estimation of capital/output ratios and the proportion of trade managed within the multinationals' systems. Since then, the proportion has risen, especially if one adds to the calculation the trade among multinationals.

14 UNCTC (1985, 1988a) and ILO (1984) provide useful discussions of the difficulties of making more precise estimates.

15 For US data, see Bureau of Economic Analysis (1985) and Whichard (1988).

16 For details of these shares in many developing countries, to the extent they are known, see UNCTC (1989: table X.1).

17 'A transnational society reveals itself by commercial exchange, migration of persons, common beliefs, organizations that cross frontiers and, lastly, ceremonies or competition open to the members of all these units (i.e., states)'. To illustrate his point, Aron used examples such as the tradition of the Olympic games, the gold standard, the free movement of people before World War I, the development of private international law and institutions like the World Bank.

18 One study of just five firms during the 1970s showed that they faced 650 conflicts, many of which were in developing countries and caused by shifting expectations (Gladwin and Walter, 1980).

19 There are major exceptions, as Bolivia found to its cost when it nationalised its tin mines, but could not change the location of the smelters for many years in the face of resistance by the multinationals. Mexico found the same problem with the development of barbasco, the raw material for steroid hormones (Moran, 1985, pp. 96–102).

20 Details of the legislative history of each of our three countries are contained in the appendix.

2 Structural changes

1 There are a few exceptions. For example, when prices declined in early 1990, Malaysia decided to protect its position as the leading producer and exporter of 60 per cent of the world's palm oil. Contrary to the spirit of World Bank policy, Malaysia combined all its palm-oil exporters into a single conglomerate, to stop them from competing among themselves in

selling to state trading houses in major consuming countries like India. Though Malaysia may not succeed, few others have equivalent power even to try.

2 There is a vast literature on the early moves of individual firms and particular industries. For excellent summaries and original data, see Buckley and Roberts (1982), Casson (1983), Franko (1976), Hannah (1976), Mytelka (1986) and Wilkins (1970).

3 Yet even the USA has felt threatened by the speed of events. Despite having one of the lowest levels of foreign participation in the domestic economy among OECD countries, a provision was included in the 1988 Omnibus Trade Act (the Exon-Florida amendment) to give the president powers to block a foreign takeover on the grounds of national security. The significance of this change can only be measured in terms of its implementation. So far, of the 100 notifications to the high-level intergovernmental committee, only two have been passed on to the president. Both have been passed, though one was amended to allow the takeover to proceed after production related to nuclear weapons had been excluded.

4 As always, such estimates, based on equity capitalisation, undervalue the multinationals' full impact. Non-equity methods of involvement are increasing, as we show later on.

5 The firms have, to be sure, been influenced by Brazilian regulations and the application of such programmes as BEFIEX (see chapter 4 for details). None the less, they would not have switched sourcing had the underlying economics been favourable.

6 Myanmar, formerly known as Burma, announced in 1990 new policies aimed at reforming the banking system. Multinational banks were to be invited into the country to provide needed specific services and skills, even if this meant the diminution of the profits of the existing state monopolists. Similarly, Albania permitted inward investment in a 1990 decree.

7 One should note that the German government whose banks had a corresponding financial involvement with Poland did not dare to do the same, and left the United States to carry a small part of the burden.

8 The only exceptions in Africa have been the role of South Africa for both strategically important minerals and its command of trade routes and surveillance of the southern Atlantic; and a few countries where there was a chance of the other gaining a predominant position – Zaïre and more recently Angola and Ethiopia.

9 There is none the less a widening array of codes and agencies setting standards and procedures for dealing with specific operational matters, including the Multilateral Investment Guarantee Agency, the Montreal Protocol on the Ozone Layer and the Basel Convention on Transboundary Movement of Hazardous Wastes. All these and others help to build a climate of consensus among nations.

10 These ideas are not new. They have been explored in different contexts by, for example, Johnson (1975a) and Thurow (1980).

11 For a similar line of argument, see Rosecrance (1986).

12 We pick up the implications of these trends in chapter 7.

13 The 1990 decision in Massachusetts to 'defend' the local firm, Norton, from

a bid by the British firm, BTR, is a case in point. The irony in this case is that Norton is itself a multinational, with relatively little of its total assets in Massachusetts, and that the defence against BTR led to eventual purchase by a more 'friendly' French firm.

14 George Robertson, in a debate at the Royal Institute of International Affairs, quoted by Julius (1990).

3 Global competition

1 For telling evidence of the workings of regional economics that do little to serve the interests of the smaller countries, see Grosse (1989).

2 The distinction between customers and consumers is important. Customers include wholesalers and others who sell to the consumers. In many developing countries, the customers for multinationals are local enterprises that can use their special knowledge of the local markets more effectively than the foreigners. Control of the channels of distribution to the final consumer has thus become an issue of debate in many countries. Indonesia, for example, used to prevent foreigners from owning local distribution, but changed their law in 1989, as part of the liberalising trend discussed in chapter 4.

3 There is much historical precedent for this effect. See, for example, Veblen (1915), Landes (1969) and Braudel (1979).

4 For some details, see 'West African mini-steel mills turn a profit', *Financial Times*, 26 July 1988.

5 Vernon's original model was defined in four stages, but was amplified in a five-stage model by Wells (1972) and further elaborated into a seven-stage model by Aggarwal (1986) to show the effects for developing countries.

6 Kojima extended his macroeconomic theories (1990) to examine the impact of national, locational advantages. He argues that Japanese investments are more attuned to comparative advantages than the American ones. His theories have, however, attracted criticism for their omission of critical, supply-side advantages within the firm and his assumption of near-perfect, cross-border markets.

7 The seeds segment of the industry has traditionally been one of trial-and-error, allowing many specialised niches for small firms. Anticipating the future benefits of bio-technology, however, the world's top chemical and foods firms have spent an estimated $10 billion during the last decade buying up seeds companies that will provide an outlet for the coming stream of biotech products. By 1989, the top twenty controlled about 35 per cent of the market, a figure that ICI has estimated in presentations at various FAO seminars during 1989 to rise to about 65 per cent by the year 2000. For an excellent summary of the trends and the forces leading to the concentration of this sector, see James (1989) and OECD (1989).

8 As much of the managerial issues involve questions of training and controlling manpower on the farms, further details are deferred until chapter 6.

9 These figures exclude the values on current account statistics for investment income, official flows and transfers.

10 For detailed reviews of the available evidence and the policy issues, see

UNCTC (1988a), Enderwick (1989), Nicholaides (1989) and Messerlin and Sauvant (1990).

11 For excellent analyses of these recent trends, see Bartlett and Ghoshal (1989), Doz and Prahalad (1987) and Porter (1986).

12 Quoted in the *Financial Times*, 29 May 1990.

13 Many observers in the USA have been concerned that alliances with Eastern competitors serve to weaken American firms. See, for example, Reich and Mankin (1986).

14 For excellent reviews of the activities of these firms, see, for example, Lall (1983), Wells (1983), Khan (1986) and Lecraw (1989).

4 Dilemmas for governments

1 For a comprehensive review of such policies, see UNCTC (1985), Business International and US Department of Commerce, annual reports.

2 Contractor's data have many problems of classification and measurement. Nevertheless, they are the most comprehensive available and accord closely with the data in the Appendix.

3 The literature on third-world debt is overwhelmingly large, so references are necessarily selective. We would pick out for particular mention Lever and Huhne (1985); Delamaide (1984); Sachs and Berg (1988); Frieden (1987); Congdon (1988) and Griffith-Jones (1984).

4 For a detailed review of both the range of possible mechanisms and recent experience, see Rubin (1989).

5 For a simple exposition of many complex arguments, see *The Economist*, 8 September 1990.

6 There are, of course, exceptions. US diplomatic pressure, as distinct from market forces, was needed to force South Korea and Taiwan to revalue their currencies, considered in Washington to be undervalued and therefore a source of 'unfair' competition with domestic producers.

7 A new study for the IMF by Tanzi (1990) was published just as we completed the manuscript for this book. In this, the complex interactions among public finance, macroeconomic policy and trade are explored in detail and support our general conclusions.

8 The effective rate of protection for finished goods differs from the nominal tariff rate, because of the impact of other tariffs on the imports of components for locally produced competitive products. An example serves to show the difference. Suppose a good faces a tariff of 90 per cent. Suppose also that local competitors have to import half of their inputs, and these incur a tariff of 25 per cent. The effective tariff becomes 155 per cent. The arithmetic is as follows:

$$\text{Effective Rate of Protection} = \frac{\text{Finished good tariff (90\%)} - \begin{bmatrix} \text{components' share of} & \text{tariff on} \\ \text{(imports (50\%)} \times & \text{components (25\%))} \end{bmatrix}}{(1 - \text{share of imported components (50\%))}}$$

9 Cartera de Comercio Exterior, the department of the central bank with

overall responsibility for import licensing. In addition, sectoral policy for some sectors has been administered by separate agencies. Thus, SEI, the Special Informatics Secretariat has administered policy in the broadly defined informatics sectors.

10 Under these tariff items, introduced in the mid-1950s, US firms pay duty only on the value added by offshore processing. Included are items ready for assembly without further processing (Item 807) and non-precious metals exported for processing (Item 806.30). This tariff programme has rapidly expanded US imports and has attracted considerable criticism in the USA. Including all the items with less than the 35 per cent added value allowed under the General System of Preferences (GSP), US imports were over $9 billion in 1987, a growth of 41 times from 1966 when the US Tariff Commission first collected data on these items (Markides and Berg, 1988).

11 *Gazeta Mercantil*, 23 June 1988, based on data from a special BNDES study.

12 There are many different terms used for the idea, each with different technical and administrative conditions. We use EPZ loosely to cover all the variations. For details, see UNIDO (1980a).

13 The ILO estimated that, since their inception, the EPZs contributed more than 60 per cent of the new employment in manufacturing (ILO/UNCTC, 1988). Even so, the total employment remains little above 10 per cent in manufacturing, less than 2 per cent of the total work force.

14 Matsushita, for example, uses Malaysia for mass assembly, leaving the more technically advanced work in Japan and to some extent Singapore.

15 Some consider that these benefits were bought at the price of gross exploitation of Malaysian labour, often female, at low wages, with no union protection. There is, however, contradictory evidence, as we discuss in chapter 6.

16 One manager in the industry, cited in *Electronics*, August 1987.

17 The same motivation has also spurred many attempts to improve trade conditions for commodities by forming Commodity Agreements, or supplier cartels. With the exception of OPEC, these attempts have failed because of the difficulties of maintaining internal discipline. We do not explore these Agreements, as our focus is limited to consideration of the added-value processing of the commodities.

18 For an analysis of the general impact of the Andean Investment Code, see, for example, Hojman (1981). The impact on firms is discussed in chapter 5.

19 For careful reviews of the possible mechanisms of privatisation, see Vuylsteke (1988) and Ramanadham (1989).

20 'Asian' in the Kenyan context refers to someone whose forebears originated in the Indian sub-continent.

21 For a clear summary of the issues, see Encarnation and Wells (1986).

22 As reported in the *New Straits Times*, 22 January 1988.

23 Quoted in the *Financial Times*, 14 September 1990.

24 The same shift from market reserve to compromise can be observed also in India's policies toward foreign computer firms. It has been a long step from the dramatic exclusion of IBM in 1976 to the recent welcome given to foreign firms to set up in Bangalore. India has also induced Bull to buy a 26 per cent share in India's national champion, PSI, primarily in order to

expand exports of hardware from India to the Middle East. Reported in the *Financial Times*, 26 July 1989.

25 Originally, the government owned 82 per cent of the equity, but this was reduced to 52 per cent in a complex refinancing package. The government, however, retains 80 per cent of the voting equity.

26 Autolatina was the result of the merger in 1986 of Ford and Volkswagen operations in Brazil and Argentina. VW had already bought out Chrysler, and Ford had acquired Willys. Other foreign firms are more specialised – Toyota in jeeps, Saab-Scania in diesel engines, Mercedes-Benz and International Harvester in vans and trucks, Bosch in components.

27 Jose Miguel de Souza and Carlos Mariano of Shell, both cited in *South*, September 1989.

28 Until the mid-1980s, even Nomura seems to have been content to tolerate a local partner with exclusive rights to purchase all output on a cost plus 5 per cent basis.

29 Under government exchange control regulations companies are obliged to take on the foreign exchange risk of overseas loans.

30 For a considered appraisal of both the technical issues and practice, see Plasschaert (1979).

31 The forgotten (and later discredited) Cecchi Report to the World Bank in 1960 produced some quite spurious figures concerning the knock-on effects of investment in tourism. It was used by the Bank's Tourism division – later closed down by MacNamara – to influence the policy making of several Pacific and Caribbean countries (Newton, 1990).

5 Local decisions for firms

1 For analyses of organisational choices, see, for example, Stopford and Wells (1972), Prahalad and Doz (1987) and Bartlett and Ghoshal (1989).

2 The attempt was in vain, for GE sold its world-wide consumer electronics business to Thomson of France in a complex deal that involved among other things GE buying Thomson's medical equipment business. Both were changing their business 'portfolios' to increase competitive advantage by concentrating corporate resources.

3 Cited in Bartlett and Ghoshal (1989), p. 180.

4 This issue has attracted research attention for decades. For examples, see Dunning (1988b) and Group of Thirty (1984). For a good description of how the French multinational, Rhone-Poulenc, balances general considerations of country conditions and risk with specific business needs, see Quarré (1987).

5 Practice on this issue varies widely, but nevertheless the trends are clear. For a careful assessment of US practice, see Markides (1990). With the exception of Japan, the same trends are pronounced in all developed countries.

6 According to a report in *Business Week*, 3 March 1986.

7 OPIC is the US government's Overseas Private Investment Corporation. Private firms can purchase insurance cover for up to 90 per cent of their foreign investments and for earnings retained abroad.

8 There is an extensive literature on the relative merits of licensing and contracts as compared to traditional forms of investment. For reviews of the general considerations, see, for example, Telesio (1979), Teece (1981, 1985), Caves (1982) and Terpstra (1983).

9 We are indebted to Lou Wells for this example that must remain anonymous.

10 For a discussion of the concept of variable defensibility of specific projects, see Poynter (1982). See also Fagre and Wells (1982) for sensitivities according to the equity percentages at issue.

11 Among a vast literature on the technical aspects of the methodologies employed, see Little and Mirrlees (1974) and Roemer and Stern (1975). For a simpler version of the issues, see Wells (1975).

12 See, for example, Newfarmer (1980) and Jacobs and Martínez (1980).

13 Cited in an interview with *Business Times* (Malaysia), 21 May 1988.

14 We omit from detailed discussion here the large question about 'appropriate' technology transfers to developing countries. For informed discussion of the issues and some evidence, see, for example Stobaugh and Wells (1984).

15 For data on Malaysia, see, for example, Chan (1983); for Brazil, see Newfarmer and Marsh (1981); for South Korea, see Cohen (1975).

16 According to *Business International*

17 Reported in the *Financial Times*, 7 September 1990.

6 Social cause and consequence

1 The Minister of Finance and the Governor of the Central Bank were, of course, also responsible for authorising the remission of the proceeds to the foreign owners.

2 One senior insurance executive with experience of indigenisation policies in Nigeria, suggested that his international company was unnecessarily angry about the Act. In Nigeria, where majority equity 'control' by locals was mandatory, it made no perceptible differences to the management of the company or, more surprisingly, to the subsidiary's profitability to the parent company. Local companies objected to the Act on the grounds that the financial requirements were set at too high a level. These, they felt, favoured foreign-owned firms which had been operating for long enough to accumulate adequate reserves.

3 For example, President Moi initiated the establishment of a large number of well-endowed secondary schools in the area where his ethnic group predominates.

4 In many developing countries that face over-abundance of male labour competing for scarce urban employment, 'good' jobs have become virtually a heritable commodity passed on from one relative to the next. This system has been institutionalised in China since before the revolution and remains resistant to reform.

5 Quantitative restrictions on imports are controlled centrally by rationing of import licences. They are hard to evade, though the rationing is susceptible to corruption. However, under a regime of Open General Licences, control

is exercised by customs officers, who may be persuaded to 'split' the duty payable on a consignment while still recording that duty has been paid in full.

6 For example, in Kenya, the average share of value added in gross output of manufacturing declined from 22.9 per cent in 1975 to 18.9 per cent in 1985. The average share of wages and salaries in gross output declined from 10.0 to 8.8 per cent during the same period, (UNIDO, 1989: table A-3).

7 See, for example, Kenya's Industrial Relations Charter (drafted 1962 and revised in 1980).

8 A similar confrontation occurred in the Manaus Free Trade Zone in Brazil in 1984 with a rather different outcome. Employers in the electronic industry attempted to sponsor the formation of a union independent from the Union of Metallurgical, Mechanical and Electrical Industries Workers, Manaus. This was successfully contested by the established union under the Labour Code, despite the fact that the local Labour Ministry office had authorised the formation of the new union.

9 Of the remaining 40 per cent, 15 per cent went to the relevant union federation (state), 5 per cent to the confederation (national) and 20 per cent to a fund administered by the Ministry. The uses unions could make of the 'tax' were regulated by law and were primarily welfare-oriented.

10 Some of the government's old ways of dealing with industrial disputes still occasionally recur. For example, in November 1988, the government dispatched troops to dislodge strikers from the Volta Redonda parastatal steel mill. Three strikers were killed and dozens injured.

11 Mathur (1989) noted a similar trend towards casualisation – or 'working non-employees' – in India, which also has stringent regulations on retrenchment.

12 David was also a Member of Parliament for the opposition Democratic Action Party and a member of the ILO Governing Body from 1985–87 (to which he has now returned). Even though the President of the International Confederation of Free Trade Unions was also the General Secretary of the National Union of (Malaysian) Plantation Workers, the Malaysian government was undeterred by the representations of the ILO and ICFTU.

13 The lobbying motives of international organisations, such as the ICFTU and the International Metal Workers' Federation, or national bodies such as the AFL-CIO, are ambivalent. Not only do they reflect general concern for worker solidarity, but also for 'unfair labour practices' that may place labour in the industrialised countries at a disadvantage.

14 Because the stability of the tobacco scheme is under threat from a new African-owned entrant into the cigarette market, BAT is attempting to persuade the government to assign them exclusive green-leaf threshing rights in Kenya.

15 Greeley and Farrington (1989) argue that governments in Third World countries should invest in biotechnological research to facilitate the acquisition of this knowledge. Unfortunately, the record of research institutes in the Third World for generating commercially viable processes or products is not encouraging.

16 The UNCTC/ILO (1988, p. 89) cites evidence that, in Singapore, three times as many women as men work on night shifts.

17 Another example of the sensitivity that top management has to display occurred in Kenya. In May 1988, the government abolished price controls on some consumer goods, including household detergents and soaps, as one condition of a World Bank structural adjustment loan. Within ten days, Unilever's subsidiary, East African Industries, increased the price of its detergents by, on average, 18 per cent: it controlled nearly 70 per cent of the local market. The next day, President Moi attacked the company for its anti-social behaviour and removed the company chairman as non-executive director of a major government research institute. A few days later, the company announced a 'special' ten per cent reduction in the price. Shortly afterwards, a group of directors was featured in the media at State House making a donation to the President for a national charity on behalf of the company.

18 For example, Malaysia's Industrial Master Plan 1986–1995 called for an increase in the proportion of engineers and technicians in the manufacturing workforce, from 2 to 8 per cent by 1995. It also recommended legislation to make in-service training for up to 10 per cent of a firm's staff compulsory every year. Achievements so far have been modest, not least because of opposition from employers, both local and foreign.

19 Under 'country of origin' rules both the USA and EC insist on the inclusion of the diffusion stage in production units to qualify DRAMs as 'local' products.

7 The way forward

1 One example where the squeeze was felt by both sides was the dispute that broke out in 1988 between the Indonesian government and its Japanese partners in the largest aluminium smelter in South-East Asia at Asahan. The Indonesians, squeezed by rising domestic demand both for alumina for local industry and for water for irrigating farms, stopped the shipments to the Japanese who had been taking nearly 60 per cent of the smelter's output. The stand-off was finally broken when the Japanese offered new cash and a rescheduling of past debt. In return, the Indonesians resumed shipments of alumina, and through a debt-equity swap increased their share of the equity from 25 to 41 per cent.

2 One striking example of such corporate diplomacy was the initiative taken by the chairman of Deutsche Bank to enlist the support of both the German and Soviet governments for a deal whereby the latter agreed to the setting-up of an export zone at Kaliningrad – formerly Königsberg in East Prussia – while the latter gave 90 per cent guarantees to commercial loans extended mainly to German suppliers hit by the foreign credit famine in the USSR: *Financial Times*, July 25 1990.

3 Political debate still rages over how governments should promote, or discriminate in favour of, national (or 'European') champions. Public opinion is still slow to adapt the idea that 'foreign' corporations can be acting more in the local national interest than home-bred ones, as we

discuss later on. Similarly, as we discussed in chapter 5, corporate boards still debate when and how a firm has to exert its control through ownership rather than by contract.

4 Small wonder that the debates over the control of trans-border data flows are now assuming heightened saliency in many countries. See, for example, Sauvant (1986).

5 That the IMF *Staff Papers* during 1990 were full of advice on how states might manage the sequence indicates the rising interest of this issue.

6 The most complete statistics, as might be expected, are collected by the leading industrialised countries. But even these have large yawning gaps. We only have rough estimates of the proportion of Japanese and US imports for which foreign-owned firms are responsible. But neither country counts or tells us what percentage of inward investment flows they account for, though we do have rough estimates of their assets, usually valued at historical prices. Even so, the data available mostly refer only to manufacturing, ignoring services. For developing countries the available statistics are often expressed in US dollars, allowing exchange rate changes to distort the picture. (See, for example, the doubling of reinvested profits by foreigners in Brazil between 1981 and 1982 in the appendix.) For a detailed analysis of the available data on forms of NFI, which also has big gaps, especially the German and Japanese data, see Graham Vickery's appendix to Oman (1984).

7 It was an American firm, incidentally – IBM – that was credited with the first use of this euphemistic adjective in the early 1960s.

8 For a useful summary of various interpretations and explanations of the superior competitive performance of Japanese firms, see Best (1990: chapter 5).

9 For example, *Holding the Edge: Maintaining the Defense Technology Base*, US Office of Technology Assessment, 1989; Senators Bingaman and McCain, *Deterrence in Decay: The Future of the US Defense Industrial Base*, 1989; and other congressional studies, quoted in Moran (1990).

10 Inoguchi and Okimoto (1988); Ohmae (1982); Abegglen and Stalk (1985); Clark (1979); Johnson (1982).

11 Krugman (1986); Grossman and Richardson (1985); Stern (1987); Zysman and Cohen (1988); Rosecrance (1986); Milner (1988). See also Richardson (1990) and Cohen (1990).

REFERENCES

Abegglen, J. C. and Stalk, G., Jr. (1985), *Kaisha: The Japanese Corporation*, New York: Basic Books.

Ackerlof, G. A. and Yellen, J. L. (1986), *Efficiency Wage Models of the Labour Market*, New York: Cambridge University Press.

Ackerman, S. E. (1984), 'The Impact of Industrialisation on the Social Role of Rural Malay Women: A Case Study of Factory Workers In Malacca' in N. Safiah Karim (ed.), *Women, A Malaysian Focus*, Kuala Lumpur: Oxford University Press.

Addison, T. and Demery, L. (1988), 'Wages and Labour Conditions in East Asia: A Review of Case-Study Evidence', *Development Policy Review*, Vol. 6, pp. 371–93.

Aggarwal, R. (1986), 'Managing for Economic Growth and Global Competition: Strategic Implications of the Life Cycle of Economics', in Farmer, R. N. (ed.), *Advances in International Comparative Management*, Vol. 2, Greenwich, CT: JAI Press.

Aggarwal, R. and Agmon, T. (1990), 'The International Success of Developing Country Firms' Role of Government-Directed, Comparative Advantage', *Management International Review*, Vol. 30, no. 2, pp. 163–80.

Aho, C. and Bayard, T. (1980), 'American Trade Adjustment Assistance after Five Years', *The World Economy*, Vol. 3, no. 3, pp. 359–76, November.

Alagandram, S. and Rahim, I. bin H. A. (1988), 'The Right to Strike and Lockout in Malaysia', in *The Right to Strike and Lockout*, Geneva: ILO/UNDP/ASEAN Programme of Industrial Relations for Development.

Aoki, M., Gustafsson, B. and Williamson, O. E. (eds.) (1990), *The Firm as a Nexus of Treaties*, London: Sage.

Ariff, M. and Hill, H. (1985), *Export-Oriented Industrialisation: ASEAN Experience*, Sydney: Allen & Unwin.

Aron, R. (1966), *Peace and War: A Theory of International Relations* (translated by Howard, R. and Fox, A. B.), Garden City: Doubleday & Co.

Austin, J. E. (1990), *Managing in Developing Countries: Strategic Analysis and Operating Techniques*, New York: The Free Press.

Australian Manufacturing Council (1989), *What Part Will Manufacturing Play in Australia's Future?*, an interim report of the Pappas Carter/Telesis Study, October, mimeo.

Ausubel, J. H. and Sladovich, H. E. (eds.) (1989), *Technology and Environment*, Washington, DC: National Academy Press.

290

Balassa, B. (1985), *Change and Challenge in the World Economy*, London: Macmillan.

Baldwin, R. E. (ed.) (1988), *Trade Policy Issues and Empirical Analysis*, Chicago: University of Chicago Press, for National Bureau of Economic Research.

Ballance, R. (1987), *International Industry and Business: Structural Change, Industrial Policy and Industrial Strategies*, London: Unwin Hyman.

Barnet, R. J. and Müller, R. E. (1974), *Global Reach: The Power of the Multinational Corporations*, New York: Simon and Schuster.

Bartlett, C. A. and Ghoshal S. (1989), *Managing Across Borders: The Transnational Solution*, Boston, MA: Harvard Business School Press.

(1990), 'Matrix Management: Not a Structure, a Frame of Mind', *Harvard Business Review*, July-August, pp. 138–45.

Basile, A. and Germidis, D. (1984), *Investing in Free Export Processing Zones*, Paris: OECD Development Studies.

Baumann, R. and Moreira, H. C. (1987), 'Os Programas BEFIEX e Alguns Mitos a Resplito', Brasilia, mimeo.

Bergsten, C. F., Horst, H. O. and Moran, T. (1978), *American Multinationals and American Interests*, Washington DC: Brookings Institution.

Berlin, I. (1990), *The Crooked Timber of Humanity*, London: John Murray.

Bernal, V. (1976), 'The Impact of Multinational Corporations on Employment and Income: The Case of Mexico', Geneva: International Labour Office, WEP 2–28, WP 13.

Best, M. (1990), *The New Competition: Institutions of Industrial Restructuring*, Cambridge: Polity.

Bhagwati, J. (1986), 'International Trade in Services and its Relevance for Economic Development', Xth Annual Lecture of the Geneva Association, London: Pergamon.

Binder, L. et al. (1971), *Crises and Sequences in Political Development*, Princeton, NJ: Princeton University Press.

Blomström, M. (1989), *Foreign Investment and Spillovers*, London: Routledge.

Blomström, M. and Wolff, E. N. (1990), 'Multinational Corporations and Productivity Convergence in Mexico', Ekonomiska Forskningsinstitutet, research paper 6392, mimeo.

Blunt, P. (1980), 'Bureaucracy and Ethnicity in Kenya: Some Conjectures for the Eighties', *Journal of Applied Behavioral Science*, Vol. 16, No. 3, pp. 336–51.

Boddewyn, J. J. (1983), 'Foreign Divestment Theory: Is It the Reverse of FDI Theory?', *Weltwirtschaftliches Archiv*, Vol. 119, pp. 345–55.

Bowie, A. (1988), 'Industrial Aspirations in a Divided Society: Malaysian Heavy Industries 1980–88', paper presented at annual meeting of Association of Asian Studies, San Francisco, 25–27 March.

Bradford, C. I., Jr. and Branson, H. (eds.) (1987), *Trade and Structural Change in Pacific Asia*, Chicago: National Bureau of Economic Research and University of Chicago Press.

The Brandt Reports, *North–South: A Programme for Survival*, Pan Books, 1980; *Common Crisis*, Pan Books, 1983; and *Global Challenge: From Crisis to Cooperation*, Pan Books, 1985.

Braudel, F. (1979), *Civilisation matérielle, économie et capitalisme, XVᵉ-XVIIIᵉ Siècle*, Paris, Librarie Armand Colin.

Brazilian Government (1986), *Politica Industrial, Relatório do Grupp Interminister-ial de Political Industrial*, Brasilia, July.

Browne, L. E. (1983), 'High Technology and Business Services', *New England Economic Review*, July-August, pp. 5–17.

Buckley, P. J. and Casson, M. (1985), *The Economic Theory of the Multinational Enterprise*, London: Macmillan.

Buckley, P. J. and Roberts, B. R. (1982), *European Direct Investment in the USA before World War I*, London: Macmillan.

Bull, H. (1978), *The Anarchical Society: A Study of Order in World Politics*, London: Macmillan.

Bureau of Economic Analysis (1985), *US Foreign Direct Investment Abroad: 1982 Benchmark Survey Data*, Washington DC: USGPO.

Business International Corp., *Investing, Licensing & Trading Conditions Abroad*, an annual periodical with data on over fifty countries.

Cantwell, J. A. and Tolentino, P. E. E. (1990), 'Technological Accumulation and Third World Multinationals', University of Reading, Department of Economics, Discussion Paper No. 139 (Series B).

Casson, M. (1987), *The Firm and the Market*, Oxford: Basil Blackwell.

Casson, M. (ed.) (1983), *The Growth of International Business*, London: Allen & Unwin.

Castro, C. M. and Carneiro, S. M. C. (1981), 'A Case Study of Training Practices of Multinational Enterprises in Brazil', in *Multinational Enterprise Training Practices and Development*, ILO, Geneva.

Caves, R. (1982), *Multinational Enterprises and Economic Analysis*, Cambridge; Cambridge University Press.

Special Commission for Manufacturing Automation/Special Secretariat for Information (CEAM/SEI) (1983), 'Aspectos Sociais, Econômicos e Trabal-histas do Automação na Manufactura', mimeo, May.

Chan, E. (1983), *Multinational Corporations, Technology and Employment*, London: Macmillan.

Chenery, H., Robinson, S. and Syrquin, M. (1986), *Industrialisation and Growth: A Comparative Study*, Oxford; Oxford University Press.

Cho, D-S. (1984) 'Government Regulation of Direct Investments Between Korea and the United States', in Moskowitz, K. (ed.), *From Patron to Partner: The US-Korean Economic and Business Relationship*, Lexington, MA: Lexington Books.

Chudnovsky, D. (1979), 'The Challenge by Domestic Enterprises to the Transnationals' Domination', *World Development*, Vol. 7, No. 1.

Clark, C. (1984), in Meier, G. (ed.), *Pioneers in Development*, New York: Oxford University Press, for the World Bank.

Clark, R. C. (1979), *The Japanese Company*, New Haven: Yale University Press.

Clegg, S. R. (1990), *Modern Organisations*, London: Sage.

Cline, W. R. (1982), 'Reciprocity: A New Approach to World Trade Policy?', *Policy Analyses in International Economics*, Washington, DC: Institute for International Economics.

Cohen, B. J. (1975), *Multinational Firms and Asian Exports*, New Haven: Yale University Press.

(1990), 'The Political Economy of International Trade', *International Organization*, Vol. 44, no. 2, pp. 261–81.

Collier, R. B. and Collier, D. (1979), 'Inducements versus Constraints: Disaggregating "Corporatism"', *American Political Science Review*, Vol. 73, pp. 967–86.

Commander, S. and Killick, T. (1988), 'Privatisation in Developing Countries: A Survey of Issues', in Cook, C. and Kirkpatrick, C. (eds.), *Privatisation in Less Developed Countries*, Brighton: Wheatsheaf.

Commonwealth Secretariat (1984), *Grenada: Development of a Cocoa-based Industry*, London: IDU/GRE/3a.

(1985), 'Foreign Investment Policy: Kenya's Experience', paper presented at seminar on foreign investment policies and prospects in Africa, June.

Congdon, T. (1988), *The Debt Threat: The Dangers of High Real Interest Rates for the World Economy*, Oxford: Basil Blackwell.

Contractor, F. J. (1990a), 'Ownership Patterns of US Joint Ventures Abroad and the Liberalization of Foreign Government Regulations in the 1980s: Evidence From the Benchmark Surveys', *Journal of International Business Studies*, Vol. 21, no. 1, pp. 55–73.

(1990b), 'Do Government Policies toward Foreign Investment Matter?', Rutgers University, GSM working paper, No. 90–15, July.

Coughlin, P. (1987), 'The Gradual Maturation of an Import-Substitution Industry: the Textile Industry in Kenya', University of Nairobi, Economics Department discussion paper, mimeo.

Cox, R. W. (1987), *Production Power and World Order: Social Forces in the Making of History*, New York: Columbia University Press.

Cox, R. W. and Jacobson, H. (eds.) (1973), *The Anatomy of Influence: Decision Making in International Organisation*, New Haven: Yale University Press.

Crook, C. (1989), 'The Third World Survey', *The Economist*, September 23.

Dahlman, C. (1984), 'Foreign Technology and Indigenous Technological Capability in Brazil', in Fransman, M. and King, K. (eds.), *Technological Capability in the Third World*, London: Macmillan.

Davenport-Hines, R. P. T. (1986), 'Glaxo as a Multinational Before 1983', in Jones, G. (ed.), *British Multinationals: Origins, Management and Performance*, Aldershot: Gower.

Deardorff, A. V. (1987), 'The Directions of Developing Country Trade: Examples of Pure Theory', in Havrylshyn, O. (ed.), *Exports of Developing Countries: How Direction Affects Performance*, Washington, DC: World Bank.

Delamaide, D. (1984), *Debt Shock*, New York: Doubleday; London: Weidenfeld and Nicolson.

de Soto, H. (1989), *The Other Path: The Invisible Revolution in the Third World*, New York: Harper & Row.

De Villiers, D. (1989), 'The Role of the State in Industrial Relations in South Africa, 1978–1988', Political Science Association of South Africa, mimeo.

Dixit, A. and Norman, V. (1980), *Theory of International Trade*, Cambridge: Nisbet.

Dixon, C. J., Drakakis-Smith, D. and Watts, H. D. (eds.) (1986), *Multinational Corporations and the Third World*, London: Croom Helm.

Doner, R. F. (1987), 'Domestic Coalitions and Japanese Auto Firms in South East Asia: A Comparative Bargaining Study', unpublished PhD dissertation, University of California, Berkeley.

Dooley, M. and Mathieson, D. (1987), 'Financial Liberalisation in Developing Countries', *Finance and Development*, Vol. 24, No. 3, pp. 31–4.

Dore, R. (1973), *British Factory, Japanese Factory*, London: Allen and Unwin.

Dornbusch, R. and Reynoso, A. (1989), 'Financial Factors in Economic Development', *American Economic Review*, Vol. 79, May, pp. 204–9.

Drucker, P. F. (1986), 'The Changed World Economy', *Foreign Affairs*, Vol. 64, Spring, pp. 768–91.

(1989), *The New Realities*, New York: Harper & Row.

Dunning, J. H. (1988a), *Explaining International Production*, London: Unwin Hyman.

(1988b), 'The Eclectic Paradigm of International Production: A Restatement and Some Possible Extensions', *Journal of International Business Studies*, Vol. 19, Spring, pp. 1–32.

(1989), 'Governments, Economic Organisation and International Competitiveness', University of Reading, mimeo, June.

(1990), 'Multinational Enterprises and the Globalization of Innovatory Capacity', University of Reading, Working Paper, mimeo.

Elson, D. and Pearson, R. (1981), 'Nimble Fingers Make Cheap Workers: An Analysis of Women's Employment in Third World Export Manufacturing', *Feminist Review*, No. 7.

Encarnation, D. J. and Wells, L. T., Jr. (1986), 'Evaluating Foreign Investment', in Moran, T. H. (ed.), *Investing in Development: New Roles for Private Capital?*, New Brunswick, NJ: Transaction Books.

Enderwick, P. (ed.) (1989), *Multinational Service Firms*, London: Routledge.

Enkyo, S. (1989), 'Financial Innovation and International Safeguards', unpublished PhD thesis, University of London.

Erickson, K. P. (1979), 'Brazil: Corporatism in Theory and Practice', in H. J. Wiarda and H. F. Kline (eds.), *Latin American Politics and Development*, Boston: Houghton Mifflin.

Ernst, D. (1987), 'The Impact of Microelectronics on the Worldwide Restructuring of the Electronics Industry: Implications for the Third World', in Dunning, J. H. and Usui, M. (eds.), *Structural Change, Economic Interdependence and World Development: Volume 4, Economic Interdependence*, Basingstoke: Macmillan.

Ernst, D. and O'Connor, D. (1989), *Technology and Global Competition: The Challenge for Newly Industrialising Economies*, Paris: OECD.

Erzan, R. (1984), *Intra-Industry Trade of Developing Countries and Some Policy Issues*, Stockholm: University of Stockholm Institute for Economic Studies.

Evans, Carol V. (1990), 'Market vs. Political Rationales for Brazilian Defence Production', *Political Economy Working Paper*, No. 49, Center in Political Economy, Washington University, October.

(1991), *Defence Industrialisation in the NICs: Case Studies from Brazil and India*, unpublished PhD Dissertation, London School of Economics.

Evans, Paul A. L. (1988), 'Organisational Development in the Transnational Enterprise', *INSEAD Working Paper*, No. 88/42.

Evans, P. (1979), *Dependent Development: The Alliance of Multinational, State and Local Capital in Brazil*, Princeton, NJ: Princeton University Press.

—— (1977), 'Multinationals, State-owned Corporations and the Transformation of Imperialism: A Brazilian Case Study', *Economic Development and Cultural Change*, Vol. 26, No. 1, pp. 78–89.

Evans, P., Rueschmeyer, D. and Skocpol, T. (1987), *Bringing The State Back In*, Cambridge: Cambridge University Press.

Fagre, N. and Wells, L. T., Jr. (1982), 'The Bargaining Power of Multinationals and Host Governments', *Journal of International Business Studies*, Vol. 13, Fall, pp. 9–23.

Faini, R. and de Melo, J. (1990), 'Adjustment, Investment and the Real Exchange Rate in Developing Countries', *Economic Policy*, October.

Fajnzylber, F. (1988), 'Technical Change and Economic Development-Issues for a Research Agenda', World Bank Seminar on Technology and Long-Term Economic Growth Prospects, Washington DC, November.

Fajnzylber, F. and Tarragó, T. M. (1976), *Las Empresas Transnacionales*, Mexico City: Fondo de Cultura Económica.

Fong, C. O. (1987), 'Wages and Labour Welfare in Three Malaysian Exporting Industries', London, ODI, mimeo.

Foreign Labor Trends – Brazil (1989), Washington, DC: US Government Printing Office, US Department of Labor, 89–39.

Foreign Labor Trends – Kenya (1989), Washington, DC: US Government Printing Office, US Department of Labor, 89–68.

Foreign Labor Trends – Malaysia (1989), Washington, DC: US Government Printing Office, US Department of Labor, 89–69.

Frank, I. (1980), *Foreign Enterprise in Developing Countries*, Baltimore, MA: Johns Hopkins University Press.

Franko, L. G. (1976), *The European Multinationals: A Renewed Challenge To American and British Big Business*, New York: Harper & Row.

—— (1989), 'Use of Minority and 50–50 Joint Ventures by United States Multinationals During the 1970s: the Interaction of Host Country Policies and Corporate Strategies', *Journal of International Business Studies*, Vol. 20, No. 1, pp. 19–40.

Frieden, J. (1987), *Banking on the World*, New York: Basic Books.

Friedman, M. (1962), *Capitalism and Freedom*, Chicago: University of Chicago Press.

Fritsch, W. and Franco, G. H. B. (1988), 'Foreign Direct Investment and Industrial Restructuring in Brazil: Trends and Emerging Issues', unpublished paper for OECD Development Centre, December.

Galbraith, J. K. (1956), *American Capitalism: The Concept of Countervailing Power*, New York: Houghton Mifflin, revised edition.

—— (1983), *The Voice of the Poor: Essays in Economic and Political Persuasion*, Cambridge, MA: Harvard University Press.

Gill, S. and Law, D. (1988), *The Global Political Economy: Perspectives, Problems and Prospects*, New York: Harvester.

Gilpin, R. (1971), 'The Politics of Transnational Economic Relations' in Keohane, R. and Nye, J. (eds.), *Transnational Relations and World Politics*, Cambridge, MA: Harvard University Press.

(1987), *The Political Economy of International Relations*, Princeton, NJ: Princeton University Press.

Giordano, R. (1990), 'Strategy as Revitalisation', Stockton lecture, London Business School, February.

Gladwin, T. N. and Walter, I. (1980), *Multinationals under Fire: Lessons from Conflict Management*, New York: Wiley.

Glover, D. J. (1984), 'Contract Farming and Smallholder Outgrower Schemes in Less Developed Countries', *World Development*, Vol. 12, Nos. 11/12, pp. 1,143–57.

Goodman, L. W. (1987), *Small Nations, Giant Firms*, London: Holmes & Meier.

Graham, E. M. (1990), 'Strategic Interaction Among Multinational Firms and Foreign Direct Investment', in Pitelis, C. and Sugden, R. (eds.), *The Nature of the Multinational Firm*, London: Routledge.

Gray, C. D. (1990), 'Protection or Protectionism', *Far Eastern Economic Review*, 13 September, p. 15.

Greeley, M. and Farrington, J. (1989), 'Potential Implications of Agricultural Biotechnology for the Third World', in Farrington, J. (ed.), *Agricultural Biotechnology: Prospects for the Third World*, London: ODI.

Griffith-Jones, S. (1984), *International Finance and Latin America*, London: Croom Helm.

Grimwade, N. (1989), *International Trade: New Patterns of Trade, Production and Investment*, London: Routledge.

Grosse, R. E. (1989), *Multinationals in Latin America*, London: Routledge.

Grossman, J. M. and Richardson J. D. (1985), *Strategic Trade Policy: A Survey of Issues and Early Analysis*, Princeton, NJ: International Finance Papers.

Group of Thirty (1984), *Foreign Direct Investment 1973–87*, New York: Group of Thirty.

Grunberg, L. (1981), *Failed Multinational Ventures: The Political Economy of International Divestments*, Lexington: D. C. Heath.

Grunwald, J. and Flamm, K. (1985), *The Global Factory: Foreign Assembly in International Trade*, Washington, DC: Brookings Institution.

Guile, B. and Brooks, H. (1987), *Technology and Global Industry: Companies and Nations in the World Economy*, Washington, DC: National Academic Press.

Guisinger, S. E. and Associates (1985), *Investment Incentives and Performance Requirements*, New York: Praeger, for the World Bank.

Gylfason, T. (1989), 'Inflation and Economic Decline: A Coincidence?', *Skandinaviska Enskilda Banken Quarterly Review*, Vol. 2, pp. 35–40.

Hamel, G., Doz, Y. L. and Prahalad, C. K. (1989), 'Collaborate with Your Competitors – and Win', *Harvard Business Review*, Vol. 67, No. 1, Jan.–Feb., pp. 133–9.

Hamilton, G. G. and Biggart, N. W. (1988), 'Market, Culture, and Authority: A Comparative Analysis of Management and Organisation in the Far East' *American Journal of Sociology*, Vol. 94, Supplement, pp. S52–94.

Hammond, G. (1989), *Countertrade, Offsets and Barter in International Political Economy*, London: Pinter.

Hannah, L. (ed.) (1976), *Management Strategy and Business Development*, London: Macmillan.

Harris, C. et al. (1990), 'International Productivity Differences in Manufacturing: the Finishing of Photographic Paper', Australian Bureau of Industry Economics, Research Report No. 34.

Hashimoto, H. (1983), 'Bauxite Processing in Developing Countries' in Vol. 1: *Case Studies on Industrial Processing of Primary Products*, Washington, DC, World Bank.

Hayashi, A. M. (1989), 'Hyundai Headache', *Electronic Business*, 6 February, pp. 25–32.

Hayek, F. (1979), *The Road to Serfdom*, London: Routledge.

Helpman, E. and Krugman, P. R. (eds.) (1989), *Trade Policy and Market Structure*, Cambridge, MA: MIT Press.

Henley, J. S. and Ereisha, M. (1989), 'State Ownership and the Problem of the Work Incentive', *Work Employment and Society*, Vol. 3, No. 1, pp. 65–87.

Henley, J. S. and Maynard, J. (1991), 'Whither Development Finance Institutions: Evidence from Kenya and Zimbabwe' in H. Singer and R. Prendergast (eds.), *Development Studies in the 1990s*, London: Macmillan.

Hennart, J.-F. (1988), 'Upstream Vertical Integration in the Aluminium and Tin Industries, *Journal of Economic Behaviour and Organization*, Vol. 9, No. 3, April, pp. 281–300.

——— (1989), 'Can the "New Forms of Investment" Substitute for the "Old Forms"?: a Transaction Cost Perspective', *Journal of International Business Studies*, Vol. 20, No. 2, Summer, pp. 211–34.

Hill, H. (1985), 'Subcontracting, Technological Diffusion and the Development of Small Enterprise in Philippine Manufacturing', *Journal of Developing Areas*, Vol. 19, No. 2, pp. 245–61.

Hirata, H. (1989), 'Production Relocation: An Electronics Multinational in France and Brazil', in Elson, D. and Pearson, R. (eds.), *Women's Employment and Multinationals in Europe*, London: Macmillan, pp. 129–43.

Hirsch, S. (1989), 'International Transactions Involving Interactions', in Giersch, H. (ed.), *Services in World Economic Growth*, Tubingen: JCB Mohr.

Hirschman, A. O. (1986), 'The Political Economy of Latin American Development: Seven Exercises in Retrospection', Working Paper for the Centre for US-Mexican Studies, University of California, San Diego and Helen Kellogg Institute, University of Notre Dame.

Hojman, D. E. (1981), 'The Andean Pact: Failure of a Model of Economic Integration?', *Journal of Common Market Studies*, Vol. 20, No. 2, pp. 139–60.

Holtfrerich, C-L. (1990), *Interactions in the World Economy: Perspectives from International Economic History*, New York: Simon & Schuster.

Horowitz, D. L. (1985), *Ethnic Groups in Conflict*, Berkeley, CA: University of California Press.

Huntington, S. (1968), *Political Order in Changing Societies*, New Haven: Yale University Press.

Iklé, F. C. (1964), *How Nations Negotiate*, New York: Harper & Row.

Inman, B. R. and Burton, D. F. (1990), 'Technology and Competitiveness: The New Policy Frontier', *Foreign Affairs*, Spring, pp. 116–34.

Inoguchi, T. and Okimoto, D. (eds.) (1988), *The Political Economy of Japan: Vol. 2. The Changing International Context*, Stanford: Stanford University Press.

297

International Finance Corporation (IFC) (1986), 'The Process of Entry Control for Foreign Direct Investment', Washington DC: IFC internal working paper.

IFC (1989), 'The Development Contributions of IFC Operations', Washington, DC: The World Bank, IFC Discussion Paper no. 5.

International Labour Office (ILO) (1981), *Employment Effects of Multinational Enterprises in Developing Countries*, Geneva: ILO.

(1984), *Technology Choice and Employment Generation by Multinational Enterprises in Developing Countries*, Geneva: ILO.

(1985), Personnel Management Seminar for East/Central/Southern African countries, October.

ILO/UNCTC (1988), *Economic and Social Effects of Multinational Enterprises in Export Processing Zones*, Geneva: ILO.

International Monetary Fund (IMF) (1985), *Foreign Private Investment in Developing Countries*, Washington DC: IMF, January.

(1988), *Supplement on Trade*, Washington, DC: IMF supplementary series, No. 15.

Islam, I. (1989), 'Industrial Restructuring and Industrial Relations in ASEAN – A Firm-level Chronicle', in Edgren, G. (ed.), *Restructuring, Employment and Industrial Relations* Geneva: ILO/ARTEP

Jacobs, E. and Martínez, J. (1980), 'Competencia y Concentracíon: el Caso de Sector Manufacturero, 1970–1975', *Economíca Mexicana*, Vol. 2, pp. 131–62.

James, C. (1989), 'Plant Biotechnologies for Developing Countries', paper presented at a CTA/FAO Symposium, Luxembourg, June.

Jenkins, R. (1979), 'The Export Performance of Multinational Corporations in Mexican Industry', *Journal of Development Studies*, Vol. 15, April.

Jervis, R. (1976), *Perception and Misperception in International Politics*, Princeton, NJ: Princeton University Press.

Jesudason, J. V. (1989), *Ethnicity and the Economy: The State, Chinese Business and Multinationals in Malaysia*, Singapore: Oxford University Press.

Johnson, C. (1982), *Miti and the Japanese Miracle: the Growth of Industrial Policy, 1925–1975*, Stanford: Stanford University Press.

(1984), 'The Idea of Industrial Policy', in Johnson, C. (ed.), *The Industrial Policy Debate*, San Francisco, CA: Institute for Contemporary Studies.

Johnson, H. G. (1975a) *Technology and Economic Interdependence*, London, Macmillan.

(1975b), 'Technological Change and Comparative Advantage: an Advanced Country's Viewpoint', *Journal of World Trade Law*, Vol. 9, Jan.-Feb., pp. 1–14.

Jones, L. P. and Sakong, I. (1981), *Economic Development and the Role of Government and Businessmen*, Seoul: Korea Development Institute.

Jones, S. and Jagoe, A. (1988), *Third World Countertrade*, Newbury: Produce Studies.

Jouet, J. (1984), 'Advertising and Transnational Corporations in Kenya', *Development and Change*, Vol. 15.

Julius, D. (1990), *Global Companies and Public Policy: The Growing Challenge of Foreign Direct Investment*, London: Pinter/Royal Institute of International Affairs.

Kaiser, K. (1971), 'Transnational Politics: Toward a Theory of Multinational Politics', *International Organization*, Vol. 25, No. 4, pp. 795–816.

Karmokolias, I. (1990), 'Prospects for the Automotive Industry in LDCs', *Finance & Development*, Vol. 27, No. 3, September, pp. 47–9.

Katz, J. M. (ed.) (1987), *Technology Generation in Latin American Manufacturing Industry*, Basingstoke: Macmillan.

Katzenstein, P. J. (ed.) (1978), *Between Power and Plenty: Foreign Economic Policy of Advanced Industrial States*, Madison: University of Wisconsin Press.

Kenya, Republic of (1986), *Economic Management for Renewed Growth*, Government Report, Nairobi.

Kergoat, K. (1982), *Les Ouvrieres*, Paris: Editions Le Sycomore.

Khan, K. M. (ed.) (1986), *Multinationals of the South: New Actors in the International Economy*, New York: St Martins Press.

Kindleberger, C. P. (1973), *The World in Depression, 1919–1939*, London: Allen Lane.

— (1990), *Historical Economics: Art or Science?*, New York: Simon & Schuster.

Knickerbocker, F. T. (1973), *Oligopolistic Reaction and Multinational Enterprises*, Boston, Harvard Business School Press.

Kobrin, S. J. (1987), 'Testing the Bargaining Hypothesis in the Manufacturing Sector in Developing Countries', *International Organisation*, Vol. 41, No. 4, pp. 609–38.

Kobrin, S. J. (1982), *Managing Political Risk Assessment*, Berkeley CA: University of California Press.

Kogut, B. (1983), 'Foreign Direct Investment as a Sequential Process', in Kindleberger, C. P. and Andretsch, D. (eds.) *The Multinational Corporation in the 1980s*, Cambridge, MA: MIT Press.

Kojima, K. (1978), *Direct Foreign Investment*, London: Croom Helm.

— (1990), *Japanese Direct Investment Abroad*, International Christian University, Tokyo, Social Science Monograph, No. 1.

Koo, B. Y. (1985), 'The Role of Direct Foreign Investment in Korea's Recent Economic Growth', in Galenson, A. (ed.), *Foreign Trade and Investment: Economic Growth in Newly Industrialising Asian Countries*, Madison: University of Wisconsin Press, pp. 176–216.

Koopman, G. (1979), 'Ten Years Andean Pact: A Re-Examination', *Intereconomics*, May/June.

Koopmans, K. and Montias, J. M. (1971), 'On the Description and Comparison of Economic Systems', in Eckstein, A. (ed.), *Comparison of Economic Systems*, University of California Press.

Krafcik, J. F. (1988), 'Triumph of the Lean Production System', *Sloan Management Review*, Vol. 30, No. 1, pp. 41–52.

Krafcik, J. F. and MacDuffie, J. P. (1989), 'Explaining High Performance Manufacturing', IMVP International Policy Forum, Massachusetts Institute of Technology, May, mimeo.

Kreuger, A. O. (1983), *Trade and Employment in Developing Countries 3: Synthesis and Conclusions*, Chicago: University of Chicago Press.

Krugman, P. R. (1979), 'Increasing Returns, Monopolistic Competition, and International Trade', *Journal of International Economics*, Vol. 9, pp. 469–80.

— (ed.) (1986), *Strategic Trade Policy and the New International Economics*, Cambridge, MA: MIT Press.

— (1987), 'Is Free Trade Passé?', *Journal of International Perspectives*, Vol. 1.

299

Kunio, Y. (1988), *The Rise of Ersatz Capitalism in Southeast Asia*, Singapore: Oxford University Press.

Kupfer, A. (1988), 'How to be a Global Manager', *Fortune*, March 14, p. 27.

Lall, S. (1979), 'Multinationals and Market Structure in an Open Developing Economy: the Case of Malaysia', *Weltwirtschaftliches Archiv*, Vol. 115, pp. 325–50.

(1983), *The New Multinationals: The Spread of Third World Enterprises*, Chichester: Wiley.

(1985), *Multinationals, Technology and Exports*, London: Macmillan.

(1987), *Learning to Industrialise*, London: Macmillan.

Lall, S. and Streeten, P. (1977), *Foreign Investment, Transnational and Developing Countries*, Boulder, CO: Westview Press.

Landes, D. (1969), *The Unbound Prometheus: Technological Change and Industrial Development in Western Europe from 1750 to the Present*, Cambridge: Cambridge University Press.

Langdon, S. (1981), *Multinational Corporations in the Political Economy of Kenya*, London: Macmillan.

(1986) 'Industrial Dependence and Export Manufacturing in Kenya', in Ravenhill, J. (ed.), *Africa in Economic Crisis*, London: Macmillan, pp. 181–212.

Lawrence, P. R. (1987), 'Competition: A Renewed Focus for Industrial Policy', in Teece, D. J. (ed.), *The Competition Challenge*, Cambridge MA: Ballinger.

Lecraw, D. J. (1989), 'Third World Multinationals in the Service Industries', in Enderwick, P. (ed.), *Multinational Service Firms*, London: Routledge.

Leeds, R. S. (1989), 'Malysia: Genesis of a Privatisation Transaction', *World Development*, Vol. 17, No. 5, pp. 741–56.

Lever, H. and Huhne, C. (1985), *Debt and Danger: The World Financial Crisis*, Harmondsworth: Penguin.

Lim, D. (1976), 'Capital Utilisation of Local and Foreign Establishments in Malaysian Manufacturing', *Review of Economics and Statistics*, Vol. 58, pp. 209–17.

Lim, L. Y. C. and Fong, P. E. (1988), 'Foreign Investment and Industrial Restructuring in Newly-Industrialising Asia', unpublished report for the OECD Development Centre, CD/R(88)9.

Lindbeck, A. and Snower, D. J. (1987), 'Efficiency Wages versus Insiders and Outsiders', *European Economic Review*, Vol. 31, pp. 407–16.

Linder, S. (1961), *An Essay on Trade and Transformation*, New York: Wiley.

Lipsey, R. and Kravis, I. (1987), 'The Competitiveness and Comparative Advantage of US Multinationals, 1957–1984', *Banca Nazionale del Lavoro Quarterly Review*, No. 161, June, pp. 147–65.

Little, I. M. D. and Mirrlees, J. A. (1974), *Project Appraisal and Planning for Development*, New York: Basic Books.

Lowenthal, A. (1987), *Partners in Conflict: The United States and Latin America*, Baltimore: Johns Hopkins University Press.

Lucas, R. (1988), 'On the mechanics of economic development', *Journal of Monetary Economics*, Vol. 22, pp. 3–42.

Lütkenhorst, W. (1988), 'Challenges from New Trends in Foreign Direct Investment', *Intereconomics*, Sept/Oct.

Maddison, A. (1990), *The World Economy in the 20th Century*, Paris: OECD, Development Centre Studies.

Maex, R. (1983), 'Employment and Multinationals in Asian Export Processing Zones', *Multinational Enterprises Programme Working Paper*, No. 26, Geneva: ILO.

Magee, S. P. (1977), 'Information and the Multinational Corporation: an Appropriability Theory of Direct Foreign Investment' in Bhagwati, J. (ed.), *The New Economic Theory of Direct Foreign Investment*, Cambridge, MA: MIT Press.

Malsch, T. (1984), 'Transfer of Technology and Plant Organisation', Wissenschaftszentrum Berlin, Discussion Paper IIVG/dp 84–209, mimeo.

Markides, C. C. (1990), *Corporate Refocusing and Economic Performance, 1981–1987*, unpublished DBA dissertation, Harvard University.

Markides, C. C. and Berg, N. (1988), 'Manufacturing Offshore is Bad Business', *Harvard Business Review*, Vol. 66, Sept.–Oct.

Marshall, J. N. (1985), 'Business Services: The Regions and Regional Policy', *Regional Studies*, Vol. 19, pp. 352–63.

Mathieson, D. (1989), *Managing Financial Risks in Indebted Developing Countries*, Washington, DC: IMF.

Mathur, A. N. (1989), 'The Effects of Legal and Contractual Regulations on Employment in Indian Industry', in Edgren, G. (ed.) *Restructuring, Employment and Industrial Relations*, Geneva: ILO/ARTEP, pp. 153–202.

Mentre, P. (1984), 'The Fund, the Banks and Member Countries', IMF Occasional Paper No. 26.

Messerlin, P. A. and Sauvant, K. (eds.) (1990), *The Uruguay Round – Services in the World Economy*, Washington, DC: IBRD and UNCTC.

Michalet, C.-A. (1976), *Le capitalisme mondiale*, Paris: PUF.

Mikkelsen, B. (1986), *Formation of an Industrial Labour Force in Kenya*, Copenhagen: Centre for Development Research, Report No. 10.

Miller, J. D. B. (1982), *The World of States*, London: Croom Helm.

Milner, H. V. (1988), *Resisting Protectionism: Global Industries and the Politics of International Trade*, Princeton, NJ: Princeton University Press.

Milner, H. V. and Yoffie, D. (1989), 'Between Free Trade and Protectionism: Strategic Trade Policy and a Theory of Corporate Demands', *International Organization*, Vol. 43, No. 2, pp. 239–72. Spring.

Moran, T. H. (1985), *Multinational Corporations: The Political Economy of Foreign Direct Investment*, Lexington, MA: Lexington Books.

(1990), 'The Globalization of America's Defense Industries: Managing the Threat of Foreign Dependence', *International Security*, Vol. 15, No. 1, pp. 57–99.

Murakami, Y. (1987), 'The Japanese Model of Political Economy', in Yamamura, K. and Yasukichi, Y. (eds.), *The Political Economy of Japan, Vol. 1, The Domestic Transformation*, Stanford: Stanford University Press.

Murphy, K., Shleifer, A. and Vishny, R. (1989), 'Industrialization and the Big Push', *Journal of Political Economy*, Vol. 97, October, pp. 1,003–26.

Myers, N. (1989), 'Environment and Security', *Foreign Affairs*, No. 74, Spring, pp. 23–41.

Mytelka, L. K. (1979), *Regional Development in a Global Economy: The Multi-*

national Corporation, Technology and Andean Integration, New Haven, CT: Yale University Press.

(1986), 'The State and Foreign Capital in the Advanced Industrialised Capital Countries', in Blais, A. (ed.), *Industrial Policy*, Toronto: University of Toronto Press.

Nankani, H. B. (1988), 'Techniques of Privatization of State-Owned Enterprises: Volume 2: Selected Country Case Studies', Washington, DC: World Bank Technical Paper, No. 89.

Naylor, R. T. (1987), *Hot Money and the Politics of Debt*, London: Unwin Hyman.

Newfarmer, R. (1980), *Transnational Conglomerates and the Economics of Dependent Development: A Case Study of the International Oligopoly and Brazil's Electrical Industry*, Greenwich, CT: JAI Press.

Newfarmer, R. (ed.) (1985), *Profits, Progress and Poverty: Case Studies of International Industries in Latin America*, Notre Dame, IN: University of Notre Dame Press.

Newfarmer, R. and Marsh, L. L. (1981), 'International Interdependence and Development', report to the U.S. Department of Labor, July 31, mimeo.

Newton, J. (1990), *The Political Economy of Tourism*, London School of Economics, Discussion Paper, mimeo.

Nicholaides, P. (1989), *Liberalizing Service Trade: Strategies for Success*, London: Routledge/Royal Institute of International Affairs.

Nunnenkamp, P. (1986), *The International Debt Crisis and the Third World: Causes and Consequences*, Brighton: Wheatsheaf.

Nye, J. (1984), 'The Multinational Corporation in the 1980s', in Kindleberger, C. and Audretsch, D. (eds.), *The Multinational Corporation in the 1980s*, Boston, MA: MIT Press.

O'Brien, L. (1988), 'Between Capital and Labour: Trade Unionism in Malaysia' in Southall, R. (ed.), *Labour and Unions in Asia and Africa*, London: Macmillan, pp. 136–70.

Odaka, K., Ono, K. and Adachi, F. (1988), *The Automobile Industry in Japan: A Study of Ancillary Firm Development*, Tokyo: Oxford University Press and Kinokuniya.

O'Donnell, G. (1988), 'Challenges to Democratisation in Brazil', *World Policy Journal*, Vol. 5, pp. 281–300.

OECD (1988), *The Newly Industrialising Countries: Challenge and Opportunity for OECD Industries*, Paris.

(1989), *Biotechnology: Economic and Wider Impacts*, Paris.

Ohlin, B. (1933), *Interregional and International Trade*, Cambridge, MA: Harvard University Press.

Ohmae, K. (1982), *The Mind of the Strategist*, New York: McGraw-Hill.

(1985), *Triad Power*, New York: The Free Press.

(1990), *The Borderless World*, New York: Harper Business.

Oman, C. (1984), *New Forms of International Investment in Developing Countries*, Paris: OECD.

(1989), *New Forms of Investment in Developing Country Industries*, Paris: OECD, Development Centre Studies.

Page, S. (1986), 'Relocating Manufacturing in Developing Countries: Opportunities for UK Companies', London: NEDO working papers, EWP 25.

Parry, T. G. (1980), *The Multinational Enterprise*, Greenwich, CT: JAI Press.

Pastore, J. and Skidmore, T. E. (1985), 'Brazilian Labour Relations: A New Era?', in Juris, H., Thompson, M. and Daniels, W. (eds.), *Industrial Relations in a Decade of Economic Change*, Madison, WI: Industrial Relations Research Association, pp. 73–114.

Pauly, L. (1990), 'Institutionalising a Stalemate: National Financial Politics and the International Debt Crisis', *Journal of Public Policy*, Vol. 10, Part 1, Jan.-March, pp. 23–43.

Pazos, F. (1985), 'Have Import-Substituting Policies Either Precipitated or Aggravated the Debt Crisis?', *Journal of InterAmerican Studies*, Vol. 27, No. 4, Winter, pp. 57–72.

Pearson, R. (1986), 'Female Workers in the First and Third World: The "Greening" of Women's Labour', in Purcell, K. *et al.* (eds.) *The Changing Experience of Employment: Restructuring and Recession*, London: Macmillan.

Perroux, F. (1950), 'Economic Space, Theory and Applications', *Quarterly Journal of Economics*, Vol. 64, pp. 89–104.

Pfeffermann, G. P. (1988), *'Private Business in Developing Countries: Improving Prospects'*, Washington, DC: International Finance Corporation, Discussion Paper No. 1.

Piore, M. J. and Sabel, C. F. (1984), *The Second Industrial Divide*, New York: Basic Books.

Pirages, D. (1988), *Global Technopolitics: The International Politics of Technology and Resources*, Pacific Grove: Brooks Cole.

Plasschaert, S. (1979), *Transfer Pricing and Multinational Corporations*, Farnborough: Saxon House.

Porter, M. E. (ed.) (1986), *Competition in Global Industries*, Boston, MA: Harvard Business School Press.

Porter, M. E. (1990), *The Competitive Advantage of Nations*, New York: Free Press.

Poynter, T. A. (1982) 'Government Intervention in Less Developed Countries: the Experience of Multinational Companies', *Journal of International Business Studies*, Vol. 13, No. 1, Spring-Summer, pp. 9–25.

(1985), 'Strategic Responses to Government Intervention in Developing Countries', in Brewer, T. L. (ed.), *Political Risks in International Business*, New York: Praeger.

Prahalad, C. K. and Doz Y. (1987), *The Multinational Mission*, New York: The Free Press.

Prebisch, R. (1963) *Towards a Dynamic Development Policy for Latin America*, New York: United Nations.

Quarré, F. (1987), *La Stratégie pour Gagner*, Paris: Masson.

Raiffa, H. (1982), *The Art and Science of Negotiation*, Cambridge, MA: Belknap Press.

Ramanadham, V. V. (ed.) (1989), *Privatisation in Developing Countries*, London: Routledge, for UNDP.

Rangarajan, L. N. (1985), *The Limitation of Conflict: A Theory of Bargaining and Negotiation*, London: Croom Helm.

Ranis, G. and Schive, C. (1985), 'Direct Foreign Investment in Taiwan's Development', in Galenson, A. (ed.), *Foreign Trade and Investment:*

Economic Growth in Newly Industrialising Asian Countries, Madison, WI: University of Wisconsin Press, pp. 85–137.

Rapoport, A. (1960), *Fights, Games and Debates*, Ann Arbor, MI: Michigan University Press.

Reich, R. (1990), 'Who is US?', *Harvard Business Review*, Vol. 68, No. 1, January–February, pp. 53–64.

Reich, R. B. and Mankin, E. D. (1986), 'Joint Ventures with Japan Give Away our Future', *Harvard Business Review*, Vol. 64, No. 2, March–April, pp. 78–86.

Reuber, G. L. (1973), *Private Foreign Investment in Development*, Oxford: Clarendon Press.

Richardson, J. D. (1990), 'The Political Economy of Strategic Trade Policy', *International Organization*, Vol. 44, No. 1, pp. 107–35.

Riedel, J. (1975), 'The Nature and Determinants of Export-Oriented Direct Foreign Investment in a Developing Country: A Case Study of Taiwan', *Weltwirtschaft Archiv*, September.

Robock, S. H. and Simmonds, K. (1989), *International Business and Multinational Enterprises*, 4th edn, Homewood, IL: Irwin.

Roemer, M. and Stern, J. J. (1975), *The Appraisal of Development Projects*, New York: Praeger.

Roesch, S. M. A. (1987), 'Public Policies towards Industrial Training: the Brazilian Programme of Fiscal Incentives', unpublished PhD dissertation, University of London.

Romer, P. (1986), 'Increasing Returns and Long-Run Growth', *Journal of Political Economy*, Vol. 94, pp. 1,002–37.

Rosecrance, R. (1986), *The Rise of the Trading State: Commerce and Conquest in the Modern World*, New York: Basic Books.

Rubin, S. M. (ed.) (1989), *Debt Equity Swaps in the 1990s*, London: Economist Publications, Special Report No. 1204.

Rugman, A. M. (1979), *International Diversification and the Multinational Enterprise*, Lexington, MA: Lexington Books.

(1986), 'New Theories of the Multinational Enterprise: An Assessment of Internalisation Theory', *Bulletin of Economic Research*, Vol. 38, pp. 101–18.

Sachs, J. D. (1981), 'The Current Account and Macroeconomic Adjustment in the 1970s', *Brookings Papers in Economic Activity*, Vol. 1.

Sachs, J. D. and Berg, A. (1988), *The Debt Crisis: Structural Explanations of Country Performance*, Cambridge: National Bureau of Economic Research.

Safarian, A. E. (1983), *Governments and Multinationals: Policies in the Developed Countries*, Washington: British North American Committee.

Salih, K. and Mei Ling, Y. (1988), 'Economic Restructuring and the Electronics Industry in Malaysia' in *The Diffusion of High-Tech and the Labour Market: Asian Experiences*, Geneva: ILO-IILS.

Sauvant, K. P. (1986), *International Transactions in Services: The Politics of Transborder Data Flows*, Boulder, CO: Westview Press.

Schelling, T. C. (1960), *The Strategy of Conflict*, Cambridge, MA: Harvard University Press.

(1979), *Ethical Theory and Business*, Englewood Cliffs, NJ: Prentice-Hall.

Schive, C. (1990), *The Foreign Factor: The Multinational Corporation's Contribution* to the Economic Modernisation of the Republic of China, Stanford: Hoover Institution.

Schneider, S. and Frey, B. S. (1985), 'Economic and Political Determinants of Foreign Direct Investment', World Development, Vol. 13, No. 2, pp. 161–75.

Schumpeter, J. A. (1942), Capitalism, Socialism and Democracy, New York: Harper & Row.

Scoville, J. G. (1973), 'Some Determinants of the Structure of Labour Movements' in Sturmthal, A. and Scoville, J. G. (eds.), The International Labour Movement in Transition, Urbana: University of Illinois Press.

Sen. G. (1984), The Military Origins of Industrialization and International Trade Rivalry, New York: St Martins.

Shaikh, R. A. (1986), 'The Dilemmas of Advanced Technology for the Third World', Technology Review, Vol. 89, No. 3, pp. 56–64. April.

Sharp, M. and Holmes, P. (eds.) (1989), Strategies for New Technology: Case Studies from Britain and France, London: Philip Allen.

Shonfield, A. (1965), Modern Capitalism: The Changing Balance of Public and Private Power, London: Oxford University Press/RIIA.

Sieh, L. M. C. and Chen, K. L. (1985), 'Redistribution of Malaysia's Corporate Ownership in the New Economic Policy', Southeast Asian Affairs, Singapore: S.E. Asian Studies Centre, University of Singapore, pp. 235–58.

Singapore (1986), Report of the Economic Committee, The Singapore Economy: New Directions, Singapore: Ministry of Trade and Industry.

Singer, H. (1989), Lessons of Postwar Development Experience, 1945–1988, Brighton: Institute of Development Studies.

Spero, J. (1988), 'Guiding Global Finance', Foreign Policy, Winter.

Spindler, A. (1984), The Politics of International Credit: Private Finance and Foreign Policy in Germany and Japan, Washington, DC: Brookings Institution.

Steinbruner, J. D. (1974), The Cybernetic Theory of Decision: New Dimensions of Political Analysis, Princeton, NJ: Princeton University Press.

Steiner, G. A. (1975), Business and Society, New York: Random House.

Stern, R. (ed.) (1987), US Trade Policies in a Changing World, Cambridge, MA: MIT Press.

Stewart, F. (1982), 'Industrialization, Technical Change and the International Division of Labour', in Helleiner, G. K. (ed.), For Good or Evil: Economic Theory and North–South Negotiations, Toronto: University of Toronto Press.

Stobaugh, R. and Wells, L. T., Jr. (eds.) (1984), Technology Crossing Borders, Boston MA: Harvard Business School Press.

Stopford, J. M. and Dunning, J. H. (1983), Multinationals: Company Performance and Global Trends, London: Macmillan.

Stopford, J. M. and Turner, L. (1985), Britain and the Multinationals, Chichester: Wiley.

Stopford, J. M. and Wells, L. T., Jr. (1972), Managing the Multinational Enterprise, New York: Basic Books/London: Longman.

Strange, S. (1971), Sterling and British Policy, London: Oxford University Press/RIIA.

(1988), States and Markets, London: Pinter.

Streeten, P. (1981), Development Perspectives, London: Macmillan.

Stuckey, J. (1983), *Vertical Integration and Joint Ventures in the Aluminum Industry*, Cambridge, MA: Harvard University Press.

Sunkel, O. (1973), 'Transnational Capitalism and National Disintegration in Latin America', *Social and Economic Studies*, Vol. 22, No. 1, pp. 132–76.

Tanzi, V. (ed.) (1990), *Fiscal Policy in Open Developing Economies*, Washington DC: International Monetary Fund.

Teece, D. J. (1981), 'The Market of Know-How and the Efficient Transfer of Technology', *Annals of the American Academy of Political and Social Science*, Vol. 458, pp. 81–96.

(1985), 'Transaction Cost Economics and the Multinational Enterprise: An Assessment', *Journal of Economic Behaviour and Organization*, Vol. 7, pp. 21–45.

Telesio P. (1979), *Technology, Licensing and Multinational Enterprises*, New York: Praeger.

Terpstra, V. (1983), *International Marketing*, 3rd edn, Chicago: Dryden Press, chapter 10.

Thomas, H. C. (1988), *A Study of Trade among Developing Countries, 1950–1980: An Appraisal of the Emerging Patterns*, Amsterdam: Elsevier.

Thurow, L. (1980), *The Zero-Sum Society: Distribution and the Possibilities for Economic Change*, New York: Basic Books.

Triandis, H. C. (1984), 'Towards a Psychological Theory of Economic Growth', *International Journal of Psychology*, Vol. 19, Nos. 1–2, pp. 88.

Tussie, D. (1987), *The Less Developed Countries and the World Trading System: A Challenge to the GATT*, London: Pinter 1987.

Tyler, W. G. (1981), *The Brazilian Industrial Economy*, Lexington, Mass.: D. C. Heath.

United Nations (1986), *World Survey of the Role of Women in Development*, New York: United Nations.

United Nations Commission on Trade and Development (UNCTAD) (1987), Statistical Survey on Insurance and Reinsurance Operations in Developing Countries, Geneva, TD/B/C.3/220.

United Nations Centre on Transnational Corporations (UNCTC) Current Studies (1987), *Technology Acquisition under Alternative Arrangements with TNCs: Selected Case Studies in Thailand*, Bangkok: ESCAP/UNCTC Joint Unit on TNCs, Series A, No. 6.

(1981), *Transnational Corporations in the Bauxite/Aluminium Industry*, United Nations, New York.

(1985), *Trends and Issues in Foreign Direct Investment and Related Flows*, New York: United Nations.

(1988a), *Transnational Corporations in World Development: Trends and Prospects*, New York.

(1988b), *Development through Partnership – Business Relations between State and Foreign Enterprise in Kenya*, Volume 2, Draft Main Report.

United Nations Centre on Transnational Corporations/International Labour Office (UNCTC/ILO) (1985) *Women Workers in Multinational Enterprises in Developing Countries*, Geneva: ILO.

(1988), *Economic and Social Effects of Multinational Enterprises in Export Processing Zones*, Geneva: ILO.

United Nations Development Program (UNDP) (1990), *Human Development Report, 1990*, Oxford: Oxford University Press.

United Nations Industrial Development Organisation (UNIDO) (1980a), *Export Processing Zones in Developing Countries*, UNIDO/ICIS, 176, August.

(1980b), 'Women in the Redeployment of Manufacturing to Developing Countries', *Working Paper on Structural Change*, No. 18.

(1985), *Current World Situation in Petrochemicals*, Vienna, December.

(1986), 'Industrial Policies and Strategies in Developing Countries: an Analysis of Local Content Rules', *Industry and Development*, No. 18 (UN sales no. E86.II.B.2).

(1989), *Industry and Development: Global Report 1989/90*, Vienna.

Vaitsos, C. (1978), 'The Role of Transnational Enterprise in Latin American Economic Integration Efforts: Who Integrates and With Whom, How and For Whose Benefit?', prepared for UNCTAD Secretariat, mimeo.

van Tulder, R. and Junne, G. (1988), *European Multinationals in Core Technologies*, Chichester: Wiley.

Veblen, T. (1915), *Imperial Germany and the Industrial Revolution*, London: Macmillan.

Vergara, W. and Brown, D. (1988), 'The New Face of the World Petrochemical Sector: Implications for Developing Countries', Washington DC: World Bank, Technical Paper No. 84.

Vernon, R. (1966), 'International Investment and International Trade in the Product Cycle', *Quarterly Journal of Economics*, Vol. 80, May, pp. 190–207.

(1971), *Sovereignty at Bay*, New York: Basic Books.

(1977), *Storm over the Multinationals*, Cambridge, MA: Harvard University Press.

(1979), 'The Product Cycle Hypotheses in the New International Environment', *Oxford Bulletin of Economics and Statistics*, Vol. 41, pp. 255–67.

(1983), 'Organization and Institutional Responses to International Risk', in Herring, R. J. (ed.), *Managing International Risk*, Cambridge: Cambridge University Press.

Vernon, R. (ed.) (1988), *The Promise of Privatization: A Challenge for American Foreign Policy*, New York: Council on Foreign Relations.

Vuylsteke, C. (1988), 'Techniques of Privatisation of State-Owned Enterprises: Volume 1: Methods and Implementation', Washington, DC: World Bank Technical Paper, No. 88.

Wad, P. (1988), 'The Japanization of the Malaysian Trade Union Movement', in Southall, R. (ed.), *Trade Unions and the New Industrialisation of the Third World*, London: Zed Books, pp. 210–29.

Wallender, H. W. (1979), *Technology Transfer and Management in the Developing Countries*, Cambridge, MA: Ballinger.

Walton, R. E. (1985), 'From Control to Commitment in the Workplace', *Harvard Business Review*, Vol. 63, No. 2, March-April, pp. 76–84.

Waltz, K. (1979), *The Theory of International Politics*, Reading, MA: Addison Wesley.

Warr, P. G. (1987), 'Malaysia's Industrial Enclaves: Benefits and Costs', *Developing Economies*, Vol. 25, No. 1.

307

Weiss, J. (1988), *Industry in Developing Countries: Theory, Policy and Evidence*, London: Routledge.

Wellons, P. (1987), *Passing the Buck: Banks, Governments and Third World Debt*, Cambridge, MA: Harvard Business School Press.

Wells, L. T., Jr. (1972), *The Product Life Cycle and International Trade*, Cambridge, MA: Harvard Business School Press.

(1975), 'Social Benefit/Cost Analysis for MNCs', *Harvard Business Review*, Vol. 53, No. 2, March-April, pp. 40–50.

(1977), 'Negotiating with Third World Governments', *Harvard Business Review*, Vol. 55, No. 1, January-February, pp. 72–80.

(1983), *Third World Multinationals*, Cambridge, MA: MIT Press.

(1984), 'Economic Man and Engineering Man', in Stobaugh, R. and Wells, L. T., Jr. (eds.), *Technology Crossing Borders*, Cambridge, MA: Harvard Business School Press, pp. 47–68.

(1986), 'Investment Incentives: An Unnecessary Debate', *CTC Reporter*, Autumn, pp. 58–60.

Welt, L. (1985), *Countertrade*, London: Euromoney Publications.

Whichard, O. G. (1988), 'US Multinational Companies: Operations in 1986', *Survey of Current Business*, June, pp. 85–96.

Wilkins, M. (1970), *The Emergence of Multinational Enterprise: American Business Abroad from the Colonial Era to 1914*, Cambridge, MA: Harvard University Press.

Williamson, O. E. (1975), *Markets and Hierarchies*, New York: Free Press.

(1985), *The Economic Institutions of Capitalism*, New York: Free Press.

Willmore, L. (1986), 'The Comparative Performance of Foreign and Domestic Firms in Brazil', *World Development*, Vol. 14, No. 4, pp. 489–502.

Womack, J. P., Jones, D. T. and Roos, D. (1990), *The Machine that Changed the World*, New York: Rawson Associates.

World Bank (1987), *Kenya: Industrial Sector Policies for Investment and Export Growth*, Washington, DC: World Bank.

(1989), *Parastatals in Tanzania: Towards a Reform Program*, Washington, DC: World Bank.

(1990), *World Development Report 1990*, Oxford: Oxford University Press, for the World Bank.

World Bank Staff (1989), 'Problems of Public Enterprises in Sierra Leone', in Meier, M. E. and Steel, W. F. (eds.), *Industrial Adjustment in Sub-Saharan Africa*, Oxford: Oxford University Press.

Zacher, M. W. and Finlayson, J. A. (1988), *Managing International Markets*, New York: Columbia University Press.

Zysman, J. and Cohen, S. (1988), *Manufacturing Matters*, New York: Basic Books.

Zysman, J. and Tyson, L. (eds.) (1983), *American Industry in International Competition, Government Policies and Corporate Strategies*, Ithaca, NY: Cornell University Press.

INDEX